Ethics as Social Science

NEW THINKING IN POLITICAL ECONOMY

General Editor: Peter J. Boettke
George Mason University, USA

New Thinking in Political Economy aims to encourage scholarship in the intersection of the disciplines of politics, philosophy and economics. It has the ambitious purpose of reinvigorating political economy as a progressive force for understanding social and economic change.

The series is an important forum for the publication of new work analysing the social world from a multidisciplinary perspective. With increased specialization (and professionalization) within universities, interdisciplinary work has become increasingly uncommon. Indeed, during the 20th century, the process of disciplinary specialization has reduced the intersection between economics, philosophy and politics and impoverished our understanding of society. Modern economics in particular has become increasingly mathematical and largely ignores the role of institutions and the contribution of moral philosophy and politics.

New Thinking in Political Economy will stimulate new work that combines technical knowledge provided by the dismal science and the wisdom gleaned from the serious study of the worldly philosophy. The series will reinvigorate our understanding of the social world by encouraging a multidisciplinary approach to the challenges confronting society in the new century.

Recent titles in the series include:

Explaining Constitutional Change
A Positive Economics Approach
Stefan Voigt

Ethics as Social Science
The Moral Philosophy of Social Cooperation
Leland B. Yeager

Ethics as Social Science

The Moral Philosophy of Social Cooperation

Leland B. Yeager
Auburn University, USA

NEW THINKING IN POLITICAL ECONOMY

Edward Elgar
Cheltenham, UK • Northampton MA, USA

Published by
Edward Elgar Publishing Limited
Glensanda House
Montpellier Parade
Cheltenham
Glos GL50 1UA
UK

Edward Elgar Publishing, Inc.
136 West Street
Suite 202
Northampton
Massachusetts 01060
USA

A catalogue record for this book
is available from the British Library

Library of Congress Cataloguing in Publication Data

Yeager, Leland B.
    Ethics as social science : the moral philosophy of social cooperation /
  Leland B. Yeager—(New thinking in political economy)
    1. Economics—Moral and ethical aspects. 2. Utilitarianism. I. Title.
II. Series.

HB72.Y43 2001
171'.5—dc21
                                               00-042968

ISBN 1 84064 5210 (cased)
Printed and bound in Great Britain by MPG Books Ltd, Bodmin, Cornwall

Contents

Acknowledgments and Preface

I thank Peter Boettke, William Butos, and Mario Rizzo in particular for encouragement in bringing to fruition a project that dates back more years than I care to admit. At a crucial stage, Glen Whitman made valuable suggestions about arranging my chapters and chapter sections, already mostly drafted. I needed such advice, for I found myself wanting to postpone almost every topic until *after* covering almost all of the others. (Ethics resembles economics in being a subject whose individual parts can best be understood only against a background of the other parts. This fact requires a spiraling treatment, with some repetition.) I have followed most but not all of Mr Whitman's advice, so he is not to blame for the organizational infelicities that remain. Nor is he to blame for the substance; for example, after some soul-searching, I disregarded his advice to omit the material now included as the appendix to Chapter 2.

More broadly, I thank several cohorts of students at the University of Virginia and Auburn University (and one at UCLA) for their patience with and helpful reactions to parts of the material of this book presented in my Seminar in Political Economy. I similarly thank my listeners at talks at the University of Virginia, George Mason University, Auburn University, and conventions of the Southern Economic Association and International Atlantic Economic Society. Cato Institute and the International Atlantic Economic Society have very kindly encouraged me to draw on work of mine that had appeared in the *Cato Journal* and *Atlantic Economic Journal*.

My text reflects which economists and philosophers have most influenced my thinking. Nevertheless, I particularly want to mention Thomas Hobbes, David Hume, John Stuart Mill, Ludwig von Mises, Friedrich A. Hayek, Henry Hazlitt, Ayn Rand, Paul Edwards, and R.M. Hare. James M. Buchanan has provided both inspiration and challenges, Murray Rothbard more particularly challenges.

Of all of Henry Hazlitt's books on many topics that I have read, the best in my opinion (and also his own favorite) is his *The Foundations of Morality*. It is also the best single book on ethics that I know of. It seems to me that Hazlitt has received nowhere near the credit that he deserves for his scholarly accomplishments, and for no better reason than that he lacked the usual academic credentials and platform. He was a profoundly educated man, but mostly self-educated. My book echoes Hazlitt's ideas, but it echoes them in different language and with different evidence and confronts them with both support and criticism from many writers other than those he cited. Important ideas deserve varied attempts to put them across.

I want to acknowledge a legacy from my late uncle Charles Bennett that I used for – that in my mind I classified as paying for – a couple of weeks at Rehoboth Beach, Delaware, where I worked on my manuscript in near-isolation, free of the usual distractions of home. Occasional examples in my text mentioning "beach and boardwalk" probably trace to that period.

When the text occasionally says what "a utilitarian" thinks or "utilitarians" think, I am obviously referring to myself; of course I do not claim to speak for all utilitarians. References to this or that chapter refer to chapters in the present book unless the citation makes it clear that the reference is to someone else's chapters. I cite works by date of publication, or by original date plus date of version used; full citations appear in the list of References at the end. When the References include two or more works by the same author and of the same date, I find it convenient to distinguish between them in citations not by appending "a", "b", and so on to the date but by appending an abbreviation of the title.

1. Ethics and economics

SOCIAL SCIENCE

To call ethics a social science is not to announce a distinct science with special techniques of its own. Nor is it a grab for the prestige of science. Instead, it recommends an attitude. Instead of being a parade ground of intuitions, revelations, and bombast, ethics can attune itself to the findings of the social (and natural) sciences and psychology. It can even suggest questions for those fields.

Social science helps check ethical intuitions against facts. It examines clashes among values and helps sort out the most fundamental ones. It recognizes that fact and logic alone cannot recommend private actions and public policies; ethical judgments must also enter in. Knowing that "good intentions are not enough", social science insists on comparing how alternative sets of institutions and rules are likely to work.

This book's subtitle, "The Moral Philosophy of Social Cooperation", is inexact for the sake of brevity. More fully it should read "Moral Philosophy Grounded in the Requirements of Social Cooperation". The book seeks to explain why people recognize ethical precepts and esteem the character traits that foster following them. Central to this explanation is what "social cooperation" requires. The latter term labels a framework of laws, customs, attitudes, and so forth that is conducive to individuals' successful cooperation with one another as they seek to make good lives for themselves in their own ways.

NONSCIENTIFIC APPROACHES TO ETHICS

The idea of ethics as social science gains clarity by contrast with other views. One of those sees ethical precepts as divinely revealed or as God's commands. Yet can terms like "good" and "evil" derive their very meaning or content from God? To call God "good", as in the Judeo-Christian tradition, presupposes criteria of good and bad distinct from God's will.

Another nonscientific approach is that of Immanuel Kant, who insisted that moral philosophy ignore all empirical knowledge of human nature and human society and root itself in pure reason (Copleston 1985, Vol. VI, pp. 312–13).

Moral laws bind all rational creatures absolutely and are valid quite apart from the contingent conditions of humanity. Moral goodness consists in the concept of law itself, which is possible only for a rational being. Reason properly serves an end far nobler than happiness. Only in conforming to duty does conduct acquire true moral worth (Kant 1785/1949, pp. 143, 147–9, 156). (Whether Kant did succeed in transcending all empirical considerations is another question; John Stuart Mill argued that he had not; *Utilitarianism*, Chapters I and V.)

Hadley Arkes (whose position receives further attention in chapter 10) provides a more recent example of antiempiricism. Although trumpeting an objective, autonomous, irreducible, and self-validating ethics, Arkes is vague about just what "the logic of morals itself" is (1986, pp. 114, 166). Moral axioms have a "universal truth ... guaranteed by their own necessity" (pp. 424–5). An objectively existing core of morality spins out its own implications and applications. It somehow demeans morality to argue for it as benefiting either the individual or society. Arkes finds it more noble – I believe this is not too harsh an interpretation – to appeal to deep-seated intuitions rather than to facts and reasoning.[1]

OVERLAPS BETWEEN ECONOMICS AND ETHICS

Economists must have some reason for their interest in ethics, for David Hume, Adam Smith, and many others have written on the topic.[2] Similarly, several distinguished moral philosophers, including John Rawls, Robert Nozick, Loren Lomasky, and Tibor Machan, have knowledgeably brought economics into their arguments. Of course, neither I nor anyone else writing on ethics thereby claims a special degree of personal virtue – only interest in the subject and possibly some competence.

This overlap of interests between economists and moral philosophers is no accident. All discussions of how people *should* behave, what policies governments *should* pursue, and what *obligations* citizens *owe* to their governments obviously involve ethics. The same conditions provide the subject matter of both fields. The fact of scarcity, man's nature as a social animal, and the benefits of cooperation require people to get along with one another somehow, even without central direction of their interactions. Ethics and social science both bear on using dispersed knowledge, promoting cooperation, easing tensions, and coordinating decentralized activities as individuals pursue their own diverse goals. Rules against lying, cheating, stealing, and coercion and encouraging benevolence and other virtues serve these functions.

The realities of human life, as David Hume explained, give rise to concepts of property and justice. First among these realities is moderate scarcity – "moderate" as opposed to both the superabundance of the Land of Cockaigne and the desperate scarcity of "lifeboat cases". The preconditions of both economics and ethics also include gains available from specialization, trade, and sociability, as well as people's genuine but limited benevolence. Concepts of justice and property derive, says Hume, "from the selfishness and confined generosity of man, along with the scanty provision nature has made for his wants" (italicized; 1739–40, Book III, Part II, Section II, p. 446 in the 1961 edition; compare 1751/1777/1930, Section III). Rules and conventions work toward "rubbing off ... rough corners and untoward affections" (1739–40, same section, esp. pp. 438, 441 in the 1961 edition). As these and other passages show, Hume finds morality far from arbitrary or subjective; it is rooted in nature, especially including human nature (cf. D.F. Norton 1993).

A contemporary philosopher rephrases these points: "Ethics, whatever else it may be, is the investigation of rationally justifiable bases for resolving conflict among persons with divergent aims who share a common world. Because resources and opportunities are not unlimited, the success of one person is often the failure of another. ... Philosophical normative ethics is the search for rationally justifiable standards for the resolution of interpersonal conflict, ..." Any theory in ethics must confront the question "How are we to live together?" (Lomasky 1987, pp. 38, 47, 52).

Scarcity requires choice. Having more of some goods, whether material or immaterial, costs having less of others. This "opportunity cost" is another of the few most central concepts of economics. Choices mean comparisons. The economist is not content with judgments that specific choices have good or bad outcomes. He asks, "Good or bad compared to what?" He is wary of supposed principles that must be carried into effect "at whatever cost". Principles are important, as this book argues throughout; but actions and policies cannot sensibly be decided on the basis of abstract principles alone, which at worst may be mere strings of noble-sounding words. What principles mean must be sought in what implementing them would require. (Hayek 1960, Chapter 6, provides a good example by examining supposed principles of distributive justice and social justice.)

Not only are goods and services, productive resources, and time scarce; so is information. People rarely have the luxury of making fully informed decisions. They must make do with information-economizing principles, rules of thumb, precedents, customs, procedures, and institutions. Sometimes they must assess alternative institutions and rules themselves.

Good reasons recommend a healthy respect for principles, as opposed to scorning them for pragmatic choice on the separate apparent merits of each individual case. These reasons refer to economizing on information requirements and costs of decisionmaking, coordination of different people's decisions and activities, avoidance of tunnel vision and self-serving self-deception, and the educational role of principles. Yet no reasonably specific principle is so compellingly right as to require its unswerving application in every single case regardless of consequences. It may clash with other relevant principles. Here, as in other matters that economists deal with, a reasonable position may fall between conceivable extremes – but to say so is not always to recommend a mindless middle-of-the-road stance.

A DOUBLE RELATION: HOW ETHICS ENTERS INTO ECONOMICS

A double relation holds between ethics and the rest of social science. (A distinction between the two directions of this relation is admittedly fuzzy and is hardly more than an organizing device.) First, ethics enters into elucidating the conditions necessary for material prosperity and progress. Second – which is more the concern of this book – social science helps clear up some central questions about the nature, grounding, persuasiveness, and appraisal of purported ethical knowledge.

Even positive economics, aspiring to scientific status, must pay attention to ethical standards, for they condition how well economies perform. Francis Fukuyama (1995) insists on the importance of trust. Institutions like property rights, contract, and commercial law presuppose suitable ethical habits. Finding the appropriate buyer or seller, negotiating a contract and enforcing it in case of dispute or fraud, complying with government regulations – all are easier if the parties can assume each other's honesty. Trust reduces the need to spell out contract terms at length, to hedge against contingencies, and to litigate if disputes still do arise. Widespread *dis*trust necessitates various formalities and so imposes a kind of tax on business. Transactions costs are likely to be lower in societies with shared moral values. A high degree of trust also allows a more flexible organization of the workplace and delegation of responsibility to lower levels. Implicit bargains can enable relaxed work rules and long-term job security to pay for one another (Fukuyama 1995, pp. 27–8, 31, 149–56, 263, 310–11, 352). (Fukuyama does not cite but might well have cited Arthur Okun 1981 and his notion of the "invisible handshake", a concept figuring in macroeconomics.)

The problem of social order, as James Buchanan says (1979, p. 208), eternally confronts people "who realize that they must live together and that to do so they must impose *upon themselves* social rules, social institutions". Economists cannot evade their task of investigating "such rules and institutions by shifting attention to trivialities". A free-market order requires, beyond property laws, "a common set of moral precepts" (Buchanan 1979, pp. 211–12, and Part 3 on the whole). "[S]ociety cannot be free, prosperous, and self-governing unless the honorable somehow outnumber the dishonorable. ... No market can work if everybody always has to count his change" (Nutter 1983, p. 55).

Many economists and political scientists, if only a minority, have voiced similar insights. Steven Rhoads chides economists for typically trying to avoid value questions by taking tastes and preferences as they find them, immune from analysis (1985, for example, p. 213). Warren Nutter criticized "the narrow view economists take of the human race and its behavior" (1983, p. xiii). "Specialization, the fetish of scientism and ethical neutrality, and the contradictory utopian spirit have moved most economists out of contact with reality" (p. 47). Nutter found formal welfare economics (a purported application of abstract microeconomic theory) nearly irrelevant to the real world; he suggested replacing it by sophisticated comparison of alternative sets of institutions – by political economy, a science for building the good society (1983, pp. 42–5). Herbert Frankel and Ayn Rand have written, separately, about the moral significance of money. Money is both tool and symbol of a society where productive men and women benefit from and contribute to one another's excellences, voluntarily trading value for value, instead of trying to live by looting or wheedling (Frankel 1978, giving heavy credit to the philosopher Georg Simmel; Rand 1957, Part 2, Chapter II, speech by the fictional Francisco d'Anconia).

Such ideas have a venerable history. David Hume judged three conditions essential to long-run planning, saving and investment, and cooperation in large projects. These are the stability of possessions, the transfer of ownership by consent (rather than by force or fraud) and the performance of promises (1739–40/1961, Book III, Part II, esp. Sections II, III, IV, V and VI).

Thomas Hobbes had already stressed the importance of peace and security, which presupposed, as he thought, a government strong enough to suppress the war of all against all. Where every man is enemy to every man and each must look to himself alone for security, "there is no place for industry, because the fruit thereof is uncertain: and consequently no culture of the earth; no navigation, nor use of the commodities that may be imported by sea; no commodious building; no instruments of moving and removing such things as require much force; no knowledge of the face of the earth; no account of time; no arts; no letters; no society" – and then follows the description of life under such conditions made so hackneyed by repeated quotation that I refrain from quoting it still again. Peace and security, however, including secure property rights and the attendant opportunities to create and accumulate wealth, permit "commodious living", which is Hobbes's term for economic development (1651, Part I, Chapter XIII, pp. 85–6 in the 1952 edition).

In these passages of 1651 Hobbes set forth the bare essentials of development economics. Many Third World countries illustrate today, by the consequences of their absence, the importance of peace and security. Wilhelm Röpke noted the frequent lack in those countries of "the spiritual and moral foundations" required for Western-style economic success (1958/1971, p. 119). Lawrence Harrison has written in detail on how the moral and social ethos conditions economic backwardness or economic development (1985, 1992; compare Naipaul 1964/1981 on India of three or more decades ago).

Despite their wide occurrence, venerability, and importance, such insights into the moral aspects of economics have been confined to the fringes of the discipline. They do not readily lend themselves to prestigiously formal and ostensibly "rigorous" mathematical modeling and econometric testing. (To suggest this reason is not necessarily to complain about it. Narrow specialization pays off in academic as in other work. Even formal and otherwise rather sterile welfare economics provides exercises for developing proficiency in the techniques of price theory.)

Unfashionable though they may be, ethical considerations do obviously bear on what is arguably the central problem of economics, which is to explain how individual units – individuals, households, business firms, and other organizations – relate to one another in the whole economic cosmos. (As Walter Eucken warned, 1954, pp. 220–21, pointillistic focus on the decisions and actions of the individual unit risks drawing attention away from the central problem of economy-wide coordination.)

Economics investigates how even persons who will never meet one another can cooperate as they pursue their own diverse goals in life. Each one plays his own particular role in a fine-grained division of labor; yet their diverse pursuits somehow fit together, and without any authority assuming the task of coordination. *Social cooperation* – a concept central to this book – operates somehow. The market, with its signals and incentives of prices, costs, profit, and loss, is a notable arena of cooperation and coordination. *Competition*, often considered the opposite of cooperation, actually serves it as a key part of the market process. But the market is only one among many institutions, practices, and beliefs that serve cooperation. Spoken and written language and the legal and political system are others; so is informal sociability; so are ethical norms.

As the economist David Levy suggests (paraphrased in Kincaid 1993), morality helps avoid losses of potential gains from trade and other kinds of cooperation, losses due to excessively narrow and short-run views, inadequate knowledge, or poor communication. In a standard example known as the Prisoners' Dilemma, two persons could jointly benefit from cooperation; yet each, hoping to take advantage of the other or fearful of being his victim, acts in a narrowly self-centered way, with a result harmful to both. In the jargon of economics, because each person aims at a local optimum, both miss attaining a greater optimum. Metaphorically, a mountain climber is so intent on moving always upward, never down, that he stops at the top of the nearest hill and is diverted from the top of the mountain range.

Since several of the writings reviewed later in this book employ the concept, the Prisoners' Dilemma is worth explaining here. It owes its name to a much-repeated example (Rapoport 1987). Two men are arrested for burglary. The prosecutor lacks enough evidence to convict them of that crime but could convict them on the lesser charge of possessing stolen goods. Hoping that one or both suspects will turn state's evidence, the prosecutor interviews each one separately, promising each one freedom in return for his decisive testimony against his associate, who will be convicted of burglary and serve a long jail sentence. If his testimony turns out not to be decisive, however, because *both* confess and implicate each other, then both will receive sentences of intermediate length. If both remain silent, both will receive a short sentence on the lesser charge.

If the two prisoners could make and enforce a deal, both would remain silent, minimizing their combined time in jail. Since by hypothesis they cannot do so, however, each must decide by himself. Each recognizes that whether his associate rats on him or remains loyally silent, the best course from his own narrow point of view is to rat. Hence both rat, and both receive longer sentences than they would have received if both had remained silent.

This example, entrenched in the literature, suffers from the distracting feature that both persons are criminals, for whom the observer may care little. It is easy to devise examples in which the observer does sympathize with the protagonists. The point of all such examples, anyway, is that individually rational self-interested behavior may yield worse results for both persons than behavior tinged by concern for the other; individual rationality and collective rationality may possibly diverge.

Two-person examples may be generalized to many persons. Each of several farmers grazing their herds on a communal pasture finds it in his individual interest to add another cow, yet the overgrazing that results may be to everyone's disadvantage. The land's being common property rather than private property causes "tragedy" (Hardin 1968/1972). Certain strands of theory suggest that macroeconomic disturbances would be less likely to throw an economy into recession if companies and workers responded to slumps in demand for their products and their labor by promptly cutting their selling prices and wage rates. With millions of separate units making such decisions in a decentralized manner, however, most of them individually have good reason to delay those adjustments. The resulting unintended overall price and wage stickiness makes the economy more prone to recession than if prices and wages were highly flexible.

Moral rules offer a way out of some Prisoners' Dilemmas, if not out of macroeconomic difficulties. Moral rules provide constraints necessary to avoid behavior from such narrow or short-run self-interest that it precludes obtaining greater or more enduring benefits. Metaphorically, they encourage taking the one step backward that permits moving two steps forward. Moral constraints deter individuals from throwing away the good life in pursuit of momentary pleasures. They deter narrowly exploitive strategies. They underpin private property and the gains from trade. They encourage cooperation on projects whose gains accrue to the cooperators collectively, or even more broadly, rather than to any person separately at others' expense. In economics jargon, they encourage cooperation in supplying public goods, goods whose benefits cannot be confined exclusively to persons who help pay for them (Kincaid 1993, pp. 328–9).

That ethical rules serve these purposes in no way shows that they were deliberately designed for them. Nor do the purposes served for members of society jointly suffice by themselves to give each member an adequate incentive to abide by the rules individually. Questions of how morality originated and of what reason the individual might have to behave morally are large ones requiring detailed discussion.

Wilhelm Röpke alludes to the intertwining of the market and other social institutions when he warns against a *déformation professionelle*, a bias toward putting a too narrowly economic interpretation onto various aspects of life. It shows up in straining to broaden the scope of purely economic analysis, coupled with inadequate appreciation of how the functioning of a market economy depends on its being embodied in a social structure and ethical framework. Attention to ethics helps avoid this "economistic" bias.

> The market is only one section of society. ... To know economics only is to know not even that. Man, in the words of the Gospel, does not live by bread alone. Let us beware of that caricature of an economist who, watching people cheerfully disporting themselves in their suburban allotments, thinks he has said everything there is to say when he observes that this is not a rational way of producing vegetables – forgetting that it may be an eminently rational way of producing happiness, which alone matters in the last resort (Röpke 1958/1971, pp. 91–2, reprinted from the 1960 edition in Schuettinger 1970, p. 76).

THE DOUBLE RELATION: HOW ECONOMICS ILLUMINATES ETHICS

Not all economists suffer from the bias that Röpke diagnosed. Many can contribute to the study of ethics because they understand, following Hume and Hayek (see References), how social institutions can sometimes originate and evolve "spontaneously", without deliberate overall contrivance. Examples besides ethical precepts include language, the common law, private property, money, and the market itself. What Hayek calls an empirical-evolutionist outlook recognizes how institutions and practices may sometimes evolve to be more serviceable than consciously contrived ones. People sometimes follow rules that they cannot fully articulate. Not all tradition is superstition. Thanks to a process of selection over time, traditional institutions and practices may be useful, even though their usefulness may not yet have been explicitly demonstrated. Dietary customs, including taboos before the days of refrigeration, provide examples.

To recognize the unplanned selection of institutions and practices is not to preach a rigid conservatism nor to scorn scientific study and possible deliberate reform of whatever exists. The point, rather, is that economists understand the advantages of allowing some institutions, practices, and rules to evolve and operate loosely and spontaneously, of leaving agreement on them tacit, and of enforcing them and penalizing violations only informally. The reasons include the incompleteness and cost of information and the costs of bargaining, transactions, monitoring, and enforcement.

Trying to enforce detailed standards of decent behavior by law would be prohibitively costly and, though bound to fail, would spell totalitarian intrusion into people's lives (cf. chapter 11). As a practical matter, codes of morality and their enforcement must be left informal, loose, and flexible. Consider the convention of walking and biking to the right on sidewalks and seaside boardwalks. If this and many similar minor conventions were embodied in actual laws, then effectively enforcing them all would be downright impossible; there would be too many of them, and too many instances of minor violations. The necessity of enforcing them only incompletely would breed disrespect for law and would offer scope to discriminate against particular persons and groups by selective enforcement, a potential weapon for tyrants.

Still another consideration recommends leaving many institutions, practices, and conventions loose and flexible. Doing so lets them respond gradually to changes in conditions and knowledge. Their continuity and dependability help economize on time and energy spent making decisions and enable people better to predict each other's behavior and so achieve coordination. At the same time they remain open to reform.

Economists are professionally equipped to deal with ethics not only because they recognize what scarcity implies for interpersonal conflict and cooperation but also because they are alert to regularities and patterns in human affairs that may not have resulted from anyone's deliberate intentions. Economists achieve additional insights into gains from specialization and trade and from both explicit and tacit agreements, including tacit agreements to abide even by incompletely articulated rules. They understand the logic of investment – of how curtailing consumption in the short run can promise a more than compensating gain in the long run. More generally, economists understand the distinction and the relation between short-run and long-run interests and how apparent sacrifice in the short run may bring gain in the longer run. Well-conceived investments illustrate the virtue of prudence, which self-interested adherence to ethical rules also probably illustrates. The rationally conceived long-run interests of different persons harmonize to a greater degree than a superficial, short-run view might suggest.

Economists are alert to the general interdependence of economic activities and, more generally, to possibilities of remote and delayed side-effects of seeking desired results. They realize that good intentions are not enough. They are alert to how present actions may affect future actions and how some persons' behavior may affect others' behavior, as by establishing precedents.

"Externalities" are benefits and costs that people confer or inflict on one another without receiving or paying full compensation. Awareness of them alerts economists to another dimension of interpersonal relations. Some types of pollution, such as noise pollution, illustrate an overlap between ethics and the economic analysis of externalities, bargaining or transactions costs, and the like. Questions of the social responsibility of business are also amenable to a blend of ethical and economic analysis.

Not only specialists in comparative economic systems but also all economists who occupy themselves with possible reforms – with comparing the performances to be expected from existing and from modified institutions – have thereby made a start on systematizing and comparing conceptions of the good society. They are equipped to assess critiques of capitalism voiced by clergymen and other moralists. Socialists, as John Jewkes reports, have always held the market economy to be immoral. The profit motive breeds selfishness, acquisitiveness, and the worship of wealth. The flaunting of wealth destroys taste. Inequality divides the community into exploiting and exploited classes. Competition fosters dishonesty, deception, and shoddiness. Big business corrupts politics. "The injustices which men create for themselves can only be removed by the State, 'which is, in fact, accepted as the nearest we can get to an impartial judge in any matter.'" (Jewkes 1968, reprinted in Schuettinger 1970, pp. 80–81. Lest his summary of socialist attitudes be thought overdrawn, Jewkes cites writings of the Webbs, R.H. Tawney, and Sir Stafford Cripps; the quoted clause comes from Cripps).

The marketplace is, by far, not the only arena of unclean motives and methods. Bureaucracy and politics, even including academic politics, provide examples. It is far from clear that shifting economic activities from the market to the political and bureaucratic arenas will raise the average moral level of motives and methods. "[D]angerous human proclivities can be canalised into comparatively harmless channels by the existence of opportunities for money-making and private wealth, which, if they cannot be satisfied in this way, may find their outlet in cruelty, the reckless pursuit of personal power and authority, and other forms of self-aggrandisement. It is better that a man should tyrannise over his bank balance than over his fellow-citizens" (Keynes 1936, p. 374).

Political economy less sweeping than comparisons of whole systems also involves ethics. Recommendations even on relatively specific strands of policy necessarily involve not only positive analysis but also value judgments. Pricing policies of public enterprises and regulated utilities, rationing, price and wage controls, minimum-wage laws, environmental and energy-conservation and other regulations, taxes, and redistributionary policies affect different persons and groups in different ways, raising issues of fairness. The relevant positive (or factual) propositions derive not only from economic analysis but also, quite probably, from sociology, political science, psychology, and the natural sciences. The values involved are notions of desirable and undesirable, good and bad, right and wrong, fair and unfair. An economist may legitimately explore such notions.

The economist Henry Hazlitt notes (1964, p. 301) that both economics and ethics are concerned with human action, conduct, decision, and choice. Economics *describes*, *explains*, or *analyzes* their determinants, consequences, and implications. But the moment we come to questions of justification or desirability, "we have entered the realm of Ethics. This is also true the moment we begin to discuss the *desirability* of one economic *policy* as compared with another".

Economists properly avoid self-deception about the possibility of purely value-free analysis. Making explicit the normative as well as positive elements in policy recommendations helps pinpoint sources of disagreement and helps open the way to possibly resolving disagreements.

The economist Joan Robinson explained that we can describe the technical operating properties of a given economic system in an objective way.

> But it is not possible to describe a *system* without moral judgments creeping in. For ... in describing it we compare it (openly or tacitly) with other actual or imagined systems. ... We cannot escape from making judgments and the judgments that we make arise from the ethical preconceptions that have soaked into our view of life and are somehow imprinted in our brains. We cannot escape from our own habits of thought. ... But we ... can see what we value, and try to see why (1963, p. 14).

It is often said that discussing values or tastes is pointless – *de gustibus non est disputandum* – and that, anyway, economists "as such" have no business discussing them. This slogan is mistaken. Thanks to their training in observation and analysis and thanks to the subject matter they deal with, economists, or some of them, *do* have special qualifications for perceiving and weeding out contradictions and redundancies in assortments of value judgments; they are equipped to wield Occam's razor. Economists have qualifications for striving for consistency among the values that they themselves may avow. (This is emphatically not to say, though, that they are entitled to *impose* their judgments.)

Most obviously, positive analysis can help ferret out contradictions among relatively specific values. Trivially, it is a contradiction to insist on eating one's cake and having it too. Economic analysis is relevant to whether one can consistently advocate full employment, price-level stability, and strong labor unions all together, or independent national monetary policies, fixed exchange rates, and freedom of international trade and capital movements.

As Ernest Nagel writes,

> The thesis that *some* sciences [he mentions astronomy] cannot determine values is ... trivially true. On the other hand, every rational appraisal of values must take cognizance of the findings of the natural and social sciences, for if the existential conditions and consequences of the realization of values are not noted, acceptance of a scheme of values is a species of undisciplined romanticism (1954, p. 34).

Neither economics nor ethics nor both together can say clearly and unambiguously what *ought* to be done in all circumstances. This is not a defect of either field of study but hinges on facts of tough, complex reality. Economists, concerned as they are with scarcity and choice, are equipped to recognize the reality of agonizing dilemmas. They are unlikely to be unduly impressed by ethical arguments or ethical skepticism relying on "lifeboat cases". They are not baffled by cooked-up cases of clash between different ethical rules, each of which might seem decisive when considered by itself. An ethical rule is not discredited by strong reasons that might recommend overriding it in exceptional cases (a point that seems to have escaped Joseph Fletcher 1966/1974).

Aware of costs, economists do not expect all good things always to hang together, with the achievement of each serving achievement of the others. Sir Isaiah Berlin (1958/1969, pp. 170–72) has eloquently identified the common misconception that all good things must be intimately connected or at least mutually compatible, that all considerations bearing on a policy issue point in the same direction, that a final solution is available.

> To assume that all values can be graded on one scale, so that it is a mere matter of inspection to determine the highest, seems to me to falsify our knowledge that men are free agents, to represent moral decision as an operation which a slide-rule could, in principle, perform. To say that in some ultimate, all-reconciling, yet realizable synthesis, duty *is* interest, or individual freedom *is* pure democracy or an authoritarian state, is to throw a metaphysical blanket over either self-deceit or deliberate hypocrisy (Berlin 1969, p. 171).

Economists understand how the principle of marginalism qualifies the notion of priorities. Tradeoffs typically arise not between two or more goods globally considered but between marginal amounts – small increases and decreases. Obtaining more and more of one good makes it less attractive to go still further, sacrificing still more of other goods. This principle applies far more widely than just to material commodities. All the more so, notions of marginalism and tradeoffs count against absolutist formulations, such as that some particular good or particular virtue has absolute priority and must be served "at all costs". Such language is foreign to an economist.

UTILITARIANISM: A PREVIEW

The central questions of ethics include these. What sorts of knowledge, if any, do ethical precepts constitute? What meaning, use, and basis do such concepts as good and bad, right and wrong, natural law, and natural rights have? How are they grounded? How, if at all, can traditional precepts and suggested changes be judged wise or perverse? Why be moral? How does ethics bear on political philosophy? In conjunction with economics and other fields of positive knowledge, how can ethics enter into the choice of public policies?

I admit to espousing a version of utilitarianism. Utilitarianism has a bad press and is widely held in contempt. Not all versions, however, deserve the contempt admittedly deserved by the narrowest, shallowest, and crudest version, which nowadays has become hardly more than a straw man and figment of critics' imaginations.

Utilitarianism as I conceive of it is a doctrine whose test of ethical precepts, character traits, legal and economic systems, and other institutions, practices, and policies is conduciveness to the success of individuals as they strive to make good lives for themselves in their own diverse ways. Its fundamental value judgment is approval of happiness and disapproval of misery.

Admittedly, neither "happiness" nor any other single word is an adequate label. Later chapters will touch on how best to describe this fundamental value judgment or ultimate criterion. In any case, one means to satisfying it is so pervasively requisite that it becomes almost a surrogate criterion. It is *social cooperation*, which means a well-functioning society – the whole complex of institutions, practices, and precepts whereby people can interact peacefully and to mutual advantage. Institutions, precepts, and traits of personal character are to be valued or deplored according as they tend to support or subvert it. (This insight is the main theme of Hazlitt 1964, who derived inspiration from the economist Ludwig von Mises.)

Any genuinely appealing ethical system must be utilitarian in this broad sense. Let anyone who disagrees state and defend an alternative. Different ethical systems are indeed conceivable, but each of them turns out, on examination, either to be utilitarianism in terminological disguise or to be downright unappealing. The fact that some genuine alternatives are conceivable (and have even been advocated by a few philosophers) shows that I am not interpreting utilitarianism so broadly as to make it empty.

Instead of organizing the discussion in linear fashion, moving straightforwardly from topic to topic, I shall have to proceed in spirals, returning with more detail to topics already mentioned. In ethics as in economics, understanding each topic presupposes understanding the others, or the whole subject; hence the necessity of spirals.

ORGANIZATION OF THE BOOK

Chapter 2 lays out some basic ideas, including the distinctions between positive and normative propositions and between specific and fundamental value judgments, the nature and possible resolution of ethical disagreements, and definitions of key terms. Chapter 3 looks at the origins of ethics, including biological and cultural evolution. Chapter 4 sets forth the substance of utilitarianism and introduces the case for indirect utilitarianism. Chapter 5 examines the meaning of utility and explores whether people's happiness or the satisfaction of their desires is a more defensible criterion. Chapter 6 faces the charge that utilitarianism is collectivistic, more concerned with some sort of aggregate utility than with individual persons and their strivings. Chapter 7 considers charges that utilitarianism is immoral in various other ways. Chapter 8 examines what if any reasons the individual has to behave ethically. Chapter 9 considers in what sense impartiality is an ethical requirement. Chapter 10 compares utilitarianism with rival doctrines, including ones centering on natural or human rights. Chapter 11 examines ethical aspects of law, government, and public policy. Three chapter appendixes deal with free will versus determinism, some strands in the history of utilitarian doctrine, and the political philosophy of libertarianism or classical liberalism.

No chapter focuses specifically on "business ethics". Familiar complaints about how "the ethics of the market" are infecting other broad areas of life are misconceived. There is no such thing as a distinct business or market ethics (although, as recognized especially toward the end of Chapter 9, a higher degree of personal solidarity is more appropriate in small, intimate groups than in the "extended order" of the market). No otherwise unethical behavior becomes acceptable by being done in the name of business. In business as in other activities, ethical precepts express restraints on what people may properly do as they pursue their own interests and the interests of other persons to whom they owe or feel special loyalty. In business as in other areas of life, ethical quandaries may arise – clashes of applicable principles or conflicts of loyalties. Economics intertwines with ethics, then, not in prescribing special rules for people in business but in helping to clarify the nature and grounding of ethical precepts quite generally.

NOTES

1. Another remark about unscientific approaches may be worth a footnote. Although ethics and social science intersect, members of the clergy appear to claim and to be accorded special moral authority more often than social scientists. (Examples occur in National Conference of Catholic Bishops on War and Peace 1983, reprinted in Castelli 1983; National Conference of Catholic Bishops 1986, reprinted in Gannon 1987; and statements of other eminent clergymen reviewed in Bauer 1981/1985, Bauer 1984/1985, and Gray 1989LS. Also consider the frequent inclusion of clergymen on committees dealing with medical ethics or other ethical issues, as well as the clerical origin of the Sullivan principles, supposed to guide American business firms operating in South Africa during the era of apartheid.)

   Many learned and honorable men and women belong to the clergy. Still, one may wonder about looking for moral leadership to persons whose profession makes an actual virtue out of faith, out of believing and teaching propositions without and even despite evidence. As Henry Simons wrote (1948, pp. 7–8), a good moral order must rest "on much the same kind of free, critical discussion as is involved in scientific inquiry. A moral order imposed by force or fraud, by authorities, or by threats of punishment in this world or the next is a contradiction in terms".

   To say so is not to ridicule moral convictions. On the contrary, they are indispensable to a healthy society. But precisely for that reason it is important to seek a sound basis for them.

   Economists are better equipped for handling moral questions, by and large, than are clergymen and women. They are less likely, I conjecture, to be content with noble-sounding words and more likely to ask what asserted principles would mean in practice and what institutions would be required to implement them. The Catholic bishops unwittingly illustrated the contrast. They actually said that "The fundamental moral criterion for all [sic] economic decisions, policies, and institutions is this: They must be at the service of *all people, especially the poor*" (1986 letter, reprinted 1987, para. 24, emphasis in the original, a passage to which Benne 1987, p. 47, has perceptively called attention).

2. These include Jeremy Bentham, John Stuart Mill, Henry Sidgwick, Francis Y. Edgeworth, Philip Henry Wicksteed, John Maynard Keynes, Roy Harrod, Ludwig von Mises, F.A. Hayek, Frank Knight, T W Hutchison, Joan Robinson, Henry Hazlitt, Kenneth Boulding, A.W. Coats, John C. Harsanyi, William J. Baumol, Murray Rothbard, Roland McKean, Robert Sugden, James M. Buchanan, and others to whom I apologize for not going on and on.

2.   Some fundamentals

LEVELS OF INQUIRY

This chapter introduces concepts and questions to which later chapters return in detail. Before considering what sorts of argument and evidence can support an ethical doctrine, we should distinguish between different levels of discussion:

1.   Prescriptive or applied ethics, ethics on the operating level.
    a. Precepts or maxims of behavior (sometimes, perhaps misleadingly, called intuitive ethics).
    b. Critical reflection on these precepts and maxims and their application.
2.   Metaethics.

This classification, being just that, does not match hard and fast features of reality. (It roughly follows Brink 1989 and Hare, cited below.) The boundaries between (1a) and (1b) and between (1b) and (2) are not sharp. Still, the distinctions can be useful.

Discussion on level (1a) takes the maxims of popular morality pretty much for granted. It judges right and wrong. It recommends what kinds of behavior and traits of character to cultivate. It condemns lying, cheating, and stealing and exhorts benevolence. Some such *prima facie* maxims are indispensable. Attempts to do without them and to calculate the consequences of every decision directly would founder on biased perception and reasoning, defects of knowledge, and lack of time.

Thinking on the critical level, (1b), becomes necessary when generally applicable maxims appear to clash, when exceptional circumstances suggest overriding a maxim, and when a person reflects on appraising, choosing, and modifying the *prima facie* maxims themselves (Hare 1981, esp. Chapters 2 and 3, 1989EiET, pp. 110, 189-90, 202-3, 221, 237-8).

Some examples of particular moral issues are these. Under what if any conditions is abortion or the death penalty justified? Should Vera keep the truth from Malcolm to spare him anguish? (David Brink evidently puts such questions on level (1a), but they arguably belong on (1b) instead.) Sissela Bok (1979) provides examples of ethics on level (1b) by reviewing various arguments that lying is morally excusable or even required in particular circumstances. Brink's examples on level (1b) include: How are goodness and rightness related? In what way should a moral theory be impartial among people? Does impartiality require maximizing aggregate welfare, or should distribution be considered? What ideal of the person should we adopt, and how does this decision affect our moral principles?

Such issues arise *within* morality. Level (2) or metaethical issues are *about* morality; they are metaphysical, epistemological, semantic, or psychological. Metaethics examines the coherence and rationale of the operating-level ethics that forms its subject matter. It considers the meanings of moral words and the logic of moral reasoning. It asks what if any sorts of knowledge ethical precepts and judgments express. Are they factual statements, tautologies, arbitrary commands, mere vents of personal emotion, or what? Can they be objectively justified? By what if any criteria does it make sense to judge some precepts more soundly based or more strongly binding than others? If there are such things as moral facts or truths, how do they relate to natural features of agents, policies, and actions (Brink 1989, pp. 1–2)? Metaethics further asks how ethical precepts might have originated. Why do people believe in them, if they do, and generally abide by them?

The present book deals predominantly with metaethics and the critical level (1b) of prescriptive ethics. Instead of just preaching the level (1) maxims of behavior and character, it considers why they command respect, if they do, and how to assess them and any of their suggested modifications or replacements. (Chapter 11, however, does consider some issues of applied ethics, as do several writings of R.M. Hare, including his 1989EoPM.)

Only incidentally, if at all, does this book discuss decision procedures and tell readers what to take account of in making their own decisions, whether the general welfare or something else. Operating on levels (1b) and (2), it is concerned instead with criteria for appraising ethical judgments and doctrines. This distinction between *decision procedure* and *criterion* will prove useful in facing certain criticisms of the utilitarianism expounded here.

THE IS/OUGHT GAP

Before answering our broad question about how argument and evidence can bear on ethical doctrines, we must make further distinctions. Value judgments, also called normative propositions, stand distinct from positive propositions of fact and logic. Yet positive propositions do bear on value judgments. Both in explaining and in appraising a prescriptive doctrine, one expects it to square with facts of reality. A doctrine holding people morally obliged to fly around flapping their arms could not be valid. No one is morally obliged to do what he cannot do. "Ought implies can"; more exactly, "ought" *presupposes* "can".

While facts of reality are relevant to ethics, they alone cannot establish any ethical proposition. Being "natural" in some sense does not by itself suffice either to justify or condemn particular behaviors. Beyond conforming to facts and to the principle that "ought presupposes can", an acceptable prescriptive doctrine must conform to fundamental value judgments. (The distinction between fundamental and relatively specific value judgments is developed below.)

Positive propositions subdivide into factual and logical ones. Factual examples are "Grass is green" and "All episodes of severe price inflation have involved rapid money creation". Because they refer to empirical reality, factual propositions cannot carry ironclad guarantees against error. Merely to classify a proposition as factual or logical – or instead as normative – says nothing about its truth or error. "All inflations are caused by the exercise of monopoly power" is a factual but false proposition.

Logical propositions are true (barring mistakes in reasoning) by virtue of logic and word usage. Here are two examples: "If X implies Y, then not-Y implies not-X"; "If A is longer than B and B is longer than C, then C is not longer than A". (The very meaning of "longer than" rules out C's being longer than A in the case stipulated.)

Strictly positive propositions, whether factual or logical, have no normative content themselves, although people may have normative reasons for stating them or for doing research on what they pertain to.

Within the class of positive propositions, a few philosophers, including Ayn Rand and Willard Quine, have tried to deny the factual/logical distinction, also called (or at least closely related to) the synthetic/analytic distinction. We need not pursue this issue here (although it is important in other contexts; see Yeager 1994).

In contrast with both types of positive proposition, normative propositions are statements about good or bad, right or wrong, desirable or undesirable, just or unjust, obligatory or permissible or impermissible, and similar ethical predicates. One example is "Lying, cheating, and stealing are wrong". Such propositions are not purely descriptive. They are neither purely factual statements nor logical tautologies nor some blend of the two alone. Observation and reasoning *alone* cannot validate them. No one can prove in a purely objective way, free of any trace of evaluation or intuition or emotion, that considerateness and kindness are good and that torture and murder are wrong. Nor can anyone objectively prove that a policy of tolerating substantial inflation is better than one of tolerating heavy unemployment, in case the supposed choice is genuine. (Challenges to Hume's Fork, as I am inclined to call this positive/normative distinction,[1] are assessed below.)

The classification as either value-free or value-loaded applies to propositions, statements, sentences. It does not apply to whole academic disciplines or varieties or aspects of them (despite what the title of Milton Friedman's 1953 *Essays in Positive Economics*[2] might seem to suggest). If a science is interpreted as the whole range of its practitioners' professional activities, then of course it cannot be value-free. Scientists necessarily make value judgments about what questions provide important, challenging, or enjoyable research topics. They make ethical judgments about their relations with other scientists. They make judgments about the results of applying or misapplying their findings: health and prosperity are good; disease and depression are bad. (As these examples suggest, even some terms and concepts are value-loaded.) That a particular procedure or drug achieves complication-free abortions in the great majority of cases is a positive, value-free proposition (and even if it happens to be incorrect, it is still a *positive* proposition). Whether complication-free (or any) abortions are desirable or morally permissible is quite another matter. That a minimum-wage law will cause such-and-such effects is another positive proposition, distinct from value judgments about the desirability of those effects. The phenomena and institutions that economists study, the reasons for their particular interests, the ways they go about their research, and the ways that policymakers and others apply (or ignore) their findings, all are shot through with value judgments. This normative aspect of economics is neither avoidable nor regrettable – and that is another value judgment.

POSITIVE STATEMENTS THAT SOUND NORMATIVE AND NORMATIVE STATEMENTS THAT EXPRESS FACTS

Positive propositions may *mention* norms without themselves expressing any. The statement that specified values prevail in a certain society is itself a factual proposition of cultural anthropology, possibly correct, possibly mistaken. Even though its subject matter is norms said to prevail, the statement *itself* has no normative content. By contrast, a proposition *expressing* any normative judgment of its own is a value judgment, even though it has factual–logical content in addition to its normative content.

Since value judgments appraise things, events, states of affairs, persons, character traits, attitudes, and other aspects of reality, either actual or imagined, a *pure* value judgment is scarcely conceivable. (Only a highly abstract fundamental value judgment, discussed below, might perhaps count as pure.) To call the steak at Barney's "nice" (Edwards 1965, Chapter V) does not merely convey an appraisal, period; it also conveys some information (or misinformation) about the steak's objective properties that the speaker deems reasons for liking it. Similarly, if I say that Smith is a scoundrel, I am saying more than that he disgusts me; I am also conveying some information (or misinformation) about his behavior or character – only vague information thus far, but information I might spell out if asked.

Paul Edwards (1965) calls evaluative words ("nice", "disgusting", "good", "bad", "exciting", "boring", and the like) *polyguous* (a term further explained below). Such words carry multiple bits of meaning, including factual information or misinformation. The particular facts referred to vary from context to context and are vague in any case – like the character traits and behavior that warrant calling a person good or bad and the subject matter and style that warrant calling a lecture exciting or boring. Still, the word conveys an evaluation *in view of* objective reality (or imagined reality) and does not express a *pure* evaluation (whatever that might be).

Edwards illuminates these and related issues. To some extent ethical judgments do indeed express attitudes or emotions. At the same time, however, they also make factual assertions (perhaps correct, perhaps mistaken) about the *objects* of those emotions. Factual knowledge is relevant to moral judgments and to whether people consider them true or false. Without overthrowing Hume's Fork (mentioned above), a scientific approach to resolving moral disagreements is intelligible and can be fruitful. In a sense, although not by strict logical entailment, "ought" judgments may indeed follow from statements of fact. Facts may enter into arguments that lead people to reconsider (and perhaps consolidate, perhaps revise) their specific judgments about good and bad, right and wrong, just and unjust.

Edwards exempts fundamental value judgments from his claim that moral judgments, because they have descriptive as well as emotive meaning, can in principle be supported or refuted. People can give reasons for relatively specific or nonfundamental judgments, such as that John should keep his appointment with James, that Bill should not occupy Jane's parking space, or that one should not bear false witness against one's neighbor. A fundamental moral judgment is one that brings its maker to the end of his capacity to give reasons. If someone cannot say why, for example, happiness is good and pointless misery is bad – if he cannot go beyond recognizing that they just *are* good and bad – that judgment is fundamental for him (as it is for me also). Fundamental judgments like that presumably are rare in real-world discussions.

Paul Edwards illustrates how ordinary value judgments have factual content in his chapter entitled "The steak at Barney's is rather nice". When someone makes that remark to a friend of similar tastes, he means that the steak is of familiar size and thickness, consists of high-grade beef marbled with fat, is broiled to the degree ordered – and so forth. The word "nice", describing food, refers to an only rather vaguely specified set of properties, and the particular ones it refers to are different in different circumstances and in the judgments of different people. Yet the properties are objective characteristics of the foods. "[I]t is our taste, our likes and dislikes which determine what features we refer to when we call a steak ... nice." Still, a statement of this sort "is an objective claim. It asserts that these features belong to the steak at Barney's. It does not *assert* that we like steaks having these features" (Edwards 1965, p. 110).

Its vagueness does not keep the remark about the "nice" steak from referring to objective properties and does not make it into a mere report of the speaker's attitude. The niceness belongs to the steak and not to the speaker or his feelings. The niceness, although objective, does not coincide with any specific single characteristic or precisely specified set of characteristics. Nor is it something distinct from or transcending the steak's characteristics; rather, the term "nice" refers *disjunctively* to a vaguely indicated or understood set of characteristics.

"Nice" is an example of what Edwards calls a *polyguous* term, one having not just one referent but several or many. (A referent is something referred to. Edwards evidently modeled the term "polyguous" on "ambiguous"; but instead of working or applying in either or both of only two ways, a polyguous word works in several or many ways, referring to an indefinite number of facts.)

Remarks like these about "nice" also apply, with modifications, to evaluative words like "fine", "splendid", "awful", "obligatory", "right", "good", and many others. They explain why such a word cannot be defined in a simple, straightforward way.

The word "good", in particular, has drawn much attention. Yet its undefinability does not mean, as sometimes supposed (as by G.E. Moore 1903), that goodness is both a simple property (like yellowness) and also a special property perceivable only by some ethical sixth sense. On the contrary, goodness refers to a set of nonmysterious properties that a person can perceive by the ordinary five senses and describe in ordinary language. The term "good" is indefinable because it refers to different particular properties in different contexts and because in each context it indicates those properties only rather vaguely.

When Paul Edwards says that a particular action or person is good or bad, he is alluding to a set of objective properties that he could spell out in some detail if required. "Good" is a term of approval, yes, but of approval in view of objective features. Similarly, when Edwards says that "X is a vicious person", he is not merely reporting his own or other people's disapproval of X. He is referring to X's personal qualities. His disapproval intertwines with which qualities he has in mind, but the word "vicious" refers to those qualities and not simply to anyone's disapproval.

The term "good" describing actions and persons and the term "nice" describing foods are instructively similar. Both terms have several referents, differing from context to context. In each context, the set of referents is somewhat vague and indefinite. (Someone might be hard put to make a precise and exhaustive list of what characteristics he has in mind when he calls a steak nice or a person good.) Yet the referents are objective characteristics in each case. Though both terms convey attitudes, the attitudes pertain to objective features. (Hare 1997, pp. 20–21, 52–3, 59, makes much the same points about the combined factual and evaluative meaning of polyguous words like "good".)

The most important point of his book, Edwards says (1965, p. 148), is this: "[W]hat determines one to regard a person or an action as good is one's approval of certain of the qualities of that person or action, but in saying that the person or the action is good one refers to the qualities and not to the approval. ... [T]he referent of the moral judgment is determined by the speaker's attitude, but it is not that attitude".[3]

A qualification may be in order about conditional or "if–then" statements containing normative words. Examples might be: "If you want to be benevolent, you should spend your time tonight elsewhere than at Jones's meeting" or "A decent person will boycott the meeting that Jones has called for tonight". Classification of such conditionals can be ambiguous and may depend on the full context. (Some further examples appear below.)

CHALLENGES TO THE IS/OUGHT GAP

Because positive propositions lack normative content and value judgments possess it, no normative proposition can rigorously follow from positive propositions alone. A normative conclusion presupposes some normative content in the premises, along with positive content. This is not to say that value judgments express nothing but mere arbitrary feelings. Often one can argue strongly for them. The arguments employ facts and logic, to be sure; but they must ultimately appeal in addition to some one or more value judgments that, for their holders, rest on intuition rather than on factual and logical argument alone. In short, no normative input, no normative output; you can't get an "ought" from an "is" alone.

David Hume so stated, on the standard interpretation of his celebrated passage.[4] Some philosophers have challenged Hume's Fork, trying to bridge the positive/normative gap. John Searle (1964/1969, 1969, Chapter 8) spills much ink purportedly deriving Jones's obligation to pay Smith five dollars from his promise to do so. R.M. Hare (1964/1970) identifies radical flaws in Searle's derivation. Besides the facts, some normative input – such as endorsement of the institution of promising, either directly or in view of its results – is necessary for the normative conclusion. In his "Reply" (1970)

Searle says that by "ought" he did not mean "morally ought". Bluntly interpreted, then, he disavows the project promised by the title of his 1964 article – "How to derive 'ought' from 'is' ". (Let me be clear. Of course I think that Jones ought to pay. But I think so not merely because Jones uttered the words conventionally considered to constitute a promise but also because I hold certain value judgments, which I am prepared to spell out.)

Ayn Rand argues that life is the only ultimate goal or end in itself, since values can arise only in the context of life (Rand 1964, p. 17; Peikoff 1991, Chapter 7; Brown 1992). Ronald E. Merrill (1991, pp. 104–9) tries to expand this purported derivation of ought from is. He finds Rand (echoed by Harry Binswanger 1990) saying that life is an "end in itself" in the special sense of an ordered collection of activities serving as means to an end, which is those activities themselves. Every action taken to support life is simultaneously a means (because it supports life) and an end (because life is the collective of such actions). Rand sees life as a vortex of values that are simultaneously ends and means. Whatever ultimate ends there may be, one can seek them only if and to the extent that one values what serves one's own life. Whether or not life is the only ultimate end, it is an end that is a necessary means to any and all other ends. A value necessarily held by one who values anything at all is not arbitrary.

In my view, identifying a precondition (namely life) for the holding of any values does not deduce those values strictly from factual and logical premises alone. After all, life is a precondition for both a specific value and its opposite; not only happiness but also misery presupposes a living being to experience it and make any judgment about it. Nor is valuing the precondition necessary for having any values anything other than a value judgment itself. I agree that valuing life is not *arbitrary*; more broadly, I emphasize that values are amenable to discussion in suitable contexts. But I do so without obliterating the positive/normative distinction.

Merrill continues by giving examples of factual statements that nevertheless look normative: you ought to format a new computer disk before trying to write to it; you ought to avoid a certain chess move; you ought to examine the equation to see if the variables are separable. Concurring with what I think is Merrill's meaning, I would call these statements conditional "ought" statements at most; they are factual statements about means to postulated or assumed ends. Although desiring some result is a normative attitude, statements about means to achieve that result are positive statements.

"So, if we can agree on what morality is to accomplish, we can develop moral rules as factual statements. For normative statements are merely factual statements about means and ends. Here is how we can get from is to ought" (Merrill 1991, p. 107).

But is it really true that all normative or apparently normative statements are merely factual statements about means and ends? What about the judgment that happiness is preferable to misery? Also, propositions about what morality is to accomplish are normative, regardless of how much agreement they may command.

Let us assert, Merrill continues, that "ought" in the operational sense (as in "You ought to format the disk") and "ought" in the normative sense are equivalent and challenge the skeptic (Hume) to prove otherwise. If the skeptic agrees to the equivalence, the is/ought problem evaporates for him. If he does not, we may ask for the meaning of the normative "ought". If he invokes tradition or religion or emotional feelings, the Objectivist (a follower of Ayn Rand) will observe that an "ought" of that dubious sort cannot be derived from an "is". Morality is a process of selecting goals; the appropriate goals are determined by the principle of sustaining human life, based on facts of human nature, the "is". Moral rules, the "oughts", merely identify the connections between ends and means. So the Objectivist argument does take us from "is" to "ought" by a logical procedure (Merrill 1991, p. 108).

Merrill recognizes a price to pay for thus bridging the is/ought gap. Saying that "ought" has only one meaning and not two compels us to agree that formatting a disk is an act of moral significance. Rand did regard essentially every human choice as a moral choice – as when d'Anconia, in *Atlas Shrugged* (Rand 1957, p. 451) explains the moral significance of a steel mill (Merrill 1991, pp. 108–9).

I disagree with the Objectivists, I think, on little of real substance; but I try to use words more carefully. Along with them, I reject ethical relativism or nihilism. Because of the kinds of creatures that human beings are, they find little scope for disagreement about fundamental value judgments. But agreement does not transform value judgments into positive propositions.

Douglas Rasmussen and Douglas Den Uyl (1991), consistent with Rand's Objectivism, try to bridge the is/ought gap by invoking Aristotelian teleology. The very nature and vital needs of each living thing dictate to it the end or function that is the source of all the values it might have. For human beings, their very nature makes self-direction or autonomy a good thing: it is the virtue that makes all other virtues possible, all human flourishing (p. 11).

But why is the natural end of a human being morally obligatory? Why *should* one live according to one's nature? Such a question "supposes that something else is required for there to be values that are good". An infinite regress in justifications is not possible, however; "there must be something ultimate; something which is simply the case" (p. 49). The proposition about living in accordance with one's nature neither lends itself to proof nor requires any. Anyone challenging this "ultimate prescriptive premise" thereby accepts it – or so Rasmussen and Den Uyl maintain (p. 50).

Remarks like these cover many pages (including 51 and 113) and obscure just what the authors may be claiming. Although their heart is with Ayn Rand on deriving "ought" from "is", they seem to acknowledge their ultimate failure but excuse it on the grounds that the project, rigorously conceived, was impossible after all. More straightforwardly, instead of struggling to *derive* their Aristotelian judgment in favor of human flourishing from facts of reality, they might have frankly *posited* it as a fundamental value judgment and invited their readers to suggest alternatives if they could.

James Q. Wilson delivers another challenge to Hume's Fork. He observes that Hume, after distinguishing between "is" and "ought", went on to argue the usefulness of rules of justice and property. But why should people care about the future transmission of their property? Because of "natural affection" and "duty" toward one's children. Repeatedly Hume extolled benevolence and other virtues as rooted in the human constitution and temper. So, on Wilson's interpretation (1993, pp. 237–8), Hume derives an "ought" statement from an "is" statement scarcely eight pages after saying that this cannot be done.

Actually, though, Hume does *not* get "ought" from "is" alone. He appeals to one or more "oughts" that are so intuitive, so naturally ingrained, as to be practically inescapable. To identify certain normative sentiments as natural and as conducive to the survival and perhaps to the flourishing of the individual or family or society is not enough by itself to constitute one's own adoption of those sentiments. Some normative judgment supporting those sentiments, unremarkable as it may be, is also necessary.

Still another attempt at ought-from-is sometimes turns up, at least in conversation. It takes this form: the proposition "Two plus two equals four" logically entails "Either two plus two equals four or Jones ought to pay Smith five dollars". The compound proposition is valid and does indeed contain a normative *word*. However, it expresses no normative *judgment*. The suggested either/or proposition is inconsistent neither with another compound proposition whose second clause *denies* that Jones ought to pay nor with a simple denial of his obligation. The purported derivation of "ought" from "is" is a transparently unsuccessful debating trick.

Why are some philosophers anxious to reject the positive/normative distinction? Perhaps some of them merely mean that it is seldom important, since reasoning and factual observation belong in scientific and ethical discussions alike.[5] I agree; still, it serves clear thinking to recognize the distinction in the perhaps rare contexts where the issue does arise.

Heeding the fact/value distinction helps avoid contaminating the scientific or objective aspect of policy discussions. Neglecting it may tend to shelter incorrect positive propositions from criticism by confusing them with matters of value or taste about which dispute is supposedly pointless.

A minimum-wage law provides an example. Ascertaining in detail how it affects the volume and pattern of employment may greatly challenge the ingenuity of researchers. Still, its effects are what they are. It would be anti-intellectual to chalk up disagreement on this factual issue to matters of taste on which there is no objective truth, as if the issue were akin to whether light or dark beer tastes better.

When disagreement over policy issues involves questions of fact and logic, research and discussion can in principle narrow the disagreement. The ideal but not completely attainable goal is to reveal all aspects of an originally disputed issue to be matters of positive science except only for an irreducible residue of value judgment on which consensus may happen to prevail nevertheless. My survey of these issues will seem terribly abstract for a while, but examples will follow in due course.

Another reason for uneasiness over the fact/value distinction, I conjecture, is the mistaken idea that it disparages normative propositions, perhaps as mere emotional outbursts, together with the correct insight that disparagement is unwarranted.[6] Some thinkers may reject the distinction, furthermore, because they mistakenly identify it with logical positivism, examined below.

Insisting on Hume's Fork in no way means that any collection of notions about good and bad or right and wrong is just as acceptable as any other. (That, if true, would leave no scope for ethics on the critical level as a discipline.) Such notions remain open to rational discussion. What the distinction does imply is that normative propositions cannot rest on facts and logic *alone*. They can indeed be examined for the soundness of their factual and logical content and for their mutual consistency. Someone might talk me out of my belief that Smith is a scoundrel or that some specific behavior is wicked by showing me that I had my facts wrong. Showing me that some of my value judgments clash with others in the light of facts and logic demonstrates error somewhere and the need for rethinking.

LOGICAL-POSITIVIST ERROR

Unlike a now-abandoned logical positivism, Hume's Fork does not classify ethical propositions as meaningless noise or as subjective expressions of mere emotion. Years ago I used to think, wrongly, that ethical propositions belong to the category of "subjective relations", along with sentences like "Life is pleasant in Walnut Grove" or "This beer is refreshing". When A calls the beer "refreshing" and B calls it "nasty", their sentences are not contradictory if each person is simply reporting his personal reaction. Sometimes, similarly, if C calls an action morally wrong while D calls it right, each may simply be reporting his personal feeling about the action or the thought of it.

Usually, though, such an interpretation does not fit a statement phrased as a moral judgment. Typically, speakers like C and D mean to say something about the action itself. They know they disagree, when they do, about more than whether each is correctly reporting his own feelings. The idea is ridiculous (Toulmin 1960, pp. 32–3) that no two ethical judgments can contradict each other because all are mere subjective reports, as about the beer.

Another weakness of the subjectivist interpretation (Toulmin continues, p. 33) is its trouble in explaining why people take others' moral judgments into account when forming their own. Yet this observation is not enough to dismiss the subjectivist interpretation. I may consider other people's judgments relevant to my actions for at least two reasons: I may be uncertain about my moral views and welcome guidance, or I may want to avoid others' disapproval if I can do so at no great cost.

Even the subjectivist interpretation of moral disagreement need not require cutting off discussion with the shrug that "Anything goes; it's all a matter of taste". People recognize that further investigation and reflection may bring them closer to agreement on complicated moral questions. Sometimes this is true even of tastes.

The example of beer is an extreme one because whether it is refreshing or nasty is so immediate to the taster that discussion would be almost pointless. (Yet it is not totally pointless, for tasters do try to persuade each other about the characteristics of different wines and even beers.) More discussible, perhaps, is the question whether a piece of music is soothing or stirring or evocative. Discussion of melodies, rhythms, timbres, and patterns may lead listeners to revise their perceptions. Similar examples could concern the attractiveness of particular pictures, buildings, and parks. The attractiveness of life in a particular city is objectively discussible in lesser degree, perhaps, because so many of the relevant considerations are quite personal.

Moral judgments, I conjecture, lie nearer the objective than subjective end of the range of judgments that involve personal feelings. Near the objective extreme, the things judged are least concerned with diverse personal circumstances. (This is true of ethical precepts but less true of the relative *weights* accorded to precepts that clash in specific circumstances, as when benevolence might seem to recommend fudging the truth.) Because the precepts themselves are quite general and are not tied to specific personal circumstances, they stand a better chance of ultimately commanding consensus than questions about beer or about life in Walnut Grove.

The position just expressed becomes clearer when contrasted with an extreme logical-positivist view that classifies ethical propositions as mere expressions of personal emotion, expressions with meanings and rationales scarcely more definite than cries like "ouch!" or "shame!". (Charles Stevenson was a notable expositor, and his book of 1944 remains admirable for many insights and strands of reasoning. Although his view initially made a splash, no one, to my knowledge, still holds it. Even so, examining extreme or abandoned views is not necessarily beating a dead horse. Drawing contrasts with them can be a useful expository device.)

As the examples of "ouch!" and "shame!" suggest, it can make sense to ask the meaning of and reason for an emotional outburst, not to mention a calm remark. The outburst might express a normative judgment in harmony with the perceived objective circumstances and the speaker's fundamental values. If this is how ethical propositions resemble ejaculations, then it is a pejorative "persuasive definition" (Stevenson's own term) to call them *mere* ejaculations. Ones that can be unpacked into appraisals of factual situations are not so mere after all.

Related to the positivist view are various versions of ethical relativism (the anthropologist Westermarck, 1960, is one adherent, at least reputedly, and Edwards, 1965, one commentator). Remarks like "It's all a matter of taste" exaggerate the relativist view only slightly. While recognizing that individuals or groups hold opinions thought to express ethical truths, relativism denies such opinions any objective content and so tends to disparage calling them to the bar of reason.

FUNDAMENTAL VERSUS SPECIFIC NORMATIVE JUDGMENTS

To pursue the question of whether value judgments are open to rational discussion, we must make a hitherto tacit distinction explicit: we must distinguish between lower-level or relatively specific judgments and higher-level or more sweeping ones. Examples of the first kind are that Jones is a good person, that Smith belongs in jail, and that stealing is wrong. One can support such judgments by appeal to fact and logic *together with* broader value judgments, such as appraisal of character traits and notions of what sorts of behavior deserve punishment by jail terms. To support the condemnation of stealing, one might explain how it tends to undercut a society of peaceful and productive cooperation and thereby impair human happiness.

To paraphrase Moritz Schlick, norms always originate outside of science. If a philosopher answers the question "What is good?" by exhibiting norms, he is only reporting what people actually understand "good" to mean. He cannot show what the word *must* or *should* mean. Asking how to validate a value judgment means asking what acknowledged higher norm it falls under. Specific moral principles may perhaps be reduced to higher principles. It is senseless, however, to ask for justification of the highest or last norm or norms, for being highest or last means that there is no further norm to appeal to. Although an absolute justification of ultimate values is sometimes said to be the fundamental problem of ethics, this formulation is simply meaningless (Schlick 1930/1961, pp. 18, 24; cf. the translator's introduction).

As the economist A.K. Sen suggests, standard remarks about the futility of arguing over values trace to thinking of *basic* value judgments only. A "basic" or "fundamental" judgment is one that a person cannot argue for but simply accepts. An example might be the preference for general happiness over general misery. Relatively specific judgments stand in contrast: approval or disapproval of a minimum-wage law or even of lying in particular circumstances can be supported with reasons. (On the distinction between fundamental and specific judgments, see Sen 1970, especially pp. 62-4, Alexander 1967, and Edwards 1965 throughout.) Often it is possible to show that a judgment in someone's value system is *not* basic. The opposite is not true, since a judgment that initially appears axiomatic and undiscussible may prove amenable to discussion and reflection after all. "It seems impossible to rule out the possibility of fruitful scientific discussion on value judgments" (Sen 1970, pp. 62-4).

Sidney Alexander, another economist, endorses the "Socratic notion" of finding ways for people to "cooperate in progressive rational inquiry" aimed at making sound normative judgments. An apparent difference in values may turn out to hinge on differences in positive analysis, as on different predictions of the consequences of the policies considered. It is premature to see irreconcilable values in issues actually capable of being resolved. "[W]ithin a problematic situation the issues are empirical. ... [A]ny purely normative question lies at the next higher level." No normative principle need be regarded as ultimate. A disputed principle will be found to depend "on still other empirical facts or on a still higher normative principle. We can repeat the process indefinitely, so long as we do not come to a normative principle that we refuse to discuss. If ... no particular principle is inherently a *first* principle, there is no necessary stopping place". This infinite regress is benign; for an impasse would force us "to the barricades". If room always remains for investigation and discussion, "we need go to the barricades only at infinity, which is never" (Alexander 1967, pp. 105-7, 114-15).

The distinction between fundamental and specific judgments translates into the language of intrinsic and instrumental values. To say that something is good or bad intrinsically, "in itself", is to express a fundamental value judgment. To hold something good or bad instrumentally, in view of consequences or considerations beyond itself, is to make a nonfundamental value judgment. Drivers want speed and power in a car not for their own sakes, presumably, but as instruments to swift and comfortable transportation, to exhilaration behind the wheel, and perhaps to safety. Good automobile performance is itself instrumental – to satisfying lives, perhaps – and is far from intrinsic. Honesty might more plausibly be considered an intrinsic good;

yet it too is instrumental – to a good life for oneself, to a well-functioning society, and so to happiness. We are back to happiness as probably the most plausible example of an intrinsic value.

Sometimes, of course, short-run pleasure may be bad because getting it causes more extensive or persistent misery, while short-run misery may be good as a necessary means of securing happiness or avoiding misery in the longer run or of wider scope. The capacity and inclination to heed longer-run and more widespread effects on happiness and misery and not be driven by immediate pleasures and pains instead – prudence, in short – is considered a good thing precisely because happiness and misery are good and bad *in themselves*.

Conceivably one might doubt whether the judgment favoring happiness and deploring misery counts as fundamental. Some people might accept that judgment but, instead of holding it as fundamental, might argue for it, deploying facts and logic and appealing to some higher value. A judgment capable of being argued for is by that very token not fundamental. Other people might reject the judgment about happiness and misery and accept some rival in its stead. This second group might express willingness to forgo happiness and accept misery if necessary for the sake of some greater or higher value (perhaps closeness to God in some sense).

I myself can scarcely imagine how the contentions of either group might go – one group regarding happiness as a *non*fundamental and offering arguments for it, the other rejecting happiness in favor of some alternative fundamental value. For each, anyway, its attitude about happiness and misery would *not* be fundamental. By the very meaning of a *fundamental* (or ultimate) value judgment, someone holding it can give no reasons for it because he has exhausted all appeals to fact and logic. Any reasons would necessarily appeal not only to facts and logic but also to one or more further value judgments, showing that the judgment argued for was not fundamental. The closest one can come to arguing for a fundamental value judgment is to employ effective rhetoric in identifying an intuition that one expects one's listeners to share.[7]

If pressed to explain why happiness and misery are intrinsically good and bad, most people (or I, anyway) would merely say something to the effect that they just *are*; one cannot explain anything so obvious; one either sees it or does not. Similarly, if a passenger sitting beside me asks how I can *prove* that I am driving the car, I'll reply that I can't *prove* it; I just ask him to observe. (Although the two propositions are alike in being unprovable by argument, the distinction remains that one is a value judgment and the other a factual proposition.) Much as the judgment about who is driving results from direct observation, so the judgment about happiness and misery results from a kind of direct observation or intuition (or emotion, perhaps). Intuition in this sense is an unavoidable ingredient in any ethical system. (Henry Sidgwick speaks of a "fundamental ethical intuition"; 1907/1962, p. xvi, and, more broadly, pp. xv–xxi, 388–9, 406–7.)

A fundamental intuition remains intuition, even though perhaps rooted in human nature (and even though recognition of its roots may perhaps be cultivated). Brand Blanshard directs attention to "what fulfills those impulses or strivings of which human nature essentially consists, and in fulfilling them brings satisfaction" (1961, p. 343, cf. p. 357). Ends, Blanshard says, are prescribed to man by his own nature. A human nature indifferent to health and to friendship would not be human nature (pp. 330–31). Aristotle and other writers in his tradition, including Blanshard, may be correct in insisting on an objective element, as distinguished from mere personal whim, in the happiness, broadly interpreted, that we have been speaking of. That view is compatible with recognizing and even welcoming great diversity in the details of personal plans of life.

Even if human nature prescribes what best makes for a good life, as Blanshard says, that fact would in no way discredit emphasis on happiness as the criterion and on social cooperation as an indispensable means to it.

David Hume distinguished clearly between fundamental and non-fundamental value judgments, though without using those terms. Just as "there are, in every science, some general principles, beyond which we cannot hope to find any principle more general" (1751/1777/1930, p. 54n.), so the ultimate ends of human actions can never be accounted for by reason. A man asked why he exercises will answer: for health. Why does he desire health? Because sickness is painful. Why does he hate pain? He can give no reason. "This is an ultimate end, and is never referred to any other object" (Hume 1751/1777/1930, p. 134). Or the man may reply that he needs to be healthy to work and earn money, the instrument of pleasure. "And beyond this it is an absurdity to ask for a reason. It is impossible there can be a progress in infinitum; and that one thing can always be a reason why another is desired. Something must be desirable on its own account, and because of its immediate accord or agreement with human sentiment and affection" (1751/1777/1930, pp. 134–5; p. 131 in MacIntyre).[8]

Hume's fundamental value judgment thus seems to be one in favor of happiness and against misery. Reason and sentiment concur, he says, in almost all moral determinations. The final judgment that "constitutes virtue our happiness, and vice our misery", probably depends on some internal sense or feeling that nature has made universal in the species (1751/1777/1930, p. 5).

Hume invokes a natural human sentiment of sympathy or benevolence (fuller discussion appears in Chapter 4 below). He thinks that people, by and large, desire happiness and regret misery not only for themselves but also, to some extent, for others. He finds the utilitarian value judgment prevailing widely (if not always as a *fundamental* judgment). His emphasis on sympathy does not render his doctrine other than utilitarian.

A much-quoted passage expresses Hume's insight into the "public utility" of "general inflexible rules" of property. They support "civil society" – his noteworthy term. Unfortunately, such rules cannot have only beneficial consequences, without ever causing hardships in particular cases. Still, it is sufficient if their good effects heavily outweigh their bad ones (1751/1777/1930, pp. 148–9; compare my Chapter 4 below).

Personal conduct and traits of character are likewise esteemed or despised for their typical public effects. On what attributes add up to personal merit, each person need only consider whether he would want this or that quality ascribed to him, and ascribed by a friend or an enemy (1751/1777/1930, p. 6). In considering whether a person counts as humane and beneficient, "one circumstance ... never fails to be amply insisted upon, namely, the happiness and satisfaction, derived to society from his intercourse and good offices" (1751/1777/1930, p. 10). The merit of possessing "the sentiment of benevolence in an eminent degree" arises in part, at least, "from its tendency to promote the interests of our species, and bestow happiness on human society" (p. 14).

ETHICAL DISAGREEMENT

If appeal to unprovable ultimate intuitions or emotions sounds fuzzy and unscientific, so be it; ethics does have such a component. However, appeals to intuition need not be *premature* and *promiscuous*. In this respect and in what it adopts as its fundamental value judgment, utilitarianism distinguishes itself from other brands of ethical theory.

In real life, disputes over courses of action almost never hinge on divergent *ultimate* intuitions about intrinsic value. It is philosophers, not ordinary people, who talk about happiness and misery as the ultimate good and bad. In real life, disputed value judgments are relatively specific ones, and arguments over them can typically and in principle be checked for factual and logical soundness (cf. Edwards 1965; Sen 1970; Alexander 1967).

For reasons like these, it can be a fruitful working hypothesis, comparable to scientists' hypothesis about the uniformity of nature, that some tastes and especially some values are objectively valid, or come close to being so (compare the exposition of "fallibilism" in Chapter 10 below). Even though we do not know whether some things are in fact objectively good or bad and some values objectively right or wrong, leaving open the possibility of objective truth on such matters promotes investigation and discussion. We need not limit discussion to how to serve or gratify tastes and values just taken as given. Analysis from economics and other disciplines can help systematize value judgments and reveal hierarchies, compatibilities, and clashes among them. Clashes, once demonstrated, can lead people to revise their relatively specific values into better accord with each other and with their more fundamental values.

An approach centering on the concept of Pareto optimality, much invoked by economists (see Chapter 11), tends to overlook these points and to take as given, and as of equal dignity, values that may not be ultimate at all. Doing so chokes off analysis prematurely. To the extent that it is not simply empty to recommend any changes that everybody or practically everybody deems desirable, then it is hasty and even unscientific. People do not automatically understand all the probable consequences of contemplated changes in policy. They do not fully understand how particular measures may eventually change the general character of their society. They do not always fully understand even their own wants or supposed wants and the ways in which gratifying some may entail frustrating other, more basic or more enduring, wants. Room always remains for investigating such matters.

G.E. Moore (1903/1960) called it a "naturalistic fallacy" actually to identify goodness with objective features or tendencies of reality (such as conduciveness to happiness). Whether or not Moore is right about this downright identification, it surely is no fallacy to check values for consistency with facts and with each other. To do so is not to try, futilely, to establish ethical propositions on purely factual and logical grounds alone, with no appeal whatsoever to any kernel of fundamental value judgment.

REFLECTIVE EQUILIBRIUM

The method of reflective equilibrium consists of testing specific judgments and broad ethical generalizations against one another and modifying any or all of them to achieve harmony, (John Rawls 1971 stresses this method, but it is not original with him. Citing Rawls favorably, David Drink 1989 advocates what he calls a coherentist moral epistemology.) How well, for example, do judgments about capital punishment, abortion, and lying or breaking promises in exceptional cases square with generalizations about the sacredness of human life, personal probity, and the intrinsic value of happiness? Both facts and logic enter into testing the mutual consistency of value judgments at different levels. Clashes indicate error in one's reasoning or factual perceptions or intuitions. Not just specific judgments and not just generalizations but in principle all of them are open to reconsideration. While mere coherence among the different parts and levels of a doctrine does not show that the doctrine is right, it may be evidence for it (admittedly weak), for *in*coherence would show that the doctrine is defective.

R.M. Hare suspects practitioners of reflective equilibrium of often *not* fully checking their specific and general judgments against one another. Instead, he suspects, they appeal elaborately to their own personal intuitions. They take their intuitive judgments on specific questions – abortion, suicide, lying, promise-breaking, redistributive policies, and so forth – as hard-core facts; and they test an overarching ethical theory by whether it entails those specific judgments (Hare 1981, pp. 12, 155-6, 1989EiET, pp. 145-6, 212-13, and *passim*, 1989EoPM, pp. 35, 74, 126-7, 189, 193, and *passim*).

That faulty approach seems to draw an analogy between theories of ethics and of natural science. Specific ethical intuitions would be analogues of objective facts found by observation and experiment. The most nearly acceptable ethical or scientific theory would be the one best accommodating the specific intuitions or the observed facts, as the case might be, and also most fruitfully predicting further intuitions or facts not already taken into account in construction of the theory.

Thus caricatured into a species of intuitionism, the method of reflective equilibrium does deserve criticism. One reason is that specific intuitions and scientific facts are *not* closely analogous: "ought" propositions and "is" propositions remain different in kind.

Kai Nielsen (who elsewhere in his book calls himself pretty nearly a utilitarian) calls the method of *"wide* reflective equilibrium" a sounder approach (1990, pp. 19-24). That method puts our various moral claims before the bar of reason. We try to fit them into a coherent whole, squaring them both with observed facts and with what, on deepest moral reflection, we could continue to commit ourselves to (1990, p. 24). Commitment at that deepest level does not mean appealing to intuition promiscuously in the way that Hare condemns.

This method of wide reflection does *not* regard specific ethical intuitions as analogues of scientifically observed facts to which an acceptable theory must simply accommodate itself. Instead, it exposes them to criticism and possible revision. It seeks a unifying theory in considered specific intuitions and overarching ethical principles that cohere with one another *and also* with facts of objective reality, including facts of physical nature, human physiology and psychology, and economics. Only for fundamental value judgments is recourse to sheer intuition appropriate – because unavoidable.

BELIEFS AND ATTITUDES

How are words like "should" and "ought" to be understood in controversies over policy? Consider "The bill ought to be passed". Writing back in the 1950s and using a bill to legalize contraceptives as his example, Paul Edwards meant more than just to express approval of the hypothetical bill. He had reasons for his attitude, reasons linked to expected consequences of the bill's enactment. Statements about those consequences were positive propositions. They might be mistaken, but wrong positive propositions still are just that and not mere reports of attitude. Edwards's attitudes toward the predicted consequences of the bill's enactment made his predictions into reasons for his favoring the bill, but his approval did not make his predictions true or false. They were true or false regardless of his attitude.

Edwards (1965) offers several examples of sensibly and perhaps success-fully trying to clear up disagreements about what *ought* to be done. He distinguishes between disagreement in belief and disagreement in attitude (compare Stevenson 1944). The former means disagreement on the truth or falsity of purportedly factual or logical propositions; the latter means disagreement on value judgments. Should Communists be allowed to teach in universities? (Recall that Edwards took his examples from the 1950s.) Disagreement on this issue hardly hinges on one or more ultimate values for which one can offer no reasons. On the contrary, disagreement hinges on such factual questions as how much and what sort of discipline the Communist party imposes on its members, to what extent Party members abuse the teacher–student relation, and how well alternatives to barring Communists might protect the integrity of academic institutions and standards.

Should mercy killing be legalized? Each answer could appeal to purported facts about, for example, incurable and agonizing diseases, the role of suffering in God's plan, botched suicide attempts, and the danger of encouraging greedy heirs to hasten a death. These "first-order reasons" for rival judgments could be supported by "second-order reasons" – reasons why the first-order ones should indeed count as reasons – and so on with third-order and higher-order reasons.

The point of Edwards's examples is that many moral disputes, though not all, may be settled by appeal to facts. The facts that might be relevant are rarely confined to a definite, closed set. Rarely, in real-world moral disputes or policy disputes, do the participants find themselves at loggerheads over ultimate or fundamental values for which they can give no further reasons. Practically never will a dispute resolve into one disputant's ultimate, unexplainable preference for human happiness and the other disputant's ultimate, unexplainable preference for human misery.

Although an ethical precept is a normative judgment and not a positive proposition, people may sensibly discuss reasons for and against accepting it as a guide to conduct. Initial disagreement over normative propositions (other than fundamental ones) may sometimes be resolved, as Edwards showed, by clarifying them or by looking further into matters of fact or logic. It is premature to chalk disagreement up to irremovable differences in values.

SOME CONTENTIOUS TERMS DEFINED

What does being moral mean? Let us try to clarify several related concepts. Doing so may at first seem like preaching, although that is not my intention.

Self-interest is not the antithesis of morality, as I shall argue later on. It means concern for one's own well-being, for the success of one's own projects, and even for the flourishing of one's own values and of the persons and causes to which one may be devoted. An excessively narrow conception of one's own interest, however, can be another matter.

Prudence means intelligent care for one's interests. It includes adequate attention to the costs as well as benefits of activities, including attention to how the pursuit of immediate pleasure may have unfortunate consequences of wider scope and in the long run.

Egoism, understood as a personal attitude rather than as a philosophical doctrine, means predominant attention to one's self-interest and in particular to narrowly conceived self-interest.

Selfishness, a related concept, often means an unduly narrow and perhaps ruthless concern for one's own well-being and advantage. Yet the word is not always used pejoratively. Ayn Rand entitled one collection of her essays *The Virtue of Selfishness* (Rand 1964). For her the word meant a healthy regard for one's own values, projects, and legitimate interests; it is not at all the same thing as eagerness to grab unfair advantages by riding roughshod over the rights of others. It means pretty nearly the opposite of altruism in the unconventional and pejorative Randian sense explained below.

Inconsiderateness is closely related to selfishness in its usual sense. At the least pejorative, it means careless unawareness of the rights and interests of others as one bulls ahead serving one's self and one's own projects. At worst, it means willfully overriding others' rights and interests as one favors oneself in ways that have scarcely any claim to fairness.

Benevolence, practically from the derivation of the word, means "wishing well" towards others and acting accordingly. As explained by David Kelley (1996), an expositor and interpreter of Ayn Rand's ideas,[9] benevolence means according other people the presumption (defeasible, of course) that they fit comfortably beside oneself in a generally amicable, as opposed to hostile, universe. Benevolence means treating other people as potential trading partners whose basic interests are more in harmony than in conflict with one's own, trade being understood in the broad sense of beneficial interaction rather than only in the narrow business sense. It includes allowing or helping other persons to have "visibility" – recognition as autonomous human beings and harmony between what they know about themselves from the inside and the way others treat them. Benevolence includes civility or good manners, sensitivity to the circumstances and perhaps even feelings of others, and generosity. Generosity includes willingness to play one's part in maintaining a society of healthily interacting members, as opposed to trying to be a free rider.

Sympathy, on Kelley's interpretation, is a virtue intermediate between sensitivity, "a purely cognitive phenomenon, the sheer awareness of another person's condition", and kindness, the desire to act on the other person's behalf (Kelley 1996, p. 42). Sympathy largely overlaps benevolence; it will be further discussed in Chapter 4 in connection with the ethical systems of David Hume and Adam Smith.

Altruism is often understood as a leading virtue, as benevolence in heightened degree. Moritz Schlick (1930/1961) used the word in some such way. Accepting its definition as "behavior which benefits others at some cost to onself", Peter Singer (1982, p. 5) finds altruism well documented in non-human animals. He mentions warning calls by blackbirds and thrushes, stotting by Thomson's gazelles,[10] food-sharing among wolves and wild dogs, help by dolphins and elephants to injured comrades, and a victor wolf's sparing a defeated rival (pp. 6–8). (Whether such behavior might have a biological basis is considered in Chapter 3.)

In Ayn Rand's writings, however, altruism is a strongly pejorative term (compare Kelley 1996, Chapter 2). She and her followers find it a widespread trait of contemporary thinking that accounts for many of the world's evils. They take altruism to mean actually subordinating one's own values to the needs and wishes of other people, together with the perverse belief that such subordination is virtuous and ethically required. It implies lack of respect for and confidence in one's own self and values and projects. Conceptions of what is good and worth pursuing and of what is bad and to be avoided are essential to successful pursuit of happiness by oneself and others. Yet someone willing to subordinate his own values presumably has no clear conception of them and no strong devotion to them. (One's values need not, of course, center narrowly on oneself; they may well require goodwill and honorable behavior toward others.)

Randian altruism implies other-directedness in the worst sense, including a self-abasing vulnerability to manipulation by others. Some of the most memorable villains of Ayn Rand's novels, pursuing power in their own warped ways, use conventional belief in the virtue of altruism as a tool for manipulating others by intimidating or shaming them into compliance with the villains' demands.

Altruism in Rand's sense is evil, furthermore, because it makes the less honorable members of society feel entitled to be on the receiving end. It encourages their grasping nature; it encourages them seemingly or actually to be in the distress that supposedly entitles them to exploit the altruism of others. More honorable people, if they take the doctrine seriously, either actually do subordinate pursuit of their own values to the probably less estimable values of others or else feel guilt about not doing so. Altruism creates counter-productive tensions.

In the more usual, non-Randian, sense, altruism means decent and even active consideration of the rights and well-being of other persons. Decency of this sort, unless carried to a degree that perverts its nature, is not what Rand condemns. On the contrary, the heroes and heroines of her novels deal honorably and fairly with each other, showing mutual respect and considera-tion. Furthermore, Rand values general goodwill toward one's fellow men. A Randian hero would rescue a drowning stranger if he could do so without undue sacrifice or risk. Showing such benevolence does not presuppose that virtue consists of sacrificing one's own values to the values or needs or wants of other persons. Rand's doctrines are not as outrageous, then, as critics often suppose. This would be clearer if she and her critics alike used key ethical terms in similar and more nearly conventional ways.

Sacrifice is another term that provokes divergent reactions. For most people, apparently, willingness to give up one's own interests for the sake of other persons is a major aspect of the virtue of altruism; yet Randians count sacrifice as evil. They interpret sacrifice as giving up a greater value for the sake of a lesser value, which is irrational to the point of being wicked, whereas giving up a lesser for a greater value is not really a sacrifice but a sensible exchange.

A *Generalization Principle*, also called a principle of universality, universalizability, or impartiality, stipulates that ethical precepts must apply equally to all persons in relevantly similar circumstances. Precepts must not discriminate *arbitrarily* in favor of some persons and against others. The meaning of this principle is further explored, along with its grounding, in Chapter 9.

MORAL RELATIVISM AND MORAL OBJECTIVITY

This concluding section takes its title from a book in which Gilbert Harman defends relativism and Judith Jarvis Thomson defends objectivity (Harman and Thomson 1996). On both authors' understanding, relativism denies that there is any such thing as an ethic's being correct and that it is possible to find about some ethical propositions that they are true. Objectivity holds that an ethic can indeed be correct and that some ethical propositions are indeed true. Cited in favor of relativism are the diversity of detailed ethical views among societies and individuals and apparently intractable moral disagreements about abortion, euthanasia, the use of animals for food, and so on. In reply, skepticism about objective truth does not follow from the fact that certain questions, including questions about the subject matter of natural science, are very hard to answer convincingly. Furthermore, people have a way of "walling off" facts and reasoning that threaten to undermine their cherished beliefs.

Relativism taken to an extreme is nihilism: ethical inquiry is a mistaken project; ethics has no subject matter; any behaviors, precepts, character traits and so forth are as good or bad as any others; or, rather, the terms "good" and "bad" are meaningless in this context. At the other extreme, moral objectivity becomes the belief that moral evaluations and precepts are "graven in stone"; although different in kind, they are just like propositions about the physical universe in referring to an objectively existing reality.

I am uncomfortable in seeming to say, lamely, that the correct position lies somewhere between the two extremes. The dispute between relativism and objectivity does appear, however, to be largely a dispute over words, over labels. I have more sympathy with Thomson's objectivity than with Harman's relativism. Still, I recognize, following Hume, that moral judgments presuppose some values – some "moral framework", as Harman says. Of course. But moral disagreement rarely boils down to undiscussable disagreement over fundamental value judgments. I agree with Thomson that moral propositions exist about which it does make sense to ask and investigate whether they are right or wrong. The truths of morality are not just the same in kind as scientific propositions about the physical world, but this difference does not justify moral skepticism.

I hope that "quasi-objective", applied to the status of certain moral propositions, is not a weasel-word. Ethical inquiry does indeed possess a subject matter.

APPENDIX TO CHAPTER 2   FREE WILL AND ETHICS

A Persistent Old Issue

I must apologize, but the very topic of ethics requires dipping into metaphysics. Although I cannot settle an old issue, I must recognize it. Are individuals' actions and even their decisions, desires, and characters fully determined by circumstances ultimately outside their own control? If that were true – if people lack free will and true choice – then personal responsibility would lack meaning. Praise and blame, reward and punishment, would have no application; and ethics as a field of study would lack any genuine subject matter.

This position, right or wrong, seems to have been the position of Immanuel Kant. Throughout his *Groundwork* (1785/1964), Kant acknowledges an antinomy between freedom of the will and the prevalence of causal laws of nature. He maintains, however, that freedom of the will is a necessary presupposition of morality. He suggests that the antinomy might somehow be resolved through his distinction between the intelligible and sensible worlds (noumenal and phenomenal worlds, in his technical terminology). Experience, filtered through the Kantian "categories" of perception and understanding, imposes the idea of tight causality; but unknowable characteristics of the noumenal world of things in themselves might make freedom of the human will genuine. Confessedly, all this is quite mysterious to me.

The terms "free will" (or "free choice") and "determinism" have no agreed precise meanings, so I cannot begin by defining them. Exploring what these terms and concepts might mean and how they interrelate is a main task of this appendix.

We must, however, avoid "essentialism". As criticized by Karl Popper (see, for example, 1985, pp. 88–94), essentialism means focusing on one or more pieces of terminology, supposing that each one labels a definite aspect of reality, brooding over these aspects or concepts to grasp the "essence" of each, and perhaps brooding further over whether the realities corresponding to two or more concepts could exist together.[11] Trying to gain knowledge in this way proceeds backward. Perceiving uniformities and diversities in the real world belongs ahead of brooding over words to label them. Conceivably, traditional formulations of the whole supposed issue of free will versus determinism will prove misconceived.

Schlick on the Issue

My admiration for two ethicists in particular, Moritz Schlick and Henry Hazlitt, predisposed me toward their solutions; yet in the end I find them incomplete or otherwise unsatisfying. Schlick regarded the supposed issue as a mere pseudoproblem: determinism and free will reconcile (1930/1961, Chapter VII). Causality can operate while leaving individuals some freedom not only over what acts they perform but also over what choices they make. The opposite of freedom is compulsion, and determination does not mean compulsion. In the words of R.E. Hobart, whose views are discussed below, compulsion implies causation but causation does not necessarily imply compulsion.[12]

Schlick identifies a confusion between descriptive and prescriptive laws. Scientific laws *describe* how the world works; they do not *prescribe* events; they do not resemble totally enforced legislation *making* events unfold as they do. Kepler's Laws describe how the planets revolve around the sun; they are not prescriptions compelling them to revolve as they do. The law of demand describes how buyers respond to alternative levels of an item's price (apart from other overriding influences); it does not compel buyers to behave in the way it describes.

These distinctions help explain, then, how a person could conceivably be choosing and acting free from compulsion even when his choices and actions are causally determined and in principle predictable. The opposite, presumably, would be choices made and actions taken by sheer chance or baseless caprice. Choices and actions need not be stochastic or capricious to be properly called free.

If their choices and actions were totally unfree, people could not properly be held answerable for them. We do not blame a person for firing a shot if someone stronger forced the gun into his hand and pulled his finger against the trigger. We do not hold someone guilty of a crime if he was genuinely insane and lacked any control over his decision and action. It would be pointless to hold the man whose hand was forcibly manipulated or the insane person accountable for an action not truly his own. Neither is responsible because neither enjoyed freedom of choice and will over his act. (Clear-cut examples like these should not, however, invite multiplying excuses to relieve persons of responsibility for their actions.)

Responsibility presupposes a point for applying a motive, such as desire to avoid blame or punishment or to win praise or reward. Frequently it makes eminent sense to apply motives to people and hold them responsible for their choices and actions. This could not be true if no grounds existed for attributing freedom to people. Hence there *are* grounds for belief in freedom in some sense associated with responsibility.

More exactly, perhaps, the whole free-will/determinism controversy is a chimerical basis for questioning ordinary ethical concepts. Schlick's argument comes across to me as I have summarized it.

C.A. Campbell (1951/1966) finds Schlick's distinction between descriptive and prescriptive laws irrelevant. The usual reason for thinking that moral freedom presupposes some breach in causal continuity is not a belief that causal laws compel in the way legislation compels but instead the belief that an unbroken causal chain leaves no one able to choose and act other than as he does.

Moral responsibility is *not* the same, says Campbell, as scope for sensibly applying motives. Dogs can be trained with punishments and rewards; yet we do not hold dogs morally responsible for what they do. We can judge dead men morally responsible for particular actions without being able to affect those past actions. Perhaps we might reinterpret Schlick as meaning that a person is morally responsible when his motive could *in principle* be affected by reward or punishment, whether or not the judges or observers are in a position to apply it. But this modification would change Schlick's theory, which links the whole meaning and importance of moral responsibility "to our potential control of future conduct in the interests of society" (Campbell 1951/1966, p. 115).

Schlick identifies "Who is morally blameworthy?" with "Who is to be punished?" – paradoxically, given his view of punishment as a purely educative measure, without retributive content. We often think it proper to "punish" a person, in Schlick's educative sense, even without holding him morally blameworthy (Campbell 1951/1966, p. 116). We punish the dog. We punish demonstrators who may be obstructing traffic from motives that even we, the judges, may think noble.

I'll try to rephrase or interpret Campbell's objection. Schlick sees instrumental, educative, value in applying rewards and punishments, which he identifies with holding people morally responsible. We could hardly do so unless we attributed some freedom to people. But is this a valid linking of ideas? Perhaps rewards and punishments and their generally good consequences are just particular events in the unbroken causal chain. Metaphysical freedom cannot be established by pointing to the apparent or genuine good consequences of reward and punishment.

Campbell suspects that Schlick and many other philosophers cannot recognize contracausal freedom as prerequisite to moral responsibility because, while denying that freedom, they do accept the commonsense belief in moral responsibility (p. 117).

His own purpose, Campbell concludes (p. 135), has been not actually to defend free will but rather to show "that the problem as traditionally posed is a real, and not a pseudo, problem".

Hazlitt's Reconciliation

Henry Hazlitt (1964, Chapter 27) tries to reconcile free will and responsibility with determinism, interpreted as omnipresent cause and effect. He agrees "that everything that happens is a necessary outcome of a preceding state of things" (p. 269). Like Schlick, however, he stresses that causation is not compulsion. Absence, not presence, of causation is what would exempt people from moral responsibility. "It is precisely because we do not decide or act without cause that ethical judgments serve a purpose. ... The knowledge that we will be held 'responsible' for our acts by others, or even that we will be responsible in our own eyes for the consequences of our acts, must influence those acts, and must tend to influence them in the direction of moral opinion" (p. 275).

Hazlitt warns against confusing determinism with materialism, interpreted as the dogma that all causation, even in human affairs, operates ultimately through physical and chemical processes alone. He especially warns against confusing determinism with fatalism, which he interprets as the dogma that events will unfold as they are bound to do, regardless of how people try to promote or prevent them. Fatalism in this peculiar sense is obviously false. Human decisions, choices, wishes, reflection, and will clearly *do* influence the course of events. If, contrary to fact, they did not do so, or if they operated only stochastically, outside of causal chains, then notions of responsibility and ethics would have no application.

Hazlitt accepts universal causation, then, but distinguishes sharply between its supposed operation solely in material ways and its operation in ways leaving scope for human decision and will. But can this distinction carry all the weight Hazlitt places on it?

Two Further Attempts at Reconciliation

Michael Slote (1990) explains how making and implementing ethical judgments could be sensible *even if* determinism prevailed, a question he does not tackle. Here I interpret Slote's argument together with a commentary by Peter van Inwagen (1990) and forgo trying to paraphrase each separately.

We may label a person or a dog and certain actions as "vicious" and guard against and "punish" them. Yet we may recognize that the person's or dog's disposition and actions trace to unfortunate genes or mental illness or previous maltreatment, which attenuates or dispels moral culpability. We are not necessarily inconsistent in both recognizing the dispositions and actions as determined yet judging and punishing them as vicious. Our judging and punishing can themselves be links in the chain of deterministic causation and may make the dispositions and actions less vicious than they would otherwise be.

Similarly, we tend to judge actual murder "more wrong" than a failed attempt; we revile and punish an actual murderer more severely than an attempted murderer. Both culprits may have had the same intentions, and only sheer luck may have frustrated one attempt. Still it may make sense to condemn and punish the successful murderer more severely. How a person is judged and punished may thus reasonably depend on more than what he freely willed. Several considerations may warrant distinguishing between actual and attempted murder. Evil intentions may be harder to prove in a failed attempt. The gradation in punishments may help emphasize the public's solemn condemnation of murder, and in subtle psychological ways it may cause more murder attempts to fail than otherwise would.

An analogy of sorts holds between these considerations and F.A. Hayek's argument (1960, Chapter 6) about merit versus value in determining a person's income. Even though the market value of a person's efforts probably does not correspond closely to his moral merit, powerful reasons argue for allowing market supply and demand to establish his income anyway. Such remuneration may usefully guide individuals on how to use their special talents and knowledge, and it may motivate appropriate kinds and degrees of risk-bearing. Above all, perhaps, alternative institutions intended to attune remunerations to moral merit appear very unattractive upon close analysis. Again, a person's free will and intentions should not be the only factors governing how other people treat him.

Admittedly, full-fledged determinism still poses embarrassment for consequentialist considerations like these. If we recognize that our making and implementing ethical judgments and adopting this or that set of institutions are themselves fully caused and are mere links in a tight causal chain, we run into awkward paradoxes. These pertain to the whole free-will/determinism issue itself, however, rather than to ethical issues in particular.

Determinism as Fatalism

Determinism in its most extreme version (commonly attributed to Pierre-Simon de Laplace) is fatalism even more comprehensive than the variety rejected by Hazlitt. It recognizes human will and decision as elements in one grand chain of universal causation. Everything that is happening or has happened or will happen has been fated from the beginning of time to happen exactly as it does or did or will. Causation operates tightly in every detail. Even all of a person's thoughts as he deliberates whether to accept a new job or break off a love affair, and even all other persons' reactions to his decision, were fated to be exactly as they turn out. Even all philosophical controversies over the free-will issue itself take an exactly predetermined course. Far from denying that ideas and choices have consequences, extreme determinism maintains that even these are links in the great causal chain.

Laplace regards the present state of the universe as the effect of its anterior state and the cause of its next state. Ineluctable necessity rules. Nothing would be uncertain for a sufficiently vast intelligence; the future and the past alike would be present to its eyes. A true act of free will is impossible. Without a determinative motive, not even the nearest thing to a free will could originate even actions considered indifferent. The contrary opinion is an illusion of the mind (Meyerson 1921/1991, pp. 563–4, citing Laplace's *Théorie analytique des probabilités*; Boyle et al. 1976, pp. 57, 86, give apt quotations from Laplace; further discussion of Laplacean determinism occurs in Popper 1982, pp. xx–xxi, 123–4 and *passim*, and Georgescu-Roegen 1971, p. 170 and *passim*).

Clarence Darrow used to defend his clients with such an argument. The accused criminal is a mere link in the chain. Even his character and his ability or inability to reshape it trace ultimately to causes outside himself, and he is therefore not responsible and not properly punishable for his crimes (Hospers 1961/1966, p. 41).

Can anyone really believe in such tight universal causation? If only Queen Victoria had been a man, the Salic Law would not have separated the hitherto linked crowns of Great Britain and Hanover upon her – his – accession in 1837; and the subsequent history of Germany, Europe, and the world would probably have unfolded much differently from how it actually did. (Reflection on the events of 1866, 1870–71, 1914, and 1917 helps explain why.) Much depended, then, on which particular sperm happened to fertilize her mother's ovum at Victoria's conception in 1818.[13] Yet this micro event and all its momentous consequences were bound to occur exactly as they did. Thus must strict determinism maintain.

No one, to my knowledge, espouses this position consistently. It is just too preposterous – though I may be mistaken in saying so.

Increasing Complexity

One reason for calling full determinism preposterous is that the world seems to be getting more complicated over time. It is hard to imagine how the less complicated past might contain all the information necessary to specify the more complicated present and future in complete detail. Such complete specification would constitute at least an equal degree of complexity *already* prevailing.

The world is getting "more complicated" by any ordinary standard of judgment. More people are living than in the past, with all their individual characteristics and thoughts and actions. The number and intricacy of the works of man are increasing, including the texts of all the books and articles ever written. The state of the world at any instant includes all the information and all the misprints in all these documents, and even the slightest details of all the flyspecks and coffee stains in individual copies.

Affairs on earth interact with affairs throughout the universe. Men or man-made instruments have disturbed the surfaces of the moon and Mars, and rockets have escaped our solar system. Eclipses, comets, planetary movements, and supernovas have affected human activities directly and through popular, religious, and scientific beliefs.

If a later state is fully determined by an earlier state, then that earlier state must contain aspects or properties or patterns or whatever – whose totality I am calling "information" – specifying that later state in complete detail. And if the world is generally getting more complicated over time, then more information is required to specify a later state than an earlier state. It is hard to imagine how all the detailed information necessary to specify the more complicated later state already existed in the simpler earlier state. It is hard to believe that even the tiniest fraction of a second after the Big Bang, the universe already contained detailed coded information about everything that would ever happen thereafter, including the exact configuration of every wisp of cloud I observed during my last airplane trip and including the exact times at which and pressures with which I would strike each key during my current session at my computer keyboard. Full determinism seems still more incredible because it involves each state's specifying not only one subsequent state but also all the infinitely many intervening states ("infinitely many" if time is continuous).

These points tell against complete causal determination.[14] Its being hard to conceive of does not, however, constitute disproof. Perhaps increasing overall complexity is a mere illusion. Perhaps greater complexity in some dimensions – in the products of the human mind and in the details of flyspecks on published pages – is offset somehow by reduced complexity in other dimensions. If so, what might they be? Perhaps greater complexity on our earth, which, like our whole solar system, is an open system, is offset somehow by reduced complexity elsewhere in the universe. Even so, wouldn't the point still hold that increasing complexity on our earth implies incomplete predictability of human affairs? By what mechanism, if any, could any offsetting reduced complexity elsewhere save the complete predictability of human affairs, if only in principle? But perhaps I am wrong about my notion of information required for complete causal specification.

Speaking of total causal determination, we may well pause to ask just what "cause" and "causality" mean. Trying to frame objection-free definitions is a sobering challenge. This very difficulty throws some slight extra embarrassment onto doctrines of a great unbroken causal chain.

In arguing for indeterminacy or openness in the universe, Karl Popper distinguishes among "three worlds".[15] World 1 contains physical objects – rocks, trees, structures, living creatures, and physical fields of force. World 2 is the psychological world of fears and hopes, of dispositions to act, and of subjective experiences of all kinds. World 3 contains products of the human mind – art works, ethical values, social institutions, the intellectual contents of books (books as physical objects belong to World 1), scientific problems, theories, including mistaken theories, and solved and unsolved puzzles. Especially characteristic of World 3 is human knowledge put into words.

Autonomous objects exist even in World 3. Human beings originally conceived of the prime numbers and conjectured about their properties, but the primes and their properties have taken on an objective existence. It is a bare fact, but a logical truth rather than a contingent empirical fact, that 143 prime numbers, no more and no fewer, exist in the range of 100 to 1000. Euclid already proved the infinitude of prime numbers: no largest one exists. But is there a largest *pair* of *twin* primes (like 17 and 19, 521 and 523, 1451 and 1453)? No one, the last I heard, has actually proved either a "yes" or a "no" answer. The problem objectively exists as a challenge to human intelligence.

The autonomous objects of World 3 interact with World 1 through the human perceptions, feelings, dispositions, and decisions of World 2. The challenges of pure mathematics lead to results that find applications in computer hardware and software, which in turn function in changing the physical world. Some challenges of her field lead a mathematician to results that enhance her reputation and win her an appointment at a prestigious university, where she has a house – a physical object – built in accordance with her tastes and increased income.

World 3 is intrinsically open or emergent, says Popper (1972, p. 5); any theory holding scientific and artistic creation ultimately explainable by physics and chemistry seems absurd to him. Moreover, interrelations among the three Worlds render the whole universe partly open and emergent.

I am not sure that Popper would agree, but his concept of World 3 in particular, the world of things like scientific theories, does help underline how preposterous it is to suppose that each later state of affairs is totally specified by earlier states. Scientific progress does occur. New knowledge, by its very meaning, was not available in advance; the notion of something being known before it is known is self-contradictory. Is it plausible, then, to maintain that all the mathematical and physical knowledge not yet achieved but that will be achieved in the next hundred years somehow already exists in latent form, already somehow coded into the current state of the universe, along with the date and other details of the discovery of each bit of that future knowledge? (Many of the associated challenges already exist as problems belonging to Popper's World 3, but this is not the same as the pre-existence of solutions both to unsolved problems and to problems not yet even formulated.)

Chance

Gerd Gigerenzer and coauthors (1989/1993, esp. pp. 59–68, 276–85) review

apparent and supposed implications of probability theory and statistics for free
will versus determinism. These disciplines have been successfully applied on
the assumption that some sheer random processes do operate in the world,
which is some evidence, if weak, that determinism in nature is incomplete.
Scientists and philosophers such as James Clerk Maxwell and Charles Peirce
have believed that airtight causality does not operate in every little detail of the
universe, that some element of randomness remains, and that free will might
occupy this gap somehow. And such gaps might not be confined to the
subatomic level that quantum theory deals with. (Here I insert the obligatory
allusion to Heisenberg's indeterminacy principle concerning subatomic
randomness.) Maxwell and Peirce (1877 article, reprinted 1958, p. 95, 1891
articles, reprinted 1955, pp. 9, 319) pointed to the statistical or probabilistic
aspect of the kinetic theory of gases, which envisages the constituent
molecules moving at different randomly determined velocities and changing
velocities as they collide with one another and with the sides of the container.
Peirce also noted the random nature of the biological mutations on which
natural selection operates.

Karl Popper also argued for the genuineness of chance events even above
the subatomic level or even the molecular level. What explains the statistical
stability of the heads and tails produced by a penny-tossing machine? Or
consider Alfred Landé's conception of dropping ivory balls onto the center of
a suitably positioned steel blade, very nearly half of the balls falling on each
side. For a determinist, barred by his doctrine from appealing to randomness
and reduced to imagining the mutual cancellation of many small causes, the
lawlike statistical process must remain ultimately irreducible and inexplicable
(Popper 1982, pp. 96–104).

Quantum-level and other small-scale indeterminacies gain relevance from
the fact that micro differences can have macro consequences. Erwin
Schrödinger gave the hypothetical example of a cat whose survival or death in
an experiment depends on an apparatus detecting particles emitted randomly
and infrequently in the decay of a radioactive element. The far-reaching
consequences of Queen Victoria's sex, already mentioned, provide another
example. This micro-to-macro principle is further illuminated by the
mathematics of chaos, even though the (hypothetical) systems used in
expounding chaos theory are fully deterministic.

An element of sheer chance in the universe appears to operate, then, along
with the causality that is also evident. Admittedly, the pervasive *appearance*
of chance or randomness does not rigorously rule out complete Laplacean
causality. (Laplace himself made contributions to probability theory.) My
statistics professor at Columbia University around 1948, Frederick C. Mills,
avoided speaking of "chance", period; he always used some such expression
as "the complex of unknown causes called chance". Perhaps he had good

reason for speaking so carefully. (In his 1938 book, p. 436, he lists three assumptions underlying the derivation of the normal curve of error. "1. The causal forces affecting individual events are numerous, and of approximately equal weight. 2. The causal forces affecting individual events are independent of one another. 3. The operation of the causal forces is such that deviations above the mean of the combined results are balanced as to magnitude and number by deviations below the mean.")

Another reservation about sheer chance or randomness requires mention. Chance poses no less difficulty for commonsense notions of human freedom and responsibility than tight causality would. To the extent that a person's actions, decisions, deliberations, inclinations, feelings, experiences, capabilities, and character traits occur by sheer chance, they are no more meaningfully his own, and he is no more truly responsible for them, than would be true if they all traced fully to external causes. Actions and thoughts governed by sheer chance are no more compatible with human dignity and responsibility, as ordinarily conceived, than their being dominated by external causes. Dignity and responsibility, if genuine, presuppose something beyond chance linking events; they presuppose a causal link in which the individual plays some independent part.

While elements of sheer chance in the world do not imply freedom of the will, "the presence of random phenomena at the quantum level does take the sting out of the argument that man cannot will freely because the material world is governed by determinism. Clearly, a completely deterministic world and a man with an absolutely free will are incompatible conditions" (Georgescu-Roegen 1971, p. 177, in part citing H. Margenau, Hermann Weyl, and A.S. Eddington). (I'll add that not merely an "absolutely" but even a partially free will is incompatible with complete determinism.) The point so far is not that indications of sheer chance in the world establish the case for free will but only that they defuse one particular kind of argument against it.

Causality as opposed to chance is required for any predictability in human behavior. Yet predictability does not rob human beings of the dignity usually associated with free will and responsibility. If anything, the contrary is true. Suppose that a friend of yours had an opportunity to steal $10000 while escaping suspicion. In fact the money remains unstolen. Which would your friend rather hear from you: "I was sure that you would not steal the money" *or* "I didn't have a clue whether or not you would steal it"? Would your friend be insulted by your thinking that his behavior is predictable? (Compare Hobart 1934/1966, p. 81, and 1934/1984, p. 504.)

Far from being vitiated by elements of stable relations – of causality – among events and circumstances, including character traits and actions, the very concepts of free choice and responsibility presuppose such elements.

Often these elements make confident predictions possible, all without undercutting notions of free choice and responsibility.

Sheer chance, in short, not only does not establish the case for human freedom and responsibility but even poses difficulties of its own. Its role in my argument is different and slighter: it undermines one particular argument against freedom of the will.

Once chance has shaken the notion of total causal determination, the path remains open for considering whether something besides chance might also contribute to the evident openness or indeterminacy of the universe. Everyday evidence, considered next, testifies to some sort of free will. That evidence can be questioned, but the questions rely precisely on the determinist doctrine that is itself open to question.

The Experience of Free Will

Everyone's experience suggests that people's decisions, talk, writings, and thoughts do influence the course of events. The thoroughgoing determinist or fatalist would not deny this personal experience, but he would question its significance. Our decisions and thoughts, influential though they are, are mere links in unbroken causal chains. Each decision, utterance, and thought is caused by other events and circumstances, including physical conditions, the previous thoughts and utterances of oneself and other people, and one's own and other people's character traits, genetic makeups, and current and past environments – according to the determinist. Each of these causal links traces to contemporaneous and earlier links – and so on, presumably, back to the Big Bang.

A hardened habitual criminal could have avoided committing each of his crimes *if* he had willed not to commit it. But could he have so willed? Well, yes, *if* his character had been different. Furthermore, it would have been different *if* his earlier actions and decisions and circumstances had been different. But could they have been different? These earlier character-influencing events and circumstances, perhaps especially including his childhood environment and his genetic makeup, were themselves links in an unbroken causal chain.

The complete determinist is unimpressed, then, by the observation that the criminal could contingently have avoided committing his crimes. Far from proving his responsibility for them, that observation is an uninformative truism. It merely says that *if* the links in a causal chain had been different from what they actually were and had been fated to be, then the outcome of the chain would have been different from what it in fact was.

Despite these assertions of the (imaginary) fatalist, we all have personal experience with making decisions *ourselves*. We decide, true enough, largely in the light of external circumstances. Often these include the expected reactions of other people. But it is we ourselves who weigh the considerations pulling one way and another. We know from our own experience with decisions, furthermore, and from what observation suggests about the decisions of other people, that people do respond to prospects of reward and punishment, approval and disapproval. (Surely economists understand about incentives.) Holding people responsible does affect their behavior.

A fatalist could accept this conclusion without abandoning his doctrine. He could agree that if juries, judges, and legislatures generally accepted the Clarence Darrow defense, crime would be more rampant than it is in fact, and the world a more miserable place. Society is fortunate, he could agree, that juries, judges, and legislatures, usually ignoring Clarence Darrow, as they are fated to ignore him, do hold criminals responsible and do punish them. We are fortunate, in other words, that his determinist theory is not generally accepted and implemented. Yet the fatalist could maintain that his theory is correct, that he is fated to propound it exactly as he does, and that – probably fortunately – you and I and most of the rest of us are nevertheless fated to reject it.

How would the theory of strict determinism interpret academic disputes over that theory itself? Taken literally, it would regard each move in the dispute – each conversation, lecture, journal article, criticism of an article, reply to the criticism, and every slight detail in each of these – as simply a particular link in the great causal chain. The determinist philosopher would agree that his latest paper on the topic was fated in every slightest detail to say what it does say, fated not only by what he had heard and read on the topic but by his genes and childhood experiences and innumerable other circumstances. All reactions to his paper are similarly fated. Yet this consideration does not necessarily lead him to abandon the whole issue and turn to some other branch of philosophy or some other line of work. He could stick to the issue, recognizing that he is fated to do so and that his work on it, and others' reactions to it, are fated to turn out exactly as they do.

This determinist position, then, may not be downright inconsistent with itself, not downright self-refuting. Rather, it is practically incredible.

The Self-referential Problem of Determinism

Joseph M. Boyle, Jr, Germain Grisez, and Olaf Tollefsen (1976) expose the self-contradictory position of one who "rationally affirms" full determinism or, as they say, denies that anyone has any "free choice". (To "rationally affirm" a proposition goes beyond merely mentioning it or considering it possible; it means holding that it is true or at least more reasonably acceptable than its contradictory.) A philosopher who argues that persons interested in the issue ought rationally to accept the no-free-choice position must believe that although they are not compelled to accept it, they *can* rationally accept it ("ought implies can"); they have some freedom of choice in the matter. Yet the determinist proposition being urged denies that the persons addressed have any freedom. Either the determinist is thus contradicting himself or else is pointlessly urging people to do what by his own doctrine they cannot do – make the free choice of rationally accepting that doctrine.

Boyle and his coauthors do in effect recognize the possibility, mentioned in the preceding section, that determinism is true and that participants in controversy over it versus free choice are behaving like fully programmed robots whose every slightest verbal move in the game is a fully determined rather than rationally chosen action. "To affirm [the determinist] position in this way, however, is to withdraw from the philosophical controversy" (p. 169).[16]

The Irrefutability of Determinism

Besides being practically incredible and besides putting its proponents in the position of either contradicting themselves or avowing themselves to be mere robots rather than rational controversialists, determinism is irrefutable or unfalsifiable – in the bad sense. It has a built-in immunity to any adverse evidence; its claim to say anything definite about how the world actually works is a sham. No perceptions of persons that they are more than mere cogs in tightly working machinery, that they have some scope for making decisions not *totally* predetermined by their genetic makeups and past experiences, count for anything; for these very perceptions have themselves been predetermined. Similarly, no number of episodes in which unexpected, astonishing, or unpredictable decisions of particular persons brought major consequences count for anything. Apparent examples of formidable exertions of will count for nothing. The theory itself rules such episodes out as evidence on the grounds that the cited decisions and exertions, as well as their being unexpected, astonishing, or apparently unpredictable, are themselves mere links in the universal causal chain. Examples in which a person seems to have changed his very character by effort of will would not faze the determinist. He would maintain that the person's exertion of will, and with what degree of success, were themselves predetermined. Determinism does not deny that praise and blame, reward and punishment, can be efficacious in influencing behavior; it simply maintains that these in turn are predetermined.

What adverse evidence of any sort is even conceivable, then, from which the theory does not protect itself in advance? A theory that can accommodate absolutely any evidence does not specify any genuine restrictions on how the real world actually works; its ostensible empirical character is a sham.

Furthermore, the theory does not carry any actual implications for how to live one's own life or for public policy. Should individuals cultivate a sense of control over their own decisions and actions or, at the other extreme, cultivate a fatalistic outlook? Some psychologists may offer the one line of advice and others the opposite line; but in any case, each is merely offering the advice he is fated to offer. A determinist philosopher is not necessarily bound to advise the fatalistic outlook; for he may recognize the benefits of feelings of autonomy and responsibility and himself feel, furthermore, that he is fated *not* to undercut such feelings and the benefits flowing from them. Each ordinary individual, similarly, is receiving the advice he is fated to receive and will respond to it, along with other influences, as he is fated to respond.

Should criminals be held more responsible for their actions and more liable to punishment than they currently are or, on other hand, should the Clarence Darrow defense be given greater heed? The first policy shift may reduce crime and make for a healthier society on that account, although it would be unfair to criminals who are, on the determinist theory, mere unfortunate links in a causal chain. (Incidentally, doesn't determinism undermine even the concept of unfairness?) In either case, policymakers will hear the arguments they are fated to hear and respond as they are fated to do.

In short, the determinist theory not only has built-in immunity to adverse evidence but also lacks implications about how to apply it in practice. It is empty. Individuals, by and large, cannot bring themselves to regard it as meaningful and to conduct their own lives and public policy in accordance with it.

I am saying not that full determinism is wrong but that it is an empty, meaningless doctrine. This conclusion is not, I believe, one of the airy dismissals of philosophical issues that used to characterize a crude logical positivism.

Extreme Positions and Partial Determinism

I have tried to show that total fatalistic determinism is empty, perhaps even absurd. We might now try to focus on the opposite extreme position, except that complete free will and absolute *in*determinism are downright inconceivable. No conceivable self is free of a biological nature and of the influences imposed by an external world. Still, let us see how far we can get in imagining a self whose will is *essentially* free.

A self whose character had been determined not by heredity and environment but only internally would be the product of a core self, a miniature self within the self, as R.E. Hobart says (1934/1966/1984). But how could that core self be free from external influences? Only by its character having been determined by a further internal miniature self, and so on in preposterous infinite regress. "To cause his original self a man must have existed before his original self. Is there something humiliating to him in the fact that he is not a contradiction in terms?" (Hobart 1934/1984, p. 505).

In some respects, of course, a person's earlier self does partially shape his later self: his earlier decisions and actions affect his capacity for and inclinations toward later experiences, decisions, and actions. But if a person does improve his qualities, what could merit praise but the ingredient of aspiration and resolution in him that made his effort possible? (Hobart 1934/1984, p. 505). What could merit praise except features of an already existing character that could not have been fully its own creation? One praiseworthy character trait is the capacity to respond suitably to praise, blame, and the concept of responsibility.

Any consistently conceivable self must to at least some extent, then – and experience suggests a large extent – be the product of external forces. What implications follow concerning the freedom, autonomy, dignity, and responsibility of the individual? Hobart faces the question: How can anyone be praised or blamed if heredity and circumstance have ultimately given him his qualities? Does the fact that a person did not create himself bar recognizing his character for what it is? If – inconceivably – someone had somehow made his own "original character", and a fine one, and if we praised him for it, we would be ascribing a still earlier character to him. Praise or blame for decisions or actions refers to what kind of person took them; there is nothing else for praise or blame to refer to (Hobart 1934/1984, p. 505).

A person's character at a particular time is what it is. It inclines him to the kinds of intentions and decisions and actions that it does incline him toward; so it meaningfully exposes him to admiration or reprehension, praise or blame. This is true regardless of just how his character came to be what it is. A reprehensible character remains reprehensible even though it can be explained, or explained away, as the product of adverse heredity and environment. The notion of character being admirable or reprehensible only to the extent that it is internally determined, free of external influences, is a self-contradictory notion.

An analogy of sorts holds with a person's wants and tastes. J.K. Galbraith (1958, esp. Chapter XI) made much of what he called the "dependence effect": many of an individual's wants in modern society are not wants that he would experience spontaneously if left to himself. Instead, his wants are created by the process of satisfying them. The consumption patterns of other members of society, and notoriously advertising, create wants. Wants that are artificial in this sense cannot be urgent or important, so the implication runs (and, in Galbraith's view, incomes that might nevertheless be spent on meeting them may properly be taxed heavily to finance really important services of the kinds supplied by government).

F.A. Hayek (1961/1967) calls this argument a *non sequitur*. Suppose that people would indeed feel no need for something if it were not produced. If that fact did prove the thing of small value, then the highest products of human endeavor, including the arts, literature, and the marvels of high technology, would be of small value. Standards of hygiene and the demand for products with which to meet them, instead of arising spontaneously within each separate individual, are likewise social products.

More generally, the individual himself is the product of social forces, operating largely through language, which conditions his thoughts, values, and activities. Recognizing the individual as a social product in no way denies that happiness and misery, success and frustration, are experienced by individuals; there is no such thing as collective happiness distinct from and transcending the happiness of individuals. Recognizing how society shapes its members in no way imposes collectivist or communitarian rather than individualist thinking and policies.

The analogy, in brief, amounts to this: a person's tastes are what they are and their gratification or frustration causes him pleasure or unhappiness, even though his tastes are themselves largely the product of external influences. Similarly, a person's character is what it is and does expose him to admiration and praise or reprobation and blame, even though his character, like his tastes, is itself largely the product of external influences.

Praise and reward, blame and punishment, are appropriate to the extent that they are capable in principle of influencing actions, decisions, and character traits, inappropriate otherwise – so Moritz Schlick persuasively argues. Having grown up in ghetto poverty is no valid excuse for robbery, mayhem, or murder; on the other hand, it is pointless to blame a person for actions imposed by congenital deformity or actual insanity. Reward and punishment, praise and blame, all implicitly acknowledge a partial determinism operating in human affairs. (Sometimes, however, a distinction holds between punishment and blame, as in the case of the unruly dog. Individual or collective self-defense against criminally insane persons, as against mad dogs, is not the same as assigning moral culpability. "Punishment" in such a case, like quarantine of a disease-carrier, is not punishment in the fullest sense.)

Praise or blame, reward or punishment, is appropriate for an act committed freely, even and especially for one committed in accordance with the agent's moral character. Its appropriateness does not hinge on the agent's character being totally uncaused, whatever that might mean. Praise or blame would be inappropriate if it would have no effect on acts of the type in question and no effect on propensities to commit them.

Partial determinism, which responsibility presupposes, is fundamentally different both from full determinism and from complete (perhaps stochastic) indeterminism. It recognizes that causality does operate in human affairs, as in the rest of the universe. It recognizes that how an individual will decide when facing a particular choice may be heavily or decisively influenced by his genetic makeup and by his past experiences. These influences include the arguments he has heard and the thoughts that have been aroused in his mind, including the concept of responsibility and prospects of praise and blame. Partial determinism does not maintain, however, that absolutely everything is fully predetermined in the minutest detail. It allows some scope for chance and possibly, also, some scope for the autonomy (or whatever it might be called) that doctrines of free will allude to.

Unlike full determinism, the doctrine of only partial determinism, recognizing scope for some sort of free will, does *not* enjoy built-in immunity to adverse evidence and is *not* devoid of practical implications. If people never experienced feelings of autonomy in making decisions – if they never experienced situations in which they felt that they personally were weighing conflicting considerations and themselves making decisions, free of *total* outside compulsion and constraint, and if, on the contrary, they always perceived themselves under identifiable tight compulsions and constraints – then the doctrine of free will would falter. Or if people sometimes did experience feelings of autonomy but could be shown in each case that the feelings were illusory and shown in detail just how their supposed free choices were in fact externally predetermined in full, again the free-will doctrine would be undermined. Most obviously, the doctrine would be discredited if people were always keenly aware of being mere links in a causal chain and if they recognized in detail just what causes were operating on them, including recognizing just how various facts and arguments came to their attention and what weight each of these commanded.

Discrediting evidence of this sort is conceivable, and the free-will doctrine itself does not rule out its significance. That very fact shows that the doctrine is not empty. The absence of such discrediting evidence suggests, furthermore, that the doctrine may be correct. But it does not, of course, prove that it is right; no doctrine about empirical reality can ever be proved absolutely.

Conclusion

Discussing free will versus determinism was necessary because many philosophers consider the issue genuine and important, intertwining with the question of moral responsibility and so with ethics in general. The fatalist doctrine of an unbroken chain of tight causal determination operating from the beginning of time, of apparently ever more complex states of the world having been fully specified in advance by the apparently less complex earlier states – that doctrine is practically incredible. The idea of some kind of sheer chance almost imposes itself. Chance enters ethical discussion not because it itself provides scope for responsible human choice but because it undermines the claims of full, fatalistic determinism. Once determinism is shaken, the idea of some sort of free will, operating alongside of both causation and chance, gains a possible foothold. Everyday personal experience supports some such idea.

One question, however, remains dangling. *Can* a person's will be shaped in any manner other than by chance and by external influences such as heredity, environment, and experiences (including exposure to ideas concerning responsibility, praise, and blame)? Is reflection in one's own mind such an "other" manner? No, or not unequivocally; for although ample experience testifies to its reality, that reflection is itself conditioned by external influences, including the actions and ideas of other people. Yet some such "other" manner of determination seems to be what the cheerleaders for free will are postulating.

One approach to a solution – to reconciling free will with the sort of determinism that science deals in – appeals to the notion of emergent properties. "Specific combinations, arrangements or interactions of components can give rise to totally new attributes. The whole is more than the sum of its parts." Diamond and charcoal possess properties quite different from those of their component carbon atoms. A drum made from flat planks can roll. An essay has meaning not contained in the individual ink dots on the printed page. Laws of grammar are quite different from but not incompatible with laws of physics. Similarly, somehow, the human mind is able "to make choices not determined solely by external or genetically fixed factors; the mind is self-programming – it modifies its own processes" (Voss 1995).

I admittedly cannot form a satisfactorily definite conception of what suggestions like that may be getting at. I claim, then, not to have settled the free-will issue but to have kept alive the possibility that if it is not merely a pseudo-problem after all, it anyway is not a problem subversive of ethics. The determinist thesis appears meaningless in the sense of carrying built-in immunity to any conceivable adverse evidence. Since no observations about the world could conceivably clash with it, the thesis does not really say anything about the world and about whether any free will operates in it.

While the free-will/determinism issue thus dangles unsettled, we all find ourselves seized with ineradicable impressions (or illusions) that we enjoy some freedom of action and choice and even of will. When we write as scholars, we simply cannot believe that our every word is precisely predetermined and will draw precisely predetermined reactions from our fellow scholars.

Sometimes we find two or more strands of theory applicable to certain phenomena without our being able – yet, anyway – to reconcile those strands, which may even appear inconsistent. An example concerns the apparent dual nature (wave and particle natures) of light and of electrons. The principle of complementarity, introduced to physics by Niels Bohr, condones applying each strand of theory where it does good service while still hoping to reconcile the different strands, perhaps by modifying one or all (Teller 1980, pp. 93, 105–6, 138–40). Economists formerly did not know, and some would say still do not know, how fully to reconcile three strands of balance-of-payments analysis, the elasticities, absorption, and monetary approaches. It makes sense anyway to apply each approach where it does good service while still seeking a fuller reconciliation among them.

Similarly, in analyzing the worlds of nature and human affairs, we find it reasonable to believe in tight causality or in causality loosened by an element of sheer chance. We also find reason – or at least the pressure of compelling personal experience – to believe in a loosening by some element of free will. The corresponding strands of theory are complementary. Since we cannot really believe that ethics is a field deprived of subject matter, let us continue investigating it.[17]

Let us condemn, though, the tactic of offering mere cheerleading for free will in the guise of argument. (Free will is good, those who doubt it are scoundrels, and we are on the side of the good.) As David Hume said, "this question should be decided by fair arguments before philosophers, [rather] than by declamations before the people" (1739–40/1961, Book II, Part III, last paragraph of Section II).

NOTES

1. Some writers (for example, Flew 1971, pp. 383–9, 404, 462; Rorty 1991, pp. 40, 42) use the term "Hume's Fork" to label not the is/ought or positive/normative distinction but instead the above-mentioned synthetic/analytic or factual/logical distinction. Since Hume expounded both distinctions, one might speak of *two* Hume's Forks.
2. One plausible interpretation of the notion of a purely positive economics is the set of factual and logical propositions expressing research results that economists have achieved. Reaching and stating such propositions surely amounts to only a part, perhaps a small part, of economists' professional activity. Furthermore, conceiving of positive economics as a set of propositions does recognize that the relevant distinction lies between types of proposition.
3. Moritz Schlick's usage of the term "good" is worth noting. According to classical utilitarianism, as he interprets it, "'The good *is* what *brings* the greatest possible happiness to society.' We express it more carefully: 'In human society, that is *called* good which is *believed* to bring the greatest happiness.'" (1930/1961, p. 87; cf. p. 85 and *passim*). Schlick's own formulation, though perhaps hard to prove, is nevertheless a positive proposition concerning how people use words to express judgments. It is different from, though not inconsistent with, the proposition that that *is* good which *does* promote happiness. Much evidence is relevant to what promotes happiness, but accepting the latter proposition presupposes a further value judgment, one in favor of happiness.
4. See *A Treatise of Human Nature* (1739–40), Book III, Part I, Section I, last paragraph. The standard interpretation has been challenged, for example by A.C. MacIntyre (1959) and Geoffrey Hunter (1963), both reprinted in Chappell (1966). R.F. Atkinson (1961) and Antony Flew (1963, 1966), also both in Chappell (1966), rebut the challenge. The standard interpretation seems victorious also to W.D. Hudson (1964/1966), who reviews the discussion, and to me.

Hudson (1964/1966, p. 296 of the reprint) warns against confusing the two questions of what Hume really meant and what the correct view is. I focus on the latter question and argue that the view traditionally attributed to Hume is correct.

5. David Brink (1989) is one philosopher who admits to not having fully made up his mind about the is/ought gap. He further says that its existence would be no embarrassment to the objective utilitarianism he espouses. He draws an analogy with an is/*is* gap among different natural sciences: for example, psychology cannot be gaplessly reduced to physics (as far as we know); yet this gap does not deprive either or both sciences of objective character.

6. Throughout this book I myself use normative language, and without embarrassment; for avoiding it would be intolerably awkward for both me and the reader. When I say, for example, that a moral code or a legal system "should" incorporate such-and-such a feature, I mean that the feature would tend to serve social cooperation and so serve happiness. When I say that such-and-such a positive proposition "should" be accepted, I imply that available evidence and reasoning point to correspondence between the proposition and the way things actually are. I also believe that acceptance of true propositions, in contrast to cheerful indifference to truth or falsity, by and large serves human happiness. (Fellow fans of George Will may notice that I have borrowed a couple of turns of phrase from his TV performances.)

7. John Stuart Mill has often been charged with the fallacy of trying to prove that happiness is *desirable* as an ultimate end from the fact that it is *desired* (*Utilitarianism*, Chapter IV). Yet Mill explicitly recognized (in the same chapter and already in Chapter I, penultimate paragraph) that "Questions of ultimate ends are not amenable to direct proof". The nearest one can come to proving that happiness is good is to present "[c]onsiderations ... capable of determining the intellect either to give or withhold its assent to the doctrine" (pp. 246-7 in Mill 1861, 1863, Cowling edition). This is what I have called using effective rhetoric in identifying a shared intuition.

8. Conceivably a person might hate pain because it interfered with his completing some work on which he set great stock. His desires might operate in a circle: he might value health and comfort to be able to work, while valuing the work, or its results, as a means to happiness. (Cf. Merrill's interpretation of Rand, summarized above.) But then isn't happiness still the ultimate criterion, though with different specific content for different persons and circumstances?

9. Ayn Rand herself gives little if any explicit discussion of benevolence in her nonfiction writings; but several of her fictional heroes, as Kelley (1996) points out, do exhibit that virtue.

10. Recent research suggests, however, that such behavior may not convey altruistic warnings after all. By jumping up and down in sight of a lion on the prey, the gazelle may be signaling that he is in too good shape to be worth pursuing; the lion might do better chasing other gazelles (Brownlee 1998).

11. Walter Eucken (1950, pp. 50-51, 329-30) effectively blasts such essentialism or conceptual realism in economics.

12. Just what is compulsion? How may we distinguish acts done under compulsion from free acts for which a person is responsible? In a sense, as Dworkin (1970/1984) notes, a person does his every act because he prefers it to any alternative open to him under the circumstances – even submitting to a highwayman. Dworkin distinguishes, then, between two sorts of desires or reasons for action. A free act is one motivated by a reason that the agent finds acceptable. A person acts under compulsion when responding to a reason that he does not want to have.

Although Dworkin may be on the right track, his distinction is inexact. One may undergo an operation, free from compulsion, while wishing that the reason for the operation did not exist.

13. This particular example is my own, to the best of my recollection; yet it is in the spirit of essays collected in Squire (1931). There, for example, Winston Churchill speculates on what would have happened if Lee had not [sic] won the battle of Gettysburg, Hilaire Belloc on what would have happened if the cart that in fact blocked Louis XVI's escape at Varennes in June 1791 had gotten stuck before reaching the crucial place, and Emil Ludwig on what would have happened if German Emperor Frederick III had lived to reign until 1914 and not

just for his actual 99 days in 1888. Such examples mesh nicely with currently popular theories of "chaos" or "complexity".

14.   Considerations resembling these appear in Peirce (1958, selection 9), an article I had read and then forgotten many years before first drafting this appendix.

My appeal to increasing complexity and information-content may admittedly appear to run afoul of the second law of thermodynamics, the entropy law, and I may be quite wrong. On the other hand, that law in its central context pertains to energy and its degradation; and its rationale is perhaps most clearly set forth with reference to the statistical properties of crowds of nonliving molecules. The law may not fully carry over to the present context. One difference from the context of inanimate processes is that in the evolution of information, as in biological evolution, selection may accomplish a kind of inner directedness. It may be that on our earth and perhaps even in the universe as a whole, neither kind of evolution violates the second law.

15.   See, for example, Popper 1985, Selections 4 and 21, 1982, Section 38, and his 1972 lecture, reprinted 1982. Earlier (in articles of 1908, pp. 358–79 and 404–5 in Pierce 1958), Charles S. Peirce had distinguished among "three Universes of Experience". Popper's World 3 and Peirce's first universe correspond fairly well, as do Popper's World 1 and Peirce's second universe, but the remaining world and universe correspond loosely at best.

16.   The argument of Boyle et al. is extremely complex, detailed, and repetitious, contains many cross-references and other obstacles to comprehension, and does, after all, occupy an entire book; so I cannot guarantee that my summary is entirely faithful to their argument.

17.   Edward N. Lorenz (1993, pp. 159–60) reminds us that we should believe even in an uncomfortable truth rather than in an appealing falsehood. That premise recommends believing in free will. If it is a reality, our choice is correct. If it is not, we still shall not have made an incorrect choice, since, lacking free will, we shall not have made any choice at all.

3.   Origins of ethics

EXPLAINING ORIGINS VERSUS APPRAISING SUBSTANCE

History scarcely shows that people deliberately invented and agreed to ethical precepts. True enough, some rules of families and other groups, including statutes enforced by governments, have been deliberately adopted. They were framed, however, against an already existing ethical background. Instead of being deliberately devised, ethical precepts evolved through largely unplanned biological and social processes.

Explaining how something originated and why it persists is not the same as appraising or justifying it: "has evolved" does not mean "is good" (Ruse 1990, p. 65). Oddly, many people seem unable to distinguish a statement of what is believed true from advocacy of what ought to be true (Dawkins 1978, p. 3). (Examples come to mind of "political correctness" requiring particular positions on what are actually questions of fact.)

A naturalistic explanation of traits and behaviors does not entail approval. Nature, so far as we know, has not been aiming at any particular results. To the question whether nature deserves emulation as the handiwork of a benevolent and omnipotent God, John Stuart Mill answered in effect: *Are you kidding?* (Wright 1994, p. 331; Mill 1874/1969). Lecturing on "Evolution and ethics" in 1893, Thomas Henry Huxley attacked the idea of deriving values from evolution. On the contrary, society's ethical progress "depends, not on imitating the cosmic process, still less in running away from it, but in combating it" (quoted in Singer 1982, p. 62; cf. Wright 1994, p. 242). Although natural selection may "want" us to be effective and prolific creatures, not happy ones, psychiatrists have no good reason to mold people that way. Understanding natural selection might even be helpful in defusing mental traits that it has stuck us with. Sympathy, conscience, obligation, and guilt can promote behaviors that natural selection might not "approve" of but that do tend to serve happiness (Wright 1994, esp. pp. 211, 226, 242, 258, 298, 328, 331). As no less tough-minded a biologist than the author of *The Selfish Gene* wrote, understanding the evolutionary principles encapsulated in his book's title may help us work toward a society that does *not* imitate those principles (Dawkins 1978, esp. p. 3; cf. Hamilton 1996, pp. 189–91, 219, 258–9).

Understanding and explanation can help change features of reality judged unattractive. Being possible is a necessary (though not sufficient) condition for something to be worth recommending: "ought implies can". A naturalistic explanation of something is evidence of its being dependably possible.

IS ALTRUISM COMPATIBLE WITH NATURAL SELECTION?

These remarks about explanation and appraisal extend to cooperativeness and generalized benevolence – "altruism" in the nonpejorative, non-Randian sense. This chapter mainly considers biological and social circumstances that might promote altruism. It only incidentally mentions how these circumstances might promote deception and predation also. This distribution of emphasis does not dismiss those evils as untypical or unimportant. Human beings do indeed share unsavory characteristics with other animals. Altruism receives special attention precisely because it is *un*natural, or superficially appears so. That ethical behavior and beliefs are nevertheless possible and do occur is what may appear remarkable and in need of explanation.

Any value judgments that people hold sincerely even after calm reflection must be consistent with knowledge of physical reality and of biological reality shaped by evolution. Innate capacities and dispositions get molded and supplemented by culture, leading us to think and act in biologically adaptive ways (Ruse 1990, p. 63). If the "sympathy" that David Hume and Adam Smith judged central to ethics is real, and perhaps even more so if it has a biological basis, that fact counts *something*, if perhaps not much, toward approving of behavior manifesting it and of precepts encouraging it: at least they are not impossible.

Morality, Hume observed, involves some near-universal human sentiment applauding some and censuring other kinds of behavior. That sentiment does not, however, call for indiscriminate equal benevolence. Nature ordains reserving our strongest sentiments of benevolence for ourselves and our relatives, friends, and associates; for directing them too widely would dissipate them. We correct the narrowness of these sentiments, however, by reflecting on the usefulness of a general standard of vice and virtue (Hume 1751/1777/1930, pp. 110, 65n.; compare the sections on sympathy with other persons and on the generalization principle in Chapters 4 and 9 below). In merely *recognizing* Hume–Smith sympathy as a fact of human nature – if it is a fact – an observer does not make a value judgment, but he does make one if he admires and shares this sentiment.

Natural selection favors traits of behavior and character that tend to preserve an organism's own life and capacity to reproduce. Or if it does not always favor the individual organism's *own* reproduction, natural selection at least favors the transmission to further generations of the genes it shares with relatives. Plainly, the virtue of prudence has survival value. As social animals, humans must have capacities for living and cooperating with one another, which presupposes genes consistent with the concern for others necessary to such cooperation.

Compatibility between self and social interest, if it holds, presumably shares a biological basis with language. The bodily and mental characteristics enabling individuals to communicate with one another enhance their prospects of surviving and reproducing. Much the same must be true of capacities to absorb the social conventions embodied in language, to understand the purposes of other people, and so to get along with them, reap the gains from trade with them, and also avoid extreme exploitation by them.

Any biological roots of ethics, including Hume–Smith sympathy, apparently reach back to before the evolution of the human race. Behavior in apparent conformity with rules of social cooperation has been observed in chimpanzees and other mammals. The evident rules concern food-sharing and other forms of reciprocity; violators are punished. "Consolation behavior" is also observed, as in embraces given to animals defeated in fights. (Work on these topics by the primatologist Frans de Waal and other researchers is reported in Marshall 1996, Cowley 1996, and "Going Ape" 1996.) Even behavior benefiting others at some cost to oneself has been widely observed in nonhuman animals (Chapter 2 mentioned examples). Such behavior can hardly be explained as mere responses to praise and blame (Singer 1982, pp. 5–8, 11).

Michael Ruse sketches some history of thinking about sociability (1990, pp. 72, 73, 75). Aristotle focused on the good life for the individual, which might seem rather self-centered except for his insisting that man is a social and political animal. Some virtues or excellences crucially involve other persons. Individuals cannot be truly happy, Aristotle thought, unless they interact properly with their fellows, as with justice, liberality, and perhaps bravery. Ruse's own Darwinism concurs with David Hume's position on several points: the rooting of morality in the subjective feeling of sympathy; the is/ought distinction; and compatibilism, the "soft" doctrine on the issue of free will versus determinism that leaves a window for morality and some element of choice, even though humans are part of nature's causal chain. Hume grasped a proto-version of kin selection but could not see, so far ahead of modern genetics, that reciprocal altruism could develop through biological as well as cultural processes.

James Q. Wilson (1993) restates the idea that human beings share an intuition about proper behavior and a disposition to make moral judgments. This moral sense includes notions of self-control, fairness, and duty. It also includes the sympathy identified by Adam Smith as the source of moral sentiments: the capacity for and inclination to imagine the feelings of others.[1] Sympathy intertwines with a desire for closeness with other persons. It appears in the attachment between parents and children. Without these bonds, human beings could not survive their long period of helpless infancy. Parents lacking the biological capacities and dispositions necessary for care of the young would tend not to pass their genes on to later generations.

Evolution selected not so much for specific behaviors as for traits predisposing people toward broad types of behavior, notably for the disposition to attachment to others and sensitivity to their feelings. We do not simply share but also judge the feelings we imagine others to have; to sympathize is to judge (Wilson 1993, p. 32). Judging others, we are aware that others are judging us. We care about reputation, respect, and being liked. We desire not only to be praised but to be praiseworthy. As Adam Smith said, "Man naturally desires, not only to be loved, but to be lovely" (1759/1976, p. 208; Wilson 1993, p. 33).

Sympathy shows up not just as tenderness or concern but also as anger and vengefulness. We would be enraged at a man torturing a baby. Accepting the torture of babies for amusement "would make it all but impossible for people to live together in an orderly society". (In saying so, pp. 239–40, Wilson implicitly appeals to the criterion of social cooperation.) Wilson welcomes Robert Frank's (1988) explanation of many otherwise puzzling human actions by appeal to the practical value of commitments visibly made and "irrationally" obeyed; emotions communicate commitments (pp. 231–2; compare Chapter 8 below).

KINSHIP SELECTION AND RECIPROCITY

Because reciprocity is necessary for social animals to cooperate and survive, evolution tends to select for individuals inclined to act accordingly. If two men attacked by a sabertoothed tiger do not cooperate, one or both will die; yet fighting together they can kill the tiger. Repeated such encounters will probably leave a population of people inclined to cooperate; the others will have been eaten (Wilson 1993, pp. 65–7, crediting Peter Singer with the example).

Among useful innate dispositions (mixed with less admirable ones), Michael Ruse counts feelings that we *should* behave in helpful and caring ways. People show some tendency to be decent moral beings, disliking cruelty and thinking that people deserve a chance. But they are not suckers: natural selection works against self-sacrifice for no benefit to oneself or to carriers of genes like one's own (Ruse 1990, pp. 63–4).

One plausible evolutionary mechanism promoting such dispositions is kinship selection: assistance to one's children or other close relatives helps them survive and transmit their genes, which are more likely to duplicate one's own and to promote behavior like one's own than are the genes of strangers. Biologists speak of "inclusive fitness" (Hamilton 1996, Chapters 2, 6, 8, 9, and *passim*). The fitness selected for is not narrowly confined to expressions of the genes of one's own body but extends to the same genes in the bodies of relatives and, as mentioned below, of reciprocators.

Being partial to the interests of oneself and one's kin is natural in evolved creatures. Rules authorizing partiality of this sort appeal to our concern for other individual persons rather than for everyone impersonally. Such rules tend toward better care for children, the sick, and the aged than the altruism of strangers would provide (Singer 1982, pp. 158-60; on overlapping networks of special regard, see Hazlitt 1964, Chapter 20).

Another biological mechanism involves reciprocity; mutual grooming in birds and primates – removing parasites and cleaning – is a standard example. (Ruse 1990 discusses both kinship selection and reciprocal altruism, as do Robert Axelrod and William D. Hamilton in their jointly written Chapter 5 of Axelrod 1984 and as does Hamilton 1996, p. 50 and Chapters 8 and 9. Hamilton credits the term "reciprocal altruism" to Robert Trivers.) The exchange of services tends to promote the survival and reproduction of individuals who are more likely than nonreciprocators to carry genes for fair dealing of that sort. "Rules encouraging reciprocity and discouraging cheating build on a natural human tendency to reciprocate good or evil" (Singer 1982, pp. 158-9). Honorable people make more reliable trading partners than ones motivated by narrow and predatory self-interest, especially in transactions in which cheating is hard to detect. Evolution would therefore favor individuals able to distinguish decency from contrary traits in others. Being recognized as a presumably reliable trading partner improves one's opportunities to reap the gains from trade, and the obvious way to receive such recognition is to deserve it (Singer 1982, pp. 43-4).

Speaking of mutual recognition, Richard Dawkins introduces the metaphor of the "green beard". Because genes may have multiple effects, it is theoretically possible for a gene to confer a visible label like the beard, together with a tendency to be especially nice to fellow carriers of it. More plausibly, not a beard but *actions* identify the carrier of an altruistic gene. It could prosper in the gene pool if it gave its carriers a tendency to rescue or otherwise assist their fellows. Especially plausible, perhaps, is altruism toward close relatives, who have an above-average chance of sharing genes. In a species whose members move around in small groups, like monkeys, whales, and dolphins, the overall probability that a random member of the group may share one's genes may make altruism worth the cost to the individual –

worth it for the survival of the altruistic gene (Dawkins 1978, esp. pp. 96–7, 108).

Dawkins introduces some useful terminology and models. "Cheats", who welcome being groomed or rescued but never spend effort helping anyone else, supposedly fare better than "Suckers", indiscriminate altruists who help just anyone. Cheats continue faring better even as, in consequence, the whole population declines. But suppose "Grudgers" appear and exhibit a third strategy, behaving altruistically except for bearing a grudge against those who have cheated them. (Singer 1982 also uses the term "grudger".) If and when Grudgers manage to reach a critical proportion of the population, their chance of encountering and benefiting each other becomes great enough to offset their efforts wasted in helping Cheats. They will start to average higher payoffs than Cheats, who will be driven toward extinction. Dawkins has done computer simulations on populations starting with Suckers strongly in the majority, a minority of Grudgers just above the critical size, and a minority of Cheats of about the same size. The Cheats prosper for a while; but eventually, as Suckers get wiped out, they encounter few but Grudgers and fellow Cheats. No longer easily getting away with exploitation, the Cheats go into decline. The shrunken Cheat population levels out as its members "enjoy the privileges of rarity and the comparative freedom from grudges which this brings". Then it slowly dwindles toward extinction, leaving only the Grudgers. "Paradoxically, the presence of the suckers actually endangered the grudgers early on in the story because they were responsible for the temporary prosperity of the cheats" (Dawkins 1978, pp. 197–202, quotation from p. 201).

To change the metaphor, people who heed the Biblical behest to turn the other cheek can actually harm decent people by letting predation be seen to pay off. Righteous indignation, conversely, can serve a social purpose.

The strategy of grudging or reciprocal altruism is pretty much the same as the tit for tat of Robert Axelrod, whose computer simulations Dawkins apparently anticipated (Axelrod 1984, discussed in Chapter 8 below). Including a propensity to repay attempted exploitation in kind, the grudging strategy is quite different from playing doormat, from turning the cheek. Grudgers (reciprocators) are valuable to other members of the group and likely to receive favorable treatment from them (sexual selection being just one possible mechanism). They are likely to have an edge in – though no guarantee of – survival, prosperity, and reproduction. Known exploiters will be shunned.

Mutual considerateness (Loren Lomasky says "deference") may develop by a kind of invisible-hand process. If each of two persons has some propensity to be considerate of the other and to reciprocate considerate actions, then exchanging benefits can escalate, even apart from any actual contract

(Lomasky 1987, Chapter 4). Even when the players (bacteria, for example) cannot literally recognize one another, mechanisms equivalent to or substituting for conscious reciprocity may be at work. Human beings, as Axelrod says (1984, pp. 188, 191), can use their foresight to speed up an otherwise blind process of evolution. Experience and moral training can reinforce behavior favoring reciprocators and sympathizers and their reproduction; a virtuous circle can operate. Morality need not be seen as actual self-sacrifice, and nothing beyond "nepotism" and direct and indirect reciprocity need be invoked to account for it (Alexander 1987, pp. 195, 77, and *passim*).

If reciprocity and sympathy are advantageous to interacting individuals, they are advantageous to a group of such individuals. The group tends to prosper relative to other groups in which those traits are less prevalent.

DOCILITY AND BOUNDED RATIONALITY

Herbert A. Simon (1990) warns against simplistic models of the "selfish gene". He finds altruism, defined either socially or genetically, an important determinant of human behavior and "wholly compatible with natural selection" (p. 1668). (Altruism as he interprets it, "a partial sacrifice of genetic fitness, may be very different from the forgoing of wealth and power that is called altruism in common discourse"; p. 1668.) Altruism is a by-product of "docility", by which Simon means teachability, or an ability and inclination to learn from others and to accept their influence. Through it, nature selects for behavior that goes beyond generosity to close kin and beyond what the hope of benefits promotes or social measures enforce. Docility can enhance fitness by causing individuals to adopt culturally transmitted behaviors even without independently evaluating how these might contribute to their own fitness (p. 1665). The individual's narrow self-interest and reproduction can come out ahead on the whole even though in some respects losing out from altruistic behavior and attitudes and values transmitted through social influence. Docility would lose much of its value if the individual spent great effort evaluating social influences. Accepting them without full evaluation is part of the mechanisms of docility and also of guilt and shame (p. 1667).

Because of what Simon calls "bounded rationality", the learning process and the individual's calculations cannot sharply discriminate between behaviors and beliefs that do and those that do not serve the individual's narrow self-interest and reproduction. Altruists can actually be fitter than selfish individuals as long as socially imposed demands for altruism are moderate compared with the advantages of knowledge and skills acquired through docility. Given this condition, the proportion of altruists can rise (pp. 1666–7).

Openness to social influence benefits both the individual and the group. In a complex environment, biological evolution cannot fine-tune the individual so exactly that his behavior and dispositions serve only the narrow interests of himself, his close kin, and individuals from whom he can reasonably expect reciprocal favors. Because the docility favored by natural selection spills over even into some genuine altruism, biology cannot entirely forestall behavior and inclinations adverse to the individual's own survival and reproduction. Benevolence hitch-hikes onto traits serving narrow self-interest. (One might wonder, however, just why evolution cannot work so finely as to select exclusively for narrow self-interest and reproduction. It does work finely in some other respects. On the other hand, perhaps the very concept of such extremely narrow self-interest is problematic for social animals, whose individual survival depends on survival of the group. As Paul Samuelson argues in an article reviewed below, rigorous selection of *anti*altruistic individual members would work against survival of the species or group and thus ultimately against survival even of such members.)

Simon's argument is congruent with Schlick's and Hazlitt's point (reviewed in Chapter 8) that cultivating a moral character serves the individual's self-interest on the whole and in a probabilistic sense, even though acting from such a character is harmful and even fatal to the individual in exceptional cases. Although morality cannot be guaranteed to pay off, it is a sound strategy.

Behaviors associated with Simon's "docility" go beyond reciprocity in a narrowly economic sense. Reciprocity need not involve exchanges of goods and explicit services, not even exchanges under wholly tacit understandings. Often it means remembering social interactions, whether in returning a favor or in seeking revenge. In a context of continuing personal relations, resentment at social bilking stands in contrast with its commercial counterpart. "When a friend lets us down, we are not just disappointed at not receiving our due; we are also upset by the failure of the friendship. This is why ingratitude is so disturbing." Attitudes of sympathy and benevolence are not based solely on narrow businesslike calculation of the likelihood of receiving future benefits or services. A narrowly economistic interpretation, one that would dismiss sympathy as apparent only, is wrong (Midgley 1994, pp. 146–7, quotation from p. 147; Midgley cites de Waal 1989, p. 207).

GROUP SELECTION

A biological account of altruism need not commit the formerly common fallacy of supposing that selection operates not just among related or closely interacting individuals but especially on the level of groups, even large groups and whole species. That would amount to supposing that individuals flourish collectively through sacrificing themselves individually. Before around 1960, "a misreading of theory" did attribute most adaptation to selection at the level of populations or species. But now biologists have become more careful with such notions. "The original individualistic emphasis of Darwin's theory is more valid" (Axelrod and Hamilton in their jointly written chapter of Axelrod 1984, p. 89; compare Rosenberg 1990, pp. 93–4). (The difficulties of a theory of biological group selection are further set forth in Wright 1994, pp. 186–8, and Rushton 1995, pp. 88–91.)

The economist Paul A. Samuelson (1993) summarizes an apparently emerging reconciliation of views among biologists. He makes some distinctions that help dispel, after all, the "dogma that group-selection arguments are somehow unclean" (p. 147). It seems obvious that altruism in the sense of a penchant for self-sacrifice tends to eliminate possessors of that trait and so eliminate the trait itself. Darwin already understood this result of natural selection operating solely at the individual level. (Altruism figures in just one of many examples of possible conflict between group and individual fitness. Darwin also understood dysfunctional sexual selection, one example being the awkward tail of the male peacock.[2]) Because economists understand the fallacy of confusing what is true of individuals or parts with what is true of aggregates or wholes and also understand the prisoners' dilemma, they tend to shy away from the concept of altruism. Samuelson wastes no ink, however, trying to avoid the concept by face-saving tautologies, as by maintaining that someone performs a heroic act only to get the good feeling of doing it. Such argumentation is boring, meaningless, and, as the physicist Wolfgang Pauli reportedly said, not even wrong.

Competition (and cooperation) occurs on a hierarchy of levels, Samuelson continues, and there is no a priori presumption that what succeeds at one level succeeds at another also. Much self regarding behavior is socially harmful. Individual genetic adaptation may work against species adaptation. Group selection or something much like it does work, however, to eliminate the results of group-adverse individual selection. In the context of competition for scarce resources, species or genetic groups whose members have traits adverse to the collective will tend to be wiped out. A mutant that sabotages an evolved elaborate cooperation will kill off its colony and eliminate itself (Samuelson cites the authority of the biologist E.O. Wilson).

Samuelson suggests, but does not actually draw up, a table categorizing mutations according to how the behaviors they trigger affect the fitness of the individual (and its progeny) and the group:

	Individual		
		Fit	Unfit
G			
r	Fit	(1) Persist	(2) Transient
o			
u	Unfit	(3) Eventually	(4) Transient
p		eliminated	

Case (1), with mutations favorable for both individual and group, is more likely to persist than the others. Cases (4) and (2) are likely to exist only transiently: individuals carrying mutations harmful to themselves are prone to die out fast. Type (3) mutants, although enjoying increased individual fitness, are unlikely to endure, for groups harmed by their individual members tend to perish. "In sum, group selection prunes from the record many of the perversities of individual selection. This ... is merely the banality of mathematics and logic applied to survivability" (Samuelson 1993, p. 147).

A restatement may help. Natural selection will not promote traits merely for the group's benefit if they would harm the individuals bearing them. Nor are traits narrowly favorable to the individual (say a propensity to take advantage of one's fellows) necessarily favorable to the group. We can predict the elimination of groups whose members have individually favorable but socially harmful traits. What is bad for the group is bad for its members, at least in the long run, since, among social animals, survival of individuals presupposes survival of their societies. (Compare Dawkins's and Axelrod's simulations – further reviewed in Chapter 8 below – in which strategies of preying on one's fellows eventually get weeded out because the predators run out of victims to prey on.) In short, no traits tend to become dominant that are bad for the individual but good for the group or good for the individual but bad for the group.

Theodore Bergstrom and Oded Stark (1993) study environments for prisoners'-dilemma games that would seem hostile to cooperation: individuals get higher payoffs from cheating or preying on their fellows than from cooperating, and high payoffs are favorable to reproduction. Even so, cooperation can persist and flourish. Individuals who inherit a biologically or culturally determined tendency to cooperate are more likely than defectors to benefit from cooperative siblings or other close associates. A mutant who defects against her cooperating sister may herself get a high payoff; but her descendants, inheriting the gene for defection, will suffer in their interactions with one another. Similarly in the other direction, the descendants of a mutant cooperator will benefit from interactions among themselves even amid a population of defectors. This point holds most straightforwardly for asexual reproduction; sexual reproduction complicates but does not reverse it. Siblings are more likely than randomly paired individuals to share the gene for cooperation or the gene for defection; and the advantages of cooperation are likely to promote the multiplication of cooperators. With cultural inheritance, similarly, organisms patterning their behaviors after a cooperative role model are more likely to interact in mutually beneficial ways than ones following a defector role model.

SELECTION THROUGH CULTURE

Although some early notions of biological selection on the group level are fallacies, cultural selection is not. Group selection can operate through a quasi-Lamarckian transmission of acquired characteristics – "quasi" because operating otherwise than through the biological processes that J.-B. Lamarck supposed. While genes pertain to individuals, members of a society share cultural traits. Groups whose institutions and traditions favor their survival and prosperity tend to fare better than groups with inferior cultural traits. It is not necessary that the favorable traits and habits had been deliberately adopted in view of foreseen and desired consequences. They might well have arisen gradually as piecemeal adaptations of actions to circumstances. David Hume understood that "the rules of morality are not the conclusions of our reason" (quoted in Hayek 1984, p. 319) – which is not to disparage bringing reason to bear in appraising and perhaps modifying inherited rules.

Traditions of fairness and honor and even of considerateness and kindness may aid the survival and prosperity of societies that respect and transmit them. Groups with contrary traditions are more likely to die out or be conquered. Alternatively, they will gradually replace their unfavorable customs and institutions by imitating those of more successful societies, transmitting these beneficial modifications to successive generations.

Herbert Spencer (1897/1978) envisaged group selection of some such kind. He recognized that "harmonious cooperation within the tribe conduces to its prosperity and growth" and spoke of "survival of the fittest among tribes" (Vol. I, pp. 345–6). Spencer's rational utilitarianism, as he called it, aimed at fulfilling the conditions of happiness, in contrast with what he called the empirical utilitarianism of Jeremy Bentham and Henry Sidgwick, which supposedly saw happiness as the immediate aim (Vol. II, pp. 260, 491–6). Although Spencer was the most famous of the so-called Social Darwinists, his work is not as crude as popularly parodied (Ruse 1990, p. 61). He did not advocate the law of the jungle to weed out inferior human beings. On the contrary, he hoped that social evolution would bring increasing harmony of interests and mutual aid (Spencer 1897/1978, Vol. I, p. 3, Vol. II, pp. 445–6; but cf. Vol. II, pp. 408–9).

Charles Darwin, more clearly than Spencer, was not a Social Darwinist, to judge from passages in *The Descent of Man*. Darwin saw "no cause to fear that the social instincts will grow weaker" in future generations; he expected "that virtuous habits will grow stronger, becoming perhaps fixed by inheritance". If so, virtue would triumph over the lower impulses (1871, Part I, Chapter IV, p. 494 in 1936 edition). Humans perform acts of sympathetic kindness to others in hopes of receiving good in return. Sympathy is strengthened by habit and increased by natural selection, for communities having the most sympathetic members flourish and rear the most offspring. It is often impossible to sort out the roles of natural selection and of sympathy, reason, experience, imitation, and habit in transmitting the social instincts (1871/1936, p. 479). The higher moral rules "are founded on the social instincts ... relate to the welfare of others", and "are supported by the approbation of our fellow-men and by reason" (p. 491). We reach the highest stage in moral culture "when we recognise that we ought to control our thoughts, and not even in inmost thought to think again the sins that made the past so pleasant to us" (p. 492, Darwin quoting Lord Tennyson). As man advanced in intellectual power and experience, "his sympathies became more tender and widely diffused, extending to men of all races, to the imbecile, maimed, and other useless members of society, and finally to the lower animals – so would the standard of his morality rise higher and higher" (p. 493). Darwin further wrote (p. 495): "The moral sense perhaps affords the best and highest distinction between man and the lower animals". The social instincts, intellectual powers, and effects of habit lead naturally to the golden rule, "and this lies at the foundation of morality".

HAYEKIAN THEMES

Advantageous rules and social arrangements may arise without ever having been deliberately planned; instead, they can emerge as unforeseen results of individuals' strivings to achieve their own particular purposes. Social selection and transmission is a recurrent theme in the writings of the economist F.A. Hayek (see, for example, Hayek 1984, Chapter 17, and 1989). Although favorable tendencies can have powerful cumulative effects over the generations, tendencies are no more than that. Nothing actually guarantees that societies with traits serving the well-being of their members will always prevail over less attractive societies. Mere survival of a cultural trait is no proof of its goodness (again, facts alone cannot yield a value judgment).

Hayek emphasizes the institutions and practices, including private property, that made wide-ranging indirect cooperation through market transactions possible. He reminds us (1984, p. 321) of Hume's "three fundamental laws of nature" concerning property and contract (discussed in the appendix to Chapter 6 below), on whose strict observance the "peace and security" of society depend. Only through individual property and competitive price determination could humanity become able to exploit discoverable resources intensely enough to support growing populations (Hayek 1984, p. 322). Group selection in cultural evolution favored groups whose traditional rules permitted market transactions yielding even unrecognized and unsought benefits. "This undesigned moral tradition", though different from reason, interacted with it and became "as indispensable for the formation of the extended order as reason itself" (pp. 321–2).[3]

Group selection even favors customs, says Hayek (1984, p. 324), whose value for survival is not perceived by individuals and which they may be unable to justify rationally. "We must learn to recognize that what the rationalists have habitually ridiculed as 'the dead hand of tradition' may contain conditions for the existence of modern mankind" (p. 329).

R.F. Harrod, another economist, sensed the role of social cooperation in ethics and anticipated (1936) some of Hayek's points about social natural selection. "The experience of generations, crystallised in moral consciousness, appears to be against the lie." The test of a breach of moral standards asks whether the breach, "if done by all in similar relevant circumstances", would undercut some established method of society's securing its ends. Only societies with strong moral emotions could attain stability; "an arbitrary and authoritarian element in the moral sphere" proved necessary. During the evolution of stable society, "those systems have survived which have established recognised practices and institutions giving effect to the Kantian principle, and allowing members to reap the additional advantages which adherence to it can yield" (pp. 295–7 of the excerpt from Harrod 1936 in Bok 1979).

Harrod also stressed that certain acts performed *n* times have consequences more than *n* times as great as those of the same act performed once. A million lies may cause more than a million times as much harm as one lie. Harrod's insight expresses one more reason for acting on principle and on notions of obligation, not just on case-by-case calculation (p. 294 of the excerpt in Bok 1979).

Katz, Hediger, and Valleroy (1974), although unaware of Hayek's argument, present an evident example. Some but not all American Indian tribes heated and dried corn (maize) and then boiled it in a solution of lime or other alkali. (These are steps in the preparation of tortillas, for example.) Tribes cooking corn this way had higher population densities and more complex social organizations than tribes that did not. The alkali treatment enhances the quality of the digestible protein by improving the relative amounts of essential amino acids. Among the 51 societies in North, Central, and South America reviewed, Katz and his coauthors found a close relation between ones cultivating and consuming large amounts of maize and those using the alkali treatment. Societies cultivating and consuming smaller quantities of maize almost invariably did not cook with alkali. The evidence implies that heavy dependence on corn without use of these cooking techniques brings serious malnutrition. These techniques were one of the chief cultural adaptations permitting the intensification of maize agriculture, which in turn favored the evolution of further social complexity. Practitioners of those techniques did not know and did not need to know the relevant biochemistry; their evolved cultural beliefs enabled them to survive and reproduce more effectively than otherwise (Katz et al. 1974; Rushton 1995, p. 87, summarizes this article but gives an incorrect citation to it).

Andrew Oldenquist (1990) summarizes the argument that ethics derives from the interaction of biological evolution and cultural evolution. The idea of group selection through cultural evolution does not incur the same difficulties as biological group selection. Cultural transmission presupposes some genetic predisposition to conformity – compare Simon's "docility", considered above – while culture, being part of the environment to which organisms adapt, helps shape biological selective pressures. Physiological characteristics of human beings, including their capacity for language, underlie their innate sociality. Natural selection favors the sympathy and regard for others necessary to a flourishing society. Unfortunately, human beings cannot have the benefits of "community" without an insider–outsider distinction, which, in its extreme form, is a source of racism and bellicose nationalism. (Alexander 1987, pp. 1–2, 79, agrees that cooperativeness within groups is paralleled by competition and aggression among them and that intergroup rivalries have played a large role in human evolution. For "a Hayekian slant on racism", as the article was originally entitled, see Yeager 1993R&C.)

THE SPREAD OF ALTRUISM

Peter Singer speculates on how human compassion may spread beyond its primitive narrow bounds. Human nature and the structure of social life, including reciprocal altruism, habituated people to justifying their actions publicly in objective terms. Once this habit is established, the "autonomy of reasoning" takes over. The idea of disinterested defense of one's own conduct takes on a logic of its own that extends it beyond the bounds of the group (Singer 1982, quoted and paraphrased in Wright 1994, p. 372; Darwin wrote similarly about the extension of one's sympathies to all nations and races;

1871, Part I, Chapter IV, p. 318 in 1952 edition; Wright 1994, p. 372 and citation at p. 425n.).

Language and the capacity for reflection, Singer suggests, gave human beings advantages in the evolutionary competition for survival. They also helped transform genetically evolved social practices into rules and precepts of conduct supported by shared judgments of approval and disapproval. Reason applied to what had been genetically dominated behavior supported social customs. Custom implies a capacity to see beyond particular events and relate the present to the past. Bringing particular events under a general rule may be the most important difference between human and animal ethics (Singer 1982, pp. 91–5).

As Singer further suggests, a reasoning being sees the rationale of making his various thoughts and actions consistent with one another, instead of granting himself exceptions to standards that he expects others to obey. (At least he sees the inexpediency of claiming a right to make such exceptions.) Human beings are uncomfortable about inconsistencies among their beliefs or between their beliefs and their actions (on this "cognitive dissonance", cf. Festinger 1962). Hypocrisy can be stressful. Discomfort over inconsistency presumably has some basis in the advantage that rational behavior conferred on human beings in the evolutionary process. Avoiding inconsistency promotes a certain impartiality in propounding standards about how people should treat one another. (This is my reading, anyway, of Singer 1982, pp. 139–45.)

Biology, then, is not the whole of James Q. Wilson's story, introduced above. Experiences within the family reinforce children's dispositions toward prosocial behavior. Conditions of settled life, with property, forced people to accept their natural inequalities, inequalities that hunter-gatherers had been obliged to overlook (Wilson 1993, pp. 75–6). Self-control and sympathy came to be admired because people generally fare better dealing with others who show these qualities, and perhaps too much rather than too little of them. Attention to etiquette is one sign of self-control (Wilson 1993, pp. 81–5; Henry Hazlitt is quoted on manners in Chapter 4 below).

Wilson perceives a slow and uneven but continuing expansion of the idea that the moral sense ought to govern a wide range and perhaps all of human interactions. Why, he asks, did the boundaries of the moral sense expand most widely in "the West" (roughly interpreted as Northwestern Europe and North America)? Why, especially there, did respect for the individual grow and the belief develop that human rights exist not just for members of one's own group but for all people everywhere? Wilson's conjectured explanation involves particular patterns of matrimony, family structure, and child-rearing, inter-twining with features of private property, land tenure, inheritance, travel, and commerce (1993, pp. 193–221).

EXPLANATION VERSUS APPRAISAL REVISITED

Michael Ruse sees a challenge, even a danger, in the naturalistic basis of ethics. As a "Darwinian evolutionary ethicist", he attributes morality or "literal altruism" to genes that "make us cooperators (biological altruists)". Although substantive ethics lacks an objective foundation and is merely "an adaptation of humankind to aid survival and reproduction", our biology makes us "objectify" it and think it has a reality "out there", beyond our subjectivity. Unless we thought so, "we would start cheating, morality would collapse, and cooperation would be at an end" (Ruse 1990, pp. 82–3).

Ruse thus appears to say that we humans must accept being deceived into belief that morality has an objective basis beyond mere biology; otherwise it would collapse. "Ethical skepticism may be the correct philosophy, but our genes are working flat-out to make such a conclusion counterintuitive" (Ruse 1990, pp. 66–7).

But *are* we being deceived? If the origin and consolidation of morality does ultimately trace to self-interest in a broad biological sense covering reproductive success and inclusive fitness, that fact still does not keep moral dispositions from being genuine. Biological evolution, together with social evolution and social conditioning, can lead the individual to see a moral disposition as in his own and his fellows' interest both, and correctly so. (As Moritz Schlick and others imply, disagreeing with several philosophers – see Chapter 8 below – we appraise a person's character by *how* he conceives of his own interest.) We can recognize the largely biological origin of moral precepts and their service to social cooperation and human flourishing, which is objective enough, while denying them any further and total objectivity. Their basis must indeed also include a fundamental, unprovable, and subjective value judgment – our approval of flourishing, or happiness. Such recognition does not turn us into ethical skeptics or demean or destroy morality. On the contrary, morality would ultimately suffer more from linkage to factually incorrect assertions. We can recognize the benefits of heeding moral precepts almost *as if* they were objectively valid while still recognizing that they do not in fact have a totally objective grounding and that an element of sheer value judgment does also enter into them. We find the value judgment compelling even though, being fundamental, it is not amenable to proof. (Here, "heeding moral precepts almost *as if* they were objectively valid" is shorthand for an available fuller description. Such language does not mean that we trick ourselves into falsely believing in purely objective precepts.) In any case, no question arises of an elite concealing the truth about morality from hoi polloi.

Humans' long memory and capacity to recognize each other as individuals suggest an important role for reciprocal altruism in human evolution. This cheerful possibility, however, is not the whole story. A seamy side warns us once more against confusing what is natural with what is desirable. Robert Trivers suggested that natural selection shaped psychological characteristics for ability both to cheat undetected and to detect others' cheating. Even feelings of envy, guilt, gratitude, and sympathy may enter into this ability. "Subtle cheats" can appear to be reciprocating while consistently paying back a bit less help than they received. Man's brain and predisposition to mathematical reasoning may possibly have evolved as a mechanism for ever more devious cheating and ever keener detection of cheating by others. Trivers further questioned the conventional view that natural selection favors nervous systems yielding ever more accurate images of the world. *Self*-deception can be advantageous if it furthers successful deceit of others. Accurate depiction of reality – to others and sometimes to ourselves – is not high among natural selection's priorities. Honesty can sometimes be a blunder in sex, reciprocal altruism, and social hierarchy (Trivers as summarized in Dawkins 1978, p. 202, and Wright 1994, pp. 264–5).

Even if nature is "trying" to maximize survival or numbers, that is no argument against our adopting an ultimately utilitarian criterion of our institutions and ethical codes. We can apply our faculty of reason, embracing investigation and logic, to appraising and perhaps revising the institutions and ethical codes of our societies. (Since reason has evolved biologically, ethics links up with biology in this further way.) Civilization, as someone has said, is largely an exercise in overcoming what is natural. Education is one way of trying to neutralize certain natural traits.

Hayek (1984, pp. 324–5) challenges the whole conception of morals as a device to serve human pleasures, "to get us what we want". By their very nature, morals are traditional restraints on the pursuit of pleasures. "[T]hey are a learned restraint which tells us which wishes we must forgo, initially to secure the survival of more men than we otherwise could, but soon in order merely to maintain the numbers of men which the extended order of human interaction has enabled us to raise" (p. 328).

Well of course morals were not *devised* to promote happiness. Even so, social scientists can come to understand why certain inherited traditions and practices have advantageous consequences. They can understand how honorable and considerate behavior serves not only the general interest but even the personal interest of one who behaves that way – if general and personal interests are indeed broadly consilient (an "if" explored in Chapter 8). We may adopt both a spontaneous-evolution theory of the origin of morals and a utilitarian metaethical theory of how to assess them.

Again we should remember the distinction between *explaining* some institution (or its origin) and *appraising* it.[4] An explanation consists of positive propositions; an appraisal requires value judgments. Whether a moral code or other institution has developed spontaneously, as through biological and cultural natural selection, is not the very test of its goodness; "natural" does not mean "good". Hayek himself, though respectful of a moral order originating neither in innate instincts nor in conscious reason, saw the legitimacy of piecemeal appraisals and of experiments "with improving its parts – not designing but humbly tinkering on a system which we must accept as given" (1984, p. 330). Reason cannot replace the "treasure" of our moral tradition but can only try to improve it by immanent criticism. Although we cannot create the system as a whole, we can try to make it serve its effects more consistently. We can judge a particular moral rule only within "a system of such rules which for that purpose we must treat as undoubted" (p. 329).

Links with biology do not predetermine ethical judgments. Of course, a credible and practicable ethical code must not fly in the face of biologically based human nature or of enduring social realities. However, "the suggestion that an aspect of human ethics is universal, or nearly so, in no way justifies that aspect of human ethics. Nor does the suggestion that a particular aspect of human ethics has a biological basis do anything to justify it" (Singer 1982, p. 53).

Far from actually validating an ethical code, then, discovering the biological or social evolution of certain precepts may help to explain them *away*. (Compare Michael Ruse's worry, cited above.) Sometimes this discovery will produce the opposite of a justification. A biological explanation of a supposedly self-evident moral rule should make us question why we accept it (Singer 1982, p. 150). What seems to be an untouchable moral intuition may be a mere relic of evolutionary history. "Discovering biological origins for our intuitions should make us skeptical about thinking of them as self-evident moral axioms." We may also "find relics of our cultural history to place alongside the relics of our evolutionary history" (Singer 1982, pp. 70–71).

Thus, something's naturalness may even support an *adverse* appraisal. Showing how a rule may have served survival or comfort in earlier stages of biological or cultural evolution may help explain why, under changed conditions, it has lost that value. Examples appear in food taboos and perhaps in sexual taboos. Hayek has traced certain deep-seated socialistic or communitarian sentiments inappropriate for the modern "great society" or "extended order" to conditions of life in small hunter-gatherer bands (Hayek 1989, pp. 17–23; more broadly, cf. Oldenquist 1990, pp. 125–6, 139, and Hamilton 1996, pp. 189–91, 217–18, 258–9). Aspects of religion may provide further examples. Monetary arrangements that evolved quasi-spontaneously over the centuries and can thus claim some degree of naturalness may nevertheless be inferior to alternatives available with improved technology and changed social conditions.

CONCLUSION

This chapter has argued against any idea that nature is working for noble purposes automatically commanding human allegiance. Ethical precepts are not objective realities naturally graven in stone or fixed in DNA.

On the other hand, it is pointless to preach norms that are hopelessly at odds with physical and biological reality, including the roots of human nature. Fortunately, the utilitarian fundamental value judgment regarding happiness and misery *is* compatible with deep-seated reality. Human beings are capable of the requisite social cooperation and of altruism (in a suitably defanged sense). Biology has shaped humans as social animals; and a kind of cultural natural selection, reinforced by reason, which is itself a biological capacity, can operate on human societies.[5] Reason can help shape the cultural conditioning that joins with biology in influencing how closely the diverse separate interests of individuals mesh with their collectively shared interests.

Considerations developed in this chapter further count against any distinctively intuitive metaethics, any doctrine postulating that we human beings simply "know" what is objectively good and bad, right and wrong, as if through some sixth sense. They count against any idea that a search for deeper foundations somehow demeans ethics. No system can utterly dispense with intuitions – which is what value judgments, especially fundamental ones, are – but the intuitions should withstand probing examination. Their examination includes confrontation with physical and biological realities. It does not constitute mere "debunking" and need not (despite the contrary view of some philosophers) undermine adherence to moral intuitions.

NOTES

1. Loren Lomasky (1993, pp. 43–4) objects to Wilson's adopting the concept of "moral sense" that he attributes to Francis Hutcheson. No such sense exists, no sense akin to sight and smell by which we perceive an objectively existing world of moral facts. (Compare trying to infer a theistic sense from widespread belief in gods.) Nor, according to Lomasky, contradicting Wilson, did David Hume and Adam Smith adopt any such concept from their teacher Hutcheson. Neither one believes in "a world of moral facts to which we have unmediated cognitive access. Instead each attempts to explain how we are able to formulate interpersonally justifiable moral judgments in the absence of a faculty of moral sense" (p. 44). Lomasky in no way rejects Hume–Smith "sympathy"; he repudiates Wilson's linking it to a supposedly Hutchesonian moral sense.
2. Recent research suggests that such features, an elk's big antlers being another example, may not be dysfunctional after all. They signal to females the male's possession of genes favorable to good health and prolific procreation (Brownlee 1998).
3. Hayek was "inclined to claim that only an economist, i.e. someone who understands the process of the formation of the extended order of cooperation, can explain the selective evolution of the morals of property and honesty – how they arose as well as what effects they had on the development of mankind. They are matters which are problems of science and not

value problems" (1984, p. 327). By "extended order", Hayek means a network of interactions ranging far beyond face-to-face contacts.

4. Darwin already distinguished between appraisal and explanation. He preferred speaking of the "Greatest happiness principle" as the standard rather than as the motive of conduct (1871/1936, p. 489). "A dim feeling that our impulses do not by any means always arise from any contemporaneous or anticipated pleasure has ... been one chief cause of the acceptance of the intuitive theory of morality, and of the rejection of the utilitarian or 'Greatest happiness' theory. With respect to the latter theory the standard and the motive of conduct have no doubt often been confused, but they are really in some degree blended" (p. 490). Distinguishing between "the general good or welfare" and "the general happiness" of the community or of mankind as "the standard of morality", Darwin inclined, with qualifications, to the former (p. 490).

5. Mayr (1997, Chapter 12) and Ridley (1996) also discuss the roles of both biological and cultural elements in the evolution of ethics. Ridley's excellent discussion of this chapter's themes came to my attention too late for me to cite it in detail.

4.   The case for indirect utilitarianism

THE MEANING OF UTILITARIANISM

Philosophers sometimes ask which takes precedence, "the right" or "the good". It seems noble to say "the right" on the grounds that nothing morally wrong can be good. But this answer is superficial and circular, failing to identify the grounds for judgments of right and wrong. Some notions of good (and bad) must enter into these judgments, so good does take precedence over right.

This is true anyway, according to utilitarian doctrine. This book expounds one version, a rules or indirect version, in contrast with act utilitarianism. (This chapter will further distinguish between varieties of utilitarianism.)

Utilitarianism compares and appraises alternative sets of institutions, laws, traditions, patterns and maxims of behavior, and personal dispositions and character traits. Only sets of realistically possible and mutually compatible characteristics and practices are in the running; a set with mutually inconsistent features is out of the question. (Again, *ought* presupposes *can*.) Positive analysis – economics, political science, sociology, psychology, and the natural sciences – helps in judging whether particular institutions, rules, practices, and character traits are or are not consistent with one another.

Utilitarianism approves or disapproves of institutions and principles according to whether they tend to support or to subvert a society that affords people relatively good opportunities to make satisfying lives for themselves. Ones that facilitate fruitful cooperation among individuals pursuing their own diverse specific ends score ahead of ones that cause clashes. (The comparative-institutions approach to policy assessment, further explored in Chapter 11, is thus closely related to, or is an implication of, utilitarianism.)

THE PENULTIMATE CRITERION: SOCIAL COOPERATION

A well-functioning society is so indispensable to individuals' effective pursuit of their own happiness in their own diverse ways that it becomes a nearly ultimate criterion of institutions, ethical rules, and so forth (Hazlitt 1964, esp. p. 36). Many thinkers in the utilitarian tradition speak of "social cooperation". Direct appeal to an actually ultimate normative criterion is rarely necessary.

Social cooperation flourishes through institutions, rules, and practices that improve people's chances of predicting each others' behavior and coordinating their activities. Voluntary cooperation accords better than coercion with each person's having projects, purposes, and ideals of his own and with his having only one life to live. Emphasis on voluntary cooperation warns against imposing unfair sacrifices on individuals for the supposed greater good of a greater number.

By the criterion of social cooperation, truth-telling and promise-keeping command approval. So does respect for justice (as John Stuart Mill emphasized in *Utilitarianism*, Chapter V); so does respect for property rights and other human rights. In many activities, an honest partiality toward oneself and one's compatriots, friends, and associates also commands approval provided that it is hedged by due respect for the rights and legitimate interests of other persons.

Though without using the specific term, David Hume clearly recognized social cooperation as the criterion of ethical judgment. Hume was a utilitarian of a particular type. (To document the sometimes challenged classification of Hume as a utilitarian, an appendix to Chapter 6 assembles several pertinent quotations.) In one of his most often quoted passages, he recognizes the utility of general inflexible rules, notably of private property, in supporting "civil society". As his esteem for private property illustrates, Hume understood how positive analysis helps assess which characteristics of persons and society serve and which subvert social cooperation.

THE ULTIMATE CRITERION

Social cooperation is only a *nearly* ultimate criterion. It serves some further value taken as desirable without argument. (Argument would have to appeal to some still further value, which would be then be the ultimate one, or more nearly so.)

Utilitarians can only take stabs at labeling what they deem ultimately desirable. It is individuals' success in making good lives for themselves, or fulfillment, or satisfaction, or life befitting human potential, or what Aristotle called eudaimonia. No single word is adequate. When one is required, however, "happiness" is the traditional choice; and "misery" is the ultimate negative criterion.[1]

Hume used both words. Reason "show[s] us the means of attaining happiness or avoiding misery"; but reason alone – fact and logic – does not determine approval and disapproval. "Reason being cool and disengaged, is no motive to action, and directs only the impulse received from appetite or inclination" (1751/1777/1930, p. 135).

The happiness criterion, being a fundamental value judgment, cannot be *proved* valid. Suggested alternatives, provided they are not self-contradictory, cannot be *proved* wrong. F.A. Hayek, as we have seen in Chapter 3, apparently preferred the criterion of "survival". It may well be true, as a fact of biological and cultural evolution, that spontaneous processes have selected for behavioral precepts and character traits tending to promote survival and reproduction rather than for ones promoting happiness. Again, however, explanation is not evaluation; what is "natural" is not automatically best. The reader should ponder which he more truly considers the greater value for himself and for humanity in general – survival, no matter in what conditions, or happiness in the broad sense indicated above. He should also consider why the quasi-ultimate criterion, social cooperation, serves survival and happiness both.

Even though choice of an ultimate criterion or value must be a matter of intuition, intuition may be cultivated reflectively: people can ponder their various intuitions, track down possible inconsistencies among them, and consider which ones they hold most deeply. Happiness or some such concept (perhaps "flourishing") will prevail over rival criteria – or so I conjecture. At issue is not how to determine or validate a fundamental value judgment but how most coherently to articulate one. So articulated, it may turn out to be widely shared.

Regardless of just what plausible interpretation we give to happiness, social cooperation is prerequisite to its effective pursuit. Lying, cheating, and stealing subvert happiness because they subvert the prerequisite cooperation. Telling the truth, keeping promises, and respecting other people's rights and property are conducive to cooperation. We come to believe propositions like these through factual and logical analysis of what conditions help individuals pursue their own diverse goals effectively.

SYMPATHY: HAPPINESS AS A WIDELY SHARED CRITERION

Every science, said Hume, contains "some general principles, beyond which we cannot hope to find any principle more general. No man is absolutely indifferent to the happiness and misery of others". In everyone's experience, "[t]he first has a natural tendency to give pleasure; the second, pain". These principles probably cannot be resolved into any simpler and more universal ones (Hume 1751/1777/1930, p. 54n.).

In our thoughts and conversations, "everything ... presents us with the view of human happiness and misery, and excites in our breast a sympathetic movement of pleasure or uneasiness" (p. 56). The sentiment that approves or censures, that "constitutes virtue our happiness, and vice our misery", probably depends on some sense or feeling that nature has made universal in the species (p. 5).

A "natural sentiment of benevolence" leads people to a regard for "the interests of mankind and society". A creature like man cannot "be totally indifferent to the well or ill-being of his fellow-creatures". Absent some particular bias, he straightforwardly pronounces "what promotes their happiness" good, "what tends to their misery" evil (p. 65). Some benevolence, however slight, is "infused into our bosom; some spark of friendship for human kind; some particle of the dove kneaded into our frame, along with the elements of the wolf and serpent". However weak "these generous sentiments" may be, "they must still direct the determinations of our mind, and where everything else is equal, produce a cool preference of what is useful and serviceable to mankind, above what is pernicious and dangerous" (p. 109).

In so describing sympathy, Hume identifies desiring happiness and regretting misery, not only one's own but also other people's, as a widely shared fundamental value judgment. (On the overlap between sympathy and benevolence, recall the discussion of benevolence in Chapter 2.) We do not know how to ground this sentiment in anything beyond itself (although, as Chapter 3 says, we may perhaps partly *explain* it by its conduciveness to the survival and reproduction of one's close relatives or even of the species). (Possible tension between sympathy and self-interest is a topic for Chapter 8.)

Adam Smith (1759/1976) also stressed sympathy, appealing as a criterion to the judgments of a benevolent "impartial spectator". Emphasis on sympathy expresses no disagreement with utilitarianism (although the affinity with it seems less clear in Smith than in Hume).

Hume finds

> that the circumstance of utility ... is constantly appealed to in all moral decisions concerning the merit and demerit of actions: That it is the sole source of that high regard paid to justice, fidelity, honour, allegiance, and chastity: That it is inseparable from all the other social virtues, humanity, generosity, charity, affability, lenity, mercy, and moderation: And, in a word, that it is a foundation of the chief part of morals, which has a reference to mankind and our fellow-creatures (Hume 1751/1777/1930, p. 66).

UTILITARIANISM IS NOT HEDONISM

The foregoing account, drawing on Hume, does not describe utilitarianism as it is often misconceived and caricatured. It does, however, briefly describe *indirect* utilitarianism. Despite what some critics charge, its fundamental value judgment in favor of happiness and against misery is not vacuous; for rival fundamental values are conceivable and have even been suggested (cf. Chapter 10).

Utilitarianism so conceived is not hedonism. The "happiness" it appeals to is not pleasure in any narrow sense, and certainly not mere carnal sensations. It comes closer to meaning fulfillment or flourishing, or satisfaction with one's life as a whole (using weasel words, one might even say satisfaction in the light of calm reflection). Individuals differ widely in their specific projects and goals in life and in their detailed conceptions of happiness – for readily understandable reasons, and to their mutual advantage. Still, what makes for happiness is not entirely a matter of personal whim; inquiry into the substance of the good life is not nonsense. Psychological, sociological, economic, and other analysis can bear on what enters into a life appropriate for human beings.

Aristotle and other ancient philosophers, Carl Menger, Ayn Rand, Mortimer Adler, Henry Hazlitt, Brand Blanshard, and many others have agreed in attributing some objectively ascertainable content to the good life, the ends of life, and true self-interest. They invoke such concepts as true and false satisfaction, desires consonant or dissonant with human nature, and narrow and short-run versus broad and long-run self-interest. Individuals may sensibly seek quasi-objective truth on such matters and seek and offer instruction. Not everyone must always regard his own and other people's desires as given beyond question. Even a little preaching may sometimes be in order.

THE PREJUDICE AGAINST PLEASURE

Moritz Schlick and Henry Hazlitt diagnose what Schlick calls a "prejudice against pleasure". Why, Schlick asks (1930/1961, p. 123), do we rebel against recognizing pleasure as one ultimate element of value, including moral value? We slip into that attitude, if we do, because we have generally encountered moral rules and training when someone wanted us to behave otherwise than we might have done (pp. 124–5). Rules of morality and of prudent self-interest sometimes require forgoing pleasure or incurring pain in the short run. Their rationale, even if we forget it, is to promote happiness in the long run or on the whole. "Suffering" may sometimes serve happiness (going to the dentist is a trivial example).

Calmness toward necessary suffering or sorrow may be a character trait that helps make one ready for happiness, as Schlick says. Since self-discipline and forgoing immediate pleasure often are *means* to long-run benefits, otherwise purposeless acts of asceticism may even be useful for keeping in practice. William James recommended keeping the faculty of effort alive "*by a little gratuitous exercise every day*" (quoted by Hazlitt 1964, p. 219). This may be good advice for young people still shaping their characters, says Hazlitt; but a mature person who faithfully performs his work, and also avoids overweight and cholesterol, "is doing a good deal. The Lord will not blame you too much for not looking around for little 'unnecessary' deprivations simply in order to develop your moral muscles" (p. 220).

The mistake is erecting means into ends. *Readiness* for hardships necessary to broader or longer-run benefits is one thing; quite another is making the extent of hardship, rather than the goal achieved, the test of morality. St Simeon Stylites "performed prodigious feats of asceticism" benefiting no one. "The striving for 'morality' or 'self-perfection' for its own sake is a perversion of true morality" (Hazlitt 1964, p. 222).

ACT VERSUS RULE UTILITARIANISM

Abstractly considered, moral rules that are specific but not tailored to individual cases might seem less sensible than sweeping advice to promote all people's interests impartially. "Following a moral rule either leads us to do what best promotes the interests of all – in which case the rule adds nothing to the basic principle – or the rule forces us to do something which does not promote the interests of all – in which case, why should we follow the rule?" (Singer 1982, p. 158). Answering Singer's question harks back to the reasons for distinguishing rules or indirect utilitarianism from act utilitarianism.

Act utilitarianism, as often described, calls for the action in each individual case that seems likely, quite apart from any general principles, to yield the best results on the whole. Each person should act in whatever way promises to contribute most to the aggregate excess of happiness over misery, taking full account of all effects of all the possible actions compared. Although this polar doctrine illuminates more plausible positions by contrast, it is hard to believe that any philosopher actually advocates it. (Joseph Fletcher 1966 comes close, however, with his act-agapeism, a version of situation ethics.) Although ethical precepts are not objective realities naturally graven in stone, a moral code could hardly be meaningful if it were open to wholesale reconsideration by each individual at the time of each particular decision. Such continual case-by-case reconsideration would come close to a situation ethics and to not having a moral code after all. Rules and codes are best appraised outside the context of immediate decisions.

Successfully applying act utilitarianism would presuppose impossibly great information and foresight about consequences of individual actions – intended and unintended, nearby and remote, immediate and delayed. Each person would have to be impossibly neutral between his own and his relatives' and friends' interests and projects and those of other persons. In effect, act utilitarianism makes each person a law unto himself; it encourages him to follow his own moral intuitions as if they were infallible and as if he had more factual and theoretical knowledge of many sorts and more prodigious ability to calculate consequences than anyone realistically could have. It overlooks the temptations and excuses that people find to take advantage of vague or pliable rules. (Suppose the rule "No dogs on beach or boardwalk" granted an exception for "dogs led or supervised by owners who do not expect their dogs to make nuisances of themselves".)

Furthermore, act utilitarianism overlooks the coordinative value of rules: confidence that people will generally observe familiar rules and conventions makes people better able than otherwise to predict each others' behavior and avoid acting at cross-purposes. A general practice of case-by-case assessments would complicate forming expectations and so would impair coordination of activities – unless individual decisionmakers could somehow take even this effect into account on each occasion.

Rules utilitarianism, perhaps better called *indirect* utilitarianism for reasons stated below, expects no such feats of prediction, calculation, and benevolence. Instead, it recommends following familiar moral rules. It values ingrained habits that resist individuals' temptations to deem their own particular cases exceptional. It saves the time and mental and emotional energy otherwise required for agonizing over each individual case. General observance of ethical rules improves people's abilities to predict and coordinate one another's actions.

Of course, utilitarianism does not occur only in two sharply defined polar versions (which no one actually espouses anyway). Besides differing in other dimensions, versions vary along a scale running between the extremes of literal act utilitarianism and highly indirect utilitarianism; they differ largely in how they distribute emphasis.

The logic of rules utilitarianism requires people to abide by the rules almost unquestioningly and automatically in ordinary cases of real life. (The economist Roy Harrod made a notable contribution of this sort, 1936, to what he called "utilitarianism revised".) The rules themselves are subject to critical scrutiny, but by people in a reflective or dispassionate mood. (R.M. Hare speaks of scrutiny on the "critical level" – recall Chapter 1.)

INDIRECT UTILITARIANISM AS AN EXTENSION OF RULE UTILITARIANISM

As already mentioned, the version that contrasts with act utilitarianism might better be called "indirect" than "rules" utilitarianism. The choice is one of labeling and emphasis, not of opposition; no one, to my knowledge, advocates either rules or indirect utilitarianism *in opposition to* the other. Indirect utilitarianism encompasses and transcends a narrow focus on rules.

John Gray, who introduces the label "indirect utilitarianism", attributes that version to John Stuart Mill. It calls for cultivating and acting from certain attitudes and character traits. "The larger part of any moral code has to do, not with the institution or enforcement of social rules, but with the inculcation of sentiments and attitudes and the instilling of dispositions and inclinations" (Gray 1983, pp. 31–2; cf. Gray 1979, Wollheim 1979). Richard Taylor (1970) recommends, similarly, that moral philosophy, instead of elaborating rules, should aim at presenting moral aspirations that "extend to the passions and to the inner man". People can do better than busy themselves day by day "doing all sorts of things in accordance with moral principles and rules, and congratulating themselves that they have, just by virtue of this, attained morally significant lives". Socrates was right: "what a man is is infinitely more important than what he from time to time does. No mere rule of morality, however strenuous and noble" can override the ultimate aspiration to be, in Taylor's words, "*a warm-hearted and loving human being*" (pp. 254–5).

Philip Rhinelander (1977) distinguishes between classical and legalistic approaches to ethics. The great classical philosophers "stressed the importance of developing *virtues*, or dispositions of character, such as courage, temperance, wisdom". Rules of conduct were secondary and derivative. This classical approach is flexible, putting weight on judgment, training, and experience. In contrast, a legalistic emphasis on rules tends to reduce virtue to living by the book; it tends toward rigidity and a delusive exactness.

Indirect utilitarianism recommends, then, rules whose application is conditioned by suitable attitudes and inclinations and dispositions. Examples include sympathy (as of Adam Smith's impartial spectator) and a sense of fairness, a disinclination to grab special privilege and to make arbitrary exceptions in one's own favor. Having and acting on such dispositions is likely, by and large, to serve both one's own happiness and the general happiness – or so run arguments reviewed in Chapter 8.

A disposition toward considerateness finds expression partly in manners, which, like morals, rest on a principle of "*sympathy, kindness, consideration for others*". Every code of manners has something deeper at its heart than its conventional and arbitrary aspects. "Manners developed, not to make life more complicated and awkward ..., but to make it in the long-run smoother and simpler. ... Manners are minor morals" (Hazlitt 1964, p. 75). "Civility or common courtesy is the most elementary form of benevolence", writes a philosopher influenced by Ayn Rand (Kelley 1996, p. 37). It typically involves observing widely understood conventions. An individualist might ask why he should conform to arbitrary social standards. The answer is that "while the forms are conventional, what is conveyed through those forms is not"

(p. 38). Considerate persons acknowledge each other's humanity and independence somehow, as by employing commonly expected words and gestures (p. 38).

Fairly specific rules have their place; benevolent intentions are not enough. People lack the time and information to decide each action by calculating afresh what seems best on the whole. Rules lessen the risk that emotions may color perceptions and that people may consciously or unconsciously bend their calculations to their own narrow interests. Rules help people predict the actions of others and help hold down the costs of coordination and transactions; they help promote informal reciprocity. "Imagine there were no commitment to telling the truth, only a commitment to doing what impartially advances everyone's interests. Then in many situations we would not be able to rely on information given to us" (Singer 1982, pp. 162-3). Rules as Richard Taylor recommends them (1970, p. 130) "are nothing but *practices* or ways of behaving that are more or less regular and that can, therefore, be expected". Not all need be the results of rational contrivance; not all need be put explicitly into words. As Hume and Hayek have maintained, useful practices and unarticulated rules can evolve gradually.

CHALLENGES TO THE ACT/RULE DISTINCTION

Some philosophers question the distinction between rules and act utilitarianism (though they would have found it harder to do so, I think, if they had fully recognized the indirect version that embraces but goes beyond attention to rules). The economist John C. Harsanyi tries to answer the "surprising claim, sometimes made even by very distinguished moral philosophers" - he cites Richard B. Brandt, David Lyons, and R.M. Hare - "that rule utilitarianism and act utilitarianism are equivalent as to their practical moral implications" because both would yield the same answers on Hare's critical level (Harsanyi 1985, p. 121; cf. Harsanyi in Seanor and Fotion, pp. 89ff.). Even on the critical level, act utilitarianism would generate less socially fortunate decisions than rule utilitarianism. Harsanyi emphasizes how rules affect expectations, confidence, incentives, and coordination.

David Lyons (1965) questions not only the rules/act distinction but some forms of rules utilitarianism itself. Versions he calls "simple" and general utilitarianism and one form of rule utilitarianism are extensionally equivalent, he says; for they always yield the same judgments. Other rule-utilitarian theories, ones not equivalent to simple utilitarianism, are different from it in ways that make them wrong (p. x). All utilities are ultimately ascribable to particular acts (pp. 99-100). Lyons repeatedly brings up the example of violating a rule against taking a shortcut across the grass. Done by assumption only once, the act will not damage the grass; but it will save the violator's time. Postulating that it goes unobserved forestalls objections about its setting a bad example, creating ill will, and so forth. By stipulation, then, crossing the lawn just once does no harm. Lyons thinks that considerations like fairness and justice also belong in the appraisal; but he calls these *non*utilitarian considerations, seeming not to understand that they are themselves grounded in utility (he fails to cite John Stuart Mill on justice).

Only glancingly at best (for example, pp. 163–4, 176–7) does Lyons recognize that the violator's gain at negligible direct cost to others is parasitic on compliance by others and that the rule being violated concerns not merely grass in particular but making exceptions in one's own favor (which, as he briefly does recognize, p. 144, people are carelessly prone to do). The violator is acting from a spirit and character that tends to undercut social cooperation.

"If such intentions, motives, or reasons for acting are relevant to the assessment of acts as right or wrong independently of the consequences produced, then utilitarianism is an inadequate doctrine in any form" (Lyons 1965, pp. 176–7). Lyons insists (p. 189) that there are rights, duties, and obligations not exclusively grounded in producing good or preventing evil. He seems not to understand how indirect utilitarianism emphatically is concerned with motives, intentions, and character traits.

Reviewing Lyons's book, Gertrude Ezorsky (1968) provides further insights into making exceptions in one's own favor. She notes how Lyons purports to solve a problem of competing descriptions. In describing an action to appraise it, he finds only its causal or consequentially significant properties relevant. It is irrelevant to assessing a lie that a six-toed existentialist philosopher told it. But if rule utilitarianism conforms to this principle of causal consequence (CC), it becomes coextensive with act utilitarianism. If a particular lie contributes to overall utility, then that fact is relevant to describing and appraising it. Rule and act utilitarianisms would seem inevitably coextensive. Suppose (with Lyons) that six people are stuck in a stalled car. Five of them would be enough to get the car going. If one refuses (or only pretends) to push, a rule utilitarian who objected would be ignoring a consequential property, namely, that enough people *are* pushing. Taking all consequential properties into account dispels the illusion of a difference in practical moral judgments between rules and act utilitarianisms.

But Lyons is wrong, Ezorsky continues, in supposing that CC is a sufficient criterion of relevance. A criterion of general utilitarian relevance (GUR) also belongs in the story: only properties that are both consequential and *nondiscriminatory* are relevant for utilitarian generalization within a given social group. Shirking a job or speaking too loud while others are complying is discriminatory. A lie is not saved from condemnation by the fact that it maximizes utility (in its narrow context). No universal agreement requires (or excuses) utility-maximizing lies. The GUR principle rules out act-utilitarian excuses for shirking or lying.

Would a rule utilitarian require a specific person to push the stalled car even though not enough others would cooperate with him? No; the doctrine does not demand a futile act. (Declining to push without adequate assistance is not discrimination in one's own favor but merely avoiding useless discrimination against oneself, or so I would add.) "RUians can claim that, if they are allowed a proper criterion of relevance, they can be independent of AU and stand by their founding principle: what other people do doesn't count" (Ezorsky 1968, p. 544).

D.W. Haslett also tackles David Lyons's objection (1965) that indirect utilitarianism "collapses" into direct utilitarianism – that the two versions are "extensionally" equivalent because the indirect one ends up justifying norms that justify the very same acts as the direct version does (Haslett 1994, p. 20). But an indirect utilitarianism that focuses on the consequences not of universal *compliance* but of being backed by social pressure does not collapse in this way. The popular objection against direct utilitarianism – that it prescribes acts contrary to moral intuitions – does not apply to the moral norms justifiable in Haslett's indirect system (p. 21). His version acknowledges human fallibility. The system must contain only a limited number of moral norms and values, ones that for the most part are simple and easy to learn and comply with (p. 20). Such norms do not always prescribe the same acts as the difficult to-comply-with, direct-utilitarian criterion (p. 21). Despite J.J.C. Smart's contention (in Smart and Williams 1973), sticking to these simple and easy norms even when one believes that contravening them would maximize utility is not mere "rule worship". If people undertook to violate these norms whenever they thought that doing so would maximize utility, then, because of mistaken calculations, rationalizations, unpredictability, and insecurity, more harm than good would result (p. 21). Here (and on pp. 19, 22–3) Haslett alludes to the point that fairly firm adherence to simple rules enhances predictability, coordination, and social cooperation.

Haslett attaches importance to whether or not norms and values are backed by social pressure (as further explained below). Changes do occur in what ones are so backed – fortunately, for otherwise there could be no moral progress. But changes occur gradually enough so as not to destroy predictability or uniformity in people's moral behavior (p. 23).

As for rights, Haslett continues, their having a consequentialist justification does not render them mere "rules of thumb". (Compare the discussion of rights in Chapter 10.) Rights are no mere heuristic devices to be considered only insofar as people, being fallible, are unable to apply some more fundamental consequentialist moral principle. Despite critics' persistent misunderstanding, rights and other norms in a properly formulated indirect-utilitarian moral code "are themselves the norms of morality; no 'deeper' consequentialist moral principle is hovering in the background, waiting to override these rights whenever the veil of human fallibility lifts". True enough, indirect utilitarianism does not entirely rule out appeals to consequences in emergencies; but the legitimacy of any such appeals is built into the rights themselves as potential exceptions of carefully limited scope, thereby precluding any general "collapse" into consequentialism or direct utilitarianism (Haslett 1994, pp. 50–51).

Rolf Sartorius (1975) calls himself an act utilitarian – curiously, for his doctrine is indeed what I would call rules or indirect utilitarianism. (He does not specifically note the latter's emphasis on dispositions and character traits, perhaps because John Gray had not yet written on the topic.) Sartorius recognizes the great value of rules and social conventions accepted as almost conclusively binding. He sees good reason for barring judges, for example, from deciding individual cases by direct appeals to utility (p. 177). Barring direct appeals helps shape the environment in which people ponder consequences and make choices; it helps create the shared expectations and resulting behavior on which a viable social order depends (pp. 211–12). Although the act-utilitarian principle must remain the ultimate criterion of a benevolent person's conduct (on Sartorius's view, anyway, as it comes across to me), the person should still participate in good faith in upholding the demands made by enlightened social norms (p. 213). Supporting norms that bar direct appeal to utility need not be inconsistent with departing from those norms in exceptional cases (p. 4).

Sartorius distinguishes, or tries to, between rule utilitarianism (RU) and utilitarian generalization (UG). RU holds an act right if and only if performing it accords with a set of moral rules whose general acceptance would have consequences at least as good as the general acceptance of any alternative set. UG holds an act right if and only if everyone's performing an act of that kind would have consequences at least as good as those of everyone's performing any alternative act (p. 12). Sartorius objects that neither RU nor UG recognizes that the effects and thus the morality of specific acts often depend on other people's behavior. Both require action on the basis of considering hypothetical situations that typically fail to obtain (pp. 15–16). Yet, despite Sartorius, indirect utilitarians *can* indeed recognize that whether a rule is binding – to keep promises, for example – depends on how generally it is observed among the people dealt with. Self-effacing benevolence would hardly have good consequences in a society of thugs. (Considerations like this one help support my point in Chapter 8 about interaction between the prevalence and the validity of moral teachings.)

Why does Sartorius call his doctrine *act* utilitarianism? One apparent reason is that he counts the adoption of rules and conventions as itself an act or collection of acts, one's done, in his political metaphor, on the "constitutional" level. The theory remains act-utilitarian if choice of the principles of justice is itself based on direct utilitarian considerations (p. 120). I'll attempt a paraphrase. Assessing possible rules involves assessing the consequences of the individual acts that the rule is likely to promote. Rules and conventions work through conditioning the decisions made about individual acts (such as whether or not to tell a lie on a particular occasion). Furthermore, Sartorius appears to interpret rules utilitarianism as a rules fetishism (see Chapter 7 below) that would never tolerate a direct appeal to utility in any individual case, no matter how unusual.

So narrow an interpretation makes rules utilitarianism a preposterous doctrine. As for act utilitarianism, Sartorius interprets it so broadly that the label covers even what most philosophers would call the rules or indirect version. Thus Sartorius merely applies labels in an unusual way; he does not actually reject indirect utilitarianism or the act/indirect distinction.

One final point in favor of this distinction will emerge in succeeding chapters: the absurdity of attacks on utilitarianism that muddle the act version and the rules or indirect version together.

THE UTILITY OF FLEXIBLE AND REFORMABLE RULES

Writings cited above turn us to the question of just what the utility of a rule means. Does it mean the benefit of its being generally accepted, even if only by lip service, the benefit of its being generally obeyed in practice, or what? D.W. Haslett, as mentioned above, says that the best-justified moral norms and values are those, roughly speaking, "that would maximize overall well-being, or utility, if backed by social pressure", interpreted broadly to include education, child-rearing, and the like (Haslett 1994, p. 43 and *passim*).

This is a felicitous formulation (apart from the word "maximize"). Recommending particular norms or rules for benefits expected even from mere lip-service to them would scarcely be credible. The same holds for rules that would be beneficial if generally heeded but that in fact could not or would not be heeded. Social pressure is more than lip-service, and its wide application testifies to widespread belief in its effectiveness. Futile pressure would be worse than useless.

Part of the rationale of ethical rules, as opposed to rigid and comprehensive laws, is that they can accommodate flexibility in their application and drift or reform in their details. Some are vague. Like rules of writing style (see Chapter 7), they offer guidance but leave much to the judgment of the person applying them, which is one reason for emphasis on dispositions and character traits. Enforcement is loose and informal. Cases may arise in which no known rule clearly applies, or *prima facie* applicable rules clash, or following the apparently applicable single rule would bring disaster. Rules and laws cannot be framed in advance and in detail to suit absolutely all cases that might arise.

It is instructive to consider whether the rule against lying is morally binding unequivocally and in all circumstances (Bok 1979 surveys the issue). A traditional example concerns a would-be murderer who asks where his intended victim is. If mere evasiveness would itself convey information, it seems to me that ordinary decency requires telling an untruth. In the episode of *NYPD Blue* televised on NBC on 12 May 1998, Detective Greg Medavoy obtains a confession from an actual murderer through skillful interrogation. Contrary to fact, he convinces the suspect that the police already have nearly conclusive physical evidence, as well as an eyewitness. Are his lies justified or excusable? One might argue that the job of the police is to solve the murder, using a variety of techniques. If the police really are seeking the truth and are putting on an act in interviews as one technique among others and if they will make due amends to the suspect if he turns out innocent, that is one thing. If they are trying to get a conviction no matter what, that is another thing, and entirely inexcusable. Furthermore, the interviews are a kind of game that the suspect presumably understands. The guilty suspect will presumably tell lies if he thinks they will work; and he understands that the police will try to expose any inconsistencies and lies, perhaps even by lying themselves. In such circumstances, arguably, the detective's lying, or acting, is no more reprehensible than bluffing in a poker game.

The example suggests, I think, that telling an untruth is not always and unequivocally wrong. In tough cases, other considerations and even other rules may pull against the rule against lying. One should be wary, of course, of sliding into the comfortable and self-serving view that lying is acceptable even in unexceptional circumstances.

The police example meshes with Henry Hazlitt's observation (1964, Chapter 10) that exceptions to rules may be justified if they themselves are rule-like and help serve the purposes of the main rules. (Hazlitt drew an analogy with cases in which fire engines, police cars, and ambulances may depart from ordinary traffic rules.) It is even a virtue of ethical rules, as opposed to rigid law, that they have a certain flexibility.

Moritz Schlick recognized that creative moralists of outstanding insight and vision sometimes do (rightly) condemn current judgments of what is morally good and seek to raise moral insights and standards. This creative work – condemnation and reform – is distinct from the likewise valuable work of explaining people's actual moral behavior. (David Rynin so interprets Schlick in his introduction to Schlick 1930/1961, p. v.)

A moral reformer must, as such, be disagreeing with prevalent beliefs about what behavior, precepts, or character traits best conduce to satisfying whatever the ultimate criterion may be (such as happiness or conformity to divine will). The reformer presumably thinks he can change prevalent beliefs if only people will pay attention to his facts and reasoning. If ethics is thus amenable to rational discussion, it must contain an objective element. Moral standards are not just matters of whim or emotion: they can be better or worse; morality contains an objective element.

Flexibility in applying rules does not mean that "anything goes". Flexibility, if a virtue, must accord with attitudes of prudence, reasonableness, integrity, and benevolence. Attitudes affect what rules people generally follow, while following rules affects attitudes. One who behaves *as if* he possessed a particular virtue may come to possess it in fact.

INDIRECT ROUTES TO ULTIMATE GOALS

If happiness is the ultimate criterion, shouldn't ordinary persons and policymakers alike strive to maximize it personally and in the aggregate? No. Dissolving the "paradox of hedonism" helps explain why not (Singer 1982, pp. 145–6). (The term is a misnomer, however, since the supposed paradox is not actual and since it is not restricted to narrowly hedonistic pleasure.) One no more achieves personal happiness by aiming directly at it than one reaches Boston by pointing the car in that direction and bulling straight ahead. People have no way of pursuing and enjoying pleasure or happiness directly. All anyone can directly pursue is fairly specific activities, accomplishments, and experiences. Pursuing goals beyond a vague personal happiness – food, clothing, shelter, knowledge, skill, accomplishment, and the welfare of one's family and community – serves both personal survival and inclusive fitness (the transmission of genes like one's own through one's children or other close relatives), as well, probably, as happiness after all.

Just as one achieves personal happiness not by aiming directly at it but rather by pursuing projects (Lomasky 1987), so one does not contribute most to general happiness by aiming directly at it. Maximum aggregate utility is a meaningful goal neither for ordinary persons nor for makers of public policy. Policy can better work for the background conditions, the institutional framework, within which individuals have the best chances of living successful lives. (F.A. Hayek 1944/1956, p. 18, suggests the analogy of a gardener's creating favorable conditions for his plants.) An ethic requiring constant direct pursuit of maximum total happiness, whatever that might mean, would be self-defeating.

This insight hinges on facts which, although deriving largely from elusive strands of psychology, are indeed facts and not sheer value judgments. An ethics of maximizing a social aggregate would cause tensions between self-interest and the general interest, arouse counterproductive guilt feelings, and tend toward a hypocritical and unpleasant society. (This proposition, though conceivably wrong, is researchable, illustrating again the empirical orientation of utilitarian philosophy.)

A realistic ethics does not require impartiality between the interests and projects of strangers and those of oneself and one's family and friends – a point developed in Chapter 9. What does tend toward general happiness is that individuals pursue their own interests, which need not be narrowly egoistic ones, within ethical rules and side constraints.

RULES AS UNIVERSAL MEANS TO DIVERSE ENDS

Detailed agreement on values is unnecessary for cooperation in a well-functioning society. As John Stuart Mill wrote, happiness is

> much too complex and indefinite an end to be sought except through the medium of various secondary ends, concerning which there may be, and often is, agreement among persons who differ in their ultimate standard; and about which there does in fact prevail a much greater unanimity among thinking persons, than might be supposed from their diametrical divergence on the great questions of moral metaphysics (Mill 1838/1968, p. 51).[2]

For example, business partners may work together even though they plan to spend their shares of profit for widely different purposes. Faculty members may hold similar conceptions of an ideal university president or dean while diverging in their teaching and research interests and in their politics. People may agree broadly on the institutions and ethical principles necessary for a healthy society even though supporting different causes and pursuing different lifestyles.

This consideration reinforces the warning not to chalk up disagreement prematurely to undiscussible fundamental values. Ending discussion too hastily could block discovery of policies commanding agreement even among people working for different ends.

Like other social institutions, ethical rules and codes are subject to appraisal by the criterion of conduciveness to social cooperation and ultimately to happiness, broadly conceived. The criterion of appraisal is not the same thing as the very *content* of an ethical code. Happiness as the ultimate criterion in no way logically entails the rule: "Arrange all of your activities in pursuit of general happiness". On the contrary, as Chapter 9 argues, such a rule would impose excessive demands on individuals, would not be credible, and would be counterproductive in further ways. Even and especially on utilitarian grounds, then, an ethical code should make less sweeping demands. An indirect utilitarianism should recommend not only rules but also and perhaps especially character traits, dispositions, and attitudes.

These rules and precepts should not only be capable of appealing to deep intuitions but also conform to fact and logic. Robert Paul Wolff (1969) considers the "empirical, experimental nature" of utilitarianism to be its most attractive feature. Its criterion of happiness turns "all our *moral* problems ... into *factual* problems. Instead of debating abstractly in philosophical journals or courts of law, we must go out and collect facts about the happiness or unhappiness produced by various acts" (p. 401).

NOTES

1. Karl Popper prefers "negative utilitarianism", emphasizing avoidance of misery or relief of suffering rather than achievement of happiness. His main reason, not inconsistent with utilitarianism in the ordinary sense, is that revolutionary or reform movements aiming at the happiness of mankind have often turned into cruel tyranny. See O'Hear (1980), Chapter VIII.
2. Further evidence on Mill's indirect utilitarianism appears in the appendix to Chapter 6.

5.   What counts as utility?

IS HAPPINESS THE SAME AS SATISFACTION OF DESIRES?

Does the utilitarian value judgment favor the actual happiness of individuals or, if there is a difference, favor satisfying whatever desires or preferences individuals may currently happen to have? Although one answer to this question may sound ominous, neither answer has any direct policy implications. (I am not about to advocate *imposing* happiness on recalcitrant subjects.) Anyway, if gratifying their actual desires would in fact make people miserable because their desires had been based on misinformation or warped by an extreme short-run outlook or were otherwise ill-considered, should philosophers nevertheless applaud such counterproductive gratification? Philosophers are unlikely, of course, to know in advance that gratifying desires would bring misery and overriding them bring happiness. Still, clarity of thought requires facing the issue.

One might object that assessing two versions of a fundamental value judgment against each other is pointless because such judgments, by their very meaning, can have no reasons offered for them. Two versions of utilitarianism, with their somewhat different underlying intuitions, simply stand in contrast. Strictly speaking, this objection is valid, but only against the way I have phrased the issue so far. Actually, the issue is discussible because a judgment that appears fundamental may turn out, under examination, not to be so (recall Sidney Alexander's remarks, cited in Chapter 2). Discussion may sharpen the intuition on which a seemingly fundamental value judgment rests.

THE ENDOGENEITY OF PREFERENCES

Paradoxes arise from the endogeneity of preferences – their responsiveness to experience, including experience shaped by policy. Similarly, policy affects what information people have and even what personal identities members of future generations will have. Citing Derek Parfit and others, Tyler Cowen (1993) makes much of these paradoxes (also mentioned in Chapters 6 and 11 below).

They fade, however, when placed in proper context. It helps clarify them to compare them with a well-known dilemma in welfare economics identified by Tibor Scitovsky (whom Cowen 1993 does cite). By one plausible criterion, situation B counts as superior to situation A if the persons who would gain from a move from A to B could still keep some net gain after potentially buying the willing consent of those who would otherwise lose. (This judgment of superiority cannot be made if the gainers from the move could not advantageously compensate the losers.) The test, to use technical jargon, is whether the gainers could potentially "overcompensate" those who would otherwise lose, to the advantage of both groups. Paradoxically, the same test of potential (over)compensation, applied to a contemplated move from B to A, might rank the two states in the opposite order. The reason is a difference in the distribution of wealth in the two states when each is taken as the starting position. The test considered so far appeals to potential, not actual, payment by the winners to buy the acquiescence of the losers. A change made without actual compensation alters the distribution of wealth. Then, conceivably, the same criterion of merely potential but not actual compensation could recommend a reverse switch: each state of affairs could count as better than the other. (Altering the contemplated test to require *actual* compensation would forestall the paradox; Little 1950, pp. 98–100.)

In a roughly analogous way, assessment of a policy-based move between two situations might depend on which of two sets of endogenous preferences is consulted, the set prevailing in one situation or in the other. Government can no more "be neutral across different preferences ... than ... across the distribution of wealth". Policies must ultimately be judged not only on grounds of efficiency but also by what preferences they favor (Cowen 1993, p. 267). Should policy seek, then, to satisfy the preferences people actually have, the "cleansed" preferences they would have if better informed, or what? Using "cleansed" preferences is not the conclusively correct recommendation, one reason being that better information is not always a good thing. "A perfectly informed life would be a curse" (p. 263). People do value suspense, anticipation, surprise, and discovery, as well as merciful ignorance of unavoidable future calamities.

That tastes are endogenous – malleable, instead of being totally predetermined – is hardly a new or underrecognized insight (Yeager 1978). Economists are not denying endogeneity whenever they find it convenient, for textbook and classroom exercises in consumer theory and welfare economics, to take tastes as given. Microeconomic theory is hard to teach and to master; and anything helpful is legitimate as an exercise, including learning the subject backward and forward – as positive economics and as welfare economics – and in words, in diagrams, in mathematics, and with unrealistic as well as realistic assumptions. In pedagogical exercises, then, economists may legitimately set aside the distinction between happiness and desire-satisfaction, interpret utility as people's getting what they want, and regard tastes simply as given from outside the context of discussion. Outside this context, however, no type of welfare analysis is operationally available other than comparative-institutional analysis (a point Cowen 1993 seems not to recognize). Penetrating comparative analysis may dissolve the supposed paradoxes deriving from the undeniable malleability of preferences.

Many philosophers, apparently including David Hume, have inclined toward the desire-satisfaction criterion, largely on the grounds that facts and logic cannot show an intrinsic desire to be mistaken. Yet desires, being affected by institutions, policies, and other people's attitudes, are not simply given. To take them as given anyway is inconsistent with philosophical discussion of what attitudes, desires, and policies are worth recommending. The desire-satisfaction theory cannot be intelligibly worked out in detail, or so Richard Brandt argues, opting for the happiness theory (1979, pp. 146–7, 247). As Brandt argues (also in his 1992, Chapter 3), it can make sense to distinguish between rational and irrational desires and aversions and to bring facts and reasoning to bear in reconsidering them. To point this out is not to claim special insight and authority for oneself about how desires should be molded. Facing up to reality is not in itself dictatorial or totalitarian.

D.W. Haslett (1990, citing Brandt; cf. Brandt 1992, esp. Chapter 9) also contrasts two conceptions of utility: having certain experiences, like pleasure or happiness, and having one's desires or preferences satisfied. Haslett compromises on satisfaction of *fully informed* preferences for *experiences*.

One can sensibly appraise whether desires and aversions are rational, for few are intrinsic or ultimate. One can consider what a person would desire if he were fully informed and if any questioned desires and aversions of his had been "fumigated", as Brandt says, by "cognitive psychotherapy". An irrational desire or aversion is one that psychotherapy could remove or weaken.

Brandt's cognitive psychotherapy confronts desires with information (1979, p. 113). If a member of Congress is letting alcohol endanger his career, successful therapy would help him recognize and heed his priorities. If a boy refuses to play with a neighboring little girl because he is squeamish about her pet rabbit, a therapist might remove his aversion by tracing it to his once being frightened by a loud noise as he was reaching to touch a rabbit (pp. 11–12). A therapist might alleviate a patient's obsession with the high or low prestige of available jobs, or anxiety about other people's judgments, or morbid drive to excel everyone else, or extreme stinginess, all by showing him how obsolete residues of childhood experiences were blocking him from goals that informed reflection would recommend (pp. 116–23).

Brandt presumably does not actually advocate imposing psychotherapy to *make* people happy; instead, he is trying to clarify discussion. Admittedly, though, the happiness theory is disquieting when expounded with terminology and examples like Brandt's.

Brandt finds the changeability of desires posing greater difficulties for the desire-satisfaction conception of happiness than for the "fumigated" or more philosophical conception (1992, Chapter 9). How should competing satisfactions of past, present, and future desires be weighted? Suppose that a young couple desire and arrange a very expensive wedding but afterwards feel the more fully considered and durable desire that they had saved the money for household goods instead. Which expenditure decision would have yielded the couple more happiness? Which one would a well-informed and benevolent observer wish for the couple? Which one would he recommend if his advice were sought in advance?

Suppose, similarly, that a father, understanding how tastes evolve as people mature and knowing his son's personality, is considering a birthday gift. To add most to his son's happiness, should the father choose the gift that the son most wants right now or the one that will contribute most to satisfying his son's desires as the father knowledgeably expects them to evolve over time?

WORRIES ABOUT PREFERENCE MANIPULATION

Such questions may admittedly sound ominous. Still, recognizing that individuals' preferences do change and can even be downright mistaken in no way recommends either government coercion or social pressures to impose the decisions or the lifestyles deemed good for people.

At least four reasons count against that idea. First, even if there were such a thing as the objectively good life, no one could properly claim infallibly to know what it is. Freedom to experiment is itself valuable. Second, the specific content of the good life is different for different people, partly because of differences in genetic endowments and early experiences. Variety in interests, occupations, and lifestyles contributes to a flourishing society. No authority can have the knowledge and ability necessary for determining the occupation and lifestyle of each person and for determining the social pattern of diversity. Third, being *forced* into a specific lifestyle makes it less good than it might otherwise be. Happiness is not the sort of thing that can be rammed down people's throats. Fourth, attempts to impose good lives on people would presuppose and would increase the power of man over man, expand the scope for power to corrupt, impair social cooperation, and thus interfere with good lives after all. History records innumerable tyrants who have inflicted cruelties on their subjects in the name of making them happy, if only in the aggregate and in the long run. Precisely out of utilitarian concern for the actual happiness or misery that individual persons will themselves experience, we are wary of institutions and indeed of doctrines that might tend toward such perverse results.

Worries about meddlesomeness or totalitarianism, although not decisive against the actual-happiness criterion, should be taken seriously. A utilitarian can recognize that letting people make their own mistakes is more conducive to happiness, after all, than letting "the man in Whitehall" direct their lives. The reasons for thinking so appeal to facts or supposed facts of human nature and human society and so may be wrong. Anyway, they illustrate the great scope for positive analysis in ethical discourse, as distinct from invocation of sheer value judgments.

Amply reasonable worries do not justify distorting the fundamental utilitarian criterion into that of people's always achieving whatever they think would fulfill whatever desires they may currently have. To misstate the criterion and link it to the factually dubious supposition that individuals always are the best judges of their own interests would be "welfare scholarship". This, in the sense explained and condemned by Warren Nutter (in conversations), means misstating or de-emphasizing what one believes to be the truth imposed by facts and logic out of fear that people may misinterpret or misapply this unvarnished truth or, most broadly, that one's audience is unfit or unready to hear it. Withholding or distorting painful truths may conceivably be appropriate in some contingencies, but not in science or scholarship.

Although questions about the good life are worthy of attention and although some may turn out to have objectively valid answers, this fact no more authorizes the government – or intense social pressure – to impose answers than it authorizes imposing answers to scientific questions. Attempts to do either would subvert social cooperation in various ways, as social science can help explain. Liberalism and modernity regard questions about the good life as systematically unsettlable – from the public standpoint – or so Alasdair MacIntyre reports, not necessarily agreeing (1981/1984, p. 112). Without inconsistency, one can be a libertarian on questions of the scope of government and an objectivist and conservative on questions of morality (see, for example, Meyer 1962; compare the discussion of truth judgment and fallibilism in Chapter 10).

Just as individuals differ in their specific conceptions of happiness, social philosophers differ in how much they focus on the individual and how much on the community (Elbert 1989). Classical liberals or libertarians prize the autonomy and freedom of the individual. Communitarians (for example, Etzioni 1988) stress the individual's membership in social groups. This difference of emphasis centers not on fundamental values but on the social arrangements most favorable to them, and disagreement is in principle capable of being narrowed by further research. Man is a social animal, and the individual is shaped by his society and its language and culture. Yet such facts do not discredit individualistic attitudes and policies. Culture is not monolithic, least of all modern Western culture. It does not fully predetermine individuals' social roles and lifestyles. Individuals pursue their own diverse projects; they experience satisfaction from success, frustration from interference. The facts of reality, including human nature, do not impose an outlook that would subordinate the interests of individuals to any supposedly distinct set of community interests. Correctly conceived, morality imposes no such subordination.

COMPARING INSTITUTIONS

In the realm of actual decisions and advice, policy has no way of aiming directly at maximizing either people's happiness or the satisfaction of their preferences, whether actual or cleansed. Policymakers have direct handles on no such things, as Rutledge Vining has eloquently argued (1984 and earlier writings); policymakers can merely tinker with institutions and practices. According to indirect utilitarianism, the goal of any such tinkering should be to preserve and improve social cooperation, which is a state of affairs allowing individuals in general (rather than specific, nameable, preferred individuals) favorable opportunities to make good lives for themselves in their own diverse ways through trade and other peaceful interactions with their fellows.

Welfare analysis of this broadly utilitarian type compares the likely performances of alternative sets of mutually consistent social, political, and economic institutions and practices, and even of character types and attitudes, especially as these are influenced by policy. Economics, psychology, political science, and other disciplines may well enter into making these comparisons. Philosophically, it may well be true that the actual happiness of persons makes a more defensible criterion of ethical rules, government policies, and so forth than does the satisfaction of whatever preferences they do have or think they have. (Suppose that preference-satisfaction would make people miserable and that some other line of action would make them blissfully happy.) Clear thinking requires that this truth, if it is one, not be obscured by individualistic horror at the idea and the likely consequences of institutions authorized to give people what they should want rather than what they do want, while "cleansing" their thinking in the process. Such institutions are ominous and would tend to subvert rather than serve people's actual happiness. But actual happiness, not preference-satisfaction, remains the philosophically more defensible criterion.

Institutions and policies can affect people's tastes and attitudes. Laws and court decisions in the United States since World War II have altered attitudes toward discrimination against blacks. Examples of "bad" effects might be found in considering how particular welfare measures supposedly tend to breed successive generations of families who grow up believing that it is acceptable not to work for a living, or in considering the idea that recipients of unemployment compensation should not be expected to take jobs felt beneath their dignity. Redistributive measures predicated on the supposed injustice of material inequality may tend to erode respect for property rights. Tariff protection tends to dignify employing government power to obtain private benefits at other people's expense. Attitudes and traditions and the policies that alter or reinforce them can even influence whether a country has a primitive or a modern economy.

Whether one likes the fact or not, then, the effect of public policies on people's tastes and attitudes may be important and foreseeable enough in some cases to count in the assessment of policies.

IS UTILITARIANISM VALUE-NEUTRAL?

Should all desires be equally eligible to influence social policy, even ill will and an itch to meddle? One might think that indiscriminately aggregating all preferences bypasses having to judge their legitimacy. But that is not true. Including them all amounts to judging them all equally legitimate and entitled to count equally, or in proportion to their intensity. This practice, however, might "sanction a policy that obligates a person to act against, for instance, his preferences in food, housing, sex, and so forth, because a majority (though directly unaffected by his doing so) intensely dislikes the thought that he should indulge them" (Baier 1967/1982, p. 291). Such indiscriminateness would hardly be liberal.

Consider a person who wants to be neutral among different people's tastes and a Nazi who wants to count some for more and others' for less. "Political preferences ... are on the same level – purport to occupy the same space – as the utilitarian theory itself. Therefore, though the utilitarian theory must be neutral between personal preferences like the preferences for push-pin and poetry, as a matter of the theory of justice, it cannot, without contradiction, be neutral between itself and Nazism" (Dworkin 1981/1984, p. 157).

I regret seeming to invoke the authority of Ronald Dworkin; but I believe that a consistent utilitarianism does countenance assessing tastes, finding some more and others less worthy of respect and gratification, ultimately on the grounds of their likely effects on happiness. More exactly, perhaps, a consistent utilitarianism yields principles implying that some particular tastes are to be judged more and others less worthy. This is not to say that anyone is infallible in making such judgments; like propositions of science, they remain always at least potentially open to reconsideration in the light of further investigation and discussion. All the less does the appraisability of tastes recommend overlooking the grave dangers of empowering some coercive authority to make the appraisals and impose its judgments.

Utilitarians can deplore equal respect for sadism, ill will, and meddle-someness on the factual (and therefore falsifiable) grounds that respecting those attitudes will encourage them and so make for a less well-functioning society. Antisocial feelings arguably detract, in a long-run probabilistic sense, from the happiness even of people who harbor them.

James Buchanan sometimes seems to present his contractarian doctrine as resting on near-neutrality among values. But equal respect for all possible values, or even for all nonaggressive values, is itself a value. Buchanan apparently realizes this in acknowledging his own individualistic value judgment. (Individualism hardly counts, by the way, as a *fundamental* value; for it derives from the facts of human nature and from a deeper judgment presumably concerning happiness and misery.) (The References list a few of his relevant writings; also see the discussion in Chapter 10.)

Once one modifies value-neutrality by individualism, why not go further and forthrightly lay out one's entire value position for inspection? Let us see how any proposed alternatives fare in discussion. (No one is likely to advocate misery.) A fully neutral stance is incoherent.

INTENTIONS OR RESULTS?

Do utilitarians judge actions and decisions morally good or bad by their consequences, regardless of the intentions behind them? Not at all. The considerations that recommend rules or indirect utilitarianism count against judging the morality of specific acts by their specific results. A utilitarian can agree with Moritz Schlick (1930/1961, pp. 89–90) "that the *decisions* (the 'intentions') alone are the objects of moral judgment". The frequent distinction "between an 'ethics of intention' and an 'ethics of result'" is mistaken. "There has never been an 'ethics of result.'"

Psychological research illustrates Schlick's point. Jean Piaget and seven collaborators (1975) told stories to children to elicit their moral judgments. A little boy in one of the stories, disobediently playing in his father's study, accidentally made a small ink stain on the blotter. Another boy, disobeying no instruction and indeed trying to be helpful by filling the inkwell in his father's absence, clumsily made a big stain. Which boy was the more wicked? In another story, one child said his schoolteacher had given him good marks that day, although the teacher had given no marks at all. A second child said he had seen a dog as big as a cow, although in fact a rather ordinary dog had frightened him. Which child told the worse lie?

Young children generally answered that the second child in each story was the more wicked. A big stain is worse than a small one; a cow-sized dog is further from possible truth than good marks. These young children mostly had a material or results-oriented conception of good and bad. Older subjects of the experiments, in contrast, understood that intentions are what count ethically, rather than material outcomes or divergences from objective possibility. It is more wicked to make a small stain while being disobedient than a large stain while trying to help; it is more wicked to lie deceitfully than to exaggerate from fright.

As persons grow in ethical maturity, they learn to judge intentions. A decision made from bad motives does not become virtuous just because a quirk of fate brings a good result, nor does a decision made with good intentions become morally blameworthy just because of an accidentally bad outcome that could not have been foreseen and guarded against. Results can be judged objectively fortunate or unfortunate, apart from whether the actor deserves praise or blame.

Saying this is not to divorce intentions and results as objects of moral appraisal. We value good intentions, attitudes, character traits, and the like because persons bear fuller responsibility for these than for actual results in individual cases and also because good intentions are generally more likely than bad ones to bring good results. On the other hand, good intentions alone are not enough to make any action praiseworthy; nor will good intentions excuse anything, for there are such things as *culpable* carelessness, ignorance, or incompetence.

It is instructive to confront Schlick's remarks about intentions and results with F.A. Hayek's points about material rewards (1960, Chapter 6). Hayek defends the kind of economic system in which people tend to be rewarded according to the market value of their achievements rather than the moral character of their efforts. A popular singer may become wealthy without great effort; he may even enjoy performing before ardent fans. A publisher may grow rich on pornography. At the same time, a brilliant scholar may toil incessantly for scant rewards; or a dedicated and innovative medical researcher, blamelessly suffering bad luck, may get into a blind alley or else may be beaten to his discovery by an unknown rival. Yet Hayek would accept market determination of incomes and would not want to carry out redistribution to achieve a pattern of rewards corresponding more nearly to the moral merit of efforts or the nobility of intentions.

Can Schlick's and Hayek's views be reconciled? Yes. Schlick and Hayek are discussing different questions. Schlick is discussing how praise and blame apply to decisions and intentions and underlying character traits. Moral judgments do not apply to individual outcomes considered apart from these volitional elements, for outcomes often contain unintended and accidental elements. It is immature to put greater blame on the well-intentioned child who made the larger ink stain in Piaget's story.

Hayek is not primarily discussing praise or blame; he is considering choice among alternative institutions. Advantages flow from letting supply and demand determine the wages and the allocations of various kinds of labor and letting prospective salaries and profits guide workers and entrepreneurs in the use of their abilities and hunches. The advantages concern enlistment of knowledge and incentives, freedom of choice, and decentralization of authority and power. What is the alternative to the market system of signals, incentives, rewards, and coordination? How attractive is that alternative?

The paraplegic of mediocre intelligence who cannot do work of much value yet struggles diligently to support himself demonstrates moral merit and deserves admiration and praise. How, though, shall it be arranged to pay him according to his merit rather than according to the value of his work? (A social safety net to alleviate distress is something different from reward according to merit.) On the other hand, a brilliant promoter may establish one innovative and flourishing enterprise after another, to the benefit of consumers and workers and fellow taxpayers, all while relishing his challenges and accomplishments. He may be admired; but his talents, capacities, and enthusiasm, being largely attributable to biological inheritance and early environment, do not constitute exceptional moral heroism. How, then, will his income and wealth be kept below the market values of his accomplishments and in line with his more nearly ordinary moral merit? What sorts of boards will decide on the respective merits and incomes of different people? When market-determined wages and profits no longer guide the distributions of efforts and talents and investable resources among various activities, what will replace those market signals and incentives?

Suppose, however implausibly, that incomes *were* somehow distributed according to accurately assessed moral merit, so that high and low incomes were seen as unambiguous badges of high and low merit. What would the pyschological consequences be? Would people really be happier than in a market system?

Confronting Schlick's and Hayek's arguments with one another helps clarify the distinction between different objects of moral appraisal – decisions and intentions and character types on the one hand, alternative sets of social institutions on the other hand.

6. The alleged problem of aggregation

THE CHARGE OF AGGREGATION

This chapter is the first of two that face some leading criticisms of utilitarianism.

One might conceivably accuse utilitarianism of being too individualistic, perhaps because its British champions of the early nineteenth century, the "philosophical radicals", generally advocated free-market policies. More recently, Ludwig von Mises forthrightly advocated both utilitarianism and economic laissez-faire. Nowadays, however, roughly opposite charges are more common. Utilitarianism is said to be collectivist in spirit: it aims at maximizing an aggregate of measurable and interpersonally comparable individual utilities, even without regard to their distribution. It would unfairly sacrifice the utility of some persons for the supposed greater utility of others. At their most superficial, critics imagine utilitarians going around looking for opportunities to murder redheads to gratify the multitude or to excuse rape when the rapist's pleasure outweighs the victim's distress (Rothbard 1982, pp. 202, 211, 212; Machan 1989, pp. 64–5, 219 n. 5).

More respectable examples of the charge surfaced at a conference held in 1989 to celebrate James Buchanan's seventieth birthday. Several participants faulted utilitarianism for taking as its criterion not the diverse welfares of actual individuals as experienced by each but rather some impersonal aggregate utility. John Gray warned against "a consequentialist or utilitarian conception of the market as maximiser of aggregate welfare" (1989BoL, p. 12).

Assessing such charges requires some distinctions, including one between identified lives and statistical lives (made by Thomas Schelling 1968). Almost any action or policy, compared with an alternative, puts some persons at a disadvantage. A program of vaccination might save millions of lives but harm or even kill a few persons who would have escaped the disease anyway. Policies concerning highway construction and safety, air-traffic density, long holiday weekends, energy generation, and drug testing necessarily involve trading off greater pleasure, convenience, economy, and even life for many against increased risk of harm or death for a few. Even a man who takes his wife and children out to dinner exposes them and other persons to some slight risk of being killed in a car crash (Hardin 1989). The French government maintains "the beautiful roadside avenues of trees" even at the cost of some additional fatal accidents (Griffin 1986, p. 241 and *passim*).

Must we say, then, that such policies and actions immorally sacrifice the interests of a few to the greater interests of the many? Could an antiutilitarian ethics remove the need for the sometimes agonizing choices just illustrated? Must we reject any policy whatsoever that might leave some persons or participants in some activities with less attractive prospects than under some alternative policy? Must we condemn any philosophical position that does not reject such a policy? Few if any policies or philosophies could pass that test.

Loren Lomasky and Jan Narveson, eminent philosophers, have made typical attacks. Utilitarianism views morality "as an unconstrained exercise in the maximization of some social value function"; it presupposes "some impersonal standard of value to which all persons have reason to adhere" (Lomasky 1987, p. 35). It treats persons merely as "convenient loci at which and through which value can be realized. Because rightness of action is entirely a function of utility production, it is necessarily utility that counts primarily, persons only derivatively" (p. 54). A utilitarian counts no individual's good for anything except as a component of the totality. Taking all value to be impersonal, "utilitarianism makes no room for individualism. It values humanity but not individuals" (pp. 196–7). Each person is but a soldier in a common cause. Individuals may fall, but the enterprise goes on. Nothing is "suspect about sacrificing one of the troops for another just so long as more impersonal value is thereby attained" (p. 53). Utilitarianism enrolls all us individuals "as partners in the human enterprise to which all our efforts must be devoted", even though no such thing exists, "only the various personal enterprises in which individuals enroll themselves" (p. 35).

Reviewing Jan Narveson's book of 1988, Lomasky contrasts utilitarianism with his own supposedly distinct position. He understands morality (correctly, in my view) "as an enterprise for mutual benefit but not as an exercise in self-abnegation. The great classical exponent of this view is Thomas Hobbes, and David Gauthier's *Morals by Agreement* is an impressive recent rendering" (Lomasky 1989, p. 46).

This supposed contrast is misleading. A utilitarian philosopher, analyzing and perhaps recommending but not *imposing* ethical codes and social arrangements, is quite able to recognize facts of reality, including the distinctness of individuals and their quite reasonable partiality to their own projects. He can recognize that no happiness is available other than the happiness of individuals. He can inquire into what arrangements will best facilitate cooperation among individuals as each pursues his own projects.

Jan Narveson also interprets utilitarianism as implying readiness to sacrifice the utilities of some persons for larger increments to the utilities of others. It supposedly calls on each person to work for greatest total utility, remaining impartial between his own and other persons' aspirations (1988, especially pp. 150–53). It invokes "equality of value to anyone of a unit of anyone's utility" (p. 92); it requires counting all utility units of all persons equally (p. 152).

Narveson's charges gain attention from his avowed conversion away from his own earlier utilitarianism. Yet his 1967 book did not espouse the version he now attacks, the one whose criterion is the maximum sum of cardinally measurable and interpersonally comparable utilities. He said something weaker: "the purpose of morality is to maximize the general happiness, which is to say, to be concerned for others as well as oneself" (1967, p. 245). "The general happiness is merely everybody living the sort of life he would find best, according to whatever conception of the good life he happens to have" (p. 256.) Perhaps Narveson found his early book unsatisfactory, without identifying exactly how, and so moved on to another doctrine.

Utilitarianism, according to J.R. Lucas, "made no concessions to the individual, treating him only as a unit; and in submerging his pay-off to an anonymous sum total, it was, in effect, inviting him to merge his individuality in a collective whole" (1980, p. 68). Utilitarian theories correspond dangerously well with "the instincts of rulers". They "encourage bureaucrats in their natural propensity to push people around, manipulating them merely as means and not regarding them as ends in themselves" (p. 149). Utilitarians tend "to regard people as pets, who have feelings and ought to be well cared for, rather than rational agents who act on their own responsibility" (p. 192). Utilitarians manifest "callous unconcern ... towards particular individuals, whose interests they are prepared to trample on without scruple, so long as the sum of good is thereby increased" (p. 185).

Alan Hamlin finds classical utilitarianism holding "that the community must be supreme over the individual. ... In this view the government has as its legitimate role the complete structuring of all activities which contribute to the good. The individual is simply the material from which community is built" (1986, p. 161). Criticizing a version that he attributed, I think wrongly, to John Stuart Mill, Jeffrie G. Murphy found utilitarianism "so obviously morally bankrupt that very few contemporary moral philosophers take it at all seriously. ... [I]t fails to pay attention to ... important *autonomy* values ... and thus fails to articulate a satisfactory conception of *justice* or *respect for persons*. It does not rule out the sacrifice of persons for the general good" (Murphy 1977, p. 232).

Judge Richard Posner (1990) echoes such criticisms: utilitarianism is "radically collectivist" because for it only the aggregate counts; one person's happiness can in principle offset another's misery; for it, as for other isms, the individual is a mere cell in a larger organism (pp. 346–7, 376). That Posner should so readily go along with standard criticisms is odd, given his own pragmatist and consequentialist predilections and his skepticism about ideas of objective morality and natural law and rights (see Chapter 11 below).

Sen and Williams (1982, p. 4) express the point starkly:

> Essentially, utilitarianism sees persons as locations of their respective utilities – as the sites at which such activities as desiring and having pleasure and pain take place. Once note has been taken of the person's utility, utilitarianism has no further direct interest in any information about him.[1] This view of man is a common feature of different variants of utilitarianism. ... Persons do not count as individuals in this any more than individual petrol tanks do in the analysis of the national consumption of petroleum.

In other words (mine), utilitarianism allegedly regards each person as scarcely more than a processing station for converting goods and experiences into contributions to an impersonal aggregate utility; he is like a mere branch factory that might properly be reconverted or closed down to serve the efficiency of some larger unit.

David Gauthier repeats the aggregation charge. Utilitarianism, he says, regards persons as passively receiving goods rather than as actively engaged in producing them and agreeing on their distribution. "[T]he utilitarian ignores, as his principles require him to ignore, the structure of interaction" (1986, p. 127). "The utilitarian relates morality to society as we relate rationality to the individual; morality is identified with collective maximiza tion. The moral actor seeks to maximize ... a strictly increasing function of all individual utilities" (1986, p. 104).

Yet especially in view of utilitarians' emphasis on social cooperation, it seems odd to accuse them of ignoring "the structure of interaction". (Further comment on Gauthier's charges comes below.)

Robert Nozick made such charges during his libertarian incarnation (1974; compare Gauthier 1985 and Sartorius 1984). In the apt paraphrase by H.L.A. Hart (1983, Essay 9, pp. 205–6), Nozick's argument

> simply assumes that utilitarianism is only intelligible if the satisfactions it seeks to maximize are regarded as those of a single social entity. It also assumes that the only alternative to the Nozickian philosophy of right is an unrestricted maximizing utilitarianism which respects not persons but only experiences of pleasure or satisfaction; and this is of course a false dilemma.

Hart develops this charge in several strands. (1) In classical maximizing utilitarianism, individuals are not important for their own sakes. They are mere channels or locations of fragments of what *is* important – aggregate pleasure or happiness. (2) Utilitarianism treats individuals as of equal worth only by treating them as of *no* worth. Only experiences of pleasure or satisfaction have worth. (3) Yet contrary to the tacit utilitarian supposition, no one experiences the net balance of happiness or misery of different persons. Society is not an entity capable of such experience. (4) Maximizing utilitarianism admits no principles of distribution to restrict tradeoffs between the satisfactions of different persons. It makes a false analogy between how a single rational individual prudently orders his life and how a whole community might rationally order its life through government. Although a single individual can rationally sacrifice some satisfactions now for different and greater ones later, one person's happiness cannot be similarly replaced without limit by the greater happinesses of other individuals (Hart 1983, Essay 9, pp. 200–202; compare James Sterba's argument, reviewed below).

Pursuing these strands of criticism, Hart says that utilitarianism has a "sinister side permitting the sacrifice of one individual to secure the greater happiness of others" (pp. 194, 202, 204). Its "arch-sin" is to ignore the separateness of persons. John Rawls compresses such charges into a sentence quoted ad nauseam: "Utilitarianism does not take seriously the distinction between persons" (1971, p. 27; cf. p. 187). While also pressing this charge, David Gauthier (1986, pp. 109–10) ironically tars Rawls with his own brush:

> [T]he utilitarian supposes that even a person's natural attributes, her physical and mental capacities, are vested in her only in so far as this proves socially convenient. ... We must expect the utilitarian to welcome the idea, suggested by John Rawls, that the talents of the naturally most favoured are to constitute a common asset for the benefit of all.

Furthermore, Rawls's theory

> violates the integrity of human beings. ... In seeking to treat persons as pure beings freed from the arbitrariness of their individuating characteristics, Rawls succeeds in treating persons only as social instruments. In denying to each person a right to his individual assets, Rawls is led to collectivize those assets (Gauthier 1986, p. 254).

Lucas (1980, esp. pp. 185, 192, 194 and 202) similarly accuses Rawls of utilitarian sins.

AGGREGATION NOT NEEDED

Having pulled these quotations together, I feel almost outrage at the slipshod scholarship they betray. Where do the critics get their notions of utilitarianism? Not directly from utilitarian writers, to judge from the fewness of pertinent citations. Seldom if ever do they come to grips with the best of Hume, John Stuart Mill, Mises, Hayek, and Hazlitt. Possibly the critics have been parroting one another. (Sen and Williams 1982 is a compendium of articles that, with few exceptions, recite further complaints of the sort already illustrated.)

The notion that utilitarianism cares only about experiences, not persons, is baseless. Any even halfway sophisticated utilitarian recognizes *facts*. Experiences cannot occur apart from the people having them. Society as such cannot experience satisfaction and frustration. Utilitarians care about experiences because they care about the persons having them.

Social science, especially economics and public-choice theory, illuminates the likely consequences of entrusting any authority with the mandate to maximize total satisfaction (whatever exactly that might be); and a utilitarian recoils in horror from those consequences. A utilitarian recognizes that the distributions of income and wealth and especially of power, as well as the features of social organization conditioning those distributions, do affect whether the character of society affords individuals good or poor opportunities to make good lives for themselves. A utilitarianism taking social cooperation as a near-ultimate criterion is not open to the charges made by the other critics cited.

Many critics seem to take it as axiomatic or as true by definition that any morally appealing and plausible doctrine just cannot be utilitarian. Utilitarianism serves them as a foil to make their own doctrines look good by contrast. Even if they were able to unearth a few actual adherents of such a straw-man doctrine, what would be the value of blowing it down? As Karl Popper has said somewhere, criticism is most useful only if it attacks a doctrine in its strongest, not its weakest, form.

AN ILLUSTRATIVE EXAMPLE

An example contrived by J.A. Mirrlees (1982, pp. 75–6) affords insight into what the critics may have in mind when complaining about aggregation (and if they are not just mindlessly echoing one another). Social welfare is the arithmetic sum of the utilities of society's two members, Tom and Dick. Both have the same utility function with plausible properties. Total utility is a positive function and marginal utility a diminishing function of income and leisure. Moreover, more income increases the marginal utility of leisure, and more leisure increases the marginal utility of income (more income increases the marginal *dis*utility of labor, and more labor decreases the marginal utility of income). Intuitively, working a lot leaves a person less time and capacity to enjoy income, and having a large income reduces one's willingness to work. The production function is very simple: 1 unit of Tom's labor produces 2 units of real income, while 1 unit of Dick's labor produces only 1 unit of income. Only in their productivities do the two men differ.

On these radically simple assumptions, straightforward calculus shows that maximizing social welfare requires Tom both to work more hours and also to receive less income than Dick. Tom, though more productive, is unequivocally the worse off of the two. An intuitive explanation invokes comparative advantage, a principle prominent in the theory of international trade. Tom has both absolute and comparative advantages over Dick in transforming labor into income. In transforming income into utility and welfare, Dick has neither an absolute advantage nor an absolute disadvantage, but he does have a comparative advantage. Tom should therefore specialize in producing income and Dick specialize in consuming it. Tom's being busy creating income leaves him comparatively little leisure for effectively transforming income into utility; Dick, allotted more leisure, is more effective in transforming income into utility. If total utility counts but not its distribution, the more productive person "should" have a lower level of utility.

Any (imaginary) utilitarian who remained content with considerations of this sort would be committing grave oversights. Most obviously, though not most fundamentally, he would be overlooking incentives, including incentives to reveal or conceal information about one's own capabilities and tastes. Considerations of fairness must also enter into any even halfway sophisticated version of utilitarianism. An ethical code cannot promote the welfares of individuals unless it commands wide adherence, which it cannot do if seen as grossly unfair. (On any plausible definition, fairness, like justice, cannot be regarded as a desideratum or criterion in *rivalry* with the utilitarian criterion of happiness, broadly interpreted. Precisely on utilitarian grounds it is desirable that social arrangements be fair and that people treat one another fairly.) More broadly, an ethical code must meet the requirements of social cooperation. What sort of society would it be in which officials and institutions had authority to make the sorts of assignments contemplated in the Tom-and-Dick example, and how would individuals like living in such a society?

WHOSE UTILITY?

Occasionally, at least in conversation, the question arises of just who the persons are whose utility is supposed to be the criterion of actions, rules, and so forth. Are they oneself alone, the narrow set of oneself and one's closest relatives and friends, one's country, all mankind, all sentient beings, or what? Such a question, in some contexts, comes close to presupposing aggregation. Well, not all utilitarian writings are intended as advice; many are analytical contributions. Utilitarian advice, when so intended, is directed, as most advice is directed, to all persons interested in it or in a position to act on it. A doctrine calling on each person always to put the welfare of all humanity above his own would be unworkable, and preaching it and trying to abide by it would probably cause more unhappiness than happiness. At the other extreme, a code calling on each person always to put his own welfare above everyone else's, always preferring a trivial benefit to himself to a huge benefit to other people, or a code arbitrarily favoring specific persons or groups at the expense of others, would hardly be an *ethical* code (see the discussion of the generalization principle in Chapter 9). Utilitarianism does not recommend direct attempts to maximize the aggregate utility of any particular group, narrow or broad. It recommends institutions, actions, principles, dispositions, and so forth that are generally conducive to well-being. The question of *whose* aggregate welfare is misconceived. Incidentally, different groups of persons overlap. If most persons behave decently toward those with whom they come into direct contact, the web of direct and indirect decent interactions becomes extremely wide (Hazlitt 1964, Chapter 20; compare Chapter 8 below).

Whatever doctrines the charges and examples just reviewed might apply to, if any, they scarcely apply to *indirect or rules utilitarianism*. That version does *not* envisage maximizing either a sum of utilities or any other definite social-welfare function. On the contrary, its focus on voluntary social cooperation rejects any maximization attempted by a central authority. Distinct individuals take center stage, bargaining among themselves to reach mutually beneficial agreements. Although the bargainers are maximizers themselves in the sense of pursuing their respective goals and ideals, the diverse particular agreements among them do not aim at any collective maximum. Indirect utilitarianism recognizes no transcendant whole of which individuals' good lives are mere parts.

Indirect utilitarianism and contractarianism, charitably interpreted (Chapter 10), reinforce each other. Both doctrines recognize the separateness of individuals as they seek success in their own projects. The function of morality and (ideally) of public policy is to facilitate cooperation among them.

DETACHMENT

Still, the social philosopher or policy advisor cannot avoid all *semblance* of a maximizer's viewpoint. Whatever his conception of the general good, he must have some notion of institutions and rules serving it better or worse. Although desiring the best in this harmless sense, the utilitarian does not envisage maximizing some quasi-homogeneous substance, perhaps even by depriving some persons of their due shares to give greater gains to others.

In a benign way, impartiality has some affinity with this faint semblance of a maximizer's view. The detached mood appropriate to a social philosopher or policy advisor *does* in a sense require regarding individuals equally as "statistics", so to speak, and according overriding privilege to none of them. Utilitarians like John Harsanyi (discussed below) and F.A. Hayek (1967, p. 163, 1976, pp. 114, 129–32, 1978, pp. 62–3; cf. Vickrey 1961) weigh the prospects of the member of society considered at random. For them, a good society is one that diverse individuals would find it good to live in, one that a person taken at random would find most conducive to his own successful pursuit of happiness. In that sense it is the sort of society in which some sort of average utility, possibly median utility rather than the arithmetic mean, is expected to be highest. Admittedly, though, the criterion of what the person taken at random would prefer is open to challenge, perhaps for inconsistency with contractarian insights (discussed in Chapter 10).

Anyway, the detached mood cultivated by such a conception does not require forgetting that each person is special to himself and within his own circle. A utilitarian recoils in horror from empowering any authority to manipulate individuals as mere statistics. Misrepresenting a detached philosophical mood as the stance of a collectivist maximizer is just that, misrepresentation. Reference to the greatest attainable fulfillment of one's criteria of a good society implies appraising alternative sets of institutions. It in no way implies a collectivist view that would deny the separateness of individuals and the specialness of each one to himself and to the persons closest to him.

The attack focusing on interpersonal comparisons, aggregate utility, and unconcern for individuals, although perhaps better than a shabby debating point, does at best rest on misconceptions. Is maximization of an aggregate of individuals' utilities a feasible or even a clearly conceivable goal of policy, distinct from facilitating mutually advantageous cooperation among individuals? No; of course not. Economic theory and experience tell against any such collective enterprise. Ludwig von Mises (1949/1963, p. 242), an emphatic utilitarian, rejects it:

> Some economists believe that it is the task of economics to establish how in the whole of society the greatest possible satisfaction of all people or of the greatest number could be attained. They do not realize that there is no method which would allow us to measure the state of satisfaction attained by various individuals.

It would be especially far-fetched to impute even the concept of aggregate utility, let alone a desire to maximize it, to utilitarian economists such as Ludwig von Mises and Henry Hazlitt, since they, in the tradition of "Austrian" economics, repudiate even such *relatively* meaningful aggregative concepts as gross national product, national income, and the total capital stock.

Whom, by the way, in the critics' view, do utilitarians expect to pursue maximum aggregate happiness? Ordinary persons cannot realistically be imagined subordinating their own diverse values and purposes to some dubious aggregate. Nor does any single mind or authority exist – or even be plausibly desired – to undertake a society-wide maximization exercise as if it were an engineering problem. Critics should at least grant utilitarians the presumption that they are not blind to reality. A realistic utilitarianism recognizes that achievement and happiness pertain to individuals, who must pursue them primarily by themselves and through others with whom they interact. As the "paradox of hedonism" recognizes, furthermore, each has better chances of success if, instead of pursuing happiness directly, he pursues his own specific and distinct goals and projects, including ones shared with others (on project-pursuit, cf. Lomasky 1987).

Since maximum utility, whether personal or aggregate, is not a goal that anyone can directly pursue, the question facing ethical philosophers and policymakers concerns background conditions instead. What self-consistent and attainable framework of institutions, rules, character traits, dispositions, and attitudes conduces best to mutual noninterference and effective cooperation among individuals pursuing their own diverse objectives? The answer, in its details, of course depends partly on the historically inherited conditions of particular times and places.

Some of the propositions invoked above deal largely in psychology and are not guaranteed correct. Still, they do concern matters of fact and are not sheer value judgments. Utilitarians are neither contemptuous of such facts nor so certain of already being in full possession of all relevant ones that their doctrine can remain unchanged even in its details and specific applications. Being oriented toward reality, utilitarianism can cope with a wider range of circumstances than a more purely a priori doctrine.

Why, nevertheless, do critics persist in imputing to utilitarians a goal that is neither feasible nor even clearly conceivable? It is true that a few economists have carried out abstract exercises of trying to imagine the measurement of individual utilities and their aggregation in some sort of social-welfare function. Although not to be taken literally, such exercises may perhaps be justified on heuristic grounds.

A doctrine that does not conceive of trying to maximize the aggregate of individual utilities is less exposed to questions about the fairness of distribution of utility than a doctrine that does so conceive. As for fairness, we value it, however exactly we may interpret it, because a society deficient in it would be a less attractive society, affording its members worse chances of leading satisfying lives – is that not so? When we contemplate the distribution of utility and of means to it, such as goods and money, we already take account of how fairness and unfairness affect utility levels and the desirability of redistributive measures. (A later section of this chapter discusses such issues.)

AGGREGATION AS A METAPHOR: AGGREGATE VERSUS AVERAGE UTILITY

Some philosophers have wondered whether aggregate or average utility should be the utilitarian maximand. As many critics of utilitarianism insist, the question is not operational. The very notions of total utility and of the total divided by population are fuzzy and vaguely collectivistic. It can be instructive, nevertheless, temporarily to *pretend* that the concepts of total and average (arithmetic-mean) utility are operational and also that they allow due respect for individuality and personal autonomy. On those nonfactual assumptions, would the total or the average criterion be preferable?

For a population of a given size, the two criteria coincide. The issue of choosing between them arises only insofar as institutions, policies, ethical precepts, and so forth can affect the number of people. To evade additional complications, let us consider either a single completely closed society or the world as a whole, not a world of multiple distinct societies; and let us postpone the question of how unequally individual utilities are distributed. Even thus simplified, the choice is difficult: which is preferable, a small population enjoying a high level of happiness per person or a large population enjoying greater total happiness but less per person?

An individualistic intuition tends to favor the higher average utility of the actual members of the smaller population. It does not care about aggregates or averages except as they correspond to the utilities of individuals. It stands opposed to the version imagined by critics that takes aggregate utility as a goal in its own right and regards individual persons as mere stations at which portions of this aggregate accrue.

Would a rational and impartial benevolent spectator give as much weight to gains in total happiness achieved by an increase in population as to gains accruing to members of a population of given size? Richard Brandt answers "no": an increase in the welfare of existing persons counts for more than producing additional persons who would be happy if they existed (1979, p. 216).

Derek Parfit (1984) takes a similar view. Persons who are or will anyway be alive are the ones whose welfare counts, not persons who do not and never will exist. A policy favoring the smaller but happier population cannot inflict deprivation on potential additional persons who remain always merely imaginary. Imaginary persons can experience no deprivation either of satisfactions or of life itself. Yet for persons who do or will exist anyway, it is a deprivation to enjoy less happiness than they otherwise might have enjoyed. This thought reflects concern for individuals as such and for their own happiness rather than concern for them as mere stations for generating increments to aggregate happiness.

Does a married couple have a duty to bring a baby into the world if it would grow up to be a happy person? No, for a baby never conceived remains imaginary. Does the couple have a duty to refrain from bringing a baby into the world who would grow up grossly deformed and miserable? Possibly yes. The deformed baby, if born, would be an actual person experiencing actual misery. Refraining from inflicting that misery arguably comes closer to being a duty than the conjectured duty to have the happy child.[3]

"Whether causing someone to exist can benefit this person" (the title of Appendix G to Parfit 1984) is a question relevant to the example of happy and miserable potential children. Derek Parfit hints at "yes". His answer does not imply, however, that someone is harmed by never being conceived; for a never-existent entity is never "someone" and so can experience neither harm nor benefit. "Unlike never existing, starting to exist and ceasing to exist both happen to actual people. This is why we can claim that they can be either good or bad for these people" (p. 489).

The average utility criterion stands in favorable contrast with what Parfit calls a counterintuitive Repugnant Conclusion: if the greatest net sum of happiness minus misery were the criterion instead, then for any large population with a high quality of life, some much larger population must be imaginable, and preferable, even though its individual members would lead lives barely worth living (1984, Chapter 17).

A Mere Addition Paradox superficially seems to support the opposite intuition (1984, Chapter 19). A population is enjoying a high quality of life. Now a noncommunicating population comes into existence with a lower yet still good quality of life. This occurrence can hardly be judged bad, even though it brings down the average quality of life of the two populations considered together. Yet if we had been comparing a larger population of lower life quality with the original smaller but happier population, the average criterion would have chosen the original population.

This Paradox does not straightforwardly bear, however, on the question we had been tackling. Its stipulation of a *noncommunicating* additional population violates the context of members of a single society contemplating their own policies affecting population size.

A distinction introduced by Peter Singer and developed by Eric Mack (1988) bears on the issues of the last several paragraphs. "Total-view" utilitarianism favors the largest balance of pleasure or preference satisfaction over pain or dissatisfaction. "Prior-existence" utilitarianism counts the experiences only of beings who do exist or will exist independently of whatever decision is being contemplated. This formulation seems inexact, however. For example, the deformed and miserable baby will exist, if he does exist beyond the fetal stage, *in consequence of* a decision to have him born; yet his misery arguably ought to count in the assessment.

Prior-existence utilitarianism, akin or perhaps identical to individualistic utilitarianism, calls not for maximum aggregate utility but for maximum average utility (or maximum utility of the member of society considered at random). A decision for the smaller but happier population benefits persons who will actually exist. It will not harm merely potential persons who in fact never do exist and so never will experience any deprivation. A decision for the larger population with lower average (though higher aggregate) utility would harm actual persons, those members experiencing less personal happiness than in the other case. (The very word "decision" warns of pitfalls. The institutions and rules necessary for influencing population size might themselves be sources of unhappiness.)

Yew-Kwang Ng (1989) suggests a modified-total criterion of population size: the maximand is not average utility multiplied by the straight-forward population figure (that is, total utility) but average utility multiplied by a figure that rises with population, but less fast, approaching an asymptote. Although Ng does not explicitly write it down, the formula for his multiplier is

$$(a^N-1)/(a-1),$$

where N is population and a is a parameter between 0 and 1 governing how much less fast than population the multiplier rises and indicating where between the extremes the compromise criterion lies. When $a = 0$, the multiplier becomes 1, and the maximand is average utility. When $a = 1$, the multiplier coincides with actual population, and the maximand is total utility. (Strictly, the multiplier is undefined at $a = 1$; but when a approaches 1 as a limit, the multiplier approaches the actual population as a limit, making the maximand total utility.)

Some such compromise, with a between 0 and 1, has intuitive appeal. Philosophers would not like a population of only a single "utility monster" enjoying enormous happiness. (That example is perhaps illegitimate, however, for it contemplates not only different sizes of population but also bizarrely different personal characteristics of the members, or rather the sole member, of the population.) Nor would philosophers like the opposite case of immense total utility shared among so enormously many people that the average person's life was only barely worth living. By Ng's compromise, when the population is small, the welfare significance of additional utility recipients (that is, their marginal significance in the eyes of the social philosopher) is relatively great; but when the population is very large anyway, the welfare significance of additional persons is slight.

This formulation does not necessarily express an anti-individualistic philosophy; for to accord slight significance to imaginary additional persons is not to harm those persons, who never are born anyway. Ng's compromise conceives of a tradeoff between average utility and number of recipients. When what is very low is average utility, the impartial benevolent spectator gives heavy weight to increments to it; but when what is very low is population, the spectator gives heavy weight to increments to *it*. As each of these factors of the maximand rises relative to the other, its relative weight declines.

Despite describing such a compromise, Ng says he proposes it only for persons who, unlike himself, cannot accept a monistic principle. Perhaps he distrusts the very idea of weighting done by persons other than those who actually experience the utilities. "[H]appy human lives are valuable in themselves and not *in the eyes* of someone else" (1989, p. 250). Ng does not like the idea of diminishing marginal significance of persons.

Yet anyone dealing seriously with the issues that Ng reviews implicitly requires himself to assign weights. He unavoidably is working with a social-welfare function, if only implicitly and with a vague and partial one. Ng himself, in giving overriding weight to total utility and none to the number of persons sharing in that total, is doing so. One cannot leave the conception of the social-welfare function up to the merely hypothetical inhabitants of the world being modeled.

The notion of great total utility being received in very small shares by extremely many persons is indeed, as Parfit says, "repugnant". Just one difficulty is the notion of measurement accurate enough for the observer to say that the average person's utility, though very low, is still positive. This difficulty is one slight additional reason not to worry over persons' loss of utility through their never being born in the first place. It seems especially odd to worry about the nonexistence of persons who, if they had been born, would have experienced utility so low that they scarcely felt it as positive.

As already implied, one might reject, as nonoperational, the very topic of the last several paragraphs. Even the question of whether life is worth living is suspect. Most of us might think that we have an answer, but a bias necessarily enters into it. Inputs into the judgment come exclusively from persons who have experienced life. In the nature of the case, no inputs can come from persons who never had the experience of living (or whose experience, in questionably equivalent words, is that of never having lived). How, then, can anyone authoritatively say whether or not it would have been better for him never to have been born or, perhaps, for the human race or the universe never to have existed?

Only in special contexts does the question of effects on size of population arise. In most ethical discussions that question is irrelevant. The live issue is what best contributes to social cooperation and thereby to happiness.

THE DISTRIBUTION OF UTILITY

Setting aside the population question, we now blur any difference between the criteria of total and average utility. Should this merged criterion be modified out of concern about the degree of inequality of distribution?[4] Yes, say some egalitarians (for example, Rawls 1971 and especially Sen 1973). They would prefer a more to a less nearly equal distribution of utilities even at the cost of a lower level. They distinguish between utilities themselves and their welfare significance or ethical worth. For them, a given increment to a fortunate person's already high utility has slighter social significance than the same increment to an unfortunate person's low level.

Their position is more extreme than a mere egalitarian slant in assessing alternative distributions of *money* or *goods and services*. That slant, along with the related notion of diminishing marginal utility of real income or wealth, is relatively plausible. A gain or loss of $100 worth of goods and services presumably does mean less to a rich person than to a poor person; it means fewer "utils" (assuming that utility is measurable and interpersonally comparable). Even nonegalitarian social philosophers should recognize this as a factual point, not a normative judgment, even though its validity may be hard to establish conclusively and although its possible policy implications are far from straightforward. The issue here is different: whether 100 utils mean less when enjoyed by a relatively happy person than when enjoyed by a relatively unhappy one. More precisely, the normative issue is whether utils should count less toward welfare at the margin – count less in a philosopher's social-welfare function – when going to the happy person than when going to the unhappy one.

In mentioning utils and wondering how they should count in assessments of welfare, I may seem to be accepting the measurement, comparison, and aggregation of individual utilities, the goal of maximizing this aggregate, and the expediency of sacrificing some persons' utilities to gain greater additions to the utilities of others. Actually, I reject this alleged version of utilitarianism for reasons already set forth. Here, however, I am temporarily acquiescing in *other writers'* concepts and language for heuristic purposes. We can sometimes make issues clear by presenting them with exaggerated sharpness. Let us suppose, then, that the concepts at issue are operational. *Even then*, any notion of sacrificing some utility for the sake of a more nearly equal distribution of what remained is very much open to question.

Although aggregate utility cannot be measured and is fuzzy even as a concept, clues to it and its distribution may be available. It is not nonsense to identify societies with greater or lesser inequalities in the distribution of happiness. It is not sheer nonsense to ask which is preferable – a society with a more nearly equal distribution but a lower overall level of utility (somehow roughly estimated) or a society with a more unequal distribution but a higher overall level. Attitudes on this question might be expressed in a social-welfare function (one more complicated than the one appearing in the Tom-and-Dick example above). Each person articulating his attitude might conceivably have a distinct social-welfare function of his own. (For reasons pertaining to value judgments and to conceptual difficulties of aggregation, there is no such thing as an objectively true social-welfare function belonging to society as a whole.)

To focus the issue of egalitarianism, let us imagine a society in which, all things considered, even including how the pattern of distribution itself affects individuals' utilities and disutilities, 99 members enjoy 50 utils each and the 100th member enjoys 80. To prefer a society in which the 99 members retain their 50 utils and the 100th has his utility chopped down to 55 is an extreme example of the egalitarian view.

John C. Harsanyi, 1994 Nobel laureate in economics, sees such a position as verging on faulty logic (1976, Chapter V, and others of his works listed in the References). The criterion of average (or total) utility already takes account of any nonproportionalities between individuals' utilities and their incomes or wealth. Their feelings about distribution are also reflected in their utilities. If people feel uncomfortable living in a society with a super-rich minority, then their discomfort is expressed in the lowness of their utilities, which holds down the average level; and that very criterion then speaks in favor of alternative social arrangements.

To insist on further egalitarianism in the social-welfare function would be to adjust twice, and illegitimately in Harsanyi's view, for feelings about inequality. In the example of reducing the utility level of society's most fortunate member without any gain in the utilities of the other members, the loss is just that, a loss. To vary the example slightly, suppose that *everyone's* utility is at least slightly higher in state A than in state B, although the distribution in A is much more unequal than in B. No unusual value judgments are needed to prefer state A, the Pareto-superior state (on the Pareto concepts, see Chapter 11). An observer preferring B on egalitarian grounds would be transcending the assessments of individuals themselves. After all, their assessments of the overall situation, including the inequality of distribution, are reflected in their utilities; and if everyone achieves higher utility in state A than in the more egalitarian state B, on what basis could an outside observer complain?

On our present assumptions, a util is a util. Attributing less significance to a util enjoyed by a fortunate person than to one enjoyed by an unfortunate person is either irrational or anti-individualistic. A social philosopher who insists on such a double adjustment and accordingly prefers the lower-utility state B to the Pareto-superior state A must be taking as his supreme criterion or ultimate moral value something other than the well-being experienced by individuals themselves; his egalitarianism must have an anti-individualistic basis.

Such a view might recommend allocating a scarce drug to a poor patient precisely because he is poor and unhappy rather than to a rich patient who would benefit more from it. The philosopher would be willing to sacrifice humanitarian considerations to his own egalitarian views. That is what it means to attribute diminishing marginal social significance to the utilities of persons.

Perhaps Harsanyi's objection to the extreme egalitarian position needs restating. Like Bentham and Edgeworth before him, Harsanyi has indeed written as if he envisaged measuring, comparing, and aggregating individual utilities. He offers what he calls "a modern restatement of Adam Smith's theory of an impartially sympathetic observer" (Harsanyi in Sen and Williams 1982, p. 46). He imagines social welfare to be a function – specifically, the arithmetic sum – of the utilities experienced by the individual members of society. Such exercises in exaggerated definiteness, involving measurable utilities and their entry into various social-welfare functions, may charitably be interpreted as heuristic devices for sharpening and examining vague intuitions. We all often make interpersonal comparisons in a rough and ready way. Harsanyi makes one when he judges which of two young boys would more enjoy a small present he happens to have with him. We need not reject such comparisons out of methodological purism.

Harsanyi challenges the notion of diminishing marginal welfare significance of individual utilities themselves, the notion that the higher a person's utility is, the less a unit of it counts socially. That notion, he maintains, makes an illegitimate *double* application of the postulate of diminishing marginal returns, which is already reflected in the individual marginal utilities. It makes sense to speak of diminishing marginal utility of income and wealth – of goods or money – but not of diminishing marginal utility or welfare significance of utility itself.

Harsanyi's is not the last word, however, on whether a util is simply a util and has the same social significance whether experienced by a happy or unhappy person. Questions arise, for example, about *risk* of winding up in fortunate or unfortunate social positions. James Sterba (1980, pp. 47–50) offers the example of persons behind Rawls's veil of ignorance (Rawls 1971; cf. Chapter 10 below) who expect equal chances of belonging to the Privileged Rich or to the Alienated Poor. Under social arrangement A, expected utilities are 55 for the Rich and 10 for the Poor, with an arithmetic mean of 32.5. Under arrangement B, expected utilities are 40 and 20, with a mean of only 30.

Sterba recognizes that the numbers are supposed to take the diminishing marginal utility of income or wealth already into account. (We might further stipulate that the utility consequences of the possible perceived unfairness of any redistributionary measures are also taken into account.) Yet, Sterba asks, might not people reasonably consider the chance of enjoying 55 utils under arrangement A rather than 40 utils under B insufficient to outweigh the danger of having only 10 utils rather than 20? Might it not be reasonable to play safe by choosing arrangement B despite its lower expected utility? Remember, a person is going to wind up definitely belonging either to the Rich or to the Poor and will never experience average utility. To choose according to the average-utility criterion, persons would have to think of themselves as destined to live, seriatim, integral parts of the lives of many randomly selected individuals. Curiously, they would think of themselves as parts of "average persons". Sterba's benevolent observer choosing in a detached mood imagines himself winding up in either the happy or the miserable class, with no chance of experiencing average utility. Sterba's emphasis on the unacceptable risk of winding up in the miserable class in higher-*average*-utility state A echoes John Rawls's (1971) maximin principle, which adopts the criterion not of average welfare but of the welfare of the worst-off class.

Still, Sterba may be committing the double-adjustment error that Harsanyi warned against. Like the random member of society in the examples just considered, the holder of a lottery ticket likewise does not experience the average of the possible utility outcomes; yet the average-utility criterion is standardly considered appropriate for choosing between alternative lottery tickets (Harsanyi 1976, pp. 72–5). As I read him, Harsanyi does say that it is irrational to prefer being a person selected at random in a society with lesser expected mean utility than being a person at random in an alternative society with a higher mean but also a greater dispersion of individual utilities. If the chooser would be unhappy about winding up as a disadvantaged person in a highly unequal society, then he already takes these feelings into account in assessing individual utility levels and their mean. He already discounts the higher individual utilities for the risk of not receiving them, much as one might discount future utilities against present ones because of their remoteness in time. The lowness of low utilities already takes full account of the danger of winding up with them, especially as items in a highly unequal distribution. Any further adjustment for risk would be an illogical double adjustment.

Again Harsanyi would emphasize just what utility means. It is the sort of thing of which more or less *means* better or worse for the affected persons. The utility function of each person in our examples already takes account of the diminishing marginal utility of income or wealth. Furthermore, it also takes account not only of risk and the individual's attitude toward it but also of the very pattern of distribution in society and of its fairness or unfairness as the individual perceives it. If hypothetical redistributionary measures achieve a pattern judged "fairer" by some external observer but also impose losses of utility on the losers exceeding gains to the gainers, a net loss of utility does occur, a loss of utility as perceived by individuals themselves. In Harsanyi's view, any basis for preferring the more egalitarian society with lower average utility would have to be an anti-individualistic basis transcending the assessments of society's individual members.

I have been summarizing Harsanyi's argument as I understand it. Admittedly, however, it might make sense to take an anti-individualistic standpoint and speak of the diminishing marginal *welfare significance* of utility. I confess to gnawing doubt. Is Harsanyi eliding some necessary distinction between the utilities of chances and chances of utilities? Does he commit an error in using the von Neumann–Morgenstern conception of measurable utility, which is defined in the context of decisions under risk, rather than a more traditional or intuitive conception? (On such technical issues, see Yeager 1988USWF.)

Whatever our judgment on such technical points, Harsanyi's heuristic exercises do not impose the goal of maximizing an actual social aggregate of individual utilities. Harsanyi presumably knows as well as anyone else that utility, by its very meaning, is something experienced only by individual persons, not by some sort of transcendent social entity. Treating individuals as mere means to maximizing a social aggregate would subvert the good society and so impair prospects for the happiness of individuals, whose happiness is the only kind available. No maximum social aggregate can be pursued directly. Attention must be paid, instead, to the institutions, practices, and character traits that make for a good society, one affording individuals the best prospects for making satisfying lives for themselves in association with their fellows. Anyway, however much (or little) utilitarians may learn from Harsanyi, they are not bound to take his views as defining their doctrine.

More broadly, it is irresponsible to rest content with mere intuitions about a social-welfare function and about possible tension between the level and distribution of happiness; it is irresponsible to rest content with mere abstract principles, such as John Rawls's (1971) "difference principle" of dominant concern for the least-well-off stratum of the population. Responsible advice presupposes inquiry into what institutions and policies would be required to carry one's intuitions or principles into practice. Philosophers, economists, and policymakers do not have any direct handle on social outcomes. The best they can do is recommend and carry out tinkering with the institutions and rules thought to affect outcomes (Vining 1984). Utilitarianism calls for comparative-institutional analysis.

Such analysis can conceivably prune away extreme versions of both egalitarianism and antiegalitarianism and so narrow the range of distributional principles, institutions, and policies left plausibly in the running. Never, I conjecture, will the time come when further factual and logical investigation proves utterly irrelevant to distributional issues and patently incapable of narrowing any remaining disagreement. The issue of average utility versus distribution of utilities dissolves, I conjecture, on a level of discourse concerned with actual institutions and ethical and other rules. Is it possible to specify a set of institutions and rules yielding greater average utility but a lesser degree of equality and an alternative set yielding a lower average level but a greater degree of equality? Arrangements aiming at or resulting in either extreme outcome, great inequality and near-equality alike, would presumably have adverse side effects on total and average utility levels and the level of the individual considered at random.

We can conceive, at one extreme, of a complete absence of redistributive measures (other perhaps than private charity) – or even of institutions and measures positively reinforcing inequalities due to heredity, inheritance, and luck. At the other extreme, we can conceive of drastically redistributionary policies. But plausible arguments suggest that either extreme would result in less utility, or less attractive prospects for average members and even for disadvantaged members of society, than some intermediate position. Such arguments would enlist facts and theory from various fields of knowledge, including psychology. Not only institutions and policies but also precepts and attitudes are relevant.

Similar comparisons could be made, if less unambiguously, between alternative policies ranked further from the extremes on the scale of redistributive ambition. We would never obtain all the detailed factual and theoretical knowledge necessary to judge that arrangements A would yield more utility more unequally distributed while arrangements B would yield less utility less unequally distributed. Further knowledge would always remain relevant to assessing the attractiveness of the contemplated society; and we would never, I conjecture, face having to make a sheer value judgment between utility and equality. The question of such a tradeoff, like some others in social philosophy, can appear to arise because we have not faced the prior question of in what *context* it would relate to a genuine issue.

Exercises in trying to conceive of total or average welfare or the welfare or utility of the person taken at random or of the least fortunate stratum of the population should make us all the more wary of trying to put those concepts to use in actual policymaking. Still more must we be wary of trying to maximize any such total or average or representative magnitude. Yet formulations mentioning such criteria can be useful for heuristic or expository purposes. Their critics surely are not advocating *less than* maximum welfare, however conceived. By the very meaning of welfare, it is almost tautologically true that less of it cannot be preferable to more.

SUMMARY REMARKS ON CRITICISMS CONSIDERED SO FAR

At their best, the critics are warning that the language of decision criteria and maximization may convey a false impression of what a good society is and how it might be sought. Such language risks directing attention to authorities and experts and diverting attention away from individuals pursuing their own goals. It risks displacing the question of what institutional framework is likely to be most conducive to individuals' successes in their own efforts. The warnings direct attention back to social cooperation. Judging what serves and what subverts it probably comes as close as is operationally possible to measuring effects on utility.

Even though some disagreement remains on distributional issues, within the range of plausibly defensible positions, a broad consensus can prevail on the basics of ethics and on the ethical principles guiding policy – so I conjecture. These include disapproval of lying, cheating, stealing, coercion, and murder; approval of honesty, courage, and sympathy; the principles underpinning legitimate government and political obligation; and support for private property and a market economy.

Utilitarianism is not defeated in favor of a rival theory, then, by its inability to prescribe all details of social organization, reaching even to the details of institutions and policies affecting the distributions of income, wealth, and happiness.

APPENDIX TO CHAPTER 6   HISTORICAL REFLECTIONS ON THE ISSUE OF AGGREGATION

Utilitarians Possibly Open to the Charge of Aggregation

Chapter 6 faced the charge that utilitarianism is an ominously aggregative doctrine. Why do critics persist in it? This appendix examines possible grounds for that charge and further answers it by reviewing some strands in the history of thought. Critics can indeed find excuses for linking some kinds of utilitarianism with some notion of maximizing an aggregate.

Jeremy Bentham

Jeremy Bentham sometimes did write as if he envisaged measuring, comparing, and aggregating individual utilities (see, for example, Bentham 1780, 1789, 1823/1948, esp. Chapter I, and 1973, esp. Chapter 14 and Appendix A). So did the nineteenth century economists Francis Y. Edgeworth (1881/1967)[5] and Henry Sidgwick (1907/1962, esp. Book II, Chapter I, and Book IV, Chapter I). Perhaps they meant that formulation literally. Perhaps they were only tamely if clumsily expressing the generalization principle, which rules out ethical precepts rigged to the special benefit of particular persons at the expense of others (see Chapter 9). Bentham himself saw difficulties with actual aggregation: "'Tis in vain to talk of adding quantities which after the addition will continue distinct as they were before, one man's happiness will never be another man's happiness: a gain to one is no gain to another: you might as well pretend to add twenty apples to twenty pears" (manuscript quoted in Halévy 1951/1966, p. 495; also quoted in Arrow 1963, p. 11n., from Mitchell 1937, p. 184). Bentham went on to call this "addibility" of the happiness of different subjects ... fictitious", although it is a successful because (presumably) heuristic fiction.

Anyway, it seems odd to take Bentham as the very prototype of a utilitarian philosopher. "Bentham's taste lay rather in the direction of jurisprudential than of properly ethical inquiry" (Mill 1838/1968, p. 38; Mill even goes on to regret the publication of Bentham's *Deontology*).

Thomas Hobbes

Do notions of aggregation pervade utilitarian writings to the extent of actually defining the doctrine? Not the writings of Thomas Hobbes, whom numerous historians of thought recognize as an early or proto utilitarian. Catlin (1939) calls him "the father of utilitarianism" (p. 236); "Hobbes and [John] Selden are the first Utilitarians" (p. 242); "Of the Utilitarian philosophy, Hobbes ... is an historical pioneer" (p. 245); "Through Helvetius and Bentham, the Hobbesian ethic, reclothed and sobered but still the same, logical, militant, returned in triumph" (p. 349).

Hobbes's fictions of the state of nature and the social contract are not the core of his doctrine. He does introduce the supposed contract as an expository device for dramatizing the great utility of acquiescing in government and political obligation to overcome the horrors of anarchy and of war of all against all (1651; see Chapter 11 below). Before introducing that fiction, however, he states what he calls "laws of nature". These moral laws recommend a disposition to seek peace when it is attainable, an accommodating nature, gratitude and forgiveness, fairness in dealing with others, forbearance from claiming special privilege, performance of covenants, and the like. Morality thus comes first in Hobbes. It consists of dispositions and behavior conducive to "peace and security" – social cooperation, in modern terms – which in turn is prerequisite to "commodious living". Hobbes was impressed by the benefits of "art, commerce, civilisation and culture which can exist only in conditions of peace". His thesis was "that peace and security, and hence the conditions necessary for the establishment of peace and security, are the all-important ends of human conduct, and the basis on which moral and political philosophy must be constructed" (Kemp 1970, pp. 24–5).

David Boonin-Vail (1994) interprets Hobbes similarly. Drawing on many of his writings and not only the best known few, Boonin-Vail makes a powerful case against Hobbes's standard reputation as a moral nihilist. Hobbes did not judge all kinds of behavior, including even predation, equally legitimate in the state of nature. He believed that even in this imaginary state without government or positive law, certain "laws of nature", although not laws in the strict legal sense, do hold. These precepts call for seeking peace and fulfilling covenants and cooperating with people who do likewise, as well as gratitude and "compleasance" (sociability, or a spirit of accommodation). Even the sovereign, once one is instituted, ought to obey the moral law (even though, perhaps, his subjects ought ordinarily to obey his edicts because their obedience is conducive to peace and security). Hobbes recommended not so much moral acts or even moral rules as, rather, habits, character traits, and dispositions conducive to smooth interpersonal relations, peace, security, and commodious living. "Hobbes insists throughout his normative writings on the existence of the just man who is motivated to do the right thing not because it serves his interests or because it serves the interests of others, but simply because it is right" (Boonin-Vail 1994, p. 46). "In Hobbes's account of virtue ... the disposition of the just person is not simply a disposition to do just acts; it is also a disposition to enjoy doing them" (p. 184).

Is it irrational rule worship for a person to forgo a gain available from violating a moral rule with impunity? No, not for Hobbes: a just person acts from a settled disposition that maximizes his prospects for security. Hobbes's approach recognizes, however, that being a virtuous person is neither a necessary nor a sufficient condition for personal success. A villain might prosper; a virtuous person could lead a miserable life. Still, the person who cultivates the virtues reduces his chances of failing to flourish (Boonin-Vail 1994, pp. 200–201; cf. the position of Moritz Schlick, reviewed in Chapter 8). Hobbes held that "the reasons of Justice and other Moral Vertues, are ... ultimately to be resolv'd into that natural support and advantage they bring to a Society and Commonwealth" (James Lowde, *Discourse Concerning the Nature of Man*, 1694, quoted by Boonin-Vail, p. 107n.). Thus, Hobbes's ethics, focusing on the requirements of social cooperation, is an indirect utilitarianism (although neither he nor Boonin-Vail uses these particular terms). Nowhere does Hobbes imagine any direct pursuit of maximum aggregate utility.

David Hume

Several historians of thought forthrightly classify David Hume as a utilitarian. "Utility is central to [his] philosophy", writes George Catlin (1939, p. 349). Hume "is the philosophic initiator, if not the popular founder, of Utilitarianism as a system" (p. 351). On whose happiness should count in guiding conduct and framing institutions, Jeremy Bentham credited Hume's *Treatise on Human Nature* with causing "the scales to fall from my eyes" (quoted by Catlin, p. 368). Bentham also credited Hume with the insight that "the foundations of all *virtue* are laid in utility" (*A Fragment on Government*, Chapter I, para. XXXVI, quoted in Flew 1986, p. 157). "Hume is not restricted to any narrowly utilitarian view of morality; for his 'utility' means usefulness for any desired end or purpose, not just usefulness for the purpose of producing pleasure and reducing or preventing pain" (Kemp 1970, p. 45). In speaking of utility Hume "did not have in mind a simple maximizing structure with a clearly defined maximand" (Simmonds 1987, p. 603).

Hume's "critique" of natural law, according to N.E. Simmonds, removes the deontological framework and leaves only utilitarian arguments. Hume removed God from the picture and used arguments of "convenience" or utility to justify rules of justice and property (Simmonds 1987, p. 603). Hume finds the key to describing and explaining men's actual moral judgments "in the basic facts of human nature, not in the supernatural realms of theology nor in the *a priori* categories of rationally determined fitnesses and unfitnesses of things" (Kemp 1970, pp. 51–2).

F.A. Hayek called Hume "perhaps the greatest of all modern students of mind and society" (1978, p. 264). "Utilitarianism appears in its first and legitimate form" in his work (Hayek 1967, p. 88).[6] Hume "insisted that the obedience to moral and legal rules which nobody had invented or designed for that purpose was essential for the successful pursuit of men's aims in society". Certain abstract rules prevailed because groups heeding them flourished as a result. Hume stressed the superiority of an order that results when each member obeys the same abstract rules, even without understanding their rationale, instead of deciding on each individual action by explicitly considering its own likely consequences. "Hume is not concerned with any recognizable utility of the particular action, but only with the utility of a universal application of certain abstract rules" (Hayek 1967, p. 88).

Hayek approvingly quotes another historian of thought to the effect that Hume attributed standards of morality and justice to the practical experience of mankind (1960, p. 436, n. 37, quoting C. Bay, *The Structure of Freedom*, 1958, p. 33). The slow test of time assesses the utility of each moral rule in promoting human welfare. Hume in effect envisaged a tendency toward survival of the fittest among human conventions – fittest for serving social utility.

Henry Hazlitt, an avowed utilitarian, calls Hume "probably the greatest of British philosophers" and the greatest of the British utilitarians from whom he has learned most, running from Hume through Adam Smith, Bentham, Mill, and Sidgwick. Strangely, Hazlitt continues, Hume's "insistence on the utility of acting strictly in accordance with general rules was ... overlooked by nearly all of his classical Utilitarian successors". Anyway, "Much of what is best in both Adam Smith and Bentham seems little more than an elaboration of ideas first clearly stated by Hume" (Hazlitt 1964, pp. viii, 53). (On Hume as discoverer of the principle of utility and on his influence on later utilitarians, also see Halévy 1955/1966, esp. pp. 11–18, 22, 33, 46, 52, 130–32, 142, 197, 201, 205.)

The economist Eugene Rotwein reads Hume's essay "Of refinement in the arts" (reprinted in Rotwein 1955/1970) as justifying a commercial and industrial society on ultimate moral grounds. He drew on "the utilitarian ethic – a position which he himself had expounded and defended in his philosophical analysis". He regarded desires for consumption, for interesting activity, and for liveliness "as major ingredients of the happiness of the individual" (Rotwein 1987, 694–5). Particularly in "The stoic" (reprinted in Miller 1985), "Hume had in mind the value that is now generally stressed in justifying a free society – the striving for self-fulfillment" (Rotwein 1968, p. 549).

Rotwein quotes and paraphrases many of Hume's references to human welfare and well-being, individual happiness, attaining happiness, utility, public utility, "felicity", "virtue and happiness", and the "pursuit of happiness". Denying that "love of virtue" is irreducible, Hume "argues that all moral judgment ultimately rests on utility considerations" (Rotwein

1955/1970, Chapter IV; quotations from pp. xciii and ci, note, citing Hume's *Treatise*, pp. 478–80).

Hume explained moral rules and practices by their utility: "The rules of equity and justice owe their origin and existence to the utility which results to the public from their strict and regular observance. ... Common interest and utility beget infallibly a standard of right and wrong among the parties concerned" (*Enquiry*, quoted in Mackie 1984, p. 98). Later Hume supplemented this explanation with hints, at least, about conventions produced by social as well as biological evolution that help resolve coordination problems and problems of partial conflict of interest. The internalization of rules of behavior then turned conventions into norms (Hume's *Treatise*, cited by Mackie 1984, p. 99, who also cites his own 1980, Chapters 6 and 9).

Hayek (1976, p. 166, n. 18) approvingly quotes Hume's *Enquiry Concerning the Principles of Morals* (1751/1777/1930, pp. 148–9):

> Public utility requires, that property should be regulated by general inflexible rules; and though such rules are adopted as best serve the same end of public utility, it is impossible for them to prevent all particular hardships, or make beneficial consequences flow from every individual case. It is sufficient, if the whole plan or scheme be necessary for the support of civil society, and if the balance of good, in the main, do thereby preponderate much above that of evil.

With regard to property and contract, Hume discerns "*three fundamental laws of nature, that of the stability of possession, of its transference by consent*, and *of the performance of promises*" (Hume 1739–40/1961, p. 467). Antony Flew (1986, p. 164) recognizes Hume's case for these principles as unequivocally utilitarian. Property transfer by consent is of "plain utility and interest" (Hume 1739–40/1961, pp. 457–9). "[T]he obligation of promises" facilitates contracts in which the parties' performances cannot be simultaneous. Hume continues speaking of "the necessities and interests of society", "public interest", "self-interested commerce of men", "mutual advantage", "consequences and advantages", "the convenience of society", and "public interest and convenience" (1739–40/1961, pp. 459–67). "'Tis on the strict observance of those three laws, that the peace and security of human society entirely depend" (1739–40/1961, p. 467, here as quoted by Flew, p. 164).

The *Treatise of Human Nature* is full of passages in which Hume rejects trying to assess consequences of decisions and their desirability case by case and instead recognizes the utility of almost inflexibly applying rules, practices, and institutions that facilitate social cooperation. He also emphasizes that whether a person is virtuous or vicious hinges on his qualities of mind or character, on his intentions or motives. (Pitson 1989 cites such passages in

Hume's writings and, although without using the term, practically credits him with indirect utilitarianism.)[7]

While looking like agreed conventions, these rules, practices, and institutions have not in general resulted from actual agreement. "[T]he rule concerning the stability of possessions ... arises gradually, and acquires force by a slow progression, and by our repeated experience of the inconveniences of transgressing it" (1739–40/1961, p. 442). Hume thus anticipates the results, for example, of Axelrod (1984) and Gauthier (1986) (reviewed in Chapter 8). He goes on to cite the gradual evolution of languages and money also.

Hume's nonaggregative utilitarianism is evident when he explains the utility of firm application of rules of justice, even though the consequences might be regrettable in special cases. The whole system of rules

> is highly conducive, or indeed absolutely requisite, both to the support of society, and the well-being of every individual. ... Property must be stable, and must be fixed by general rules. Though in one instance the public be a sufferer, this momentary ill is amply compensated by the steady prosecution of the rule, and by the peace and order which it establishes in society. And even every individual person must find himself a gainer on balancing the account; since, without justice, society must immediately dissolve, and every one must fall into that savage and solitary condition, which is infinitely worse than the worst situation that can possibly be supposed in society. ... [T]he whole system of actions concurred in by the whole society, is infinitely advantageous to the whole (Hume 1739–40/1961, p. 448).

Adam Smith

One might plausibly argue that Adam Smith's *Theory of Moral Sentiments* (1759/1976), with its emphasis on sympathy (reminiscent of Hume), reconciles nicely with utilitarianism. Since Smith is not usually classified as a utilitarian, however, I will devote little space to defending him against the charge of aggregation, except to mention his concept of the impartial benevolent spectator. The judgments of this imaginary personage serve as a surrogate criterion of morality. Smith's spectator may be interpreted as a device for putting the social philosopher, and possibly an acting individual, into a detached mood of moral reflection. So may John Rawls's device of original position and veil of ignorance (see Chapter 10 below), even though Rawls himself does not see this similarity and even mistakenly suggests (1971, pp. 184–8) that Smith's device implies conceiving of some single individual or committee trying to maximize some well-defined social goal.

John Stuart Mill

John Stuart Mill's understanding of utilitarianism, already introduced in Chapter 4, deserves special weight. Although Jeremy Bentham had apparently coined the word, Mill popularized it after finding it, as he said, in a novel by John Galt. He established the Utilitarian Society in 1822-23 and later entitled a book *Utilitarianism* (Mill 1863/1968, pp. 248-9n.; Anschutz 1981, p. 197).

H.L.A. Hart (1983) apparently dissents from the interpretation of Mill as an indirect utilitarian. With a sweeping reference to "classical maximizing utilitarianism", Hart cites Mill along with Bentham on the principle of counting everybody for one and nobody for more than one, but he names no contemporary or recent writer open to his criticisms. He does recognize (pp. 17, 188-9, 192-3) that Mill tried (in *Utilitarianism* and *On Liberty*) to reconcile respect for fundamental rights with utilitarian political morality. Mill sought a utilitarian grounding for justice, respect for individual rights, and protection of the freedom and basic interests of individuals. Yet despite Mill, says Hart, an unbridgeable gap remains between maximizing aggregate welfare and recognizing the rights of individuals as constraints on the maximizing aggregative principle.

Hart may find Mill's arguments inadequate, but their inadequacy would not make Mill a maximizing utilitarian of the sort he criticizes. He practically says so in recognizing that "[g]eneral utility" plays no operative part in Mill's construction and that Mill's arguments rest ultimately "on a specific conception of the human person and of what is needed for the exercise and development of distinctive human powers" (p. 17). Hart comes close to suggesting that if Mill is not open to the standard criticisms of utilitarianism, he is not really a utilitarian. Yet Mill's concern for "what is needed for the exercise and development of distinctive human powers" is indeed a utilitarian concern, though not of the straw-man variety.

Admittedly, Mill does make some stray apparent allusions to aggregating utilities. The utilitarian standard "is not the agent's own greatest happiness, but the greatest amount of happiness altogether" (*Utilitarianism*, Chapter II, 1968 edition, p. 253). "As between his own happiness and that of others, utilitarianism requires him to be as strictly impartial as a disinterested and benevolent spectator" (p. 258). According to the "Greatest Happiness Principle", one person's happiness counts for exactly as much as another's (Chapter V, p. 302). Mill does not actually call for aggregation, however, or say how it might be accomplished. His remarks perhaps just awkwardly express the generalization principle (discussed in Chapter 9 below).

Mill's emphasis on rules, sentiment, dispositions, and character traits further helps show that he envisions no actual exercise in aggregation. His Principle of Liberty, although defended in utilitarian terms, is a utility-barring principle that attaches rights to individuals and says nothing about maximizing or even promoting any particular value (Gray 1983, pp. 7-8). Further evidence against a maximizing conception is Mill's prizing of individuality and even eccentricity (notably in *On Liberty*). For an adult of sound mind, happiness is served by autonomy – taking responsibility for one's own life and character and being able to formulate and pursue one's own projects (cf. Gray 1983, Chapter IV). Evidently referring to the happiness of an individual person, Mill observed that "The ingredients of happiness are very various, and each of them is desirable in itself, and not merely when considered as swelling an aggregate" (*Utilitarianism*, Chapter IV, 1968 edition, p. 277).

Now if Mill thus disavows aggregation even for an individual, would he not all the more disavow aggregation of the happinesses of different individuals? Ordinarily the person need not concern himself with promoting "the good of the world" (made up of the good of individuals); it suffices that he take care not to violate "the rights, that is the legitimate and authorized expectations, of anyone else" (*Utilitarianism*, Chapter II, 1968 edition, p. 260).

Mill's conception of utilitarianism further appears in his essay on Bentham (1838/1968, esp. pp. 37, 51–3). Bentham, he said, did not appreciate the "generalities contain[ing] the whole unanalyzed experience of the human race"; he did not see that happiness is "much too complex and indefinite an end to be sought except through the medium of various secondary ends"; he gave inadequate attention to the formation of one's own character and will and to how actions affect one's frame of mind; he did not understand the legitimacy of appraising people's tastes.

Mill brought murder into a discussion of what we would nowadays call act versus rules utilitarianism. There are many persons whose murder would be greatly beneficial. "The counter-consideration, on the principle of utility, is, that unless persons were punished for killing, and taught not to kill; that if it were thought allowable for any one to put to death at pleasure any human being whom he believes that the world would be well rid of, nobody's life would be safe." The mischief from violating a rule will generally far outweigh any good expected from the individual act – "generally, not universally; for the admission of exceptions to rules is a necessity equally felt in all systems of morality" (Mill on Whewell in Ryan 1987, pp. 246–7).

Critics have alleged an inconsistency between Mill's utilitarianism and his insistence (in *On Liberty*) on the "one very simple principle" of liberty. How can happiness really be the criterion if the principle of liberty sweepingly restricts its application? Hasn't Mill fallen into a sentimental muddle?

No; John Gray (1983) finds no contradiction. Far from being an act utilitarian, Mill believed that direct appeals to utility to settle practical questions are self-defeating. He gave reasons "partly by reference to the distinctive characteristics of human happiness and partly by claims about the necessary conditions of stable social co-operation" (Gray 1983, pp. 46–7). Consequently, "a utilitarian may have reason to act on a secondary maxim", even when, paradoxically, "doing so appears to result in a loss of achievable happiness". "[S]econdary maxims – precepts distinct from utility and having implications other than those resulting from a straightforward calculation of consequences – are not just helpful but actually indispensable to the utilitarian's practical life" (Gray 1983, p. 13). Mill emphasized reasons for following general rules, especially of justice. Mill's doctrine has at least two distinctive features: (1) neither the general happiness nor the agent's own happiness is the object of direct pursuit; and (2) utility, in conjunction with its action-guiding corollary, expediency, serves as a principle of evaluating whole systems of precepts of art. Mill viewed morality as a social instrument for coordinating human activities (Gray 1983, pp. 38–9). He thought that "The larger part of any moral code has to do, not with the institution or enforcement of social rules, but with the inculcation of sentiments and attitudes and the instilling of dispositions and inclinations" (Gray 1983, pp. 31–2).

Mill's utilitarian argument for the moral right to liberty rests on three claims. First, the direct pursuit of happiness is self-defeating. Second, persons derive satisfaction from autonomous thought and action and from exercising individuality. Third, a liberal social order affords persons wide opportunities to develop their powers and discover indefinitely many forms of happiness (Gray 1983, pp. 15–16).

In both *Utilitarianism* and *On Liberty* Mill in effect argues that utility itself demands the adoption of weighty side-constraints to protect rights (Gray 1983, pp. 59–60). Mill sought to give respect for moral rights a utilitarian grounding (this seems to be a leading theme of Gray's book). In Mill's view, "a higher maximum of utility is attainable in a world where policy is bounded by the constraint of the Principle of Liberty than could be attained by the direct and unconstrained pursuit of utility" (Gray 1983, p. 65).

Herbert Spencer

Herbert Spencer (1897 and earlier, reprinted 1978) espoused what he called "rational utilitarianism", evidently akin to the rules or indirect version; and he distinguished it from what he called Bentham's "empirical utilitarianism". He emphasized social cooperation, occasionally employing that very term. (On his not being a social Darwinian as usually criticized, recall the observations about him and Darwin in Chapter 3 above.) Spencer saw unacceptable implications in Bentham's supposed view that the legislature should aim directly at the greatest happiness of the greatest number. Rational utilitarianism, instead of taking happiness as the immediate object of pursuit, urges conformity to the principles and cultivation of the conditions necessary for attaining happiness (Vol. I, pp. 194–200, Vol. II, p. 260 in particular). Deploying insights expressed earlier by Hume and Adam Ferguson and developed later by Hayek, Spencer recognized that useful institutions and ethical and other rules have to a large extent evolved gradually through a kind of unplanned cultural selection.

No tenable ethical doctrine, Spencer insisted, can rest on some ultimate criterion contradictory of happiness or conduciveness to it. (Like Mill, he identified even Kant as a crypto-utilitarian; Vol. II, p. 68.) He subjected purportedly antiutilitarian doctrines to a *reductio ad absurdum*. The intuitionist school "teaches that courses recognized by moral intuition as right, must be pursued without regard to consequences. But on inquiry it turns out that the consequences to be disregarded are particular consequences and not general consequences" (Vol. I, p. 89). Conduct counts as good or bad according as its consequences for oneself or others are pleasurable or painful; pairing the words in the opposite way would be absurd. Whether perfection of nature or virtuousness of action or rectitude of motive is adopted as the supposed standard, it must ultimately appeal to happiness experienced in some form, at some time, by some person. Even persons suffering pains or forgoing pleasures to propitiate God do so to escape greater pains or receive greater pleasures ultimately. They would no longer hold some action a duty if performing it promised not eternal happiness but eternal misery. Any persons thinking they ought to be unhappy to gratify their creator must still envisage a utilitarian standard or end, "the pleasure of their diabolical god". "Pleasure somewhere, at some time, to some being or beings, is an inexpugnable element" of an ultimate moral aim (Vol. I, pp. 79–80).

Contemporary Utilitarians

As for contemporary utilitarian economists and philosophers, none known to me is guilty of what critics parroting one another sweepingly allege. None recommends the actual pursuit of maximum aggregate utility, supposed to be measurable, and countenances sacrificing individuals and their interests and denying or overriding their rights for the sake of such an aggregate. (Only on one possible but questionable interpretation of his heuristic exercises, reviewed in Chapter 6, is John C. Harsanyi an exception.) None regards individuals as mere processing stations for converting goods and experiences into contributions to social utility. The history of philosophical thought provides scant warrant for trying to foist such an interpretation onto utilitarianism in general. Such an interpetation simply does not fit the indirect utilitarianism of, say, Hume, Mill, Mises, Hazlitt, and their intellectual heirs.

NOTES

1. Here Sen and Williams cite Rawls (1971) as a fellow critic of utilitarianism.
2. The example also introduces the concept of a social-welfare function (SWF), a heuristic or

expository device that is fairly common in the literature of welfare economics and that will appear again below. An SWF represents some indicator of social welfare as a mathematical function of various arguments, notably, the utility levels of members of the society.

3. Having to decide on abortion in such a case is tragic. It is all too easy to settle the issue with reference to a right of the deformed unborn child not to be discriminated against. But whose interest does such a remark serve – that of the facile moralizer, who may enjoy a cheap feeling of nobleness, or that of the child, who, by hypothesis, will have a painful existence thrust upon him? There is no way to leave the decision to the unborn child himself. The prospective parents, duly counseled, cannot shed their moral responsibility for the decision.

Philosophical discussions may properly take into account the likely further consequences of acceptance of abortion in such cases, including the possible stretching and extension of the doctrine.

4. Objections are sometimes raised to the very word "distribution" in contexts like this one. It allegedly reflects or promotes a collectivist mindset. The word derives from *dis-*, apart, and *tribuere*, to allot or grant. It calls to mind some person or authority parceling out a stock of good things. The question then arises whether the parceling out was done properly – whether the process or its result was fair. If it was unfair, perhaps the process should be redone or its result modified: *re*distribution is in order.

Typically, however, the pattern of how much wealth or income or utility each person enjoys is *not* the result of a distribution in any such literal sense. Instead, the pattern is the unintended result of innumerable decentralized physical, biological, and economic conditions and processes. It is far from clear what it might mean to say that the combination of all those processes has gone wrong and should be rectified by a redistribution. (I do not flatly deny, however, that if the spontaneous pattern were deemed clearly unsatisfactory and if some authority, say the government, could assuredly remedy it without unacceptable side effects, then setting the remedy nevertheless aside might in some sense be called unfair or unjust. Nor do I mean flatly to reject any social safety net for the most unfortunate members of society.)

Although the words "distribution" and "redistribution" are open to the objections just mentioned, they are too deeply entrenched and too convenient for me to take pains trying to paraphrase them away.

5. Edgeworth called the central conception of his utilitarian calculus "the greatest possible sum-total of pleasure summed through all time and over all sentience" (1881/1967, p. vii). "[T]he pure Utilitarian, ... admitting no ultimate ground of preference but *quantity of pleasure*, 'takes every creature in and every kind,' and 'sees with equal eye,' though he sees to be unequal, the happiness of every sentient in every stage of evolution" (p. 131). Utilitarianism for him connotes *Vivre pour autrui* (p. 136), implying extreme altruism.

6. Was Hayek, winner of the 1974 Nobel prize for economics, a utilitarian himself? He did come to reject that label (see, for example, Hayek 1994, p. 140), apparently because he pretty much identified utilitarianism with its Benthamite version. Nevertheless, a strong argument can be made ("Walker 1906, Yeager 1984) that Hayek was indeed an indirect utilitarian in substance if not by label. Marlo Lewis (1985), apparently from an intuitionist point of view, actually criticizes Hayek for being a utilitarian.

7. Several passages from *An Enquiry Concerning the Principles of Morals* (Hume 1751/1777/1930) further document Hume's indirect utilitarianism (page numbers below refer to the 1930 edition).

Any "humane, beneficent man" is praised for "the happiness and satisfaction, derived to society from his intercourse and good offices" (p. 10). "[T]he sentiment of benevolence [derives] ... part, at least, of its merit ... from its tendency to promote the interests of our species, and bestow happiness on human society. ... The happiness of mankind, the order of society, the harmony of families, the mutual support of friends" owe themselves to the social virtues (p. 14).

"[E]verything which promotes the interest of society must communicate pleasure, and what is pernicious give uneasiness" (p. 67). "[W]hatever conduct promotes the good of the community is loved, praised, and esteemed by the community, on account of that utility and interest, of which every one partakes" (p. 79).

"[E]verything, which contributes to the happiness of society, recommends itself directly to our approbation and good-will. Here is a principle, which accounts, in great part, for the origin of morality" (p. 54). "In all determinations of morality ... public utility is ever principally in view... ." Disputes over duty "cannot, by any means, be decided with greater certainty, than by ascertaining, on any side, the true interests of mankind" (pp. 12–13).

Hume traces the concept of justice to "public utility" and "the beneficial consequences of this virtue" (p. 15). The sole foundation for the virtue of justice is its necessity for the support of society. "[S]ince no moral excellence is more highly esteemed, we may conclude that this circumstance of usefulness has, in general, the strongest energy and most entire command over our sentiments" (pp. 37–38). Even in daily life we appeal to "the principle of public utility", asking, "What must become of the world, if such practices prevail? How could society subsist under such disorders?" How could private property ("the distinction or separation of possessions") have arisen if it had been entirely useless? (p. 37).

7. Is utilitarianism immoral?

UNWORTHY PLEASURES AND SCHADENFREUDE

Critics charge utilitarianism not only with pernicious aggregation but also with miscellaneous immoralities. Rolf Sartorius sees three "central and unanswerable" objections to "any form" of utilitarian theory (1984, p. 197). His making them is remarkable because he had published an eminently sensible book on utilitarianism in 1975. His first objection is familiar: utilitarianism aims at maximizing an aggregate measure "totally insensitive to distributional considerations except insofar as they are causally relevant". Second, it takes all sources of dissatisfaction and satisfaction at face value, including both envy and "what Bentham without any apparent embarrassment described as 'pleasures of malevolence.'" Third, it reduces all moral considerations "to one common dimension such as preference-satisfaction or happiness in the sense that Bentham understood it". It does not distinguish between urgent objective needs and strong subjective preferences and does not recognize that family members have any greater claim on a person's property than strangers in equal need.

Although applying his charges to all forms of utilitarianism, Sartorius specifically cites no writer here other than Bentham (1789/1948, p. 36). He says that all utilitarians conceive of happiness as Bentham did, even though John Stuart Mill provides an obvious counterexample (recall Chapter 4 and the appendix to Chapter 6). Sartorius's sweeping charges exemplify the familiar error of defining utilitarianism by some of the worst strands of its worst versions.

Sartorius's second charge invites elaboration. Nicholas Rescher had already made it in 1975, also failing to name specific guilty utilitarians. Rescher noted paradoxes arising from interdependent utility functions – from people's feelings toward one another of sympathy or of antipathy, including envy and Schadenfreude. Sympathy with each other's miseries compounds unhappiness felt directly. If, conversely, unhappy people reap malicious pleasure from each other's miseries, then this second-order effect would count as reducing total unhappiness. In its handling of such "vicarious affects" [sic], Rescher maintains, utilitarianism does not properly value sympathy and deplore malice. More generally, it does not adequately recognize that people's attitudes and preferences, instead of being sacrosanct, are themselves properly open to ethical appraisal (Rescher 1975, Chapter 5).

Bernard Williams similarly accuses utilitarianism of trading on the illusion that preferences are already given and that the social decision process just follows them. Yet there is no such thing as just following; to "follow" preferences is to endorse them, at least tacitly. People's preferences hinge partly on their expectations, which in turn hinge partly on what government does (Williams 1973ACU, pp. 147–9). Probably for reasons like these, Samuel Brittan (1983) says that utilitarians should qualify their doctrine to rule out counting satisfactions gained from envy and malice.

But why speak of qualifications? A social-science-oriented utilitarianism already recognizes that people's character traits, attitudes, and tastes intertwine with the characteristics of their society. Emphasis on social cooperation implies taking this interpenetration seriously. Only in certain contexts, as in textbook exercises in microeconomic theory, are consumers' tastes properly taken as given and not subject to second-guessing. A society that regards tastes for Schadenfreude as just as worthy of satisfaction as any other tastes thereby tends to damage the characters of its members in their formative years. Even though catering to envy and Schadenfreude might (just conceivably) appear to contribute to some persons' happiness in narrow and short-run contexts, institutions and policies according respect to such feelings will impair people's capacities for happiness, at least broadly and in the long run. The sympathy valued by Hume and Adam Smith may well contribute more to happiness considered broadly and in the long run than it might appear to contribute in immediate contexts. At issue here are researchable matters of fact, on which I might be wrong. Anyway, utilitarianism is empirically oriented and simply does not require taking tastes as given and exempt from critical examination (Yeager 1978).

Assessing a supposed counterexample to utilitarianism will amplify these points. (Moore 1903/1960, pp. 209–10, alludes, rather abstractly, to an example of this kind; compare comments by Smart 1961/1973, pp. 25–6.) Mr A would relish gloating over an enemy's misfortune, which in fact has occurred. Is it desirable that A should learn about it and reap his enjoyment? One might answer "no" on the grounds that A's malicious pleasure will impair his character and his capacity for future enjoyment, or that it will worsen the tone of society. A is about to die, however, so harm to his character is irrelevant. Furthermore, no one else will learn of his malicious pleasure. Wouldn't his having it then add to the sum total of happiness?

In what real-world context, however, could such a question arise? Who would be asked whether A's Schadenfreude would be a good thing? What difference for anyone's action could the answer make? To approve or disapprove of A's malicious pleasure, we would have to know of it. Wouldn't our approving of it, if we did, tend to impair our own characters and capacities for satisfaction? Stipulations detailed enough to outflank even considerations like these would make the example far-fetched indeed.

Why do we disapprove of someone's malicious pleasure even when it is not offset by less pleasure or more suffering for anyone else and so does, by stipulation, add to net total pleasure? The reason probably is that we cannot bring ourselves fully to imagine the peculiar circumstances postulated. Our ethical judgments involve estimates or intuitions of how acts and attitudes generally tend to work out in the world we live in. We cannot force ourselves to consider each individual case in complete isolation from others. We can hardly help thinking that in general and on average, a readiness to take pleasure in others' misfortunes will promote misfortune. (For example, such an attitude may lead a person to pass up even otherwise-almost-costless opportunities to lessen the misfortunes of others.) In any case except one specially cooked up to rule out the point's relevance, harboring and gratifying such an attitude will probably tend to impair the person's capacity for pleasure over the long run, assuming, with Schlick (see Chapter 8) that cultivation of the social impulses generally conduces to happiness.[1]

Here we have been harking back to our distinction between act utilitarianism and rules or indirect utilitarianism. It would be an either vacuous or downright unacceptable ethical code that prescribed, in each individual case considered by itself, whatever actions seemed to promise the best results on the whole. An ethical code hardly counts as a *code* unless it prescribes, instead, general rules of behavior, principles of character development, and criteria for appraising institutions and choosing policies. Rules or indirect utilitarianism does not recommend the actions, types of character, and institutions and policies that give ample scope to Schadenfreude. Positive analysis, psychological and other, suggests that such behavior, character types, and institutions and policies would give an unhealthy tone to society and be subversive of happiness on the whole.

Rescher (1975, Chapter 5) more or less recognizes that utilitarians may adopt a defense like the one just sketched out, but he dismisses it as an unworthy, *ad hoc* maneuver suggesting how feeble the utilitarian position is in the first place. Yet despite Rescher, the world is a complicated place; and what contributes to and what detracts from happiness cannot be described in a few simple and obvious propositions. Utilitarianism invokes social science and psychology to compare how well alternative sets of institutions and practices function. Well, science is neither guaranteed to be easy nor refuted if it is not.

ESOTERIC MORALITY

Commenting on the act utilitarianism of J.J.C. Smart in particular, Bernard

Williams objects that such a theory lacks openness as a practice. It would in some degree cease to work if the practice were openly known in society. Williams goes on to hint at manipulation by a utilitarian elite (Williams 1973ACU, pp. 123-4, 139; cf. Williams 1972/1993, p. 98). On utilitarian principles, as Henry Sidgwick similarly interpreted them, it may occasionally be right to do and privately recommend, or recommend to a particular set of persons, what it would not be right to advocate openly. Yet the plain man repudiates esoteric morality, agreeing that secrecy does not make an action good that would be bad if done openly. Utilitarianism seems to recommend secrecy even for the opinion itself that secrecy may render an otherwise bad action right; the doctrine that esoteric morality is expedient should itself be kept esoteric (Sidgwick 1907/1962, pp. 489-90, with the qualification that these perplexities and paradoxes vanish in an ideal community of enlightened utilitarians).

Yet utilitarianism does not require secrecy to be workable. Adherence to moral principles is bolstered, if anything, by general understanding of their basis and benefits. For ease of understanding or teaching or for some other convenience, one might wish that the truth on some topic were other than what it is in fact. The truth nevertheless remains what it is, and one only impairs its ultimate persuasive force by offering a supposedly more convenient substitute. Admittedly, though, tough cases may arise in which pertinent rules clash and no particular action is unequivocally best. In a rare instance of such a case, it may even be least bad to take or recommend an action without openly justifying it. But this consideration in no way discredits utilitarianism in favor of some rival ethical doctrine. Incidentally, an action taken openly and the otherwise same action taken secretly are different actions, at least in some contexts; it is not as if secrecy makes good a specific action that would otherwise be bad.

UNCONSCIONABLE ACTS

Philippa Foot (1988) sees utilitarianism and morality as almost at loggerheads. Most versions of utilitarianism, she says, combine consequentialism with welfarism. Consequentialism appraises an action and its consequences together. Welfarism employs some criterion such as pleasure, happiness, or satisfaction of desires. Although mentioning familiar criticisms concerning the distribution of welfare and the pleasures of malice, Foot focuses on the consequentialist aspect (1988, esp. pp. 224-6). Writing in the same volume, Samuel Scheffler (1988, pp. 243-60) allies himself with her attack.

Consequentialists, say Foot and Scheffler, see a good outcome as the goal of decisions and actions and so make benevolence the chief virtue.

Consequentialism requires the actor to promote what he thinks, or perhaps what an impartial benevolent spectator would think, is the best state of affairs, all with little regard to the moral aspect of what counts as a good state. Yet benevolence should sometimes give way to demands of justice, fairness, truth, personal rights, friendship, and other special obligations to particular persons. When promoting the good of others would transgress some rule of justice, it is not meaningful to say that the prohibited action would produce a better overall state of affairs than its alternative. Such a claim for an unjust act lacks any clear sense in ordinary nonconsequentialist moral thought (Foot 1988, 235–6; Scheffler 1988, pp. 246–8, interpreting Foot).

Suppose that by violating the rights of one innocent person, as by *torturing* him, I could save many innocent persons from similar tortures. Suppose, further, that my action is the *only* way to prevent the multiple tortures. Isn't a state of affairs involving only one act of torture better than an otherwise similar state with multiple tortures? Isn't my duty then clear?

Foot and Scheffler berate consequentialism for its presumed answer – that inflicting great harm on an innocent person may indeed be permissible if that is the only way to keep someone else from doing more bad things of the same kind (p. 226). They question the consquentialists' very notion of best, better, or good states of affairs. A state with more happiness or less misery is not unconditionally better than one with less happiness or more misery. The goodness of a state cannot be assessed apart from its moral quality. A state resulting from my presumptuously inflicting torture (even to prevent worse atrocities) is less satisfactory, on that grounds, anyway, than a state in which I refrain from the immoral action.

Foot recognizes that situations may arise in which the consequentialist will describe his critic as insisting on accepting a worse rather than better overall outcome. But the consequentialist either is talking nonsense or is giving his words some special question-begging meaning. Nonconsequentialists walk into a trap when they let their opponents press the question whether it can ever be right to produce something other than the best state. Apparent common sense is delusive. What is the meaning, anyway, of best state of affairs from an impersonal point of view or "from a moral point of view" (Foot 1988, pp. 227, 232–4; Scheffler 1988, p. 248)?

A state cannot count as good, Foot continues, merely because people are happy in it; it cannot really be good if it involves violation of a moral duty. No "good state of affairs" stands outside morality as the general criterion. Many requirements and prohibitions of our ordinary moral code may clash with benevolence. Offhand, we have no reason to think that any action meant to make people better off will even be morally permissible (pp. 235–6).

Scheffler, in particular, introduces the concept of agent-centered restrictions. Each person bears special moral responsibility for his own actions

– so he seems to mean – and may not excuse a wicked deed by claiming that it achieves a better overall state through blocking vaster wickedness of other persons. In at least some cases, violating an agent-centered restriction is impermissible even when doing so would "minimize total overall violations of the very same restriction, and would have no other morally relevant consequences" (Scheffler 1988, p. 243). In such a case, what an apologist might call "the minimization of morally objectionable conduct" could itself be morally objectionable (p. 244; cf. p. 250).

Similarly, and in the same volume, Conrad Johnson (1988) also invokes agent-centered restrictions: an individual does not have authority to flout moral rules even in exceptional cases; he may not murder one person to save five from being murdered. In this respect he is like a judge, who has no authority to override established law (changing the law is the province of the legislature instead). Even if consequentialist considerations do ultimately govern the content of moral rules, the individual agent has no authority to disregard the rules and appeal directly to such considerations. He has no business playing God.

As Johnson knows (for he cites Hare 1981 to this effect), consequentialists recognize good reasons for inculcating deeply ingrained compunctions against violating moral restrictions. A person should think long and hard before violating one and should feel guilt afterwards even if the violation turns out to appear right. Yet for Johnson, anguished deliberation and a sense of guilt are not enough. The violation remains downright impermissible – or so he seems to mean (1988, p. 264).

In saying so, Johnson appears not to have faced up to the exceptional character of full-fledged dilemma cases. In such a case, by the very way the critic has constructed it, circumstances have thrust the burden of an agonizing decision onto the agent. He cannot evade a decision, for deciding to stand idle is a decision. With the unavoidable burden of making one tragic decision or another necessarily goes the authority to make it – to "play God". This is an implication of the exceptional situation that the critic himself has constructed.

One major objection to Foot's position, as she recognizes (1988, pp. 240–2), embraces the notion of morally better and worse states of affairs; it sees moral rules as a kind of tacit legislation adopted by the community for the general good, legislation that the individual agent does not have the moral authority to violate. But, Foot replies, this consequentialist view of morality and its goal seems neutral and inevitable only insofar as utilitarianism and other forms of consequentialism dominate moral philosophy. Precisely this (supposed) domination is what she is questioning. Who is supposed to have the end that morality is supposed to serve? Perhaps no shared end appears in the foundation of ethics; instead we may find individual ends and rational compromises among the persons pursuing them, or perhaps basic facts about how individual human beings can find the greatest goods they are capable of possessing. "The truth is, I think, that we simply do not have a satisfactory theory of morality, and need to look for it. ... [T]he real answer to utilitarianism depends on progress in the development of alternatives. Meanwhile, however, we have no reason to think that we must accept consequentialism in any form" (pp. 241–2).

In thus recognizing that "we" have not yet found a satisfactory alternative to utilitarianism, Foot makes a major concession. Perhaps she takes it for granted that only someone taking a perversely synoptic, anti-individualistic view can accept utilitarianism or consequentialism. She seems to agree with other critics that any such doctrine cares about states of affairs rather than persons, does not take the distinctness of persons seriously, and does not recognize individuals' pursuit of their own diverse projects. In addition, she also seems to complain that consequentialism pays too little attention to personal or agent-centered virtues, almost as if she held these virtues desirable in themselves, apart from their belonging or contributing to desirable states. Nevertheless, her remark about individual ends and rational compromises does remind us of the emphasis of utilitarianism on social cooperation.

Foot concludes with an exhortation to resist consequentialism's key idea. The idea of the goodness of total states of affairs plays no part (fortunately, in her view) in Aristotle's moral philosophy, in John Rawls's account of justice, and in the theories of more thoroughgoing contractualists such as T.M. Scanlon (1982). If we accustom ourselves to seeing simply a blank where consequentialists see "the best state of affairs", we may better give other theories the hearing they deserve (Foot 1988, p. 242).

Foot and Scheffler come close to narrowly identifying consequentialism with *act* consequentialism or *act* utilitarianism. They do not adequately recognize the rules or indirect version and the arguments for it. They pay scant attention to inadequacies of human knowledge, foresight, and calculating ability and to the resulting necessity of acting on mere probabilities. Ultimately utilitarian considerations do recommend that people develop strongly ingrained aversions to inflicting torture (say) and that they not be distracted by hypothetical cases in which one must inflict torture to keep others from inflicting greater torture. Such cases are unlikely to arise and would scarcely be recognized even if they ever did. Things work out better on the whole if individuals internalize an almost absolute prohibition on inflicting torture. More generally, things work out better if individuals feel and bear much more responsibility for their own actions than for the actions of other people. (R.M. Hare has made points like these.)

A more specific answer to Foot and Scheffler focuses further on their imaginary case in which inflicting torture would prevent greater torture, and without overridingly unacceptable side effects. If the case did arise and if the person onto whom the burden of decision fell did fully and confidently understand it, then, by hypothesis, he would face a tragic dilemma: either his intervening or his standing aside would be wrong by some standard, and the critic in the ivory tower would be presumptuous to moralize against his choice.

A utilitarian (or I, anyway) would share Foot's revulsion at killing one innocent person even as the only way to prevent mass killing (as postulated in another of her examples). A disposition to be repelled by the very idea has great value, ultimately on utilitarian grounds. But suppose the postulated dilemma has arisen and the burden of decision falls on me. How can Foot be so sure that morality requires me to stand aside and let the mass killing occur?

LIFEBOAT CASES AND IMPOSED SACRIFICES

Critics employ lifeboat cases to make points like those of Foot and Scheffler. Taken literally, these are hypothetical cases involving overloaded or underprovisioned lifeboats. The term is stretched to cover many situations in which not all endangered persons can be saved. Critics contrive many such cases (see, for example, McCloskey 1984; Williams 1973CI/1988; Whewell as discussed by J.S. Mill in Ryan 1987; Finnis 1983, p. 131; and Harman 1977, pp. 154-7). A mob is bent on massacring blacks to avenge a murder supposedly committed by an unknown black man. The sheriff is sure he can pacify the mob and save many lives by framing and executing one innocent victim. A South American tyrant is about to shoot twenty captives when a Yankee traveler happens onto the scene. The tyrant offers to free all his other captives if the traveler will personally kill one of them. A fat boy is stuck in the mouth of a cave, blocking the escape of spelunkers menaced by rising waters. Should rescuers employ explosives, sacrificing the boy to save the others? Gilbert Harman (1977, p. 156) carries his attack so far as to consider whether a doctor should cut up one patient and use his organs for saving five other patients.

Utilitarians allegedly recommend sacrificing the innocent victim in each scenario, all for the sake of greater aggregate utility. The critic, so runs his veiled hint, would never act so shamefully; he is nobler than the crass utilitarians.

Some stories feature deathbed promises. On a desert island, a companion promises a dying man to erect a tombstone for him in his home town if he ever can. The promisor eventually is rescued. The dead man has no living relatives or friends. Keeping the promise would have no happy consequences and would require some slight trouble and expense (d'Amour 1976, pp. 89-90). In a variant of the story (noted by Smart 1956/1970, pp. 255-6, 1973, p. 62), the dying man exacts a promise that his fortune be turned over to a jockey club;

but his rescued companion learns that a hospital could put the money to better use. Utilitarian theory would argue against keeping the promise. On the other hand, utilitarians, when not looking through their theoretical glasses but facing the case head on, would generally agree with other ethicists that the promise should be kept (thus d'Amour 1976, pp. 89–90).

But *would* utilitarian theory argue against keeping the promise? No, not indirect utilitaranism. Hare's distinction between intuitive and reflective levels (Chapter 2 above) is relevant here. Part of the very logic of ethics is that ethical precepts, absorbed to the extent of being intuitive, should ordinarily govern behavior in actual cases; decisions should not ordinarily be open to all-things-considered reflection. Character, furthermore, is relevant. Utilitarianism recommends cultivating and encouraging the sort of character that would promote keeping the promise. (Gilbert Harman, cited above, does acknowledge utilitarian reasons for training people to have ordinary, nonutilitarian intuitions in his case of the potential organ transplants.)

Bernard Williams's (1973ACU) use of two favorite cases requires closer attention. George could not support his family without taking a job in research on chemical and biological warfare. He conscientiously opposes the research, but an enthusiast for it would take the job if George refuses. Jim, a wandering botanist, faces the choice posed by a South American tyrant: shooting one captured Indian himself or seeing their captor shoot twenty. What should George and Jim do?

Williams distinguishes, at length though vaguely, between states of affairs occurring without one's own active participation and states hinging on it. He believes – and so of course do I, so far as the point carries weight – that a person bears greater responsibility for his own than for others' behavior. Williams suggests that the goodness or badness of resulting states of affairs does not alone determine what action is right; on the contrary, the rightness or wrongness of the actions involved may also determine whether or not a state of affairs is good or bad. (Compare Philippa Foot's point, reviewed above.)

Williams makes much of "integrity" (pp. 108–18 and *passim*). He implies that George or Jim impairs his integrity by making the allegedly utilitarian choice. But, as Hugo Bedau (1995–96) asks, does utilitarianism indeed make the recommendation that Williams imputes to it? Can any other ethical system give unequivocal advice? Can Jim believe that the tyrant will keep his word to free the nineteen remaining captives? What if all twenty captives urge Jim to accept the tyrant's offer, each willing to risk being the one chosen at random for sacrifice? Would their urging have any moral significance in the situation? Can Jim have any hope of reasoning or negotiating with the tyrant, perhaps by offering himself as the single victim? Would Jim's compliance with the tyrant's demand give some moral sanction to a despicable regime and so increase the likelihood of future outrages? (Compare readers' letters and

Bedau's response in the Spring 1996 issue listed in the References.) Finally, we should remember that the scenario was specifically cooked up to put Jim in exquisite moral agony, and it is mere evasion to imagine alterations in it that would point to a relatively easy decision.

Williams does recognize that Jim's refusal to save nineteen persons by killing one might look like self-indulgent and even dishonorable squeamishness. Williams sees this not as a fresh consideration, however, but merely as a reaffirmation of precisely the utilitarian view under attack. We are at least partially not utilitarians, he says, and cannot regard our moral feelings merely as objects of utilitarian value. So to regard them is to lose our moral identity and literally our integrity (pp. 102–4).

A man's moral outlook, says Williams, might well make certain courses of action unthinkable for him. Seriously to ponder them is dishonorable or morally absurd. Situations supposedly forcing them into consideration might be logically or empirically conceivable but not morally conceivable. Having to make a choice in such situations would represent not a special problem in a person's moral world but something lying beyond its boundaries. The idea is insane that moral rationality could yield an answer in such monstrous situations. They "so transcend in enormity the human business of moral decision that from a moral point of view it cannot matter any more what happens. ... [T]o spend time thinking what one would decide if one were in such a situation is also insane, if not merely frivolous" (p. 92). Furthermore, "unless the environment reveals minimum sanity, it is insanity to carry the decorum of sanity into it. Consequentialist rationality, however, and in particular utilitarian rationality, has no such limitations: making the best of a bad job is one of its maxims, and it will have something to say even on the difference between massacring seven million, and massacring seven million and one" (p. 93).

Yet who if not Williams himself, a few pages later, trots out his examples of George and Jim? (Williams might better have remembered the maxim "Hard cases make bad law".) I am tempted to wonder whether his frequently repeated word "integrity" means something like "moral purity" and hints at a claim of being "purer than thou".

Williams concludes (p. 150) by insisting that

> the demands of political reality and the complexities of political thought are obstinately what they are, and in face of them the simple-mindedness of utilitarianism disqualifies it totally.
>
> The important issues that utilitarianism raises should be discussed in contexts more rewarding than that of utilitarianism itself. The day cannot be too far off in which we hear no more of it.

Is this not a remarkable conclusion after all that has gone before? Williams has done hardly more than snipe at utilitarianism, has not laid out a persuasive alternative, and has relied heavily on hinting at (without straightforwardly asserting) his own moral superiority over the utilitarians.

I dare not give full voice to my outrage. R.M. Hare, however, has identified the "fraudulence" of much use of lifeboat cases (1981, p. 139). He speaks of critics "playing trains", referring to "their examples in which trolleys hurtling down the line out of control have to be shunted into various groups of unfortunate people" (p. 139). Hypothetical dilemmas are easy to cook up, but what force do they have? It is indeed fraudulent for a critic to hint that he, in such a case and in contrast with a utilitarian, would preserve his own moral purity – somehow. (In a slightly different context, Donald Regan 1980, p. 208, speaks of "Pontius Pilatism".) Tragic cases can arise in which *prima facie* principles can clash and in which one or more of them must be overridden; yet the overridability of principles does not keep them from being moral principles. (See Hare 1981, pp. 59–60; and on the case of the sheriff pondering whether to frame an innocent man, see Rawls 1955/1968.)

Christina Hoff Sommers (1993, esp. pp. 6, 11–12) comments further on cases like those of the poor man tempted to steal the drug needed to save his dying wife or of the seven people in a lifeboat with provisions only for four. Overemphasis on such cases, particularly in teaching young people, tends to breed ethical relativism or skepticism. In a moral dilemma "there are no obvious heroes or villains[,] ... no obvious right and wrong, no clear vice and virtue". The characters lack moral personality, existing outside of traditions and social arrangements. The finely balanced issues only marginally engage students' minds, emotions, and moral sensibilities. "[L]isteners are on their own and they individually decide for themselves" (Sommers 1993, p. 12).

CLASHES OF PRINCIPLES

The most plausible cases in which it is sensible to override an otherwise controlling rule are ones in which applicable rules clash. Several of the preceding examples illustrate clashes of principles, but the point deserves the emphasis of a separate section. Honesty might clash with kindness (as in the case of the polite fib), or rescuing an endangered person might require taking or trespassing on someone else's property.

Ethical rules have more force than rules of writing style, but an analogy holds between them. Style books tell writers to use active verbs, avoid abstract nouns, and express main points in principal rather than subordinate clauses. But clashes occur, as between "give concrete examples" and "be brief". No one solution will resolve all clashes, and a person must sometimes draw on his practiced attunement to ethical problems or to language. (Ludwig Reiners 1975, pp. 91, 193, invokes *"ein gewisses Fingerspitzengefühl"*.) Clashes discredit neither moral rules nor rules of style. Situation ethics – "Do the best thing in each particular case" – is as empty as advice always to write in the most effective way.

Suppose you are a captured prisoner of war or are honor-bound to keep a friend's confidence. You are questioned in such a way that your mere silence would convey information and so breach your duty to your country or your friend. You cannot avoid either breaching your duty or lying.

It is an error, says Nicolai Hartmann, to believe that such dilemmas may be resolved theoretically. Every such attempt leads either to inflexible rigorism putting one value ahead of the rest or to fruitless casuistry. Trying to avoid choice when values conflict violates both those values and is moral cowardice (Hartmann 1932/1970, pp. 41–2). A man ought to "decide according to his best conscience; that is, according to his living sense of the relative height of the respective values, and to take upon himself the consequences, external as well as inward, ultimately the guilt involved for the violation of the one value. He ought to carry the guilt and in so doing become stronger, so that he can carry it with pride" (p. 42).

That one must sometimes settle conflicts by one's own free sense of values, Hartmann continues, "should be regarded as a feature of the highest spiritual significance. ... Yet one must not make of this a comfortable theory, as the vulgar mind makes of the permissible lie, imagining that one brings upon oneself no guilt in offending against clearly discerned values. It is only unavoidable guilt which can preserve a man from moral decay" (p. 42). "In some unusual situations we should break ethical rules", says Peter Singer in a similar spirit, yet be censured for doing so; for censuring violators is an important way of publicly supporting the rules. "Though ethical rules have no ultimate authority of their own, there are some ethical rules that we cannot do without" (Singer 1982, p. 167).

Hartmann means, then, with Singer apparently agreeing, that there is no complete escape from guilt in a moral dilemma. Yet one should not let that fact destroy all sense of guilt and make one an amoral person. One must accept guilt for one action or another, and in accordance with one's own moral character, but without brooding excessively about it. A moral person will accept guilt without letting it destroy him.

INTUITIONS AND UTILITARIANISM

Easy though it is to invent alleged clashes between utilitarianism and deep moral intuitions, to set them at loggerheads is fallacious. (Intuitio*nism*, the doctrine, is a different matter, considered especially in Chapter 10 below.) Intuitions inculcated into us from early childhood may well have a deep utilitarian basis. As Henry Hazlitt explains (1964, Chapter 19), if most of our moral judgments seem to force themselves upon us without our thinking of consequences, the reason is that they have been built into us from our earliest infancy. We absorb them with our language, which conditions our thought and even our perceptions. Words like "lying", "theft", and "murder" mingle judgments with descriptions. Henry Sidgwick admired the morality of common sense as embodying the experience of immemorial generations. "The morality of common sense is a sort of common law, with an indefinitely wider jurisdiction than ordinary common law" (Hazlitt 1964, p. 181). A traditional moral rule is open to criticism, but it ordinarily carries a presumption of usefulness. "We should never refuse to abide by an established moral rule merely because we cannot understand the purpose of it." No one can know "all the experiences, decisions, and considerations" that have shaped it (Hazlitt 1964, p. 184).

Are any moral axioms self-evident? Perhaps so, if they are tautologies or if they clearly serve a recognized goal (but are they then *axioms*?). The rule against torturing a child is self-evident in the sense that no person of normal feelings would ever ask what justifies it. The ethical philosopher is well advised, however, not to multiply alleged intuitions or direct cognitions unnecessarily (Hazlitt 1964, pp. 186–7). (To quibble, though, it is odd to speak of a *rule* against torturing children; no such rule is what makes people refrain. The direct intuition involved does, however, have an ultimately utilitarian basis.)

These considerations equip us to face remarks such as that morality "has an autonomous legitimacy that demands to be dealt with on its own grounds; it is neither at odds with rationality nor amenable to a reduction to prudential considerations. Above all, ... the worth of altruism is intrinsic rather than reducible to utilitarian maneuverings" (Rescher 1975, Summary, p. x; compare Hadley Arkes's position, discussed in Chapter 10 below).

Well, what are morality's "own grounds"? And how is the worth of altruism "intrinsic"? Isn't the issue between utilitarianism and rival doctrines just *what* the grounds of morality are and *how* various attitudes and principles can be appraised? Rescher does say (1975, p. 90n.) that he elsewhere "espouse[s] a rival ethical theory (one that deploys a complex combination of intuitivist, pragmatist, and idealistic ideas)". One suspects intuition-mongering. In his 1966 book, Rescher demotes utility to just one criterion among several. But what might those other criteria be? Is justice one of them? Equality? Communal spirit? Isn't it true that any such supposedly rival criteria would owe any plausibility to serving social cooperation and thereby ultimately happiness?

RULES FETISHISM

Replies to criticisms focusing on malice, lifeboat cases, and the like invoke the distinction between immediate act utilitarianism and rules or indirect utilitarianism. This emphasis on rules draws another and quite different charge, of fetishism[2] (even though indirect utilitarianism emphasizes attitudes and character traits also). J.J.C. Smart explicitly alleges "rule worship" (1961/1973, p. 10), rather questionably calling his own position *act*-utilitarian. Herbert McCloskey (1969, p. 191) suggests that a rules utilitarian in Australia would follow that country's drive-to-the-left rule even when violating it could avoid a crash. If keeping a promise here and now would produce worse results than breaking it, my duty nevertheless to obey the rule cannot derive from its general utility, since the many cases in which obeying it does produce greater utility are different from the present exceptional case precisely in this consequence (Quinton 1973, pp. 108–10, reporting the views of J.J.C. Smart and David Lyons; cf. Harsanyi 1985, p. 121).

If a critic cooks up a case in which overriding an ordinarily applicable rule is clearly the best thing to do when absolutely all relevant facts and considerations are taken into account, then overriding the rule is indeed, by the critic's very stipulation, the best thing to do. But how much is supposed to follow from such cases? A rules utilitarian would point to the cooked-up nature of the critic's case. He would insist that case-by-case calculations are usually impossible or highly inexpedient. Recognizing reasons for violating otherwise applicable rules in exceptional cases does not mean abandoning rules utilitarianism and returning to act utilitarianism (which just cannot be taken literally).

The supposed alternatives – one doctrine recommending fresh utility calculations from scratch in each individual case, with no line of conduct enjoying any presumption over any other, and another doctrine demanding undeviating adherence to rigid rules for their own sakes – are the horns of a false dilemma. A realistic rules utilitarianism stresses the impossibility of full knowledge and accurate case-by-case prediction of consequences. It stresses the coordinative value of rules generally obeyed. Instead of insisting on rigid and heedless obedience, it cautions against violating an applicable rule on whim or fragmentary information. No sensible version of utilitarianism erects rules into supreme ends in their own right, to be followed always no matter how much misery results. Interpreted too rigidly, rules can do mischief, even providing supposed moral justification for puritanical sadism. (Edwards 1965, Chapter VII, describes hypothetical persons who consider themselves paragons of virtue but delight in applying their moral standards to make other people miserable.)

No rule short and clear enough to guide action can cover all cases that might possibly arise. Human nature and human life are too complex. The attempt to bar exceptions is foredoomed. The way to avoid dishonest wriggling around rules while still giving them lip-service is to drop any pretense that they are unchallengeable absolutes (Singer 1982, pp. 164–5).

Morton Kaplan already (1959–60) suggested how to reply to the kind of question asked by J.J.C. Smart: why follow a rule of thumb that has a bad result in a particular case if an easy calculation could establish a better course of action? Well, calculating the consequences of individual acts is often undesirable, even though doing so might bring a "better" decision in particular individual instances. Calculations are undesirable in social situations dependent upon diffuse attitudes of the participants. The stability of a marriage would suffer if each spouse was always coldly calculating the chances of finding a richer or handsomer mate or worrying that the other would leave if the first became ill. Certain important relationships require attitudes that are diffuse and noninstrumental if they are to achieve their purpose (Kaplan 1959–60, pp. 228–9). In the standard prisoners' dilemma also, the outcome would be better for both persons if both were acting from ingrained cooperative attitudes (pp. 229–30).

Ordinarily the drive-left rule of McCloskey's Australia helps avoid accidents; but if a freakish situation should require swerving right to avoid a crash, a rules utilitarian would of course swerve. A violation is acceptable if it serves the purpose that the rule itself normally serves. Fire engines, police cars, and ambulances may violate traffic rules under specified conditions. But exceptions to ordinarily applicable rules, instead of being made *ad hoc*, should have a rationale and should themselves conform to rules, if necessarily vague ones (Hazlitt 1964, Chapter 10). (Traffic rules and their exceptions, being legally enacted and enforced, are not entirely satisfactory examples for our purposes. The rules of morality have wider scope than statutes and also are looser, more flexible and adaptable, and more open to exceptions.)

For a rules utilitarian as for an act utilitarian, results are what count. The issue is whether good results are best pursued afresh case by case. Rules are recommended not for their own sakes – not as fetishes – but for their usual good results. To say otherwise is to ignore or caricature the rules-utilitarian argument.

Utilitarianism does not recommend rules as mere rules of thumb, as mere generalizations or summaries of act-utilitarian calculations, as poor substitutes for the case-by-case calculations that would be preferable if time, information, and freedom from bias permitted. No, positive analysis recommends them as likely to promote social cooperation. Undeniably, different rules may clash in their application to particular hard cases. In such cases – in a complicated and "morally messy" world (Gordon 1976, p. 589) – conforming to some rules may require violating others. That fact does not keep the rules violated in exceptional cases from still being moral rules.

Taking rules seriously also helps people develop personally and socially useful habits, attitudes, dispositions, and inclinations. These dispositions include the sympathy of Hume and Smith and a disinclination to grab special privilege and make unfair exceptions in one's own favor. Such dispositions may condition the application of rules in particular cases. Rules utilitarians, like other ethicists, understand why the characteristics that distinguish ethical rules from the requirements of actual law are desirable; they understand why it would be undesirable legally to codify and enforce all precepts of decent behavior. It is scarcely fair, then, to accuse them of insisting on conformity to rules, come what may.

CONCLUSION

This chapter has faced charges that utilitarianism would recommend actions in violation of deep-seated moral intuitions, as well as the charge that one version turns ethical rules into silly and harmful fetishes. Discussion of one further charge – that utilitarianism is vacuous – had best be left to Chapter 10.

NOTES

1. Arthur Schopenhauer recognizes that actual *malice* does exist. This *"malicious joy at the misfortune of others* ... is the really devilish vice. For it is the very opposite of compassion and is nothing but impotent cruelty. Unable itself to bring about the sufferings it so gladly beholds in others, such cruelty thanks chance for having done so instead". For Schopenhauer, the highest virtue is compassion, manifested in natural justice and loving kindness (1841/1965, quotation from p. 162; cf. Richard Taylor's "Introduction", esp. pp. xxii–xxiii).

    Despite Schlick, Schopenhauer, and others, my condemnation of Schadenfreude cannot be absolute and categorical. As Robert Frank explains (1988; cf. Chapter 8 below), emotions can often usefully give a short-run payoff to actions and attitudes that would otherwise be advantageous for the individual only probabilistically and in the long run. Feelings of satisfaction at one's own benevolence are an obvious example. But it is also desirable on utilitarian grounds that individuals not routinely tolerate predation against oneself or others. In particular cases, however, resistance or retaliation might not seem worth the cost; but prospective feelings of shame at letting oneself be walked over and of satisfaction at helping give a predator his just desserts can help tip decisions against the socially undesirable inertia. Schadenfreude – specifically, satisfaction at the culprit's deserved pain – can thus occasionally be useful.

    The complications that bar a sweeping condemnation even of something as unsavory as Schadenfreude count among the reasons why some flexibility must hedge the application of ethical precepts to individual cases.

2. Chapter 4 above faced the rather different objection that the rules version "collapses" into act utilitarianism.

8. Altruism and self-interest

AN INTRODUCTORY APOLOGY

A benevolent impartial observer would want individuals to abide by an ethical code if he thought that their doing so would be good in itself or would benefit people in general. To have good results, however, an ethical code must actually *work*, which presupposes that individuals find abiding by it in their own interests, by and large. A workable social system must stand what John Rawls called the "strains of commitment" (1971, Section 29). Furthermore, individuals *ought* to abide by an ethical code only if they *can* do so; and if they could do so only at great personal cost, that fact would weaken their moral obligation.

Traditional ethical rules do seem to command wide respect, or at least lip-service. Even villains often try to excuse their actions, to themselves and others, in ways that tacitly acknowledge those rules. Some feel twinges of conscience.

Such a consensus, if in fact it exists, suggests that ethical training and dialogue can be effective. The person who can only be coerced, never conditioned or persuaded, must be rare (but this is a falsifiable empirical proposition). Explaining ethical consensus will further invoke, presumably, cultural or biological selection. (Propositions about consensus on values and precepts and about how they evolved are positive propositions. Yet the values and precepts themselves remain value judgments.)

Group acceptance of ethical precepts, along with a mental makeup conducive to individuals' internalizing them, presumably had survival value during the course of human evolution. (To "internalize" a value or precept is to absorb it as an integral part of one's attitudes, beliefs, or character. These topics occupied us in Chapter 3.)

Now, what reasons of his own, if any, does the individual have for behaving morally? This question brings to mind a distinction between motive and standard. The standard or criterion for appraising an ethical precept or system is one thing; the motive that an individual might have for abiding by it is a different though related question.

Why be moral? One might deny any reason. Less implausibly, one might reply that morality tends to serve the individual's self-interest: although the payoff is not certain, morality offers the better bet. Such an answer, even if not wrong, is incomplete and seems hard-hearted. It suggests disregard for the "sympathy" of David Hume and Adam Smith or for "altruism" in an acceptable sense of that equivocal term.

Expanding and supplementing the hard-boiled answer leads, however, into awkward territory. This chapter, more than any other, risks taking on a maudlin, preachy tone. Examples occur in passages from John Stuart Mill, Moritz Schlick, David Schmidtz, and other ethicists, passages that I quote or closely paraphrase out of squeamishness about stating their substance in my own words. I do not want to preach, and I apologize if I seem to do so. I am concerned, instead, with the nature of ethical precepts and their role in a functioning society.

A note written to myself many years ago provides an embarrassing contrast to writings by others that I have since come to admire. My old note suggested something like the following as the fundamental ethical rule: in deciding one's own actions, one should weigh their direct and indirect effects not only on oneself but also on other people, whose welfare should count along with one's own. Trying to validate ethical propositions by appeal to self-interest, my note continued, is almost self-contradictory. The essence of ethics is concern for the welfare of others. An appeal ultimately to one's own interest alone has no ethical value, and heeding it is mere expediency. The attempt to root ethics in religion, for example, fails for this reason. If people do good and refrain from evil to reach heaven and avoid hell, they are behaving no more ethically than when wearing rubbers in rainy weather to avoid (supposedly) catching cold.

W.D. Hudson expresses similar ideas. The notion that ethical behavior tends to be in one's own interest misconceives morality. "The conclusive reason for being just is not that it pays or that it is what any man, or all men, want, but that it is being just" (1970, p. 275). R.F. Harrod calls acts morally good when they promote the ends or interests of other people, bad when they frustrate them (1936, pp. 142–3). According to common moral consciousness, a good man "concerns himself with promoting the ends of others and that is what is meant by calling him good" (p. 143). Considering the ends of others is the essence of morality. "If the group of persons included is one more or less closely associated with the self, the moral principle is still cloyed with egoism" (p. 143).

Statements like these seem dangerously close to endorsing altruism in the sense condemned by Ayn Rand – the subordination of one's own interests, purposes, values, and affections to those of other people (a sense mentioned in Chapter 2 and further examined below). Or perhaps those statements are mere carelessness, and Harrod's overall position merits a more charitable interpretation.

Altruism in the condemned sense is unworkable for several reasons. One is the problem of knowledge conveyed by the metaphor of people always giving each other Christmas presents without ever choosing what they want for their own selves. Another reason is the invitation to hypocrisy and the psychological strain linked with such an exigent notion of moral obligation.

A more workable notion leaves individuals free indeed to pursue their own interests, purposes, and affections, rather than those of miscellaneous other persons, but free to pursue them only within ethical limits. Within them, self-interested activities can indeed serve the interests of other persons, as Adam Smith's metaphor of the invisible hand recognizes (1776/1937, Book IV, Chapter II, p. 423). But service to others, genuine though it can be under suitable social arrangements, does not thereby become the individual's overriding purpose. He properly pursues his own interests, purposes, and affections. So much the better, perhaps, if these should come to include the interests of other persons with whom the individual has particular ties of affection (realistically, they could not include the interests of all other persons indiscriminately).

The central question of this chapter is not, then, what reason the individual has to behave altruistically in the problematic sense further spelled out below. He has no such reason. The question, rather, is what reason he has to behave within the standard ethical restraints and further, perhaps, to admire and even cultivate the standard virtues.[1]

"To prize one's own happiness and be indifferent to another's is a clear case of irrationality", writes Brand Blanshard (1980, p. 295). Although occurring amidst an otherwise eminently sensible discussion, that is surely an overstatement. Narrow concern only for one's own happiness is not irrational, not downright logical error. Rather, it reflects misperception of reality. Given the realities of the world, human society, and human nature, one cannot effectively pursue one's own happiness while remaining indifferent to that of other people. One can indeed get along well while indifferent to the happiness of particular other persons and to other persons in general, but not while sweepingly indifferent to that of absolutely all others. This is an empirical generalization, of course, and as such conceivably wrong.

Writings reviewed below, including those of John Stuart Mill, Moritz Schlick, and Henry Hazlitt, have led me to reject the thinking quoted from Hudson, Harrod, and my former self. Why not demonstrate harmony, if one validly can, between self-interest and the general interest? What is so "mere" about "mere expediency"? Not all expediencies are the same. Expediency as an overriding narrow regard for what seems to promise the best result for oneself on the immediate occasion is one thing; quite another is regard for the precepts and character traits and interactions with one's fellows that offer the best prospects of a satisfying life as a whole. Expediency of the latter kind coheres best with reconciling individual interest with the common interest.

SELF-INTEREST AND ALTRUISM

An ethical code not appealing to self-interest but instead preaching self-*sacrifice* would not be workable and so would serve the interests neither of individuals nor of their society. "Altruism", as Ayn Rand pejoratively labels such a moral code and as was discussed in Chapter 2, calls on individuals to subordinate their own values (if indeed they have any of their own) to the values of other persons.

Ordinary, non-Randian, language conceives of altruism less sharply. Receiving widespread lip-service in our society, altruism means due concern, or even special concern, for the rights, interests, and welfare of other persons, or the character traits evoking such concern.

We must get another terminological annoyance out of the way. It is sometimes said that everyone always acts from self-interest. Whatever a person does, even yielding to an armed robber, he does because he thinks it best for himself under the circumstances. Even an altruist expects a payoff for himself, if only in self-esteem or a warm glow. A frequent implication seems to be that since all actions are self-interested, none are particularly virtuous.

But interpreting self-interest so as to make it always the controlling factor yields a tiresome tautology. It suppresses meaningful distinctions of ordinary language. *How* does a person conceive of self-interest, and *how* does he pursue it? *What sort of character* does one act from and cultivate? A narrow, short-run-oriented, grasping, ruthlessly pursued self-interest is one thing; quite another is the wider, long-run-oriented conception of Aristotle's great-souled person.

Self-interest is not to be condemned. Baier reminds us of the old quip that "everyone is his own nearest neighbor" (1965, p. 146). Barring special obligations, emotional ties, or similar special reasons for putting someone else's interests ahead of one's own, "*everyone's* interests are best served if *everyone* puts his own interests first". By and large, each person best knows his own plans, aims, ambitions, and aspirations and is more diligent in promoting them than those of other persons. "Enlightened egoism is a possible, rational, orderly system of running things, enlightened altruism is not." Each person can look after one person better than after two or more. "And if he has to look after only one person, there is no advantage in making that person some one other than himself" (p. 147).

Aristotle and other ancient Greeks were concerned with a rational, satisfactory human life. They emphasized the character and dispositions that ultimately support ethical values and the virtues that serve human well-being. What is ethical is so much part of the good person's self, in their view, that ethical considerations take precedence over other wants; goodness comes naturally. John Maynard Keynes, similarly, gravitated to an ethics emphasizing individual character development. Before the Christian era, Keynes noted, all "thoughtful and reflecting persons" were egoists. It never occurred to them that a person could have a goal except his own well-being (Helburn 1992, pp. 32–5).

Francis Y. Edgeworth, a nineteenth century economist, evidently thought differently. He (mis)conceived of utilitarianism, apparently with satisfaction, as requiring at least impartiality between one's own and other persons' interests; it demanded *vivre pour autrui* (Edgeworth 1881/1967, pp. vii, 131, 136; compare the appendix to Chapter 6 above). But surely such a doctrine of extreme altruism cannot be put into general practice. It is psychologically unrealistic to expect each person to weigh others' interests equally with or more heavily than his own. As Robert G. Olson says, urging someone to act against what he rationally sees as his own best interests will probably either "embitter him or ... inspire contempt for reason" (1965, p. 12). People who believed such a doctrine would feel tension between it and their own actual thoughts and actions; hypocrisy and feelings of guilt would result. The general level of happiness would fall below what sounder doctrine could have permitted. (More follows elsewhere on these quasi-Randian points.)

WHY BE MORAL?

In a book review of 1998, Paul Heyne finds Richard McKenzie (1997) recognizing that suitable ethical rules are essential to a prosperous society, yet fearing that the moral infrastructure of American society has begun to collapse. "... McKenzie makes the problem even more difficult than it is by assuming that ethical behavior will regularly be irrational and contrary to the interests of the person acting." Although wicked groups will ultimately fail, "the morality which is such an important prerequisite for the effective functioning of a market economy ultimately cannot be defended or argued for. Individuals and societies either have it or they do not" (quoted by Heyne from the last page of the book). This formulation, as Heyne recognizes, poses a key question sharply. Is it true that morality "ultimately cannot be defended or argued for"? Is it true that no persuasive reason can be offered to the individual for obeying ethical rules and cultivating the consonant character and dispositions?

Ludwig von Mises (1927/1985, p. 165) observes that since "the peaceful course of social cooperation ... is in the interest of everyone", everyone has an interest in doing his own part to preserve it. Left without elaboration, such a claim would be fallacious. The target of that ethical sermon might respond: "Yes, I understand why it is in almost everyone's interest for almost everyone to behave as you say. I understand the sorry consequences of what you call unethical behavior. But I am only one person among many. My own violations will scarcely affect the general level of ethical conduct, so I will hardly suffer any backlash through that channel. I benefit from other people's honesty, but my lapses will hardly drag down its general level. And on particular occasions I can gain from dishonesty. So you have given me no reason to abide by your principles". The person so replying wants to take a free ride on the decency of his fellows.

Mises, however, says more. In requiring the individual to forgo a personally advantageous but socially detrimental action, "society does not demand that he sacrifice himself to the interests of others". It imposes only a provisional sacrifice: trading away "an immediate and relatively minor advantage ... for a much greater ultimate benefit" (Mises 1927/1985, pp. 33–4; cf. pp. 155ff.).

Mises does not and could not deny all possibility of tension between self-interest and the general interest. In effect, rather, he postulates a long-run and probabilistic harmony. His friend Henry Hazlitt makes this postulate explicit. What best harmonizes with the general interest is not narrowly focused short-run self-interest but considered, long-run self-interest. Even over his entire lifetime, a person's interests are never *identical* with those of society. Over the long run, however, the actions and especially the rules of action that serve self-interest tend to coalesce with those that serve the public interest. In the long run it is in the individual's greatest interest to live in a society characterized by law, peace, security of property, respect for others' rights, promise-keeping, goodwill, cooperation, and helpfulness. Everyone has an interest in promoting fidelity to such a code of conduct, and any individual's infraction endangers its maintenance (Hazlitt 1964, p. 96).

Again, however, such considerations do not fully answer the would-be free-rider. Although the individual's observance or violation of the moral code tends to promote or undercut its general observance, with beneficial or adverse repercussions on himself, these effects must be slight except in small groups. In a large group, one individual's violation will only negligibly undermine others' observance of the rules. If he takes a narrow view of his self-interest, he can look for a free ride on the moral behavior of other people (cf. Buchanan 1965). As Hazlitt recognizes and as is further argued below, more must be said to make the case for long-run coalescence of self-interest and general interest.

PLATO'S CLEVER DEVIL, HOBBES'S FOOLE, AND HUME'S SENSIBLE KNAVE

In Plato's *The Republic*, Glaucon plays devil's advocate in a long conversation with Socrates. Is it always better, he asks, to be just than to be unjust? Which is better: to be a truly just man yet have the (erroneous) reputation of being a scoundrel and so be reviled and abused, or to be a scoundrel yet have the (undeserved) reputation of being a just man and so be admired and favored? Plato's Socrates replies in effect that the truth cannot remain unknown indefinitely; at least the gods will know it. The just man will fare well in this life eventually, and in the afterlife; the scoundrel will be found out and scorned. "Wherefore my counsel is that we hold fast ever to the heavenly way and follow after justice and virtue always, considering that the soul is immortal and able to endure every sort of good and every sort of evil." (Plato's discussion in *The Republic* starts at the beginning of Book II and strings out piecemeal to Book X, the last one; the quotation comes from the book's last paragraph.)

Socrates does not explicitly say that being just provides a more satisfactory mental state than being unjust, although he perhaps hints at that claim in saying (early in Book II) that justice belongs to the highest class of goods, those desirable both for their own sakes and for the reward or results flowing from them. Nor does Socrates explicitly make Moritz Schlick's point, developed below, that the probabilities recommend morality.

Socrates's position has drawn much comment over the centuries. Xenophon, living four decades later (430?-355? BC), interpreted Socrates (470?-399 BC) as saying that it pays to seem upright, and the easiest way of seeming so is actually to be so. Glaucon's challenge to Socrates was: "Given a choice between being a morally good person and being a person who remains open to acting immorally when so acting would serve one's interests, might one not maximize one's expected happiness by choosing the latter and so be entirely rational to do so?" (Copp 1985, p. 8). Yet in the real world, an ordinary human being (as opposed to an impossibly clever devil) best serves his own interest – even if he cares for nothing else – by acquiring moral language and moral thinking as ingrained habits (Hare 1989EoPM, p. 89).

Hobbes's "foole" (*Leviathan*, Part 1, Chapter 15) "says in his heart that he will violate the obligations of justice whenever doing so would be in his own interest" (Copp 1985, p. 8). Hobbes argues that the chance of being detected and uncertainty about the size and probability of the benefits and costs of violations renders violations of duty irrational (Copp 1985, p. 8).

Hobbes (as interpreted by Baier 1965, Chapter 7) saw a point later urged by Bentham: laws and punishments serve, ideally anyway, to help reconcile self-interest and social interest. In a lawless "state of nature", with its actual or ever-threatening war of all against all, no one benefits if only one or a few persons follow the rules of morality; for their doing so brings their ruin. Reason can support morality only when the presumption that other people are immoral is reversed. Hobbes thought that only an absolute ruler could achieve this result; but it can also be achieved – so Baier suggests (1965, p. 152) – if the group teaches and enforces morality, so that each member reasonably expects his fellows generally to obey its moral rules. (A later section of this chapter pursues this point.)

David Hume also faced Glaucon's challenge. In exceptional cases, self-interest may seem to recommend vice above virtue: "[A] man, taking things in a certain light, may often seem to be a loser by his integrity". Given the imperfection of human affairs, "a sensible knave, in particular incidents, may think that an act of iniquity or infidelity will make a considerable addition to his fortune, without causing any considerable breach in the social union and confederacy". It might seem wisest to follow the general rule of honesty as the best policy while taking advantage of exceptions (Hume 1751/1777/1930, Section IX, Part II, pp. 121–2).

Hume sees the difficulty of persuading someone "whose heart rebel not against such pernicious maxims" (p. 122). Scoundrels do exist with whom his arguments carry no weight. He then makes explicit (p. 122) the reply that Socrates only hinted at.

> But in all ingenuous [= straightforward, candid] natures, the antipathy to treachery and roguery is too strong to be counter-balanced by any views of profit or pecuniary advantage. Inward peace of mind, consciousness of integrity, a satisfactory review of our own conduct; these are circumstances, very requisite to happiness, and will be cherished and cultivated by every honest man, who feels the importance of them.

Furthermore, honest and reflective persons have "the frequent satisfaction of seeing knaves, with all their pretended cunning and abilities, betrayed by their own maxims ...". They plan to cheat only moderately and secretly; but "a tempting incident occurs, nature is frail", and they wind up losing all reputation and forfeiting "all future trust and confidence with mankind". Even if their secret cheating succeeds, the knaves "are, in the end, the greatest dupes, and have sacrificed the invaluable enjoyment of a character, with themselves at least, for the acquisition of worthless toys and gewgaws". Very little is required to supply *necessities*, while the greatest satisfaction is "peaceful reflection on one's own conduct" (pp. 122–3).

What actions a person finds in his own interest, said John Stuart Mill, depends on his character. The improvident man cares only for present interests and not for distant but weightier ones.

> On the average, a person who cares for other people, for his country, or for mankind, is a happier man than one who does not; but of what use is it to preach this doctrine to a man who cares for nothing but his own case, or his own pocket? He cannot care for other people if he would. It is like preaching to the worm who crawls on the ground, how much better it would be for him if he were an eagle (Mill 1861/1991, pp. 296–7).

Like Hume, Mill emphasized the individual's state of mind:

> When people who are tolerably fortunate in their outward lot do not find in life
> sufficient enjoyment to make it valuable to them, the cause generally is caring for
> nobody but themselves. To those who have neither public nor private affections, the
> excitements of life are much curtailed, and in any case dwindle in value as the time
> approaches when all selfish interests must be terminated by death; while those who
> leave after them objects of personal affection, and especially those who have also
> cultivated a fellow-feeling with the collective interests of mankind, retain as lively
> an interest in life on the eve of death as in the vigor of youth and health.
>
> Next to selfishness, the principle cause which makes life unsatisfactory is want
> of mental cultivation (Mill 1861, 1863, Chapter II, p. 255 in Cowling edition, pp.
> 144–5 in Gray edition).

Henry Sidgwick judged cultivating the "sympathetic susceptibilities" in
one's "enlightened self-interest". Bishop Butler had rightly rejected "the
vulgar antithesis between Self-love and Benevolence". "[N]o imprudence [is]
more flagrant than that of Selfishness in the ordinary sense of the term."
Excessive concentration on one's own happiness "tends to deprive all
enjoyments of their keenness and zest ...". It excludes "the more secure and
serene satisfaction" available from activities directed toward more
prospectively stable ends than one's own happiness. It loses "the peculiar rich
sweetness, depending upon a sort of complex reverberation of sympathy,
which is always found in services rendered to those whom we love and who
are grateful" (Sidgwick 1907/1962, p. 501).

Moritz Schlick is still another ethicist whose ideas, for reasons already
mentioned, I would rather quote and paraphrase than state in my own words.
Schlick recognizes that virtue does not guarantee happiness; nothing can. Still,
it tends to improve the probabilities.

> The blows of fate cannot be influenced, and have nothing to do with morality; but
> what our *mood* is under given external conditions, and what kind of influence the
> blows have upon us, does depend upon our impulses and behavior. The virtuous
> man and the scoundrel are equally subject to chance, the sun shines upon the good
> and the evil; and therefore the assertion regarding the relation between virtue and
> happiness says only that the good man always has better *prospects* of the joyful life
> than does the egoist, that the former enjoys a greater *capacity* for happiness than
> does the latter.
>
> If the virtuous man has better prospects, that is, a greater probability of joy,
> then, on the average, good men must be happier than egoists. And experience so
> clearly confirms this that it must be visible to every open eye (Schlick 1930/1961,
> pp. 193–4).

Schlick suggests as a central moral maxim: "At all times be fit for
happiness" or "Be ready for happiness" (pp. 197–8). Kant, he reminds us, said
that one should strive not to be happy but to be *worthy* of happiness. But what

Kant called worthiness is nothing but *capacity*. Thus Schlick's formulation need not imply, as Kant's seems to do, that happiness must always be earned and is suspect when due to luck.

Being fit for happiness involves, in Schlick's view, sympathy and considerateness toward one's fellows. "The social impulses constitute a truly ingenious means of multiplying the feelings of pleasure; for the man who feels the pleasures of his fellow men to be a source of his own pleasure thereby increases his joys with the increase in theirs, he shares their happiness; while the egoist is, so to speak, restricted to his own pleasure" (p. 189).

Sympathy with others makes them, metaphorically, receivers or antennae of joy for oneself. This does not mean turning others into mere instruments of one's own pleasure; for the "ingenious means" that Schlick speaks of does not work unless the sympathy is genuine, unless one values others and their joys partly for their own sakes and not merely for one's own sake. One can perhaps share especially in the joys of others, or the relief of their sorrows, to which one oneself has contributed.

Returning thus to David Hume's and Adam Smith's old theme of "sympathy" does not imply that concern for others should be one's chief preoccupation. Schlick's doctrine of the multiplication of pleasures also implies a warning against too much brooding over the misfortunes of others. Feeling guilt over all the suffering in the world does no good and in itself impairs happiness. This consideration also recommends trying to cultivate a cheerful outlook so that sympathy will serve to spread happiness more than misery.

MORE RECENT DISCUSSIONS

For psychological and other reasons, it is unrealistic to expect an individual to participate equally in the joys and sorrows of all other persons. It is enough for a healthy society that individuals have genuine sympathy with small circles of relatives, friends, colleagues, and acquaintances, coupled with mostly passive goodwill toward humanity in general. Against this background of diffuse benevolence, the small circles within which special sympathy prevails will overlap in a network of direct and indirect sympathetic ties (Hazlitt 1964, Chapter 20).

Philippa Foot, like Schlick and Hazlitt, argues that even though ethical behavior and dispositions cannot guarantee happiness, the probabilities recommend them. It is impossible to show that justice is more profitable than injustice if particular acts are considered in isolation. To someone prepared, in very evil circumstances, to face death rather than act unjustly, his justice brings him disaster. Even so, he had good reason to be a just and not an unjust man. He could not have it both ways and while possessing the virtue of justice hold himself ready to be unjust should any great advantage accrue. The man who has the virtue of justice is not ready to do certain things, and if he is too easily tempted we shall say that he was ready after all (Foot 1958/1973, p. 213).

Foot's remark returns us to the idea, explored by James Buchanan (1965), that violating ethical precepts might be in one's own interest in exceptional cases. (Buchanan was not issuing advice, cynical or otherwise; he was concerned with predicting people's behavior in various situations, as in large and small groups.) Conceivably, the best state of affairs for an individual is one in which everyone else conforms to ethical standards while he alone retains freedom in his own mind to act as he finds expedient in each particular situation. This is not to say that the individual will act immorally often, or ever. He simply retains a wider range of choice than if he resolved *never* to permit himself an exception to the rules followed by other people.

A wider range of choice, however, is not always better than a narrow one. Sometimes a person can benefit by having his options narrowed, or by narrowing them himself and being seen to have done so, or by internalizing self-denying ordinances of personal character. (I welcomed the rule at the University of Virginia forbidding a professor to change a course grade except to rectify an actual error in calculating or reporting it.)

Further to meet Buchanan's point, let us postulate a case more exceptional than any he specifies. You have an opportunity to reap a huge gain by committing one single evil act, say a murder certain to go undetected. You will become so wealthy for the rest of your life that you will resolve, sincerely and successfully, never to repeat any such act. Thus you will experience no repeated adverse influences on your character and will not on that account worsen your relations with other people. Nor will your crime undermine other people's observance of ethical rules, for its secrecy will prevent repercussions on you through any such channel.

By hypothesis, in short, you will suffer no direct or indirect harm from your one single wicked act. Why, then, should you obey the rule against murder?

An answer hinges on considering the context in which such a question could genuinely arise. In what real-world context could someone issue or accept advice to stay alert to a truly exceptional opportunity for great gain from an evil deed while meanwhile behaving so as to deserve a reputation for decency? A person alert to such an opportunity – whether or not he ever found and exploited one – would have a different character than someone free from such immoral alertness. That sort of character would impair the individual's relations with others and impair his chances for a good life generally. It would not worsen his prospects for certain; but, as Schlick, Hazlitt, and Foot argued, it would worsen the probabilities.

For reasons that Kurt Baier reviewed in a passage excerpted above, people have often "thought that enlightened egoism is a possible rational way of running things" (1965, p. 147). Baier does not entirely agree (possibly in part because of divergent interpretations of "enlightened egoism"). He then tries to show that everyone has reason to act in the way required for a stable society and that, accordingly, Hume's immoralist knave is irrational.

Baier's attempt fails, says Kai Nielsen (1985, esp. pp. 220–26; cf. Copp's introduction to the volume, p. 19). Baier does not demonstrate irrationality in free-riding on other people's support of sound moral institutions. Granted, the immoralist wants morality to prevail generally, but he also hopes to gain from making exceptions in his own favor while escaping public notice of his immoral character trait or maxim. He could coherently reject Baier's "point of view of reason", itself a questionable concept. Only from a particular point of view – technical, prudential, self-interested, moral, aesthetic, and the like – does it make sense to speak of what action is rational. On an occasion of conflict between narrow self-interest and what morality requires, no point of view of reason dictates that self-interest give way. "One can understand the moral point of view without being moral just as one can drive fat oxen without being fat." Baier has not shown that the immoralist's power of reason must be weaker than that of a person of sound moral principle (Nielsen 1985, p. 225). Baier answered the easy question of why we want people in general to be moral but not the question "Why should I be moral?"

Nielsen evidently refers to Baier's 1965 book. In its concluding chapter, "Why should we be moral?", Baier does indeed place moral reasons above reasons of self-interest. The universal supremacy of self-interest would lead to Hobbes's state of nature. "Moral rules are universal rules designed to override those of self-interest when following the latter is harmful to others" (p. 149). "The very *raison d'être* of a morality is to yield reasons which overrule the reasons of self-interest in those cases when everyone's following self-interest would be harmful to everyone" (p. 150). "Moral rules are not designed to serve the agent's interest directly. Hence it would be quite inappropriate for him to break them whenever he discovers that they do not serve his interest" (Baier 1965, pp. 155–6).

But the issue is not what moral rules were designed for (if indeed they ever were actually designed). Even if violating them is "inappropriate", "inappropriate" is not the same as "irrational". Baier does seem to have left himself open to Nielsen's criticism. In effect he argues that following moral rules overcomes a prisoner's dilemma. Yes, but what reason does the individual have to do his share in overcoming it when his own behavior is far from decisive? What reason does he have for not free-riding on the morality of others? An answer, if any is available, must follow other lines, like those of Hume, Mill, Sidgwick, Schlick, and Hazlitt.

RECIPROCITY

Peter Singer (1982) brings reciprocity and emotions into the story. Ethical behavior tends to reinforce itself. (So does unethical behavior: a small ethical minority would have a hard time in a pervasively immoral society.) People will be more willing to have business and social relations with me if I am known to be honest and considerate than if I am known habitually to lie, cheat, and steal. "Cheats" (as Singer calls them, following Richard Dawkins; recall Chapter 3) accept help but give none. Cheats may prosper, but only until enough persons bear grudges against them and act accordingly. "Grudgers" – Dawkins's and Singer's perhaps unfortunate term for reciprocators – take help and also give it, except to those who have refused to give it; they play tit for tat (as explained below). One grudger in a population of cheats will fare poorly; but the more of them exist, the more often will a grudger be repaid for help and the less often be cheated. Once enough grudgers exist, it pays to be one of them rather than a cheat. So while reciprocal altruism should understandably prosper once established, "it is less easy to see why the genes leading to this form of behavior did not get eliminated as soon as they appeared" (Singer 1982, p. 18).

Singer then suggests a kind of group selection (not species selection). Occasionally within a small separate group, enough members may happen to have the gene for reciprocal altruism to make that behavior work well among themselves. This group may then have an advantage over other groups, especially if it finds ways of dealing with free-riders within itself (pp. 18–22). This is not a group-selection argument of the fallacious kind; for under the postulated circumstances, reciprocal altruism is advantageous for the individual as well as for the group.

Just as we develop friendship and loyalty toward people who help us, Singer continues, so those who exploit us arouse our moral indignation and desire to punish. If reciprocal altruism operated in human evolution, an aversion to being cheated would be an advantage. We resist being cheated, even at high cost, because of "the principle of the thing". One possible reason why we care about the principle is that although being cheated once may cost little, being cheated repeatedly costs much over the long run. Identifying and shunning cheaters is worth the trouble. Personal resentment becomes moral indignation when other members of a group share it and bring it under a general principle. Our personal feelings of resentment may solidify into a group code, with socially accepted standards of what constitutes adequate return for a service and what should be done to cheaters (Singer 1982, pp. 40–41).

Robert Frank (1988) elaborates on how emotions can reinforce reciprocity. A person can benefit from emitting signals of being a fair cooperator, yet no easy mark for predators. Faking these signals may be difficult or costly. The best course may be actually to *be* a fair cooperator, who expects fair treatment in return (recall Xenophon's interpretation of Socrates). Corresponding emotions help transmit the signals. They also help overcome a tendency to underrate long-run relative to short-run interest, for the feelings they arouse themselves provide a short-run payoff to behavior that might otherwise pay off only probabilistically in the long run.

Sometimes it may appear in one's own interest to seize an opportunity for unfair gain or to spare oneself the cost of retaliating against unfairness. Narrow, calculating rationality might then seem to counsel being a predator or a doormat, as the case might be. In such cases, however, having appropriate emotions may in effect bring long-run considerations into the short run. Prospective feelings of guilt might check one's own predation; rage and the prospect of satisfaction might prompt retaliation against a predator. And perhaps biological natural selection works in favor of an appropriate emotional setup, since having it increases one's long-run probabilities of reaping one's share of the gains from cooperation and of avoiding being the victim of predators. Not only biological selection but also social conditioning may promote appropriate emotions.

Cooperativeness is not everything. An aversion to unfairness, as well, and even a disposition to take revenge in extreme cases, all with the supporting emotions, tend to serve both the private interests of individuals and their shared interest in a good society. Stewart Alsop (1970) showed better understanding than preachers of turning the other cheek when he wrote that "the man who makes a justified fuss does a public service".

Robert Axelrod (1984) formalizes some of these insights about reciprocity. He shows how individuals can rationally, out of self-interest, develop cooperation with one another, even absent an enforcement agency. His framework is an iterated prisoners' dilemma. His method is entirely theory and simulations, apart from descriptions of two computer tournaments, a chapter on live and let live in World War I trench warfare, and a coauthored chapter on biological aspects.

Participants in the two tournaments submitted computer programs embodying rules or strategies governing whether, on each move, to cooperate with one's fellow player or "defect" against him. Typically a rule took into account the other player's recent actions. The possible payoffs to a player on each move were Reward (if both players cooperate), Punishment (if both defect), Temptation (to the defecting player if the other cooperates), and Sucker's payoff (to a player cooperating while the other defects). Temptation is larger than Reward (but will pursuing it continue to succeed?), and Sucker's payoff is worse than Punishment. Another key parameter is w, expressing how much the payoff on the next move is discounted relative to the payoff on the current move. The further w falls below 1, the stronger the incentive for shortsighted behavior.

A strategy is "nice" if it involves never defecting first, "mean" if the player tries to exploit the other through nonretaliatory defection.

"Tit for tat" is the strategy of always cooperating unless the other player has defected on the last move, in which case one retaliates. It proves to be remarkably robust in winning. It conforms to several intuitively plausible precepts. (1) Don't be envious. Cooperation brings gains; the Prisoners' Dilemma is a positive-sum, not zero-sum, game. (2) Don't defect first; be nice. (3) Pay back cooperation and also defection. Demonstrate, quickly and emphatically, that you will not be walked over. Don't, however, bear a grudge too long: make it worth while for a noncooperator to reform his ways. (4) Don't be too clever. You don't want the other player to misinterpret your strategy. The tit-for-tat strategy, in short, is nice, provocable or retaliatory, forgiving, and clear.

Taking the game as an analogue of the real world, Axelrod suggests how a reformer might change it to promote cooperation and its benefits. (1) Enlarge the shadow of the future, the value of looking ahead (increase *w*). (2) Change the payoffs (for example, add an external penalty for defection). (3) Teach people to care about each other (as by emphasizing the points of Mill and Schlick reviewed above). (4) Teach reciprocity. (Turning the other cheek can not only hurt you but also, by encouraging predators, hurt innocent bystanders; Axelrod 1984, p. 136.) (5) Improve people's abilities to recognize other players and remember their past behaviors.

Axelrod also runs "ecological" simulations, analogues of biological selection, in which high-scoring strategies multiply themselves in subsequent rounds while low-scoring ones are weeded out. Again tit for tat fares well. Exploitative strategies may do well in early rounds but falter later as the victims they depend on perish.

Axelrod describes how a new strategy can invade. Even a world of always-defect could be successfully invaded by players of tit for tat if they came in a large enough cluster to flourish by cooperating with each other (compare Singer's similar point, noted above). Once the tit-for-tat invaders got established, it would be hard to dislodge them; a beneficial ratchet operates.

Axelrod also casts his discussions into a territorial context. Territoriality can be a device for "enlarging the shadow of the future", as by improving players' ability to recognize one another. Imitation of successful strategies can play a role in their spread.

Axelrod's message, in short, is that cooperation can get started, thrive in a variegated environment, and protect itself once established. No heroic assumptions are necessary for these results. Individuals need not even be rational: successful strategies can thrive even if the players do not understand just how. Players need not exchange words or commitments: their actions speak for them. Even in the absence of trust and altruism, the strategy of reciprocity can make defection unproductive and can elicit self-policing cooperation. No central authority is needed (Axelrod 1984, pp. 173–4).

In more recent work (gathered in his 1997 book), Axelrod further pursues his computer experiments on populations of members whose behaviors are governed by analogues of genes, subject to occasional mutations, and whose gains or losses in interactions with one another promote or impede reproduction. "Noise", including errors in one's own behavior and in interpreting the behavior of others, complicates the simulated environments. In these circumstances, strategies can evolve that are more complicated than straightforward tit for tat, involving, for example, behaviors that in effect probe for further information about one's fellow players. Still, reciprocity remains a key to success.

Ken Binmore warns against excessively confident or sweeping interpretations of work like Axelrod's (1994, esp. pp. 175, 194–203). Axelrod's games and tournaments had specific simplified features, and different ones might yield different results. So might novel developments analogous to biological mutations. Still, such work does stylize some real aspects of society. Additional twists of reality allow players to "opt out" of moves or to shun undesirable partners. Would-be exploiters get eliminated by others' refusal to play with them, and more cooperation results than in the original game (Flam 1994, reporting work of Philip Kitcher, John Batali, and Ann Stanley; Gordon Tullock had already made this point pithily in 1985).

THE RECONCILIATION PROJECT

"The Reconciliation Project" is Gregory Kavka's name for the attempt to reconcile morality with self-interest. Hobbes, he thinks, appealed solely to social rewards and punishments. Relying on such external sanctions alone to make crime unprofitable may require too much sacrifice, however, of liberty, privacy, and safety from state and police power (Kavka 1985, p. 304; cf. remarks on the law in Chapter 11 below).

Hobbes saw that violations of morality will occasionally turn out beneficial *in retrospect*, as when people take lucky actions for wrong reasons. That possibility, though, does not recommend violations. Hobbes also distinguished between offensive or aggressive violations and defensive violations. The latter, he thought, are not contrary to moral duty. He did not expect sacrifice of our own interests to immoral people. He advocated what Kavka (1985 p. 303) calls the Copper Rule: "Do unto others as they *do* unto you".

Morality sometimes requires sacrificing one's life, which cannot be in one's interest. Kavka replies (pp. 307–10) with remarks reminiscent of Henry Hazlitt's position, reviewed above. (1) Some fates are worse than death. (2) A moral way of life can be consistent with prudence, even though it involves some risk of sacrificing one's life. Besides, many immoral lifestyles impose higher risks of death. Suppose an immoralist gloats that it does not pay him to be moral. This claim shows no victory over us. "It is more like the pathetic boast of a deaf person that he saves money because it does not pay him to buy opera records" (p. 307).

An individual does not require the aid or cooperation of *all* other persons, only of enough others. What follows regarding group immorality? What reason do strong groups or countries have to treat weak ones decently? We cannot prove that decency is narrowly prudent in all historical or conceivable circumstances; at best we can show its prudence in actual (or attainable?) ones. Why should rich and powerful people treat others decently? They, or more likely their children, may be poor some time, Kavka argues. Offering opportunities to members of all groups widens the pool of talent available to fill socially useful jobs. "Decent treatment of all promotes social stability and cohesion and discourages revolution" (pp. 310–12).

Why should a wealthy and powerful nation aid poor, weak nations? Allies, even poor ones, are useful. Economic development of poor nations should benefit richer ones also, while continued poverty in the Third World is likely to produce continued war and turmoil. Reciprocity occurs between powerful and weak groups because of interdependencies in economic and security matters (pp. 312–13; I do not necessarily endorse the views just summarized; for distinct questions arise concerning foreign policy and foreign aid, including factual questions beyond those arising in ordinary ethical discussions).

Kavka further asks (pp. 313–15) what interest we the living have in acting morally toward future generations. Most people, he suggests, care about the happiness of their own children and grandchildren. People have a psychological need for concerns and projects that will continue after their deaths and so give meaning to their own lives and endeavors. One problem, though, is that these self-transcending concerns need not be directed toward the distant future. On the other hand, it may be a psychological fact that enterprises promising to continue into the indefinite future are better able to provide meaning for our lives or consolation for our mortality. Kavka admits that he finds these arguments for coincidence of self-interest and concern for posterity only partly convincing.

He then moves on to the wider project of reconciling morality with practical rationality. On any use of words that does not define all motives as self-interested, people sometimes do act otherwise than from self-interest. Almost everyone has altruistic and nonselfish ends to some degree. These ends may make the requirements of reason and morality coincide beyond the range of cases in which prudence and morality coincide. Carrying out duties to future generations, for example, fulfills nonselfish ends of our own, besides contributing to our happiness. Parents who care about the well-being of their children strongly and of others moderately have reasons for raising their children to be moral. Thus morality can be potentially self-sustaining from generation to generation. "While it is normally prudent to be moral, it is sometimes rational to be moral even if it is not prudent" (Kavka 1985, pp. 315–17).

Neera Kapur Badhwar (1993) further develops ideas of Hume, Mill, and Schlick (and others, including Adler 1970). She argues that self-interest and altruism (in the non-Randian, nonpejorative sense) often reinforce each other. Without a due sense of self, even altruism would be no virtue. Certain character traits are commonly regarded as morally deficient, like blind deference to and abject self-sacrifice for a more intelligent and talented person. Someone leading such a life has abdicated any judgment and ends of her own or has never developed them. She sees herself only as a means to the ends of others; and if they did not wish to use her for their ends, she would have nothing to live for (Badhwar 1993, summary on pp. 116–17).

Self-affirming motivations – acting from a certain kind of character – may support the *depth* and *strength* of a person's altruistic motivations. Rescuers of Jews in Nazi Europe, says Badhwar, had altruism as a central part of their very identity. They helped other persons not just for the sake of those others but also to be true to themselves. Self-interest can be moral because it "includes the interest in being true to oneself and affirming one's altruistic dispositions"; without that interest one could not act "in a wholeheartedly altruistic manner" (pp. 115–16).

David Schmidtz (1993) also echoes arguments of Mill and Schlick, although apparently unaware of them. We can nurture our sense of purpose and our self-regard by taking part in something larger than our own narrow selves. Thrasymachus (a Sophist of unconventional ethics) has narrower goals and fewer reasons to live than most people; he cannot act out of regard for others; his life is impoverished (p. 68).

Having goals beyond pure self-regard and preferences worthy of satisfaction, "becoming an important part of something bigger than ourselves" – all give us more to live for (pp. 58, 61–3). We want a sense of being peaceful, productive, and esteemed members of our society and the satisfaction of deserving the esteem of our fellows (pp. 57, 63). "We seek real rapport with others, not merely a sham." We want it for our real selves, "not merely our false facades" (p. 64). If we deceive other people, we keep them from affirming our real selves (p. 68n.). In having a principled character, we become selves worth struggling for (pp. 60–61). Although our character is not directly under our control, our choices and actions do create habits and so shape the accumulation of dispositions that constitutes our character.

For Schmidtz, (non-Randian) altruism necessarily means self-sacrifice only for purely self-interested persons. Despite Kant, getting joy out of an action does not keep it from being altruistic. In exchanging a lesser for a greater value, as a person who cares for others often does in an altruistic act, one is not sacrificing oneself. Altruism will involve self-sacrifice in exceptional cases, but not routinely. It can be in one's own interest to develop the sort of character that would lead one to "fall on grenades" in an exceptional situation, which quite probably will not arise anyway (Schmidtz 1993, pp. 64–6 and notes, citing Gregory Kavka on the grenades).

Schmidtz realistically observes that people have only so much capacity for genuine concern. Trying to care about everyone would probably impoverish rather than enrich our lives (p. 66).

David Kelley, a philosopher influenced by Ayn Rand, expounds "the selfish basis of benevolence" (as he subtitles his 1996 book). He argues that treating other people with consideration and respect, as potential trading partners, and behaving as a worthy partner oneself, contributes to a society of beneficially interacting persons and to one's own interest even more specifically. (Recall his exposition of benevolence as summarized in Chapter 2.)

Viktor Vanberg (1987) echoes some now familiar points, though in insightfully different terminology. By analogy with government and politics, he distinguishes between the level of specific decisions and actions and the constitutional level – between particular actions and the moral *disposition* guiding them. The moral person constitutionally internalizes moral precepts. He recognizes that a particular situation may arise from time to time in which *im*moral behavior would be to his own advantage – provided that, contrary to fact, he could keep such misbehavior from having repercussions on other situations and on his own reputation and character. Aware of such repercussions, however, the moral person adopts a constitutional decision to cultivate character traits that bar him from pursuing narrow self-interest in immoral ways. He senses that such a course serves his own probabilistic long-run self-interest.

At least three reasons recommend heeding rules rather than making case-by-case decisions: saving on decisionmaking costs; lessening the risk of mistakes resulting, for instance, from inadequate information; and bypassing the tendency for case-by-case decisions to be biased in favor of short-term interests at the expense of long-term interests (Vanberg 1987, pp. 20–21). While arguing that sticking to moral routine and *not calculating* in particular choice situations can be rational, Vanberg does not say that acting morally must be rational even in a situation when the individual somehow *has* calculated and has properly accounted for all consequences and still finds the immoral choice to be the "maximizing" one (p. 27).

CHARACTERS OF THE INDIVIDUAL AND OF SOCIETY

Like Hobbes, Frank, Kavka, and others, Vanberg notes that consilience of morality and constitutional self-interest depends on the nature of society. Where people prey on each other and where moral characters are too scarce to be recognized and valued, the exceptional moral person would be a sucker and victim; constitutional morality would not serve his own interest. Consilience holds only in a society of generally moral persons (or, as Axelrod might say, only in the presence of a sufficient number of moral potential trading partners, even if not an actual majority).

The internal sanctions of emotions and conscience cannot, in Vanberg's view, enforce morality quite independently of external and social sanctions, direct or indirect (p. 31). People will perceive morality as sensible for themselves only if rewards and punishments do adequately occur. A community's current level of morality reflects past enforcement of the rules, and maintaining it requires ongoing enforcement. In this sense morality is *social capital* that depreciates in the absence of reinvestment. Where informal enforcement fails, formal enforcement may serve as a substitute, although inadequate. Life would be miserable in a society where rigorous formal enforcement ensured that moral behavior was advantageous even in each individual situation (p. 33). (In a footnote Vanberg says he is ignoring issues arising from dissent over moral rules; his entire essay assumes that morality is a disposition to follow rules generally considered binding.)

Frank van Dun (1994) also focuses on institutions. Self-interest and social interest do not coincide automatically. An appeal to the individual's sense of natural justice and to his sympathy will work only in a suitable setting. The continued existence of social order requires institutions that make the individual "self-interestedly concerned to behave in accordance with the natural laws of justice" (van Dun, pp. 278–9). A major test of institutions, then, is whether they promote or undercut the consilience of self-interest and social interest.

The characters of a society and of its individual members interact. What an individual sees as his own interest and whether he sees it as compatible with the social interest depend partly on society's ethical tone and partly on internalization of values and on emotions. These in turn depend partly on how children are raised.

It might be dishonest to preach that self- and social interest generally coincide to children somehow implausibly but actually destined to spend their entire lives in the stereotypical urban ghetto. Amidst pervasive immorality, the exceptional ethical person risks being a patsy. Something like a knife edge or a critical mass may prevail: above it, self-interest and the general interest increasingly coincide; below it, they diverge. Below it, more exactly, ethical behavior is increasingly futile for serving both the general interest and one's own.

Things are different in a society where parents *generally and successfully* teach the compatibility of self- and social interests, at least probabilistically and in the long run. There, ethical preaching can help make itself true. Words and the character of society can reinforce each other.

I have not fully worked out a coherent set of arguments about cheating, as on tests in school. Even so, this issue may still illustrate my general point. Where practically everyone cheats, honesty hurts its rare practitioner, unless he also happens to be an exceptionally good student. But where most people are honest, acquiring the character of a cheater tends to work out to own's own disadvantage.

"GREED"

A.B. Cramp (1991) expresses concern about "greed" in assessing, from an avowedly Christian point of view, the philosophical foundations of economics and particularly its assumption of rational utility maximization.[2] Concerns like his invite some reflection on an issue at the intersection of economics and ethics.

Familiar preachments about attending less to self-interest and more to the common weal sometimes forget that the term need not be restricted to *narrow* self-interest. In a plausibly broad sense, it also covers special concern for one's friends, relatives, and associates and for esteemed values, projects, and causes. Preachments against "greed" also often confuse pursuit of self-interest with unacceptable *methods* of pursuing it. Suspect methods include lying, cheating, stealing, and coercing. The latter includes trying to enlist governmental coercion on one's own behalf, as to obtain tax-financed benefits or special privileges or shelter from competition (cf. Horwitz 1996, pp. 729–30). Narrowly self-serving behavior also deserves suspicion within intimate "face-to-face" groups like the family, the circle of close friends, the military unit, the sports team, and perhaps the church and the small business. Within such a group, behavior reflecting a certain solidarity is in the interest not only of the group but also of the individual member (cf. Hayek's discussion reviewed in Chapter 9 and also Horwitz 1996).

It only compounds the confusion if, instead of deploring illegitimate means, one calls in effect for more of the same – coercion intended to subordinate individuals' own interests to some supposed transcendent social interest. Preaching might better aim not at condemning people's pursuing their own projects but at urging side constraints on that pursuit: each person should respect others' rights and otherwise obey the ordinary precepts of morality.

The *American Heritage Dictionary* (second college edition) defines greed as "excessive desire to acquire or possess, as wealth or power, beyond what one needs or deserves". This definition helps illuminate what gives greed a bad name. The word "deserves" alludes to illegitimate *methods* of grasping wealth or power. No one "deserves" the fruits of activities tending seriously to subvert social cooperation. The words "excessive desire" allude to personal character: the greedy person acts from a conception of self-interest too narrowly or materialistically oriented toward wealth or power for himself.

Both these aspects legitimately concern the moral philosopher, and the resulting behavior in its most flagrant forms also concerns legislators and the police. The latter two groups have the job of identifying criminal actions, ones unambiguously subversive of social cooperation. The moral philosopher's job includes trying to appraise character traits, attitudes, dispositions, and even tastes and preferences.

As with certain other words ("democracy", for example), clear thought and communication suffer when several distinct concepts bear a single label. It invites confusion to label as "greed" not only the two aspects of its dictionary definition but also ordinary attention to self-interest, even material self-interest, or diligent work, venturesomeness, and other kinds of zeal in the pursuit. Should the person studying for a professional career be stigmatized as greedy? What about the shopper at a bargain sale? The fledgling politician cultivating his personal contacts? The creative business entrepreneur? Wealth does not come out of a fixed pool that somehow just exists; people create it. As Adam Smith taught, people pursuing their own interests in honest transactions also serve the interests of other people. Great material success does not in itself betoken depravity.

If the word "greed" ever does serve clear thinking and communication, it implies something beyond self-interest, something ranging from a severe character defect to immoral or downright criminal activity. Fuming in general, then, about the "greed of the eighties" or the "greed of pharmaceutical companies" undercuts necessary distinctions; it muddles activities and character traits meaningfully called greedy together with others merely conducive to material success.

What do complaints of greed in society mean, operationally? What if any remedy is proposed? Is the complaint really about lying, cheating, and stealing employed in pursuit of wealth and power? Incidentally, do all improper methods fit into those three categories? What about dirty office politics employed to advance one's own career at others' expense? If the greedy careerist tells lies, the matter is clear. Or he may be cheating, in a broad sense, through using methods subversive of a healthy society or work group. So doing, he might be deemed in violation of an implicit contract to behave decently in return for other persons' decency. Such violation of tacit rules of interpersonal relations arrogates unfair privilege onto oneself and is a kind of free-riding.

If the complaint is not about unfair methods but about faulty personal character – about self-interest conceived excessively narrowly as wealth and power for oneself alone – then, again, what is the complainer proposing? Are the proposed remedies likely to work as desired without unacceptable side effects? But perhaps the complainer is merely urging people to reconsider their own characters. Perhaps he is a prophet, a psychological and ethical teacher. If so, more power to him. (Occasionally, however, fuming about greed may convey a suggestion that the complainer has a more noble character than the people condemned.)

It takes all kinds of (decent) people to make a world. Social cooperation and gains from trade thrive on some people's narrow pursuit of material wealth.[3] Provided they do not lie, cheat, steal, and coerce, Adam Smith's invisible hand leads them to serve a broader interest as well. If they are employing coercion or intimidation to maintain a monopoly position, their method is what deserves condemnation; but if their monopoly is noncoercive and therefore temporary, a benevolent spectator would only wish that other people were equally zealous in finding and serving in profitable niches.

Perhaps the slaves to material accumulation would be happier if they had a broader conception of self-interest, but that is basically their own problem. Anyone wanting to preach about happier lifestyles is free to do so. Psycho-therapists, teachers, clergy, novelists, playwrights, book reviewers, movie and drama critics, talk-show hosts, and friendly conversationalists have wide scope for such preaching, outside the exercise of governmental coercion.

To recapitulate, "greed" is a vague charge by itself. Suggesting a remedy might help clarify the complaint. Once one is proposed, we may compare the likely states of affairs before and after its application. If no remedy is conceivable, the complaint is empty, like complaining about gravity. While character appraisal and ethical/psychological preaching can be useful, it is doubtful whether government is best suited to perform those functions.

CONCLUSIONS

The considerations reviewed in this chapter emphatically do not recommend altruism in the Randian sense of sacrifice of one's own interests and values to those adopted from other people to curry their supposed favor. Several considerations count against making a virtue of such altruism. First, it is psychologically unrealistic to expect people to subordinate their own interests (which need not be limited to narrow personal pleasure) to the interests of other persons with whom they have no special ties. To require at least lip service to such altruism would create tensions between professed standards and actual behavior and so would create guilt feelings and unhappiness. Second, altruism, if generally practiced, would spell an inefficient pursuit of happiness; for people cannot generally know and serve others' interests as well as their own. The result would be somewhat as if people were continually giving each other presents while forbidden to buy what they really wanted for themselves. Third, wide lip service to altruism would bring some people to expect *being* served and *having* sacrifices made for them. The moochers of Ayn Rand's novels would seek whatever they themselves wanted by flaunting their own distress and by trading on the guilt feelings of avowed altruists. The tone of society would become unhealthy.

Rejecting altruism does not mean exalting selfishness – not if selfishness means favoring oneself over others by unfair means and in disregard of others' rights, nor if it means behavior ranging from inconsiderateness to downright predation. (Rand rejects any such attitude as that of "looters". She invites misunderstanding, however, by using the word "selfishness" in an unusual way to designate an actual good.)

The attitude that harmonizes self-interest and the general interest, then, is neither altruism nor selfishness. Nor is it some perfunctory splitting of the difference. Rather, it is the attitude of the trader, as Rand would say, coupled with the sympathy with others observed by Hume, Adam Smith, Mill, and Schlick and with the generalized goodwill approved (though not stressed) by Rand herself. Rand's trader, the Randian hero, relates openly and honestly to others as he pursues his own goals fair and square. He neither sacrifices himself nor expects others to sacrifice themselves for his sake. In business relations, he expects both himself and his trading partners to share in the gains from trade.

Conceivably, an individual might gain by lying, cheating, stealing, and gross inconsiderateness, all while maintaining the appearance of decency. He might benefit both from taking unfair advantage of others yet having a good reputation. Maintaining this divergence between appearance and reality, however, would require constant vigilance. He would have to conceal his unfair dealings and keep track of his lies, trying to keep them consistent. Maintaining his deception would divert time, skill, and energy from other and perhaps more rewarding activities.

One's own behavior presumably draws surer responses from other people in small groups of frequently interacting members than in large groups of changing membership and personal anonymity. A possible illustration is the inconsiderateness alleged – how validly I do not know – to be more prevalent in large cities than in small towns. No one, anyway, not even a potential scoundrel, can count on interacting with others only anonymously in large groups; everyone also belongs to small subgroups.

Even if a scoundrel does make out well over the long run, his success is likely to flow from his intellect, talents, and effort rather than from his immorality, without which his success might well have been greater. Another factor counting against the strategy of being a scoundrel while cultivating the opposite appearance involves self-esteem. Being able to conceive of oneself as a person of integrity serves one's sense of well-being better than awareness of perpetrating a sustained deception. Furthermore, repeated immoral behavior is likely to impair the individual's character and so his capacity for happiness, particularly by curtailing the sharing and multiplication of joys through what Schlick (1930/1961, p. 189) called the "social impulses".

A disposition to behave honestly, cooperatively, and fairly, and even to express justified indignation, serves the individual's own interest, even though merely as a long-run and uncertain tendency. Examples do exist of people flourishing through dishonesty and predation and of people ruining or even losing their lives through honesty and decency. This world gives no guarantees that morality will pay off. We must act on the probabilities. As Schlick, Robert Frank, and others argue, however, the probabilities do recommend morality.

These points about what serves a person's carefully considered, long-run-oriented self-interest gains support, by contrast, from Edward C. Banfield's diagnosis (1970) of criminals, drug addicts, and others who make a botch of their lives: they tend to have short time horizons. They cannot or do not take account of how their misbehavior harms not only their victims but themselves in the longer run.

Some persons, true enough, care nothing for integrity and even relish successful deception. They are a minority, however – and this conjecture provides another point where ethics is open to empirical research. They form a subset of scoundrels, ones who feel satisfaction rather than remorse.

Why are such scoundrels rare (if in fact they are)? Perhaps social processes and even biological processes have selected against them. Perhaps most persons have been conditioned in many ways from early childhood to value ordinary ethical precepts. They are taught that a decent character generally serves one's own interest. Even if (contrary to what I think is true) such conditioning had no prior basis in objective reality, its prevalence would tend to make its teachings true after all. General belief that decency serves one's own interest would affect people's expected and actual reactions to each other's behavior and so would affect what behavior did serve one's self-esteem and sense of well-being.

This chapter's propositions about interaction between the characters of individuals and of their society and about self-reinforcement of vice and virtue are positive propositions and may perhaps prove wrong. If right, they have an important bearing on issues of economic development and economic backwardness.[4] Right or wrong, they are amenable to research, difficult though it may be. They illustrate, again, the empirical and scientific character of utilitarian ethics.

Even if self-interest and moral behavior are compatible, by and large, the question remains of the relation between self-interest and the *impartiality* plausibly regarded as a defining characteristic of ethical propositions. The next chapter faces this question.

NOTES

1. This chapter's central question is related, then, to what Moritz Schlick calls "the fundamental question of ethics, 'Why does man act morally?'" (1930/1961, p. 30). (For me the fundamental question, or the one tackled throughout this book, is rather different: what is the nature of ethical propositions – how do they combine factual, logical, and normative content – what are they based on, and why, if for any reason, should they be heeded?)

   Schlick's approach to his fundamental question tends to deny the autonomy of ethics, assimilating it to psychology and other positive sciences. But why should that be disturbing? Does not science try to forge links among previously distinct phenomena and theories? For Schlick, an answer resting on psychology is "no degradation of, nor injury to, science, but a happy simplification of the world-picture. In ethics we do not seek independence, but only the truth" (p. 30; cf. pp. 25, 28–9).

   Without emphasizing the distinction, Schlick characterizes the descriptive or explanatory part of ethics, not the evaluative part. In the passages cited, he is concerned with what people actually do and think, and why, not with what they *should* do and think. What Schlick reduces to psychology is not what actually *is* right but the aspect of ethics (related to the question "Why be moral?") that concerns how conscience and other influences operate on the individual to encourage behavior generally regarded as ethical. One can will and act only in line with one's impulses. The Kantian imperative "that one act wholly independently of one's inclinations" is impossible to obey. "It goes contrary to the facts of psychology and therefore has no interest for us. Moral conduct is either impossible or it is derived from natural inclinations" (p. 62).

2. Cramp (1991, pp. 60–61) credits both St Paul and William Law, an eighteenth century Christian writer, with the insight that rationality and greed are opposites, not correlates. Mentioning Karl Marx, Cramp conjectures that greed as a motive force in Western culture – the goal of "more, without limits" – may trace more to collective cultural forces than to inborn instincts of individuals (pp. 58–9).

3. John Stossel made several of the points of this section in an ABC television program called "Greed", 3 February 1998, 9–10 p.m. US central time, defiantly using the term in a neutral or even laudatory sense. Other participants included David Kelley, Ted Turner, T.J. Rodgers, and Walter Williams. Kelley, a philosopher, observed that Michael Milken, the inventor or promoter of junk bonds, did more good for the world than Mother Teresa. Sure, Mother Teresa suffered; but what is so good about suffering? Kelley is probably right, but choosing between the two character types is unnecessary. It takes all kinds of (honorable) people to fill the world's different niches, and little is to be gained from badgering people to divert their energies and talents away from the niches where they have a comparative advantage. Activities motivated by "caring" rather than "greed", observed Williams, an economist, are frequently disasters. "Greed helps build civilization", said Stossel in closing.

4. Banfield (1958) shows the role of "amoral familism" (an excessively narrow and short-run concern for the material welfare of the nuclear family), together with dishonesty, suspiciousness, and envy, in impeding social cooperation and economic development in a town of southern Italy around 1955. Fukuyama (1995) gives a more general discussion of the importance of trust. Also recall other writings mentioned in Chapter 1.

9. Duty and universalizability

KANT'S AND OTHER VIEWS OF DUTY

The remark about "falling on grenades" (quoted in Chapter 8) brings to mind the view that *duty* is the centerpiece of ethics. Why be moral? Because duty so requires. An act is especially virtuous, on this view, if done *contrary* to one's own interest and inclination.

Duty, by the word's derivation, is action that is due, owed. It concerns fulfilling obligations to other persons (and arguably to oneself). On a utilitarian view, the concept and sense of duty are instrumental: ideally, dutiful behavior serves happiness. Duty for its own sake is senseless. Contrary to Kant, the type of personal character that leads to specific behavior only from a sense of duty is less estimable than character that leads to it from inclination. Moritz Schlick agrees with Marcus Aurelius, who said: In the stage of perfection "thou wilt do what is right, not because it is proper, but because thereby thou givest thyself pleasure" (quoted in Schlick 1930/1961, p. 207, and *passim* for similar remarks; cf. Taylor 1970 and Olson 1965).

Suppose one man has a joyful interest in other people and their welfare; he helps his distressed neighbor because he likes him, feels his distress, and takes satisfaction in helping. A second man dislikes his neighbor yet grudgingly gives the same help because he feels a moral obligation. On the view being criticized, he is the more virtuous, for his sense of duty overrides his inclinations. The first man is not particularly praiseworthy; for he is following his inclinations, which just happen to be benevolent. Someone doing good because of duty is more admirable than someone "who does it because of an inclination, to whom it has become quite natural" (Schlick 1930/1961, p. 207, paraphrasing a view he rejects).

This view is commonly attributed above all to Immanuel Kant (see, for example, Hazlitt 1964, Chapter 16; Walker 1978, Chapter XI; my own reading of Kant 1775–80/1963 and 1785MFM/1949 bears out this interpretation). For Kant, the only truly moral act is one done from a sense of duty. A kind deed done from inclination rather than from a sense of duty, however right and amiable it may be, still lacks genuine moral worth. More exactly, on Kant's view, it is not the action but the agent who lacks moral worth (Walker 1978, p. 159, quoting Kant's *Grundlegung zur Metaphysik der Sitten* [1785], Volume IV, p. 398, *Gesammelte Schriften*, Berlin: Georg Reimier, 1911).

Richard Taylor says that if he were ever to encounter someone who claimed really to *believe* and practice Kant's metaphysical morals, "then my incredulity and distrust of him as a human being could not be greater than if he told me he regularly drowned children just to see them squirm" (Taylor 1970, p. xii).

What is the nature and source of duty? For Kant, the moral law and duty exist as objective aspects of a reality independent of human desires. The virtuous man perceives the moral law and autonomously imposes it upon himself. Trying to justify it as serving human happiness would tarnish its grandeur. Morality is not to be pursued for any value outside itself. The commands of moral law may make certain ends worth pursuing; but no independent value in the ends, nor anything independent of morality, can give the moral law its value (Walker 1978, pp. 151–2, interpreting Kant).

How does one know what the moral law commands and what one's duty is? In one strand of explanation, Kant invokes his categorical imperative: "Act only on a maxim by which you can will that it, at the same time, should become a general law" (Kant 1785MFM/1949, p. 170; Flew 1971, p. 122, quotes a trivially different translation). In effect Kant asks: Would you like everyone in your situation to act on the maxim you now propose to act on, regarding it almost as a law of nature? (my restatement of Walker's paraphrase, 1978, pp. 154–5). We need not dwell on whether Kant's highly abstract precept yields clear rules for all circumstances. Oddly, it is a command issued by no commander; as an aspect of reality, it issues itself. Oddly, again, it is *categorical*. A categorical imperative comes with no *if*s, *and*s, or *but*s attached; it contrasts with a hypothetical imperative, such as "Take this medicine if you want to get well". Kant's imperative does not say: "Act on such and such a maxim *if* you want to serve human happiness or *if* you want to get to Heaven". It says: "Act in such and such a way, period".

Despite its illuminating contrast with the very different doctrine urged in this book, Kant's test does ask, in effect, whether one could *acceptably* will general adoption of a proposed maxim. But "acceptably" in view of what? Isn't acceptability a utilitarian criterion? Plausibly, then, John Stuart Mill imputes disguised utilitarian premises to Kant. From his principle concerning whether the maxim of an individual's action could be adopted as a law by all rational beings, Kant cannot deduce any actual duties of morality. He fails to show that it would be logically contradictory or physically impossible for all rational beings to adopt "the most outrageously immoral rules of conduct". All he shows is that no one would like "the *consequences* of their universal adoption" (Mill 1861, 1863, Chapter I, p. 246 in Cowling edition, p. 134 in Gray edition).

When Kant propounds his fundamental principle, Mill continues, he virtually acknowledges that an agent conscientiously deciding on the morality of some act must have the interest of mankind in mind. Kant could not plausibly maintain "that a rule even of utter selfishness could not *possibly* be adopted by all rational beings – that there is any insuperable obstacle in the nature of things to its adoption". If Kant's principle is to have any meaning at all, it "must be that we ought to shape our conduct by a rule which all rational beings might adopt *with benefit to their collective interest*" (Chapter V, pp. 292–3 in Cowling edition, p. 188 in Gray edition).

How might Kant's exaltation of duty have ever seemed plausible? Hazlitt (1964, Chapter 16) suggests an answer. No matter how morally required an act may be, when we perform it out of personal inclination, love, or spontaneous benevolence, we are not *conscious* of acting from duty, nor do we associate our underlying character traits with duty. When, however, we dutifully force ourselves to overcome personal inclination, we are more likely to be aware of a link between duty and moral merit.

Still, the concept of duty, its performance, and the requisite character traits would be pointless unless they ultimately tended to serve happiness. Actually, they have value as instruments to a good beyond themselves. Kant's mistake was to suppose that respect for duty is superior to whatever good it might serve and superior to and even subject to contamination by other virtues like sympathy and kindness. He thus confused instrumental with ultimate good (Hazlitt 1964, Chapter 16).

Duty-centered morality exalts *renunciation*: it calls for repressing one's own purposes in favor of obedience to a ghostly but objective moral law or, in its altruistic variant, in favor of the desires of other persons. Schlick recommends, instead, "the Socratic, Stoic, and Epicurean" morality of self-realization and affirmation, which asks "How must I live to be happy?" Although condemnation of selfishness does not form its core, this morality does value considerateness toward others and does reject narrow egoism "with all desirable distinctness, although usually not in the form of an original, ultimate obligation, but as a derivative demand" (Schlick 1930/1961, pp. 79–81).

By no means do I ridicule the very concept of duty. In making agreements and in other interpersonal relations, people incur obligations that, by ordinary ethical standards, they ought to fulfill. Public offices and other jobs carry duties; so even does driving a car. It might not stretch the concept too far to say that people in general have duties to obey the law (with rare exceptions) and to cultivate the recognized virtues. Conceived of in a properly non-Kantian way, duty is instrumental: taking it seriously serves social cooperation and so ultimately serves happiness. (In case the context has not made its meaning clear, I understand a duty to be a moral obligation incumbent on a person in especially clear and strong degree, and sometimes a legal obligation. People have duties to respect the rights of others, as discussed in Chapter 10.)

COMPLIANCE IN EXCEPTIONAL CASES

We can understand the general utility of a rule requiring a person, in rare extreme cases, to sacrifice his interests and even his life for others' sake. Such a duty might be part of the terms of employment of a police officer, fire fighter, or soldier. To such a person the combined rules of general morality and terms of his job say in effect: "You must be prepared to run this risk and make this sacrifice if the extreme occasion should arise, even though doing so then defeats even your own long-run enlightened self-interest". Morality can require fulfilling responsibilities even when, in exceptional extreme cases, doing so is ruinous to oneself. Holding oneself and others to the rules is in the long-run interest of *everyone*. Once we tolerate anyone's making an exception in his own favor, we subvert the purpose that the rules serve (Hazlitt 1964, Chapter 14, partly analyzing a passage quoted from Kurt Baier).

But suppose that one of these extreme cases had actually arisen and that you, a superior officer, were in radio contact with the person whose self-sacrifice you now required. How could you persuade him to perform his duty? You could hardly argue that his doing so would be in his own interest as well as in the general interest, for his own interest would be to save himself. You might appeal to his interest in being remembered as a hero rather than surviving as a coward despised by himself and others. But that argument is hardly compelling: it amounts to denying, after all, the postulated exceptional but genuine clash between self-interest and social interest.

The valid comment on such a situation could hardly be directed especially to the unfortunate duty-bearer who found himself already in it. If he had a deeply ingrained moral character, he would perform his duty anyway. Furthermore, it would have been in his own interest throughout his life up to the time in question to have that sort of character, as opposed to the character of someone ready to shirk his duty whenever shirking seemed expedient.

The rules calling for self-sacrifice in the exceptional case are directed to persons in the abstract who might conceivably some day find themselves in the postulated exigent roles and situations. They are not especially directed to specific persons whose lives are already at stake. However, the rules requiring heroic sacrifice from abstract persons in abstract extreme cases would lose their meaning and credibility if they ceased to be considered binding whenever the question arose of actually applying them to a definite person at a definite time and place. Such rules *do* have utility; taking them seriously does make happiness greater on the whole than it would otherwise be.

Thus, the question about conflict between individual interest and social interest in postulated cases must be answered with due attention to its context. (Compare Ayn Rand's remarks about context-dropping reprinted in Binswanger 1986, pp. 104–5.) We have another instance of the point already made about how morality serves happiness, not without exceptions but by and large. The evidence may not be overwhelming, but the point does again illustrate how ethics affords scope for empirical inquiry. The association between morality and happiness is probabilistic only, and tragic exceptional cases do not disprove it. No line of behavior and no type of personal character can actually guarantee happiness.

THE GENERALIZATION PRINCIPLE

Many ethicists[1] put forth a generalization principle, also called a principle of universality, universalizability, impartiality, or neutrality: ethical precepts must apply equally to all persons in relevantly similar circumstances. Precepts must not discriminate *arbitrarily* in favor of some persons and against others. "[A] normative proposition ... fails to comply with the generalization principle and so cannot be regarded as morally valid, if it applies only to some men, and not to all, in respects in which they are all essentially alike" (Adler 1970, p. 149). Of course, any two persons and their circumstances always are different: perhaps one weighs more or less than the other, was born on a different day of the week, or, unlike the other, is a friend of a specific person. But if a putative precept calls for treating the two persons differently, plausible argument must be available to show how the difference between them matters. In Peter Singer's example (1982, p. 93), if I say I may take the nuts someone else has gathered but that no one may take mine, I will be asked how the two cases differ. Not just any reason will do. The reason must seem sufficiently disinterested.

A precept would be suspect if it gave special weight, in interpersonal relations and policy decisions, to the welfare of specific individuals identified either by name or by characteristics specified merely to confer that special privilege. I might propose my own personal well-being or that of relatively few persons sharing specified personal characteristics with me as the supreme criterion to which the interests of all other persons must yield. Other persons would not take me seriously, for I could not explain *why* I or my narrow group deserved such special favor. To be taken seriously I would have to offer a bona fide argument – as in the postulated case I cannot – showing that following my suggested criterion would be more widely beneficial. Another example of nongeneralizability would be a principle approving the torture of redheads for the amusement of others, all without any argument showing that such victimization and pandering to sadism would benefit people in general. Justifying discrimination in favor of (or against) named individuals or specific groups requires more than a bald assertion that their well-being counts especially heavily (or slightly) toward the general welfare.

The generalization principle does not rule out (nor does it necessarily require) special consideration of persons in particular predicaments or with special needs. Nor does it rule out each person's preferring his own interests and the interests of the persons whom he cares most about, like family members, friends, fellow workers, and associates in cherished causes. Special preferences of that sort are practically unavoidable and indeed are necessary for happy lives and a good society. Recognizing the legitimacy of special interests and loyalties can be a *general* principle: *each person*, not just discriminatorily selected persons, is entitled to favor his own. Further general principles still restrict the means by which and extent to which one may legitimately practice such favoritism. (The section on "Partiality and universalizability" below continues this strand of discussion.)

UNIVERSALIZABILITY AS A LOGICAL OR LINGUISTIC REQUIREMENT

How is the generalization principle *grounded*? Perhaps impartiality follows almost tautologically from the very meaning of ethics – although something is suspicious about trying to settle substantive issues by definitional maneuvers. Or perhaps the generalization requirement follows, instead or also, as the conclusion of a substantive argument with utilitarian aspects.

According to R.M. Hare (1989EiET, p. 44), a moral judgment about one situation commits the speaker, on pain of logical inconsistency, to the same judgment about any relevantly identical situation. The central use of moral statements is to *prescribe* actions, attitudes, and so forth. In making a moral judgment we are prescribing universally for all similar cases (Hare 1989EoPM, pp. 128-9). Linguistic fact, Hare maintains, makes ethical propositions prescriptive and universalizable. Saying that a person with specified characteristics in specified circumstances ought to act in a specified way calls on all persons with the same characteristics in the same circumstances (including me, if I fit the description) to act in the same way. If someone says that he is in the same situation as I am, even possessing the same psychological characteristics and so forth, yet that he ought to behave one way and I another, he is twisting the very meaning of "ought". His offense against language is similar to saying, "All the books on the shelf are blue, yet there is one which isn't" (Hare 1989EoPM, p. 86).

Joel Kupperman takes a similar position. Citing David Hume's discussion (1751-77/1930, Section IX, Part I, para. 6), he notes the sense inherent in moral judgment "that the judgement should be shared: that others, from their perspective, should see roughly what one sees from one's own perspective. This distinguishes moral judgements from judgements purely of self-interest"

(Kupperman 1983, p. 35). Kupperman "agree[s] with Hume that to make a genuine moral judgement is to make an implicit appeal for the agreement of others (an appeal which thus must rest on impersonally statable considerations), and with Hare that moral judgements are subject to the logical requirement of universalisability" (p. 98).

Logic requires imposing the same moral requirements on any one person as on all others unless the differences between their situations are demonstrably relevant (p. 44). Relevance is partly a matter of fact and consequences, not of logic alone. Whether Gauguin was justified in deserting his family to paint in the South Seas may depend partly on whether he was a great or a mediocre painter (p. 44).

Supposedly, then, it is a logical and linguistic error to state a rule but make an arbitrary exception for oneself or other selected persons even though they do share the characteristics and circumstances covered by the rule. Suppose I say that two situations morally permit or require different behaviors, yet I cannot say why. I am both asserting a difference, for I recommend different behaviors; yet I am at least implicitly admitting that there is no difference, for I cannot say what it is. Or if I do state a difference, I expose myself to the question of why the difference matters. Suppose I point to some trivial difference between the two cases – some people in the one but not in the other case have curly hair – but I cannot say how that justifies the different recommendations. Then I am still commiting a logical inconsistency – both asserting a relevant difference yet conceding that there is none after all.

UNIVERSALIZABILITY AS A UTILITARIAN CONCLUSION

But is it a sheer dictate of logical consistency or something else after all that requires ethical precepts to be universalizable? It would be strange indeed to say that all persons with specified characteristics and in specified circumstances ought to act in a certain way *except* Gordon Tullock or *except* polymath autodidact economists who have published books with specified titles and who are skilled in the art of the humorous insult. (I am elaborating on a kind of joke that Tullock has used himself.) If in some circumstances or respects Tullock or other skilled insulters were to be treated differently than other people, then anyone saying so would be expected to explain what relevant differences called for the special treatment. (Cf. Bruce Ackerman 1980 on the role of discussion in justifying special treatment.)

One might conceivably argue, for example, that it is permissible to tell insulters like Tullock falsehoods about their actions, characters, or reputations that could not properly be told to others. A possible reason might be that insulters like Tullock would be more likely amused than hurt by what they would recognize as moves in a game that they themselves were playing. But some such relevant reason for differential treatment must be offered or at least be available.

It would be very peculiar, similarly, to postulate satisfying the wishes of Gordon Tullock as the supreme criterion of behavior and policy – or satisfying the wishes of a few persons who share specified characteristics with him – all without any bona fide argument that such a criterion is beneficial generally and not only to Tullock or his narrow group.

But does that peculiarly discriminatory postulate actually contradict itself? Do the very meanings of normative terms rule it out? The peculiar postulate is of course unlikely to be widely heeded, but considerations of acceptability go beyond the sheer meanings of words and requirements of logic.

Since the requirement of impartiality is bound up with a value judgment, it cannot be strictly proved. In fact, however, a precept blatantly resting on someone's narrow self-interest would not be credible, would not be heeded, and would not work. A doctrine could not be effective – for it would be laughed out of court – if it gave especially high or low weight to the interests of specific persons solely because of who they were.

An ethical doctrine could not be beneficial unless it could be expected to guide behavior, by and large. A doctrine, along with the practices and institutions it recommends, should be capable of becoming *transparent*, of being publicly and seriously espoused. People should be able to accept it even after reflecting on its meaning and grounding. A doctrine's credibility would suffer if it required each person routinely to subordinate his own interests to those of other people (cf. Chapter 8). Its credibility would suffer, also, if it were patently rigged to the differential advantage of specific individuals or groups at the expense of people in general.

A doctrine would not be laughed out of court merely for allowing special concern for persons suffering particular hardships, performing particular functions, or possessing particular virtues. The rules could still be impartial in favoring not specific persons but *anyone* in the position or with the characteristics described. Such special attention might arguably serve the interests of people in general. (Consider Rawls's 1971 argument for favoring the worst-off category of persons.) One might imagine special deference to a priestly caste on the grounds that the priests' work and the comfort it presupposes are essential to the community's enjoying divine favor. In certain past times and conditions – or perhaps only in peculiar imaginary conditions – it might even have been possible to argue sincerely that slavery or the subjugation of women promoted a workable society and served the interests of its members in general, perhaps even of the subjugated groups. If such arguments found wide acceptance, the doctrines defending those practices would not necessarily have counted as *arbitrarily* partial or nongeneralizable; and they might even have been workable. More plausibly, parents' partiality to their own children or rules barring women from the combat infantry might be defensible by bona fide argument and so would not violate generalizability. Arguments defending some such precepts against suspicion of arbitrariness might be hard to verify or falsify, but they would be open to discussion and empirical investigation.

Of course, generalizability in the sense indicated is not enough to justify a rule or ethical doctrine. As the examples of slavery and sexism suggest, it alone cannot guarantee that practices or arguments are sound or acceptable. Generalizability is a necessary but not sufficient condition for ethical validity.

Utilitarian considerations test the generality and workability of putative ethical precepts in broadly the same way that they test their more specific content. Richard Brandt asks whether a perfectly selfish or self-centered but rational person would advocate a moral code discriminating in his favor at others' expense. Well, there would be no point to his advocating a system that could not enlist others' loyalty. To be capable of producing consequences that others would like, a moral system must make the same demands on him as on them (Brandt 1979, pp. 218–19). For a morality to function effectively over the long run, Joel Kupperman says, "It must be perceived as not making appreciably heavier or lighter demands on anyone. Heavier demands lead to resentment; lighter demands lead to envy" (1983, p. 44).

A restatement may be helpful. R.M. Hare (cited above) needs some excuse if he maintains that ethical propositions are, *by their very meaning*, not only prescriptive but also universal or universalizable. Propositions with a serious claim to general acceptance do tend to prescribe restraints on how individuals may pursue their own interests, but these restraints are likely to serve social cooperation and so the long-run interests of both the individual himself and others generally. Antiuniversal propositions like the one favoring Gordon Tullock are poor candidates for acceptance. Lacking credibility, they fail the test of whether urging them is likely to serve social cooperation and happiness. They fail on other than purely definitional and logical grounds. The universalizability criterion is, after all, part of a value judgment; and to represent it as following from the very meanings of words is to *sneak* a value element into the discussion.

Admittedly, though, I have nagging doubts about the foregoing paragraphs; I am uncomfortable in disagreeing with Hare on the narrow, quasi-epistemological issue involved. Anyway, it is not central to the main doctrine of this book. I leave the question still dangling whether generalizability or impartiality is required by the very concept of ethics and by the test of logical consistency or is required on utilitarian grounds. Either way, it *is* required.

PARTIALITY AND UNIVERSALIZABILITY

In contrast with preposterous and impermissible partiality, two concepts of universality or generalizability must be distinguished. We have already surveyed the first, which requires that ethical precepts *not* especially favor or burden arbitrarily specified individuals or groups. On this first conception, it still may be a relevant difference between two situations that one does and the other does not involve oneself or one's own family and friends. A general rule could still recognize that *all* persons are entitled to show a certain partiality toward themselves, their friends and relatives, and their favorite projects. Everybody, not just specific individuals and narrowly specified groups, is allowed to behave this way. Allowing such favoritism can be defended on utilitarian grounds; and the generalization principle, sensibly interpreted, remains intact.

A less plausible conception would require each individual to treat all people alike, without special concern for his own or his friends' and relatives' interests and purposes. (Blum 1980/1982 attributes this position to Kant and Kierkegaard. To Edgeworth, similarly, utilitarianism connoted "*Vivre pour autrui*"; 1881/1967, p. 136.) Occasionally R.M. Hare seems to move beyond impartiality in the first sense toward this stronger second one, deploring a person's caring more for his own interests and projects than for someone else's: "[W]e have to love our neighbour as ourselves, which means treating his or her preferences as of equal weight to our own" (1989EoPM, p. 64).

Later, though, Hare calls it an elementary mistake to think that universalization precludes particular duties to particular persons or groups, as to one's own children or country (1989EoPM, pp. 69ff.). Complete impartiality at the critical level can justify principles requiring partiality at the intuitive level if those principles will serve the good of all, considered impartially (p. 71). (On the two levels – of philosophizing and of application – recall Chapter 2.)

Several factual considerations count against impartiality in the second, exaggerated, sense.

1. Individuals have their own values and projects, and they experience satisfaction or sorrow from progress or frustration in pursuing them. Not letting people give priority to their own values and projects would impair their own and thus general happiness.
2. Individuals know more about their own values, interests, projects, abilities, needs, preferences, and other "particular circumstances of time and place" (Hayek 1945), and about those of persons they especially care about, than they know about those of other people. Individuals can use

this special knowledge more effectively on behalf of their own interests and affections. (Contrast "giving each other Christmas presents".)

3. Use by individuals and business firms of their own special knowledge, including knowledge even of temporary and local conditions and production possibilities, is the only way of applying to the service of human wants the vast diverse knowledge scattered about the world in millions and billions of individual minds. In the anonymous Great Society – the "extended order", as Hayek sometimes calls it – this use of knowledge must be coordinated by relatively impersonal market processes involving prices, profits, and losses. "It is not from the benevolence of the butcher, the brewer, or the baker, that we expect our dinner, but from their regard to their own interest." So wrote Adam Smith (1776/1937, p. 14); Horwitz (1996) nicely expounds this theme.

4. According priority to one's own values and projects need not mean an excessively narrow conception of one's own interests, a narrowness that would tend to work even against one's own happiness. Individuals can and should favor their own interests within the bounds of morality and law.

5. Taken as the criterion of action, the well-being of people in general would tend to be regarded as a public good (in the technical sense of economic theory), with inefficient allocation of resources toward it in consequence. Property belonging to everyone collectively and to no one in particular is likely to receive inadequate care.

6. Demands for impartiality in the exaggerated sense run counter to human nature, would generally receive not actual compliance but lip service at most, would tend to breed hypocrisy, would victimize the complying public-spirited minority to the advantage of the noncompliers, and might arouse counterproductive feelings of guilt among the more conscientious of the noncompliers.

F.A. Hayek (1989) offers some insights bearing on these points, including the psychological ones. He distinguishes between the behaviors and mindsets appropriate to the worldwide "great society" or "extended order" of arms-length market relations and those appropriate to small, intimate groups. The extended order requires no special solidarity or loyalty among participants – nothing beyond ordinary decency, honorable dealing, and refraining from lying, cheating, stealing, and coercion. Indeed, market-oriented attitudes are positively conducive to impersonal cooperation and coordination ranging widely over space and time. In intimate groups, however, the attitudes of solidarity and altruism presumably inherited biologically from prehistoric life in small hunter-gatherer bands are more appropriate. Even or especially within an impersonal extended order, the intimacy available within small, close-knit groups has great psychological value. Within them, emulating market behavior, pursuing narrow self-interest, and insisting on cost/benefit calculations and careful measurements of quid pro quo would be destructive. Such misplaced market-oriented behavior would subvert the solidarity and loyalty of such groups and threaten to "crush" them (Hayek 1989, p. 18). It would be counterproductive if the same attitudes guided behavior both in the impersonal extended order and in intimate groups, whether the attitudes common to both arenas were those of universalist utilitarian altruism in the style of Edgeworth or the quite different commercial attitudes of the marketplace.

David Hume, recognizing human nature, already spoke for the first and against the second, exaggerated, conception of impartiality. The notion of morals does imply some common sentiment, extending to all mankind, about what actions and conduct deserve applause and what ones censure (1751/1777/1930, p. 110). Even so (p. 65n.),

> It is wisely ordained by nature, that private connexions should commonly prevail over universal views and considerations; otherwise our affections and actions would be dissipated and lost, for want of a proper limited object. Thus a small benefit done to ourselves, or our near friends, excites more lively sentiments of love and approbation than a great benefit done to a distant commonwealth: But still we know here, as in all the senses, to correct these inequalities by reflection, and retain a general standard of vice and virtue, founded chiefly on general usefulness.

Peter Singer also accepts the first, sensible, conception of universalizability, but with deviations toward the second. All ethical systems recognize special obligations to kin and neighbors only "within a framework of impartiality which makes me see my obligations to my kin and neighbors as no more important, from the ethical point of view, than other people's obligations to their own kin and neighbors" (1982, p. 118). (Singer's "ethical point of view" resembles Hare's critical level of thinking.) The next step, Singer continues, is to ask why the interests of my society are more important than the interests of other societies. If the only answer is that it is *my* society, ethical reasoning will reject it (p. 118).

But "more important", we may ask, from whose point of view? From the most universal viewpoint conceivable, perhaps, no society is more important than any other. On earth, one must make distinctions. Impartiality of ethical rules does not mean impartiality of concerns and decisions. Within the restraints of impartial ethical rules, each member of a particular society may usefully have special regard for his own relatively narrow circle. Family solidarity, friendship, and personal loyalty are admirable precisely on utilitarian grounds.

Similar considerations justify the members of each society in having special regard for fellow members. Patriotism can be a virtue. What can still be impartial is recognition of each society's legitimate and indeed healthy partiality to its own members – subject, of course, to further precepts about fairness, benevolence, and respect for rights, including the rights of members of other societies.

Singer maintains that ethical reasoning always pushes us toward a still more universal point of view. When our ethical horizons are fully expanded, we will take the interests of all sentient creatures into account (1982, pp. 119, 124). But again the distinction holds between impartiality of precepts and impartiality of decisions. It would be just too far-fetched to require each member of each species to treat all members of all species impartially. (The very idea of addressing ethical precepts to nonhuman animals is far-fetched anyway.)

An equal regard for all sentient beings is not credible. It violates the requirement (grounded ultimately in utility) that an ethical system be capable of public espousal in all seriousness, without hypocrisy. Saying this is not to make truth depend on palatability. With reference to a purely positive proposition of fact or logic, that would indeed be an error. Factual and logical truth cannot be determined by opinion polls or popularity surveys. At issue here, however, are value judgments.

Here we may find an answer to extreme claims about animal rights. We can hardly expect a human being to be impartial between a fellow human and a lion, any more than we can expect a lion to be impartial between a human and a fellow lion. Many animals are predators; the world of nature is cruel. Animal-rights advocates, in reply, may want to hold humans to a higher standard than lions and other predators because we, unlike they, are rational creatures. *Noblesse oblige*. Yet when the question is what ethical rules should bind human beings in their treatment of animals, it is circular reasoning to appeal to a standard simply postulated as already valid. Impartiality between human beings and animals fails the test of credibility and of being able to be publicly espoused without suspicion, at least, of hypocrisy.

What *can* pass this test is an extension in favor of animals of the general precept of benevolence, though not unlimited benevolence. We should spare animals pointless suffering and not inflict great suffering on them for slight benefits to ourselves.

CONCLUSION

This chapter has argued that a duty-centered ethics in the style of Kant is paradoxical and unpersuasive. A sensible ethics must almost surely conform to some sort of principle of generality or universalizability. Whether this is a sheer logical or linguistic requirement or instead a conclusion of utilitarian reasoning may still be open to discussion, but the chapter inclines toward the latter interpretation. Sensibly interpreted, the principle does not bar persons from showing partiality to their own selves, projects and causes, relatives and friends, and fellow countrymen, nor to responsibly preferring the interests of fellow humans over those of other animals.

NOTES

1. Including R.M. Hare; see Seanor and Fotion (1990), particularly the contributions of Thomas Nagel and Peter Singer and Hare's replies.

10. Rivals of utilitarianism

CLASSIFYING DOCTRINES

Often the exposition of a doctrine gains from contrast with alternatives. Duty-oriented ethics claimed attention ahead of the other rivals examined here. Rival ethical doctrines may differ in their epistemologies and in their perceptions of reality. Disagreements over empirical fact and over chains of reasoning can in principle be narrowed by further observation and discussion, since reality and logic must ultimately be the same for all competent and honest investigators willing to revise their judgments as knowledge accrues. Even the doctrine whose supreme value is conformity to God's will must attend to the existence of God, what his will is, how it is known, and how the facts of our world condition the details of its application. With errors of perception and logic capable in principle of being corrected, enduring doctrinal differences must ultimately trace to fundamental value judgments. (Admittedly, though, "ultimate" agreement on all questions of fact may lie only in the remote future.)

This chapter's closing section faces the charge that utilitarianism is "vacuous". It lists some alternatives to the utilitarian fundamental value judgment. The question of an alternative attitude is illuminating, particularly when pressed onto adherents of natural-rights and contractarian approaches to ethics.

Within the category of utilitarianism, alternatives exist to the rules or indirect version expounded here. "Consequentialism" is a broader category: actions, institutions, precepts, character traits, and so forth are to be appraised by their *consequences*, understanding which requires empirical analysis. One can imagine versions of consequentialism that differ in their specific conceptions of what sorts of consequences are deemed supremely good and what sorts bad. Since the various forms of utilitarianism dominate the class of consequentialist doctrines, it is not ordinarily important to distinguish between utilitarianism and consequentialism.

No classification of doctrines is ideal for all purposes. One leading classification focuses on epistemology, on views about the nature and sources of ethical knowledge. To start, I review Paul Edwards's rather broad classification, then take note of R.M. Hare's classification of a narrower range of doctrines. Finally I review several doctrines not specifically named in either of those classifications.

Edwards (1965) groups ethical theories (strictly, *meta*ethical theories) under four headings: (1) objective nonnaturalism or intuitionism, (2) objective naturalism, (3) subjectivism, and (4) emotivism. No one of these four categories represents a coherent school of thought formulated to stand in clear rivalry with utilitarianism. Each one, rather, features a trait that may be lurking in several doctrines.

INTUITIONISM

Objective nonnaturalist theories hold that being good or right or obligatory (or whatever the normative term may be) is an objectively existing property of reality, like being hot or cold, hard or soft, blue or yellow. Unlike these natural properties, however, ethical properties are held to have a distinctive, "nonnatural" character: people perceive them not with sight or touch or other ordinary senses but with an ethical sixth sense or *intuition*. People can directly and intuitively perceive, even without considering consequences, that some things, actions, character traits, and so forth just *are* objectively good or right or obligatory, while others just are bad or wrong or impermissible.

Deontological or duty-based theories typically fall into this intuitionist category. According to them, we directly perceive that certain kinds of behavior are morally obligatory, at least *prima facie*. The category also includes some doctrines of natural law or of natural or human rights. One might perceive a self-evident truth that all people have certain unalienable rights. Separate sections of this chapter will survey these doctrines.

Probably the best known intuitionist theory is G.E. Moore's (1903). In a way it straddles utilitarianism and intuitionism and so is sometimes called "ideal utilitarianism". More exactly, it is consequentialist but not utilitarian. It appraises institutions, precepts, and so forth according to how they contribute to or detract from a fundamental value, which, however, it takes to be not utility or happiness but "the good" as identified by intuition.

Several facts seem to support intuitionism. People make judgments to the effect that a certain person is "morally blind" or "morally insane" or that one person has a finer moral sensibility than another. Such statements are intelligible and often true (Edwards 1965, p. 91). The speaker intends to report facts of objective reality and not just his own emotive reactions. People engaging in a moral dispute often genuinely disagree, although they would not disagree if merely comparing their own states of mind. Furthermore, we come to hold moral views, especially about our own duties and obligations, with a certain immediacy, as if we were perceiving moral truth directly, almost as we perceive that grass is green; we sometimes experience what feels like an objectively binding obligation. (This fact does not discredit rules utilitarianism, however. We may have learned summary appraisals of the consequences of lines of conduct so thoroughly, as by earliest training and by experience, that they seem like intuitions to us. Many activities, like swimming and typing, may become natural or instinctive or intuitive, even though they originally had to be learned.)

Another fact appearing to support intuitionism is that ethical terms cannot be analyzed into nonethical terms. "Good" cannot be defined, or so G.E. Moore famously maintained. In being a simple, unanalyzable property, "good" is like "yellow": one simply perceives that something is good or is yellow. (To associate yellow with light of certain wavelengths is not to define the color itself as people perceive it.) The point about the indefinability of "good", "right", and similar ethical terms loses most of its force, however, when we consider the *polyguous* character of such terms (as explained in Chapter 2).

R.M. Hare jabs at intuitionism throughout his *Essays on Political Morality* (1989EoPM). Never in their whole thought process, he says, do intuitionists ask whether their intuitions are the ones we should have. Depending on their position on the abortion issue, they assume that women or fetuses have rights and that we can intuit what they are if only we pay close enough attention to our own navels (p. 126). They appeal to our intuitions or prejudices in support of widely divergent methods or patterns of distribution of income and wealth. But intuitions and general consensus prove nothing. We want arguments but in this field seldom get them (p. 193).

John Rawls centers his system (1971) on what parties ignorant of their own particular roles in society, negotiating in an "original position" behind a "veil of ignorance", would supposedly agree on. This system, says Hare (1989EoPM, p. 35), rests on nothing more than Rawls's private intuitions or prejudices, which Rawls hopes his readers will share. His method must yield results consistent with his intuitions in reflective equilibrium; else he will tinker with it. "In particular, it has to yield results different from those yielded by utilitarianism; for one of Rawls's firmest intuitions is that utilitarianism is wrong" (p. 127). Someone employing the method of reflective equilibrium, as Rawls avowedly does, could still be dealing in mere prejudices rather than philosophical argument.

While Rawls has an unsatisfactory procedure, Hare (1989EoPM, p. 189) finds Robert Nozick (1974) having none at all, or none but a variety of miscellaneous considerations, all in the end based on intuition. Introducing his Wilt Chamberlain example to make a point about income distribution, Nozick simply assumes that the snap answers most of us give are the right ones. We already know, by intuition, that Chamberlain should be free to exchange his basketball performances for whatever fees he can get from willing spectators. Nozick plays down the fact that the general application of this idea would bring results at odds with other of our intuitions (Hare 1989EoPM, p. 126).

Some critics "smear" utilitarians, Hare observes, with the charge that they could condone slavery in certain peculiar but imaginable circumstances in which the practice would serve happiness and abolishing it would cause misery. But if the critics' doctrine grinds out the same recommendations regardless of the facts (or postulated facts) of reality, that very characteristic suggests its emptiness (1989EoPM, Chapter 12). While utilitarians can show what is wrong with slavery in realistic circumstances, intuitionists in effect congratulate themselves on sheltering their noble conclusion from any conceivably embarrassing confrontation with facts.

The appeal to numerous specific intuitions is the opposite of disciplined argument. The tenets of intuitionist ethics, wrote Ludwig von Mises (1922/1981, p. 360), "are irreconcilable with scientific method" and "have been deprived of their very foundations". Mises (1957/1985, pp. 52ff.) criticized intuitionists who believed in a perennial ideal of absolute justice, known by an inner voice, and in man's duty to make all human institutions conform to this ideal. Its supporters did not look into the consequences of trying to implement their doctrine. "They silently assumed either that these consequences will be beneficial or that mankind is bound to put up even with very painful consequences of justice" (p. 53).

Such ethicists forgot that people disagree on interpreting the "inner voice" and that no "justice" exists outside or before society. The distinction between just and unjust emerges in the requirement that the individual abstain from conduct subversive of social cooperation. "Conduct suited to preserve social cooperation is just, conduct detrimental to the preservation of society is unjust" (Mises 1957/1985, p. 54). A free society can function even though its members disagree on many more specific judgments of value (p. 61). "[T]he peaceful functioning of society" is an overriding criterion. "Even rigid supporters of an intuitionist ethics could not help eventually resorting to an appraisal of conduct from the point of view of its effects upon human happiness" (p. 62). Mises cites Kant as an example; compare a similar remark by J.S. Mill, cited in Chapter 9. Also compare Herbert Spencer's dismissal of intuitionism, summarized in the appendix to Chapter 6.[1]

AN EXAMPLE OF INTUITIONISM

Hadley Arkes's (1986) alternative to utilitarian ethics exemplifies intuitionism, even though he does not so label his doctrine. What is good or just can never be equated with "that which makes most people happy". Some people even find pleasure in torturing humans and animals (pp. 371–2). Arkes blurs the distinction between act and rules utilitarianism and seems unaware of the indirect utilitarianism that John Gray attributed to John Stuart Mill (though evidently sympathetic to Mill, Arkes curiously denies that Mill was a utilitarian, pp. 121–7). His brief and scattered arguments against utilitarianism (like the one about torture) seldom rise above the level of debating tactics. Arkes shuns consequentialist arguments; he disdains "the tendency to reduce the understanding of morals to nonmoral measures, such as 'happiness,' pleasure, prosperity, or even 'harmony' and civic 'cohesion'" (pp. 168–9). He seems to think that trying to demonstrate its benefits, either for the individual or for "society", somehow demeans morality.

Making frequent admiring references to Immanuel Kant, Arkes finds it more noble to take morality as a self-validating ultimate. Scorning "nonmoral formulas of morals", he urges a "logic of morals itself" (p. 114, also p. 166). "[K]nowledge of what is good must be higher than any other kind of knowledge" (p. 164). The existence of morals is a momentous, ineffaceable *fact* and *truth*. The propositions implied by the logic of morals "may not be consigned to the domain of opinion or feeling, as though there were some doubt about their cognitive standing as *true* propositions" (p. 119). "Moral propositions are grounded ultimately in facts or truths, but they can be derived only from the necessary truth which affirms the existence of morals or explains its essential logic" (p. 168; Arkes repeats this formulation on p. 373, suggesting how much importance he attaches to it).

All this is circular reasoning, if it is reasoning at all. Unless morality is already deemed good for some reason or other (such as being beneficial), what is so good about adhering to it? And what is so noble about refraining from argument for an institution deemed good?

Back to summarizing Arkes. Condemning injustices, complaining about faults, despising what is hateful, loving what is admirable – all, he says, indicate a capacity for moral judgment (p. 74). The terms "moral" and "immoral" refer to things that are universally good or bad, right or wrong, justified or unjustified. All definitions presuppose some irreducible terms, and in morals these are words like good and bad, right and wrong, just and unjust (pp. 161–2 and footnote). (Arkes should be reminded of Paul Edwards's analysis of *polyguous* words, discussed in Chapter 2 above.)

The principles of moral judgment derive ultimately "from (1) the logic – or the idea – of morals itself and from (2) the nature of that creature who alone has access to the pleasures of moral understanding" (p. 127, where Arkes says that John Stuart Mill had abandoned utilitarianism and drawn these principles from the same two points that Kant had set forth as the ultimate foundations of moral judgments).

Arkes recognizes only one moral system. Its rudiments are acknowledged everywhere whenever an injured person feels outrage and demands a justification. By demanding a justification, one acknowledges all the groundwork necessary for extracting categorical propositions in the domain of morals. There is no society in which the demand for justification is not heard and the logic of morals not acknowledged (p. 157).

In morals as in mathematics, some axioms or first principles or necessary truths are virtually indifferent to variations in culture and geography. They hold true of necessity and do not merely express "Western values". They make having *some* right answers possible. The moral understandings they support are as independent of the vagaries of local opinion as the Pythagorean theorem. The validity of moral axioms cannot be affected in any way by the presence or absence of a consensus. "Their universal truth is guaranteed by their own necessity, and that truth must be indifferent to the question of whether it is universally recognized" (pp. 6, 130–1, 424–5, quotation from 424–5).

Ostensibly siding with Aristotle and against Hobbes, Arkes argues for imbuing politics with ethics. Chapter 11 below summarizes his apparently even wanting government to accomplish an amalgamation of law and ethics.

Though my knowledge of cultural anthropology is rudimentary, I am inclined to accept Arkes's point about the similarity of ethical first principles across a wide range of cultures; but I question its force as an argument for an intuitionist ethics.[2] That similarity is explainable by what is necessary for a viable society and so for the survival of human life (as discussed in Chapter 3). Furthermore, an explanation does not by itself warrant any normative judgment.

As for "axioms" whose "universal truth is guaranteed by their own necessity", what could that phrase mean? Propositions that can be argued for and shown to be necessary or whose truth is somehow guaranteed are not *axioms*. And what makes Arkes's "axioms" necessary? If they are necessary for a viable society, which in turn is necessary for human happiness, we are back to utilitarianism. As for truth not depending on its universal recognition, well of course.

In respects other than his calls for governmental activism (noted in my Chapter 11), much of what Arkes says, as in attacking moral relativism, seems unobjectionable to me. I object not so much to his conclusions as to the feeble and unsatisfactory grounding he offers for them. His method of argument is the method of emphatic reassertion.[3] Although he trumpets the existence of an objective, autonomous, and self-validating ethics, he is singularly brief and vague on just what "the logic of morals itself" (pp. 114, 166) is. He seems to envision some objectively existing hard core of morality that spins out its own logical implications and applications. He treats ethics as axiomatic or irreducible. Such a treatment boils down to intuitionism.

OBJECTIVE NATURALISM

Doctrines belonging to Edwards's second category purport to reduce moral judgments entirely to claims about *natural* qualities or relations. Criticizing those doctrines, R.M. Hare employs the apparently equivalent labels "descriptivism" and "cognitivism". Apart from a partial or doubtful exception urged by Ayn Rand, mentioned below, and apart from the "Aristotelian" doctrine described later in a section on rights, I am not aware that any philosopher deliberately expounds an objective-naturalist theory. The type is worth mentioning, however, for its instructive contrast with other theories.

A far-fetched example of the type would be a metaethical theory interpreting "good" as identical with "yellow in color". Determining whether anything is good would then be a straightforward matter of inspection. A less preposterous theory might interpret "good" as "conducive to social cooperation" or "conducive to happiness". Determining whether something was good might then require elaborate investigations in psychology and social science, not just simple inspection; but the theory would still purport to reduce judgments about goodness entirely to matters of fact and logic without any normative component, not even a value judgment about happiness. On that theory, "good" would be a purely descriptive, not evaluative, term.

Utilitarianism, in contrast, recognizes that ethical judgments cannot rest on fact and logic alone but must also appeal, ultimately, to a fundamental value judgment that is simply postulated or intuited. Although utilitarianism thus does contain some element of intuition, it does not appeal to intuition in the *ad hoc* and promiscuous way of intuitionist theories.

M.J. Perry (1988/1990) sketches a neo-Aristotelian understanding of "moral", calling his own doctrine "naturalist" and "cognitivist". Yet his and Hare's positions may perhaps be reconciled. Hare rejects the idea that ethical propositions can be purely descriptive of objective reality, without any admixture of sheer value judgment, while Perry (like Paul Edwards) emphasizes that ethical propositions do indeed have some descriptive content. To be a distinctive doctrine in this respect, "cognitivism" or "objective naturalism" must insist that ethical propositions have *nothing but* descriptive content. One must be careful with labels in this area.

A full-fledged objective naturalist would commit the fallacy of trying to get an "ought" from an "is". The "objectivist" theory of Ayn Rand is the closest to an actual example that I know of. Rand and her expositors seem to pride themselves on avoiding any appeal to value judgment at all. If I understand them correctly, they regard "conduciveness to the maintenance of one's own life" (or some such formulation) as a criterion imposed by the very context of ethical discussion and practice and not as a criterion freely adopted as a value judgment. (See Rand 1979/1990, especially pp. 33–4, and Binswanger 1986, especially s.v. "Life", "Happiness", and "Ultimate Value".)[4]

SUBJECTIVISM

Subjectivism in its various versions interprets moral judgments as reports of subjective reactions, whether of the speaker himself or of certain groups. Or, according to "causal subjectivism", moral judgments assert that a certain object or action does or did produce a certain feeling or attitude in the person making the judgment. Rather similarly, the error theory asserts that moral judgments purport to refer to something outside the speaker's mind but are false, since nothing pertinent exists for the speaker to describe except his own feeling or attitude. The error theory, as well as "naive subjectivism", are forms of moral skepticism, according to which no moral judgment is both an objective statement and true.

The strongest argument for naive subjectivism, says Paul Edwards, is that people often would accept rephrasing a moral judgment as a subjective report. For example, "mercy killing can be a good deed" might translate into "I approve of mercy killing under certain circumstances". But even so rephrased, a moral proposition is far from undiscussible: the speaker may give reasons for his attitude, supporting it with objective facts. Ordinarily, furthermore, the speaker intends more than a mere report on his own state of mind; he intends to say something about the moral quality of mercy killing itself. When people call an action right (or wrong), they cannot mean merely that it awakes in them an emotion of moral approval (or disapproval), since to have the emotion they must already be thinking of the action as right (or wrong).

Subjective feelings do not turn into objectively binding moral precepts merely by being held in common by large numbers of persons. That most devout Hindus used to hold suttee – a widow's self-cremation on her husband's funeral pyre – morally obligatory may be a valid positive proposition of cultural anthropology, but whether suttee actually is morally obligatory (or morally impermissible or morally optional) cannot be settled by factual and logical investigation alone.

EMOTIVISM

According to theories in Edwards's fourth category, moral judgments have "emotive meaning" only: they have no referent; they describe nothing. Instead, they are either outbursts expressing attitudes or imperatives prescribing actions, or both. Probably the best known expositors of this doctrine, associated with logical positivism, were A.J. Ayer (1936) and Charles Stevenson (1944). To say "Stealing is wrong" amounts to saying "Stealing – ugh!" or "Don't steal"; the words simply convey repugnance to the idea of stealing. Like "naive subjectivism" and the "error theory", emotive theories express an ethical nihilism.

Such nihilism is almost surely wrong.[5] In most cases what are alleged to be mere emotional outbursts on misconceived ethical issues can nevertheless be argued for (or against) by appeal to facts of reality. The emotions, if such they are, are responses to perceived reality; and how appropriate they are to reality can be investigated.

A theory is not nihilistic merely because it attributes emotive character or, almost equivalently, intuitive character to one or possibly more fundamental value judgments. Like utilitarianism, such a theory can express emotion or appeal to intuition only parsimoniously; it can restrict its emotive or intuitive aspect to fundamental value judgments, keeping the bulk of its content positive. The contrasting feature of theories like Ayer's and Stevenson's is that they attribute *nothing but* emotive character to ethical judgments.

Paul Edwards describes his own ethical doctrine as combining features of both objective naturalism and emotive theories. He stresses that ethical judgments typically have factual content while also conveying emotions. (Without disagreeing on points of substance, I would rather speak of the *intuitive* character of a fundamental value judgment.) While Edwards's doctrine thus does appeal to emotion or intuition, it does not do so *promiscuously*; Edwards explicitly rejects intuitionism. (The present book obviously incorporates much of Edwards's doctrine, holding it compatible with utilitarianism.)

AN ALTERNATIVE CLASSIFICATION

R.M. Hare classifies theories more narrowly than Edwards. His classification ignores implausible theories and restricts itself to versions of utilitarianism and related theories. The five that he describes have no important differences, he says, *for practical purposes* (1989EoPM, pp. 46–50).

1. According to the ideal observer theory, we should think like a person making no factual or conceptual errors and giving equal weight to the interests of all parties and to nothing else.
2. The rational contractor theory recommends the principles that would be agreed on by rational people prudently considering their own interests and knowing everything about the society they are to live in *except* each one's own particular role.

3. Specific rule-utilitarianism admits principles of unlimited specificity provided that they do not cease to be universal.
4. Universalistic act-utilitarianism recognizes that moral judgments about individual acts commit their makers to principles applying to all precisely similar acts. This position is tantamount to specific rule utilitarianism.
5. Universal prescriptivism includes Hare's own theory, for which, in various places, he accepts the label "utilitarian". In deciding what I ought to do, I am deciding what to prescribe for all cases exactly like the present one in their universal properties. This requires seeking knowledge of the consequences of acting on alternative prescriptions. Impartiality and prescriptivity recommend benevolence.

Elsewhere (1989EiET, especially the early sections), Hare offers a different but not inconsistent partial classification. Descriptivism, also called cognitivism, interprets moral statements as mere descriptions. This view has two subcategories. A subjectivist interprets moral statements as descriptions of somebody's – his own or other people's – preferences, attitudes, states of mind, utterances, or the like. An objectivist interprets moral statements as descriptions of more or less ordinary features of objective reality, free of any value judgments. Hare himself does not think that moral statements are *purely* descriptive; ordinarily, they combine some and perhaps much descriptive content with a prescriptive or normative element also. The congruence with Paul Edwards's formulation is obvious.

Employing his own categories, Hare classifies himself as a nondescriptivist Kantian utilitarian, as distinguished from a descriptivist intuitionist deontologist. (What, though, does that mean? "Nondescriptivist" is fairly clear; so is "utilitarian" as opposed to "deontologist". But what does "Kantian" versus "intuitionist" mean? And how can he be Kantian without being deontologist? Possibly Hare meant to refer to Kant's insistence on the universal character of ethical propositions.)

In his writings on the whole, Hare blurs act and rules utilitarianism. More exactly, he recommends that people follow applicable rules on the intuitive level, while on the critical level they may properly weigh the consequences of following alternative rules and indeed the consequences of alternative individual acts. (On this distinction between intuitive and critical levels, recall Chapter 2.) Because knowledge is incomplete and partial, because people are tempted to make exceptions in their own favor, and for other reasons, the policy of treating each case on its own apparent merits will not in general produce the best acts. It is better to follow principles, ones likely to work out for the best in all but truly exceptional cases. Ideal-observer and rational-contractor theories turn out to be utilitarian when we pay attention to the *grounds* on which the observer or contractor would approve of or agree to such-and-such principles or arrangements. The concepts of ideal spectator or impartial benevolent spectator, and especially of the prudent rational contractor, emphasize the separateness of persons and their interests and projects; they stand opposed to making a goal of maximizing some sort of impersonal aggregate utility.

CONTRACTARIANISM

Several or most of the ethical systems reviewed in this chapter rest on one or more propositions or values taken as foundational by the theorist himself. One type of doctrine, however, tries to relieve the theorist from commitment to scarcely anything more specific than that any foundational values should be those of the diverse individual members of society. This doctrine is contractarianism, called "contractualism" by some British writers. It judges ethical correctness by what all affected parties, applying their own possibly divergent values, do agree on or might have agreed on or would agree on under ideal conditions. In many writings James Buchanan, Nobel laureate economist, seems to say that the social philosopher has no business endorsing anything except what can command agreement.[6] The processes of negotiation and agreement are more important than results or substance. This idea parallels the idea that people's free individual choice is more important than what they choose. People must be assumed to know best, and a contractarian deplores attempts to press choices on them.

Contractarians scarcely claim to appraise principles and institutions solely by what people do in fact agree on. Actual negotiations and explicit agreement on broad principles and whole social institutions, as distinct from legislative tinkering with details, are infrequent. Contractarianism requires theoretical, not actual, agreement (or so many interpret it, for example Reiman 1990). It asks what it *would be reasonable* for people in general to agree on.

Yet appealing to this "conceptual" agreement – to what people *would* agree to or *might have* agreed to – draws skepticism. What is binding about merely potential but never actual agreement? Suppose I would have agreed to buy a particular house if it had been offered to me at a particular price. That fact scarcely obliges me to buy it.

What people would consent to depends on what they believe about reality and about how attempts to satisfy their various desires would cohere or would clash. What might command consent is not flatly given, unaffected by any attempts at enlightenment. Agreement on the basis of current knowledge and ignorance and error alone is hardly worth prizing. People engage in discussion partly to have their own and other people's ideas examined and possibly set straight. Anyone taking part is bound to use his own judgment – improved, one hopes, by the discussion – about which of the alternatives under consideration is likeliest to perform well and *therefore* eventually to be agreed on. People give their consent in view of how they expect the measures to affect their interests or happiness. The criterion of consent does not clash with the criterion of performance.

T.M. Scanlon, calling himself a contractualist, "takes the fundamental question to be whether a principle could reasonably be rejected (for application in our imperfect world) by parties who, in addition to their own personal aims, were moved by a desire to find principles that others similarly motivated could also accept" (Scanlon in Seanor and Fotion 1988/1990, pp. 137–8). Well, *in view of what* could a principle "reasonably be rejected"? Principles and arrangements that people quite probably would reject are indeed ruled out, but they are ruled out because of *why* people would reject them – their unacceptable consequences. And why does one seek principles that others could also accept? Unless principles are accepted – at least in practice if not by explicit words – they cannot work and so cannot be useful (compare the discussion of universalizability in Chapter 9). On this point contractarianism and utilitarianism converge.

Some terminology of David Schmidtz's bolsters my criticisms of contractarianism. Schmidtz (1990/1996) distinguishes two methods of justifying a state or some other institution – or, we might add, a set of ethical principles and practices. The *teleological* approach seeks justification in what an institution or set of principles accomplishes. An *emergent* approach focuses on its pedigree, on its origin or adoption by an acceptable process. Mere hypothetical consent cannot in itself provide emergent justification, since it does not refer to an actual process. If someone tells me that such-and-such is justified because I and others *would have* consented to it, I might reasonably ask, "What makes you think I would have consented?" The reasons offered, if persuasive, do the job of justification. They do it along the lines of the teleological approach, appealing to the expected results of the arrangements in question. A story about hypothetical negotiations and hypothetical agreement adds nothing but decoration; and even its apparent force hinges on the teleological – that is, consequentialist – strand of the argument.

Actual consent does have "justificatory force over and beyond the teleological force of the reasons people have for consenting". Something gains an additional warrant if all affected parties do freely consent to it, as by contract (Schmidtz 1990/1996, p. 89). The institution of contracting is warranted on utilitarian grounds. Typically and questionably, however, contractarian theorists impute some sort of binding character even to merely imaginary contracts. Realistically, though, any persuasive force flows not from imaginary contracts but from the reasons why people supposedly would have agreed to them. And these reasons, if valid and persuasive, are utilitarian reasons.[7]

Contractarians sometimes suggest that the status quo is an "implicit social contract" (see, for example, King 1988, p. 43, referring in part to writings of James Buchanan). It possesses "legitimacy" – not, to be sure, through actual consent but because it is a starting point. Any change must start from the status quo – agreed – but what sort of "legitimacy" does that truism describe? Denying the legitimacy of the status quo is often an effective way of arguing for change, as William Wilberforce argued against slavery in the British colonies in the early nineteenth century and as American civil-rights campaigners argued in the twentieth. The likely consequences of proposed reforms also require attention, including possible resistance to them and reasons for resistance. Straightforward discussion of all this requires no fictions about implied contract and legitimacy. Fictions may sometimes be heuristically useful; still, it would be instructive if contractarians occasionally dropped their assertions about what is only "conceptually" but not actually true and expressed themselves in straightforward language.

My criticisms of contractarianism so far pertain more to its style than to its substance. In substance, contractarianism of James Buchanan's type is similar to the utilitarianism expounded in this book (King 1988, esp. pp. 47–52; Yeager 1988EHD). In political philosophy, both call for comparing alternative sets of institutions; both appeal to the same kinds of evidence about how institutions work (on the contractarian theory of political obligation, see Chapter 11). Both reject the notion of a collective or legislative exercise in maximizing the sum of utilities; both recognize the diverse goals and projects of individual persons; both harbor individualistic values.

Contractarianism emphasizes that it is individuals who reap the benefits and costs, satisfactions and frustrations, and happiness or misery resulting from their interactions with one another. No aggregate net utility exists distinct from the satisfactions and frustrations that individual persons feel as they live their own lives and pursue their own projects. Except conceivably in peculiar cases, an individual cannot take satisfaction in a sacrifice imposed on himself or on persons he especially cares for to achieve a putatively greater gain for others.

Contractarians have no monopoly, however, in recognizing these facts. Here again utilitarianism and contractarianism intersect. The very term "social cooperation", referring to the near-ultimate criterion of utilitarian ethics, emphasizes cooperation and contract among individuals pursuing happiness in their own distinct ways. Emphasis on social cooperation further dissolves tensions between the two doctrines.

Although both share individualistic values, one might conceivably try to make this distinction: while utilitarianism derives individualism as a theorem, contractarianism simply postulates it as an axiom. On this interpretation, the contractarian's "first principle in political philosophy is the individualist principle of consent" (King 1988, p. 39, again referring to James Buchanan in particular). But is consent (along with choice) really a *first* principle, an ultimate value? We value consent and choice because we care about outcomes and deplore the likely consequences of empowering authorities to override individual choice and govern people without their consent. We recognize that being pushed around detracts from people's happiness. Is that not true? We can support our individualistic attitude by appeal to facts of reality, whereas an ultimate or *first* principle would be one for which we can offer no argument. Individualism is instrumental to human happiness, not a downright ultimate value. If human beings were creatures quite different from the ones they in fact are (like social insects, perhaps), concern with their free individual choices and voluntary agreements would be absurd.

Utilitarian reasoning invokes the above-mentioned facts of individuality. True enough, no more than anyone else can utilitarians perform the feat of deriving values from facts alone, of getting an "ought" from an "is". As John Stuart Mill wrote (quoted in note 7 to Chapter 2 above), ultimate ends cannot be proved, but considerations can be adduced for accepting or rejecting a doctrine. Facts can influence how someone reconsiders and articulates his values.

The contractarian and utilitarian doctrines differ mostly in their rhetoric and conceivably also in their epistemology. On the interpretation of Charles King (1988), the contractarian philosopher adopts the stance of an actual participant in interactions among individuals. He must get along with people whose purposes and specific values differ from his own. His knowledge of their desires must come mainly from how they act and from what they do and do not agree to. As a practical matter, the contractarian-as-participant must accept as fair or just whatever result emerges from existing procedures for making choices, decisions, and agreements provided he regards those procedures as just on the whole. The utilitarian, in contrast, supposedly adopts the stance of an outside observer. Not restricted in that role by any need to accommodate himself to what people will and will not agree to, the utilitarian observer is free to gain information and insights about what will serve social harmony and human happiness from whatever sources occur to him, including introspection, social science, and moral philosophy.

This contrast of roles is overdrawn. In writing on ethics and its applications, both the putative participant in negotiations and the detached observer are social scientists or philosophers. For them, the role of impartial spectator (if one accepts that term) is appropriate. Someone engaging in academic discussion can best do his job by not restricting the sources of his information and insights. His job includes straightforwardly laying out his own recommendations and reasons, exposing them to possible refutation or correction. His job is not to impose his views on anyone, and he should not be intimidated by charges of nevertheless aspiring to impose them. While he may have good reason to notice what participants in practical affairs are and are not agreeing to, he need not force his own thinking into conformity with theirs. Unlike the politician's, it is not his job to practice political "realism" in the pejorative sense diagnosed by Philbrook (1953). The role of academic observer and commentator is not identical with and cannot be replaced by the role of participant in practical affairs seeking agreement with his fellows.

The job of academics includes trying to be clear about what arrangements they think best, and why. Their reasons properly include not only positive analysis but also their values, including fundamental ones, which they should state clearly when necessary to forestall misunderstanding.

"TRUTH JUDGMENTS" VERSUS FALLIBILISM

This readiness to assert and discuss values, expecting that some may prove quasi-objectively valid,[8] stands in some tension with contractarianism. It is sometimes suspected of ties to intolerance and authoritarianism (as by James M. Buchanan 1975, pp. 164, 167, 1977, pp. 75-7, 143-4, 1984, pp. 29-30). Stigmatized as a "truth-judgment" approach, it allegedly postulates a unique conception of the good society that must command the allegiance of informed and intellectually honest men and women. Political philosophers who believe they have attained this truth implicitly claim the right to impose it on persons mired in error.

Further criticizing this alleged view, some contractarians make process and consent, not outcome or substance, the criterion of goodness or desirability in human and especially public affairs. " 'Truth', in the final analysis, is tested by agreement. And if men disagree, there is no 'truth'." Even among scientists, "the 'truth' of [a] proposition emerges only from ... agreement and not from some original objective reality" (Buchanan 1977, pp. 113, 145n.).

Its expounders consider this extreme relativism necessary to avoid authoritarianism about truth. Actually, these are not the only alternatives. A third position is distinct from both. The authoritarianism of someone claiming an infallible pipeline to objective truth is the position of the baseball umpire who insists that he calls balls and strikes as they objectively *are*. The relativist-nihilist position of rejecting all absolutes for a radical skepticism is that of the umpire who says that pitches are neither balls nor strikes until he calls them. The third position, "fallibilism", combines metaphysical or ethical objectivism with epistemological relativism. The fallibilist umpire says, "I call 'em as I see 'em". He tries to call each pitch as, by the rules of baseball, it objectively *is*; but he knows that his calls are not infallibly correct, nor do they actually cause pitches to be balls or strikes (Davis 1967/68; cf. Peirce 1955, esp. Selection 4, and Wiener 1968).

On this view, it makes sense to seek truths about reality, even about moral and political values. Yet no person or group infallibly possesses such knowledge. Each searcher contributes what he can, aware that his contribution is incomplete and perhaps wrong. In science, culture, and philosophy, including ethics, fallibilism calls for free competition of ideas, evidences, and arguments. Far from being authoritarian, a willingness to state clearly what one believes and why, exposing one's views to inspection and possible refutation, is essential to constructive discussion.

This fallibilist position adopts the scientific attitude and method. Belief that it is meaningful or heuristically fruitful to seek objective truth through research and discussion need not entail an arrogant eagerness to force one's beliefs onto others. Belief that one type of society and one type of moral code is more conducive to human happiness than another in no way entails a zeal to implement one's vision with force. A concern for *how* decisions are made and implemented, an aversion to having policies, even good ones, rammed down one's own throat or down other people's throats, may well be a major element in one's conception of the good society. Such a concern is hardly the private property of extreme relativists.

Fallibilism is akin to what W.W. Bartley (1985) calls "pancritical rationalism". His book's title, *The Retreat to Commitment*, refers to what he identifies as an irrationalist debating tactic linked to "justificationism". This is the insistence that all propositions be justified by some authority or other, to which nonrational commitment is supposedly unavoidable (Bartley 1985; cf. Bartley 1990, Chapter 15). A pancritical rationalist, in contrast, holds all propositions, laws, theories, and beliefs open to critical examination. (Framing any of them to give it built-in immunity to any adverse evidence or argument empties it of substance.) It is rational tentatively to accept propositions that have so far stood up to evidence and argument and for which no more attractive alternatives have yet appeared. Tentatively accepting such propositions is not the same as considering them actually proved, for airtight justification is downright impossible. Not even the simplest analytic propositions of logic, though seen as almost indubitably correct, are totally immune to reconsideration. Not all propositions can be reconsidered all at the same time, of course; but any of them is open to reconsideration in view of pertinent others.

Fallibilism or pancritical rationalism rejects any claim of infallible access to truth and also rejects the relativist denial of an objective reality against which propositions might be checked. Yet this third position is no mere compromise between those views; it is distinct. It endorses the procedure of science, which, while disclaiming infallibility, finds it a meaningful enterprise to devise conjectures about reality, to try to weed out errors, and thus to approach ever closer to truth. (Bartley's position shows the obvious, and acknowledged, influence of Karl Popper.)

Forthrightness even about one's own values need not, then, express arrogance, a claim to a special pipeline to the truth, and an itch to impose one's own vision of the good society by force. Laying out one's own vision follows from the professional obligation to be clear about what one is saying. Clarity in discussion facilitates inspection of one's views, exposure and correction of one's errors, and the comparison and possible reconciliation of contending views.

JOHN GRAY ON CONTRACTARIANISM

John Gray's judgment helps to wrap up our survey of contractarianism.[9] Gray distinguishes between the scarcely tenable actual-agreement model and the hypothetical-consent model. The notion of "bargaining and agreement in a hypothetical initial position" is a "heuristic fiction" at best. Dropping it still leaves the criticism standing that rational-choice theory fails to show why reason requires complying in the real world with restraints on conduct that would be rational in ideal circumstances (Gray 1989LEPP, p. 191). Even so, says Gray, the contract method works better in deriving principles that no one could reasonably reject than principles that all must reasonably accept (p. 172).

But are those alternatives really distinct? Anyway, I would press my central question: *on what grounds* does the contractarian theorist suppose that reason would bar people from rejecting or would require their accepting certain principles? Those grounds would seem to play a more fundamental role than merely hypothetical acceptance or nonrejection.

Gray finds the arguments against all varieties of contractarianism overwhelming. Without a vast background of shared understandings, contractarian method yields nothing. Typically, it yields liberal results only where liberal practices are already presupposed. It is "a rationalist illusion ... that social or political order can be the product of agreement. We are on far surer ground if we affirm ... that social life is primordial, and agreement ... a possibility only within the framework of a common life" (1989LEPP, p. 254). "[T]he contract method in all of its varieties is destitute of prescriptive content" (p. 191).

NATURAL OR HUMAN RIGHTS

Many critics of utilitarianism offer, in supposed contrast, an emphasis on natural or human rights. Not every doctrine of rights poses this challenge, for rights can be defended precisely on utilitarian grounds. Some versions, however, do reject this grounding and take rights almost as axiomatic or foundational. To seek a further grounding for rights, as in utility or happiness, is to show scant respect for them – or so hard-core rights theorists appear to think. It is to leave rights contingent on mere empirical circumstance.

Though often invoked, the US Declaration of Independence, with its stirring and admirable rhetoric about self-evident and unalienable rights, hardly establishes this position. The Declaration is an exercise in political philosophy – in the application, not the grounding, of ethics. It is concerned with guarding life, liberty, and the pursuit of happiness against violation, especially by governments. It is not an invitation to invent all sorts of rights to the good things of life that some people shall be compelled to deliver to others.

Robert Nozick comes close to the foundational view: "Individuals have rights, and there are things no person or group may do to them (without violating their rights)" (1974, p. ix). Although Nozick does cite John Locke's concepts of self-ownership and of homesteading of previously unowned resources (cf. the appendix to Chapter 11 below), he essentially just postulates rights. He avowedly "does not present a precise theory of the moral basis of individual rights"; he hoped to write on that topic later (p. xiv).[10]

H.L.A. Hart also interprets Nozick's position this way. "For Nozick, the supreme value is freedom – the unimpeded individual will" (Hart 1983, p. 208). He assumes that a social philosophy can draw its morality only from a single source, the rights of individuals, and that their violation is the only moral wrongdoing. Rights are side constraints on what other people may do to an individual; they protect him as he shapes his own life for himself (p. 207). "For Nozick a strictly limited set of near-absolute individual rights constitute the foundations of morality" (p. 202). These rights "express the inviolability of persons" and "reflect the fact of our separate existences" (p. 202, quoting Nozick).

Further, Nozick's moral landscape

> contains only rights and is empty of everything else except possibly the moral permissibility of avoiding ... catastrophe. So long as rights are not violated it matters not for morality, short of catastrophe, how a social system actually works, how individuals fare under it, what needs it fails to meet or what misery or inequalities it produces (Hart 1983, p. 203).

Like Nozick, J.L. Mackie (1978/1984) also asserts that moral theory not only can but must be based on rights. Oddly, he interprets John Stuart Mill as offering such a theory. The moral rules that Mill recognizes in Chapter V of *Utilitarianism* affect utility of such an "extraordinarily important and impressive kind" as to turn a difference in degree from the more common cases of utility into "a real difference in kind". They are maxims "more vital to human well-being than any" others (Mackie 1978/1984, p. 176, quoting

Mill). Mill "take[s] as central the right of persons progressively to choose how they shall live" (Mackie's paraphrase, p. 176).

Although Mill does indeed consider rights important, he still grounds them in utility. Why, then, doesn't Mackie take Mill at his own word as a utilitarian? Mackie does face the question whether his right-based theory and some form of utilitarianism might be extensionally equivalent, yielding the same practical prescriptions. He hopes, but admits he is not sure, that his "right-based theory" is distinct from utilitarianism (Mackie 1978/1984, p. 180); at least he hopes that it is a distinctive version.

Another but not necessarily incompatible version of rights doctrine derives rights from man's Aristotelian *telos*: rights flow from the nature of the human being, from each individual's natural obligation to seek a good life for himself, and from the need for a protected moral space if he is to meet this obligation. (We shall look further at this position below.)

Murray Rothbard (1973, 1982) tries to derive many detailed propositions about ethics and law from his conception of rights, purportedly derived in turn from John Locke's axioms of self-ownership and homesteading. (Yet even for these he offers utilitarian arguments, without acknowledging the label.) John J. Piderit, writing while an economist at Georgetown University, champions what he calls a natural-law approach: correct reason ascertains what actions are "natural" and therefore ethically acceptable by reflecting on the nature of human beings, their shared aspirations and fundamental values, and their interactions in community (Piderit 1993). Yet he can scarcely mean that whatever is natural is right and good. Civilization is largely an exercise in taming natural behavior. Of course, any acceptable doctrine must conform to nature in the sense of not requiring impossible actions or behavior enforceable only at excessive cost. Respecting the facts of nature and human interaction does not distinguish the natural-law approach from utilitarianism. Yet Piderit repeatedly insists that his approach is very different from it. But if it is, then it boils down to a promiscuous if tacit appeal to specific intuitions.

WHAT ARE RIGHTS, AFTER ALL?

In case the context has not already made it clear, a definition of "right" is now in order. Although objective reality does not predetermine what words mean, the following definition does seem to cover how the word is used in its primary contexts: one person's right is his entitlement to behavior toward him by other persons that binds those others with a special degree of moral force, and often with legal force. ("Behavior" covers not only positive actions but also forbearance or noninterference.) Entitlement in "special degree" goes beyond mere desirability. It might be nice if Jones would do some favor for me, but that fact does not itself give me a right to it or obligate Jones to do it.

One person's right implies a corresponding duty of one or more other persons. "[W]hat it *means* to say that someone has a certain moral right is to say, no more and no less, that some or all people have certain moral obligations with respect to the person said to have the right" (Brandt 1992, p. 356). The opposite relation does not necessarily hold: one person may have a duty without anyone else having a corresponding definite right.[11]

The interpersonal character of rights and duties illuminates what it means to say that rights exist. One cannot observe whether human beings have rights in the same way that one can observe whether they have legs. Rights are normative, not empirical, attributes. They "do not exist in the fashion of the sun, the moon, or even the law of gravity. Rather they exist in the way an obligation, a responsibility, or a duty might exist" (Machan 1975, p. 255; cf. p. 108 and Machan 1989, p. 1). To assert a right means that a compelling moral or legal argument can specify how other persons should treat the rights-holder (compare Gewirth 1984EHR, pp. 3-4, 31). Since rights can be argued for, assertions about them are not *fundamental* value judgments. Arguments for them appeal to facts and logic and to value judgments that *are* fundamental, or more nearly so.

Some rights call for positive action by others, as in fulfilling contracts or promises or in supporting one's own infant children. An example of Lomasky's (1987, p. 96) illuminates the question of positive rights. A small child falls into a swimming pool as the only other person on the scene, an able-bodied adult, sits nearby working a crossword puzzle. Does the child have a right to be rescued, and does the adult have the corresponding duty? My reaction is "Yes, of course". The right and the duty flow from broad moral principles, the situation itself, and the resulting special relation between the two persons, accidental and temporary though it may be.

One must beware, however, of basing sweeping assertions about positive (or "welfare") rights on exceptional cases like that of the drowning child. To move to some notion of a right to benefits unmatched by anyone's clear duty to provide them is vague and unsatisfactory. Any general notion of positive rights – people's entitlements to have certain of their wishes fulfilled or of their efforts to succeed – threatens, by its implausibility, to discredit the whole concept of rights. Rights unmatched by clearly corresponding duties hardly square with the central conception of a right.

Negative rights, in contrast, are more clear-cut and more capable of being heeded and therefore more credible. "Basic" rights (as Lomasky 1987 calls them) do not presuppose any contractual or other special relation between the rights-bearer and other persons. They include, prototypically, rights to *forbearances* by others: others must refrain from taking or coercively or fraudulently interfering with one's life, liberty, and property. The right to personal freedom is the right not to be interfered with in activities that do not trespass on the rights of others; that right implies the duty of others not to interfere. Negative rights are likely to hold with the special degree of moral force necessary to count as rights because they are especially easy to respect: they demand merely that others forbear from forcible interference with the rights-bearer.

My suggested definition is consistent with a person's having a right to do something that it is morally wrong to do (see note 11). His right implies *others'* obligation, not his own obligation or freedom from obligation. He has a right to insult others gratuitously, barring special circumstances or agreements to the contrary, in the sense that others are bound to refrain from forcibly interfering with his freedom of mere speech; yet gratuituous insults are not morally right. My definition is also consistent with a person's not having a moral right to commit some action merely because the law does not forbid it; all the less does the law's silence make the action morally acceptable.

Precepts concerning rights, Lomasky (1987) explains, identify restrictions on what individuals may legitimately do to others in pursuit of their own purposes. Recognition of basic rights may well emerge as the unintended product of rational accommodations or mutual considerateness among countless individuals. Individuals find it in their own interests, probabilistically, to cultivate the habits and attitudes and character traits that lead them to respect the rights of their fellows and to share in the projects and feelings of some of them (1987, pp. 245–6). (Lomasky's explanation largely overlaps that of Moritz Schlick; recall Chapter 8.)

Richard Brandt and Loren Lomasky warn, separately, against promiscuously dragging rights into discussions of morality or policy. Discussion of whether a person should be treated in such-and-such a way gains nothing from the assertion that the person has a *right* to that treatment, for to assert the right is simply to answer "yes" to the question being discussed. "All the discussion about who has rights and what exactly they are is only a detour that brings us around to the very same questions with which we started, none the wiser for the detour" (Brandt 1992, p. 356). To treat some issue as one on which good and evil are unmistakably delineated and on which the moral obligation to opt for the good is especially binding is to deploy some pretty heavy artillery. A proliferation of supposed rights tends to undercut the spirit of accommodation and the civility of discourse appropriate to democratic politics (Lomasky 1987, pp. 4–8, 14; Glendon 1991; Sumner 1984 also eloquently deplores "the population explosion of rights-claims"). As if to illustrate these points, a "Survey on the Protection of Your Individual Rights", dated 5 November 1991, arrived in my mail from the National Association to Protect Individual Rights, Bethesda, MD. The "Inalienable Rights" listed on the cover are: Taxpayer's, Retirement, Lifestyle, Victim's, Employee's, Personal Privacy, Sportsman's, Environmental, Smoker's, and Citizen's.

Without trying to taboo the language of rights, M.J. Perry recommends "Not Taking Rights-Talk Too Seriously" (the title of his Appendix A, 1988). Rights-talk seems reducible to ought-talk, may-talk, and duty- or obligation-talk without remainder, but the latter sorts of talk do not seem reducible to rights-talk without remainder (1988, pp. 186–7). In R.M. Hare's words, "Rights are the offspring of prima facie, intuitive principles, and I have nothing against them; but the question is, What prima facie principles ought we to adopt? What intuitions ought we to have? On these questions the rhetoric of rights sheds no light whatever" (1989EoPM, p. 194; Chapters 7–9 discuss rights).

Jeremy Bentham dismissed the notion of nonlegal moral rights as nonsensical or indeterminate (Hart 1982, especially Chapter IV; Sumner 1984). (John Stuart Mill, disagreeing, thought he could give natural or nonlegal rights an indirect-utilitarian foundation.) Particularly in criticizing the US Declaration of Independence, Bentham thought that the whole conception of a nonlegal right or of rights antecedent to law and limiting law's proper scope was nonsense; men resort to talk of nonlegal or natural rights when they wish to get their own way without arguing for it (Hart 1982 p. 57). Bentham had two main objections to the doctrine of natural rights not created by positive law but usable in criticizing and opposing it: (1) it was a gross conceptual confusion, and (2) it corrupted political argument and thought, especially when embodied in political documents intended to restrict the action of legislatures and government (Hart 1982, p. 80). Alleged natural rights lack criteria; appeals to them in political argument must either result in unsettleable controversy or create a gap which men are prone to fill by identifying as natural rights whatever 'political caprice' they have to gratify (Hart 1982 p. 82). Bentham did grudgingly acknowledge, however, that natural rights might possibly be given what I would call an indirect-utilitarian interpretation; at its most respectable, talk of nonlegal and natural rights might be understood as an obscure way of asserting that men *ought* to have certain legal rights.

TRANSCENDENTAL ARGUMENTS FOR RIGHTS

This section surveys some attempts not so much to base morality on rights as to validate rights by verbal maneuvering. In criticizing classical liberalism if offered as a universally valid political ideology, John Gray (1989LEPP) singles out two recently prominent theories of rights. To him they illustrate the failure of various projects that sought to ground liberal universal principles in some comprehensive moral theory such as one based on rights. John Stuart Mill departed from his older liberalism, which had been influenced by Scottish thinkers, and de Tocqueville and Constant, and moved toward the "sentimental religion of humanity and abstract individualism" that Gray finds pervading the conventional dominant liberalisms of our own time (Gray cites his own 1986, esp. Chapter 5). Gray also finds such thinking in Alan Gewirth's "vain attempt ... to ground positive welfare rights in the necessary conditions of human action" and in Ronald Dworkin's appeal to "an inchoate right to equal concern and respect ... as part of a programme of elevating to the status of universal truths the current banalities of American political culture" (1989, p. 230).

Let us look, then, at the theories of Gewirth and Dworkin. Gewirth recognizes assertions of rights as ethical propositions amenable to being argued for (1978, 1982, 1984ATAAR, 1984EHR). His Principle of Generic Consistency, "unlike utilitarian and material deontological theories", supposedly "contains within itself the ground of its necessity; it is self-justifying" (1978, p. 203). To pursue his own purposes effectively, each person needs respect for certain rights. He could not consistently claim those rights for himself while denying them to persons affected by his actions when his very reasons for claiming the rights for himself hold for those other persons also. He would be contradicting himself, in effect saying: "All persons for whom such-and-such reasons hold, including me, have such-and such rights"; yet he would deny, when expedient for himself, that other persons have those rights even though the stated reasons do hold for them also.

Gewirth rephrases his argument in various ways. Human beings act voluntarily and purposively. By the very fact of acting, every person implicitly judges his purposes good. To act successfully, he must have freedom and well-being, so he has rights that other persons not interfere with those conditions. The reasons he could give for his claim to this noninterference apply to those others also. He could not consistently affirm these reasons for himself while denying them for others. To put Gewirth's own summary of his argument still more briefly, each person must recognize that he needs rights to freedom and well-being to take any action. On pain of being inconsistent, he must recognize that the same rights belong to all humans, since they are all actual, prospective, or potential agents.

Sometimes Gewirth names relatively specific rights. If I could have certain *basic goods* - life, physical integrity, health, mental equilibrium, food, clothing, shelter, medical care - without excessive sacrifice by others, then I have a *right* to them. If I denied that people relevantly similar to me also have rights to such goods, I would be running afoul of the Principle of Generic Consistency. Gewirth's rights to "basic goods", including positive rights to benefits somehow to be supplied by other people, are quite different from "basic rights" (so called by Lomasky, as noted above). After some obeisance to private charity, Gewirth (1987) wonders whether private philanthropists have a right to all their wealth and a right to give it away as they choose. Perhaps a duty to let their "surplus" be taxed away for the benefit of poorer people overrides their supposed right to keep or dispose of it as they wish.

Supposedly "self-justifying" principles like Gewirth's arouse suspicion. Just what is the logical contradiction whose avoidance figures so prominently in his argument? An egoist might consider it expedient to claim certain rights for himself and deny them to others if he could get away with it. *He* does not necessarily take his own statements about rights as objectively true; *he* is not committing logical error. Instead, he encourages other persons to hold certain beliefs about rights, hoping that they will not notice internal contradictions in those beliefs. If he can thereby further his own purposes, why should he worry about other persons' faulty thinking? The insincere rights claimant might tacitly be trying to get ethical precepts accepted that violate the principle of generalizability or impartiality. He might be a scoundrel, which is not the same as being a poor logician. (In recognizing what he calls "the Machiavellian case", 1978, pp. 196–8, Gewirth does try, but ineffectually, to rebut a counterargument roughly similar to mine here.)

Of course individuals need certain kinds and amounts of freedom and well-being to lead satisfying lives. But why, as Gewirth asserts, must they believe in actual rights to what they need? Even if they did believe in them, how would that belief assure the actual existence of the supposed rights? Why may not people merely make claims or demands that they expect or hope will be granted for any number of reasons? (Golding 1984, p. 134.) Without actually believing their own arguments, individuals might speak of rights to strengthen their claims. One can recognize in one's own mind that other persons would be equally entitled to the treatment claimed for oneself, all without publicly recognizing and even while denying others' similar entitlements if one thought one could get away with doing so. Implicitly thus to claim special privilege might be outrageous, but that is not the same as logical error. The mere requirements of logical consistency do not establish the concept of rights.

Furthermore, Gewirth could hardly argue that absolutely all interferences with a person's freedom and well-being are morally impermissible. His abstract argument gives no guidance as to what particular rights "exist". An argument for rights of an unspecifiable nature is empty. To have any content, an argument for a moral obligation to respect rights must say something about their substance. Mere verbal maneuvering cannot establish substantive points.

Ronald Dworkin takes equality of concern and respect as the supreme value (Dworkin 1977; Hart 1983, Essay 9). For him, people have rights only to specific liberties, not a general or residual right to liberty. Dworkin's strategy of "deriv[ing] rights to specific liberties from nothing more controversial than the duty of governments to treat their subjects with equal concern and respect ... has a certain Byzantine complexity" (Hart 1983, Essay 9, p. 212). Interpreting denials of freedom as denials of equal concern or respect is especially implausible when a utilitarian decision or a majority vote has weighed a minority's preference for liberty equally with a majority's preference to deny liberty (pp. 214–15 and esp. p. 217). "The evil is the denial of liberty or respect; not *equal* liberty or *equal* respect": ill-treatment of the victims, not their being treated less fairly than others, is what is deplorable (p. 221).

The section on "Equality", below, looks further at Dworkin's theory. Meanwhile, it seems backward to try to derive rights from a duty of government, especially if one believes, as the Declaration of Independence states, that government's central function is to protect rights with which people are already endowed.

AN ARISTOTELIAN GROUNDING FOR RIGHTS

One line of argument for human or natural rights stresses duties that human beings naturally owe to themselves. They have a duty to strive for an Aristotelian perfection or fulfillment, to make something of themselves and become truly human. Each person is responsible for his own moral character and his own happiness through a good life. As rational and social and political animals, humans find their good in lives that develop and employ their potentialities in mutually beneficial interactions. What is good for man flows from his nature and is not simply whatever he may unreflectively desire. The individual has no higher moral purpose than his self-initiated and self-maintained achievement of the best that is in him.

Because of this responsibility for his own character and his own virtuous life, each individual needs a sphere of personal jurisdiction or moral space protected by rights from coercion or aggression by others. These protections include rights not to be deprived of life, liberty, and property. Private property is one great bulwark of a moral space secure from trespass.

Once the rights appropriate to each individual are identified, the principle of universalizability lays on all human beings the obligation to respect them. Pursuit of one's own good runs in parallel with pursuit of the common good, meaning the good that the members of a society value in common. Respect for rights and furtherance of social cooperation support one another.

The foregoing paragraphs, heavy in noble-sounding abstractions, try to distill the theme of three representative books in the natural-rights tradition (Veatch 1985, Rasmussen and Den Uyl 1991, and Machan 1989). These books employ an Aristotelian rhetoric about the individual's duty to build his own moral character and to flourish in ways prescribed not by arbitrary personal caprice but by human nature itself.

Recognizing the objective element in a good life does not justify its imposition by some external authority, for the doctrine further recognizes that a virtuous character cannot be imposed and must be each person's own achievement. Respect for rights is necessary to the self-development of individuals and to healthy interpersonal relations.

Such "Aristotelian" arguments diverge from utilitarianism less in substance than in rhetoric.[12] One possible substantive divergence is that they try to avoid simply postulating a fundamental value judgment (in favor of happiness or flourishing or whatever, as utilitarianism does) and try instead to derive "ought" from "is" through reference to man's Aristotelian *telos*. Well of course human beings have characteristics that distinguish them from other animals,[13] including their conscious pursuit of goals and their need, if they are to flourish, for cooperation within functioning societies. But these are empirical facts, recognized by utilitarians as well as by rights theorists; and they do not *by themselves* establish rights or generate any other normative propositions.

CAN RIGHTS BE FOUNDATIONAL?

This section pulls together some further thoughts about whether rights can serve as the very foundation of ethics. While recognizing reservations about "rights talk" expressed by Glendon, Brandt, Lomasky, Hare, Perry, Bentham, Sumner, and Gray, I do not reject the very concept of rights. Invoking rights can be a shorthand and often rhetorically effective way of reminding listeners and readers of the results of ethical inquiry. Rights are indeed important, but invoking them is no substitute for that inquiry. All the less does rights talk establish or identify the grounding of ethics.

Rights, validly conceived, derive from and are concepts arising *within* an ethical theory and so cannot serve as its very foundation (cf. Sumner 1984). If propositions about especially binding requirements were taken as the basis of morality, how could we derive less binding moral judgments, such as that particular actions would be admirable? If, on the other hand, we take something other than rights as foundational, we can move from considerations merely recommending certain kinds of behavior to considerations so emphatic as to establish actual moral requirements (as Mill 1861/1863 in effect does in Chapter V of *Utilitarianism*).

Joseph Raz is another political philosopher who denies that morality is based on rights. Theories of the sort he rejects fail on three counts: they do not allow for the moral significance of reasons for action other than rights; they do not allow for the moral significance of supererogation; and they cannot accord intrinsic moral value to virtue and the pursuit of excellence (Raz 1984, pp. 42-5). A rights-based morality must seem impossible especially to theorists who, as discussed in Chapter 11, regard rights as legal *rather than* moral concepts.

The main reason for rejecting rights as the basis for ethics is that ethics, like rights themselves, has a more plausible grounding.[14]

AN EXAMPLE OF APPEAL TO FOUNDATIONAL RIGHTS

Further to clinch this rejection, I'll review an unsuccessful attempt to settle a particular issue by appeal to rights conceived of as the very foundation of ethics or at least of a theory of justice. George Smith (1996) tackles the issue of capital punishment. Every person, he asserts, possesses inalienable rights that cannot be transferred, abandoned, or forfeited. Even a brutal killer possesses them. The death penalty violates his inalienable right of self-sovereignty; so libertarians, among whom Smith counts himself, must oppose it. Otherwise, which would be "catastrophic", they must give up their theory of justice, for which inalienable rights are the indispensable foundation (p. 48).

Agreeing with John Locke as he reads him, Smith maintains "that reparation (restitution) and restraint (self-defense) are the only justified uses of violence in a free society". Conceivably, Smith concedes, one might argue for executing a villain whose past crimes showed him to be a "standing threat" to society in general. Doing so would be an act of self-defense, not punishment (pp. 68-9; also see Chapter 11 below). Quite incidentally, Smith tacks on a couple of unavowedly utilitarian arguments: the death penalty makes a murderer more willing to commit further murders and more reluctant to save someone wrongly condemned for a murder that he in fact committed (p. 54).

John Goodman (1997) notes that Smith's rights-based argument, if valid, would hold not only against capital punishment but also against imprisonment. It assumes that all actions belong to either of only two categories: those that people *do* have and those they do *not* have a right to take. Actually, rights do not work so straightforwardly. If either of two persons in a one-person lifeboat has a right to try to survive, then the other has a corresponding obligation to yield, sacrificing himself. If the community has a right to imprison Murphy, judged guilty of a crime beyond all reasonable doubt, then people, including Murphy himself, have a corresponding duty not to interfere. But if Murphy is in fact innocent, does he still have no right to try to escape? In another case, an official is about to hang McCoy, who has committed a thoroughly reprehensible crime and arguably deserves that punishment. McCoy, lying, claims to be innocent. What is the duty of bystanders – to let him be hanged anyway or to rescue him?

The point of Goodman's examples is that supposed rights can clash. Clashes of rights, or supposed rights, are no more mysterious than clashes between *prima facie* moral principles in exceptional cases (compare Chapter 7). The concept of rights therefore cannot serve as the very foundation that settles all issues of ethics and justice.

In a true lifeboat-type situation, ordinary notions of morality and rights cannot apply. None of its victims has a decisive moral obligation to sacrifice himself to another's survival, or not apart from special relations between them; and each will behave according to his already developed character. In many other cases, the moral obligations of the persons involved depend largely on their knowledge and on other specific circumstances. In the cases of the duly convicted but actually innocent suspect and of the actually guilty convict, the community's right to punish the prisoner means an obligation on the part of members of the general public not to interfere forcibly or otherwise illegally unless they happen to have extremely strong reasons for believing him innocent after all. They must not be so presumptuous as to interfere on the basis of mere personal feeling or of less than near-decisive evidence; they must respect a certain division of authority and responsibility in society.

This obligation follows from the obligation to help uphold social cooperation, including a decent legal system that does work, by and large, to maintain justice and peace and security, an obligation whose basis is ultimately utilitarian. The moral obligation not to interfere with punishment does not fall, however, on people in the exceptional position of actually knowing a convicted person to be innocent, including that person himself (or, arguably, any such obligation is much attenuated).

The conception of a right suggested earlier in this chapter does work even in the contexts just considered: a right is a person's entitlement to behavior toward him by other persons that those others are obliged, by exceptional moral force, to accord to him. The specifics of their obligation depend on general ethical principles and also on the facts of the individual case, including the knowledge possessed by the persons involved. No conception of rights, taken as foundational, can displace or override these ultimately utilitarian criteria.

The notion of "inalienability" requires a further remark. Even an "inalienable" right, if there is such a thing, can be violated or "alienated" in the straightforward sense that other persons can in fact deny the rights-holder the treatment to which he is morally entitled. Even though the rights-violators scorn their moral obligation, it does remain, along with the rights-holder's moral entitlement. That is the sense in which a right may be "inalienable". Again, rights presuppose morality and cannot be its very grounding.

On the issue of capital punishment, the real question is whether the government of the relevant jurisdiction – and thus ultimately the sovereign citizenry – is morally bound not to execute even a convict guilty of a heinous murder. Utilitarian considerations underpin the moral principles central to answering this question. To try to settle the issue, as George Smith does, by invoking the criminal's supposed inalienable right of self-sovereignty is a question-begging attempt to bypass the required analysis. (Timothy Virkkala 1997 also criticizes George Smith for trying to apply a philosophical tool – the concept of inalienable rights – to a purpose for which it had not been forged.)

A UTILITARIAN GROUNDING FOR RIGHTS

Similarities between utilitarianism and an Aristotelian case for rights have already been noted. The utilitarian case draws on the indirect utilitarianism of David Hume, Henry Sidgwick, and especially John Stuart Mill (this, anyway, is the perception of John Gray, 1983 and 1984). Reviewing it will further clarify nonutilitarian rights theories by contrast. For Hume, general facts of the human condition – the limited sympathies of human beings and the scarcity of most human goods – rule out pursuing maximum welfare directly. The peace and security of human society must be sought through strict observance of the laws of justice, whose usefulness depends on their *not* being threatened by case-by-case utilitarian calculations. In Mill's indirect utilitarianism, the principle of utility, specifying what alone has intrinsic value, is the supreme standard for evaluating ethical codes and character traits; but it is not itself a criterion of action. Happiness eludes persons who make directly pursuing it their dominant concern. Each of us instead finds happiness in successfully pursuing valued projects. Successful social cooperation among persons pursuing their own goals requires respect for justice and rights. Mill saw rights as necessary for protecting personal autonomy and the security of persons and property. His stress on his "one very simple principle" of liberty[15] is quite in accord with his general doctrine. Jan Narveson (1979, esp. p. 157) also inquires whether the rights doctrine and utilitarianism really are antagonistic. Suppose two situations: (1) rights are fully respected but people are miserable; and (2) rights are taken casually but people are happy. Which situation is preferable? The critic of utilitarianism might reject the suppositions and affirm that happiness and respect for rights are congruent. But wouldn't his attack on utilitarianism then collapse? If, faced with the need to choose, one is unwilling to prefer rights over happiness, isn't one giving up any claim that a rights approach is distinctive and takes precedence?

A utilitarian approach can readily handle the distinction between negative rights (to noninterference) and positive and welfare rights (to actual benefits, perhaps including a decent job and vacations with pay). A negative right entails the duty of *all persons* to refrain from the sort of interference in question. A supposed positive right raises the questions, however, of who in particular has the corresponding duty of supplying the rights-bearer with the specified benefits, and why and under what conditions and on what terms.

Douglas Laycock, law professor at the University of Texas, expounds "the ultimate unity of rights and utilities" (1985). Rights are good things, and some are so good that they should be overridden only for compelling reasons. "But no one good thing can always trump all other good things" (pp. 409–10). The various components of an overall good state of affairs must be weighed against one another. We should neither pursue rights regardless of consequences nor overlook that if an act violates rights, that itself is an intrinsically bad consequence to be taken into account along with all other consequences of the act (p. 413). Laycock expects many rights theorists to reject his "effort to absorb rights into consequentialism. They may say I misunderstand the nature of rights. But I do not misunderstand their view of rights; I disagree with it" (p. 410).

John Gray (1984, pp. 88–91) sees some difficulties in a utilitarian derivation of rights, or at least in John Stuart Mill's derivation. How does Mill propose trading off one vital interest against a competing interest? Can he tolerate some violation of rights for their greater protection on balance? These difficulties regarding tradeoffs between fundamental rights are not very serious, Gray nevertheless suggests; for *any* plausible theory of rights and their grounding faces the same difficulties. Another objection to a wholly instrumental account of the value of rights, even the indirect-utilitarian account, is that it does not capture our sense of the moral importance of fundamental rights. But does our moral sense not ultimately derive from what respect for rights is efficaciously instrumental to, namely social cooperation and thereby happiness?

EQUALITY AS A FUNDAMENTAL VALUE

Some philosophers maintain that every plausible normative political theory rests on the same ultimate value, presumably transcending even freedom and well-being, namely that all persons should be treated "as equals" (Kymlicka 1990, p. 4, citing Ronald Dworkin's postulate of "equal concern and respect", already mentioned above). But is equality in this deep sense (let alone equality of income and wealth) really plausible as an ultimate value? Would Dworkin really prefer general unhappiness to everyone's being very happy, though with the happiness of some being just slightly impaired by their enjoying slightly less concern and respect than some others? Isn't emphasis on equality, even of "concern and respect", just a rhetorical flourish, not to be taken literally?

Furthermore, who is supposed to accord this equal treatment to all persons? Each individual can hardly be expected to show equal concern and respect for all others with whom he comes in contact. It is not only unavoidable but healthy that individuals show special concern for their relatives, friends, and associates. Does the supposedly supreme value of equality refer, then, to how a central authority should treat persons under its jurisdiction? A government-imposed caste system is indeed repulsive. It hardly seems plausible, however, that some precept about government's attitude and behavior be the fundamental value of ethics. Arguments for having any government at all presuppose one or more already accepted principles; as argued in Chapter 11, ethics takes primacy in political philosophy. Undoubtedly we do not want the government arbitrarily allocating special privilege to some of its subjects and special burdens to others, but we can explain why we deplore such differential treatment without making its rejection our ultimate value.

Does the supposed ultimate value of equality boil down to the requirement that ethical precepts be universalizable or generalizable? Plausibly they should be, either on R.M. Hare's ground that universalizability or generalizability inheres in the very concept of ethical precepts or on the utilitarian ground that principles calling for arbitrary discrimination would not be broadly acceptable, not be workable, and so not promote social cooperation and happiness (recall Chapter 9). On the first ground, equality as universalizability is a logical or tautological requirement and so not an ultimate *value*. In the broad sense to which the second ground refers, equality is a means to a value more ultimate than itself and so again is not itself an ultimate value. Anyway, different ethical systems could conform to the requirement of universalizability or generalizability without all appealing to the same ultimate value, so equality in that sense could not itself be the ultimate value. Of course, one might give a peculiar meaning to the word "equality", interpreting it to mean something like happiness; but that would be a disreputable maneuver.

In short, equality is not plausible as an ultimate value.

IS UTILITARIANISM VACUOUS?

Many critics (including Rescher 1975, as already noted in Chapter 7) see the defensive maneuvers available to utilitarians as evidence of how feeble their position is in the first place. Utilitarianism is called plastic or vacuous or tautological, evading any challenge by transforming itself or wriggling away. In this respect it resembles its own criterion, "happiness".

If happiness is interpreted narrowly, hedonistically, as pleasure and the absence of pain, then it just does not always count as good in itself or as the ultimate good. Sore muscles may be an integral part of one's welcome total experience after a satisfying day's work. If, at the other extreme, happiness means whatever people seek or value, then that criterion is allegedly irrefutable and therefore empty or tautological. (Taylor 1970, pp. 96–101, argues roughly that way. Happiness interpreted as *eudaemonia*, or well-being, is no doubt good for its own sake; but saying so is an empty claim.)

Words like "happiness" have indeed sometimes been used in tautological ways, as in saying that whatever a person does, even at gunpoint, he does because he expects the results to make him happier than whatever else he might do. But this straining at accepted meanings of words is not what adopting the utilitarian criterion means.

What a person thinks will make him happiest, especially from a short-run perspective, is not necessarily what will best serve his prospects for a satisfying life as a whole (Adler 1970). What a person currently supposes his interest to be may well diverge from his true long-run interest. Responsible social philosophers go beyond any criterion of some sort of aggregate of the short-run imagined interests of individual persons. They are prepared to distinguish between the kind of society likely to result from policies of gratifying individuals' casual short-run suppositions and the kind that seems likeliest in fact to serve people's prospects of making satisfying lives for themselves.

Saying this admittedly sounds ominous. Yet one should beware of letting one's overall policy orientation distort perceptions on particular questions of fact or distort analysis. A libertarian orientation does not settle the factual question of whether each person is always the best judge of his own interest. Sometimes he probably is not, but no paternalistic conclusion automatically follows. (Chapter 3 already faced this question of happiness versus desire-satisfaction.) A robust libertarianism accepts the facts of reality, including the fact of individual fallibility. This fact scarcely recommends providing each person with a bossy nursemaid to overrule choices she deems bad for him. The social philosopher, or a libertarian one anyway, is concerned with the framework within which individuals both pursue their own ends and enjoy opportunities to reconsider and improve them. The philosopher can be keenly aware that individual choice and freedom from bossy supervision are essential to satisfying lives; he can properly fear linking paternalism with power.

Utilitarian defensive maneuvering, if such it is, accords with the world's complexity. No single word or short slogan can describe the ultimate utilitarian criterion of good and bad, desirable and undesirable. On what contributes to and what detracts from "happiness" and its near-prerequisite, social cooperation, utilitarianism must invoke social science to compare how well alternative sets of institutions and practices are likely to function. Sociology and psychology suggest that matters of fairness, unfairness, and interpersonal distribution do affect a society's functioning and its members' happiness.

The criterion of a society affording good prospects for happiness has the form of a value judgment, not a tautology. Contrasts with possible rivals further clarify it. Here is a list of several alternative criteria.

1. A just society in the sense of John Rawls (1971), for whom justice is nobler than a mere means to happiness. His just society would be structured in accordance with his "difference principle", which focuses on the well-being (strictly, an index of Rawlsian "primary goods") of the least-well-off stratum of the population.

2. Service to God or conformity to his will, somehow ascertained, regardless of cost in other goods forgone. Conceivably God might disapprove of what he considers too much human happiness.[16]

3. Obedience to moral law, somehow known apart from all empirical considerations, out of sheer goodwill to obey it and apart from other inclinations and even regardless of consequences (Kant 1785GMM/1964, pp. 24-5, 57, 78, 109, 130-31, *passim*, and esp. pp. 93-4).[17] A perhaps somewhat more specific version of this intuitionist formulation requires performance of duty for duty's sake. Conceivably, duties objectively exist, quite apart from utilitarian considerations; and their fulfillment holds top priority, even at heavy cost in forgone happiness not only of oneself but of people in general.

4. Knowledge or, alternatively, beauty, commanding priority for its own sake rather than for happiness gained through it or its pursuit.

5. Perfection or excellence, interpreted as the flourishing of the best and noblest specimens of the human race, regardless of how ordinary persons might then fare. (This position is sometimes attributed to Friedrich Nietzsche, as by Rawls 1971, pp. 25, 325).

6. Obedience to natural law, somehow ascertained and heeded otherwise than by consideration of consequences for happiness or misery.

7. Deference to natural, human, or individual rights, taken as axiomatic and likewise ascertained and respected on other than utilitarian grounds.

8. Autonomy and flourishing of the individual. His development of his character and fulfillment of his potential on his own responsibility and initiative might be prized quite apart from consequences for his own and other persons' happiness – if that is conceivable, which I doubt.

Some of these ostensibly rival doctrines, and perhaps others that do not now come to mind, may turn out, on examination, not to be truly *rival* doctrines.

The criteria they appeal to either may not be as ultimate as happiness or may be equivalent to it after all. Some differing doctrines, on the other hand, may be too unattractive to be realistic contenders.

CONCLUSION

To choose happiness or one of its rivals as the *ultimate* criterion is to make a fundamental value judgment, which, being fundamental, is incapable of having reasons offered for it. The ultimate choice must be a matter of intuition. A fundamental intuition remains intuition, even though perhaps deeply rooted in human nature. We need not brood at length over precisely how to interpret the criterion of happiness; for, on any plausible interpretation, social cooperation is prerequisite to its effective pursuit. That means a framework of institutions and practices within which individuals can cooperate effectively in working toward their own diverse goals.

Approaches to ethics in actual or supposed rivalry with utilitarianism include various types of subjectivism, emotivism, and objective naturalism. This chapter has also reviewed contractarianism and contractarian objections to utilitarianism, as well as theories of natural or human rights. If some of these doctrines, instead of being utilitarianism in disguise, turn out to be irreconcilable with it, that very fact helps refute the charge that utilitarianism is vacuous. Having rivals shows that the criterion of happiness is no mere vacuous tautology. The unattractiveness of its rivals leaves it looking even better.

NOTES

1. Russell Hardin (1995, pp. 18–19) also delivered a blunt appraisal:

   ... ethics was long dominated by intuitionism. In intuitionism, there are no principles to apply and no deductions to make. I know some action or something is good or right, bad or wrong, when I see it – or at least I would know such things if I had gone to the right elite boys school in England at about the turn of the twentieth century. This was one of the emptiest moments in all the history of philosophy. ... Upon thorough analysis or deconstruction, intuitionism has turned into nothing.

2. Intuitionist absolutists of Arkes's stripe are not alone in rejecting ethical relativism. Moritz Schlick suggests that differences among societies in specific moral rules reflect mere differences of positive judgment about the *means* conducive to the welfare of society under their different objective circumstances. More basic moral precepts do exist that are held in common by "the most dissimilar of nations and eras" (Schlick 1930/1961, pp. 13–14, 30, 90, 195–6; quoted words from the latter pages).

3. Although Arkes's book is repetitious and tedious in spots, it is generally well written and offers much to admire. His discussions of the morality of US intervention in Vietnam and of abortion are interesting as exercises in mustering evidence, argument, and legal citations; it is enjoyable to watch a keen mind at work.

4. To avoid misunderstanding, I want to say that I regard Ayn Rand's teachings as admirable on the whole. In rejecting purported avoidance of even the slightest element of sheer value judgment, I think I am making a minor clarification of or repair to Randian doctrine. Randians whom I know, however, say I am downright wrong on a crucial point.

5. Though associated with the Vienna school of logical positivism, Moritz Schlick rejected this positivistic denial of any cognitive content to ethical discourse and this almost exclusive focus on its *rhetorical* aspect. Schlick understood that it does make sense to seek truth in ethics (1930/1961 and translator's introduction).

6. See Buchanan's works listed in the References and, for further citations, quotations, and discussion, Yeager 1985, King 1988, and Vanberg 1994.

7. We can judge states (governments) by how they came into existence, by how well they actually function, or by how well they would function if established. John Rawls and Robert Nozick, however, propose judging states (or their underlying principles) by whether they would emerge from a suitable hypothetical starting point. Schmidtz asks what such an exercise has to do with justification. Nozick's (1984) account of how a (minimal) state might have arisen by an invisible-hand process without violation of anyone's rights cannot provide an emergent justification, for it does not describe how the state actually emerged (Schmidtz 1990/1996, pp. 93–4). Neither does it provide a teleological (consequentialist) justification, for it looks backward to a merely hypothetical process in the past rather than forward to expected operating properties.

8. Of course value judgments cannot claim the objective validity of facts. I call value judgments *quasi* objectively valid if they hold up well under examination, cohering well with facts of reality, with each other, and with any fundamental value judgments that participants in sober discussion seriously maintain.

9. I cannot guarantee that these are his current views. Throughout his abundant writings, Gray has been ready to rethink his positions in the light of new evidence and argument.

10. In his 1989 book (especially Chapter 25) Nozick abandons the libertarian political philosophy of his 1974 book. Nevertheless, that earlier book, like the earlier Nozick, has acquired an enduring place of its own in the literature.

11. I may have an ethical duty to be benevolent without any particular persons' having an actual right to my benevolence. Joseph Raz (1984, pp. 56–7) suggests that the owner of a Van Gogh painting may not only have the right to destroy it (meaning that other persons have the duty not to prevent his doing so) but also have the duty *not* to exercise that right (perhaps a duty of piety toward art and human accomplishment). Yet the owner owes his duty to preserve the painting to no particular person; no one has an actual right to prevent its destruction.

    This example helps illuminate the interpersonal character of rights. One person's right to particular actions or forbearances by others by no means implies that its holder is morally obliged to exercise his right and to invoke the corresponding duties of others. It does not even imply that it would be morally acceptable for the holder to do so. Quite the contrary may be true, as with the right to destroy the painting coupled with the duty to preserve it.

    Again, I am not describing objective reality. I am noticing how certain ethical terms may function consistently with established usage and with each other.

12. John Stuart Mill insightfully refers to "the judicious utilitarianism of Aristotle" (1859, Chapter II, p. 142 in Cowling edition).

13. What little I have to say about animal rights comes in Chapter 9 above.

14. Some readers might expect to see, in an appraisal of foundationalist rights theories, some mention of L.A. Rollins's *The Myth of Natural Rights* (1983). Rollins has fun with rights theorists like Ayn Rand, Murray Rothbard, Tibor Machan, S.E. Konkin, and others, catching them in logical errors, self-contradictions, and reliance on sheer assertion. He skewers arguments that purport to derive rights from what man needs to live, flourish, pursue purposes, or whatever. As Ayn Rand sometimes herself said, need is not a claim.

    Although Rollins scores some debating points against natural-rights theorists, he does not establish an alternative position. His rejection of natural rights is part and parcel of a sweeping rejection of morality; he is an avowed amoralist, explicitly referring to "us amoralistic egoists" (p. 19; cf. p. 9). He calls morality a myth invented to promote the interests of its inventors (pp. 8–9). He does not justify his amoralism, holding it nonsense to try to argue for morality or against it. (His stock in trade is demolishing particular arguments for particular conceptions of morality.) He does not even show that he has thoroughly thought through his amoralist position; at bottom, he just asserts it. His book is not merely unsatisfactory but distasteful.

15. Namely, "that the sole end for which mankind are warranted, individually or collectively, in interfering with the liberty of action of any of their number is self-protection, that the only purpose for which power can be rightfully exercised over any member of a civilized community, against his will, is to prevent harm to others. His own good, either physical or moral, is not a sufficient warrant" (Mill 1859, Chapter I, p. 129 in Cowling edition).

   I make no blanket endorsement of Mill's ethical doctrines. He was a subtle writer, and he appears to have changed his mind on important points (cf. Himmelfarb 1974).

16. I have not tried to categorize the theological approach to ethics. It comes in several versions, and vague ones. Perhaps God makes his will known and achieves obedience, more or less, by threatening dire punishment. Perhaps he implants sympathy, consonant with utilitarianism; or perhaps he implants suitable specific intuitions.

   A contrast between two attitudes toward the theological approach is instructive. Dean L. Overman states one, R.M. Hare the other. "If the universe was an accident, there are no absolutes, and without absolutes, as Plato stressed, morals do not exist. Right and wrong have the same meaninglessness" (Overman 1997, p. 177). Without a personal God, "all meaning dissolves into absurdity. There is no real basis for ethics; everything ultimately merges into chaos" (p. 178). "[I]f there is no God, and if the beginning of the universe was accidental or impersonal; then everything is ultimately the same: evil is not evil and good is not good. ... The very fact that one sees wrong and distinguishes it from right means one rejects an impersonal beginning to the universe. For Jewish, Islamic, and Christian theists, God is the moral absolute of the universe" (p. 179). Overman simply makes these assertions; he does not argue for them.

   Some irreligious people think that if God does not exist, everything is permitted. So observes R.M. Hare. But "God or no God, the attitudes that make us revere the laws of morality are a social necessity; we could not live in communities without them. ... [S]ociety would collapse unless children were brought up to feel bad when they do bad things...". Furthermore, "a reflective critical morality can *justify* these laws or rules or principles and our attitudes to them" (Hare 1997, p. 20).

   Bernard Williams also eloquently expresses skepticism about the theological approach (1972/1993, unnumbered chapter entitled "God, morality, and prudence").

17. Yet in testing moral axioms by the consequences of generalizing them and so by engaging in a bit of tacit social science (see, for example, Kant, 1785GMM/1964, pp. 90–91), Kant was revealing himself, inconsistently, to be a crypto-utilitarian, or so John Stuart Mill remarked in *Utilitarianism*, Chapters I and V (1861, 1863, pp. 246, 292–3 in Cowling edition). R.M. Hare (1997, Chapter 8) asks "Could Kant have been a utilitarian?" and answers more "yes" than "no".

11. Law, government, and policy

JUSTIFYING POLITICAL POWER AND OBLIGATION

This chapter considers relations between ethics and political philosophy, law, and policy. What is the rationale of government? If people have any obligation to obey government and law, what is its source? Does democracy have special moral status? Does some sort of natural-law doctrine, as distinguished from legal positivism, make sense? Should judges feel free or feel obliged to consult notions of morality in interpreting – or in going beyond – the legal documents governing the cases before them? What can ethics and economics contribute on issues of crime and punishment? Is formal welfare economics (including the concept of Pareto optimality) a useful guide to policy?

Questions about the moral status of law, the legitimacy of government and its activities, and the mutual obligations of citizens and their rulers are ethical questions. This is true both of the legislator's practical problems and of theoretical problems of justifying and organizing government. So Brand Blanshard (1966) maintains. Ethics takes primacy in political philosophy.

What is government? As mentioned later about "democracy" also, no one is authorized to decree the meanings of words. Still, one notable feature of government as ordinarily understood is coercion or compulsion. Far from being a voluntary arrangement, government – or the state – has compulsion as its essence. It relies as a last resort on its power to seize goods and persons, to imprison, and to execute. Anyone who doubts this point should ponder the consequences of doggedly trying to flout an order of government and to resist all penalties.

Government provides protection against predators in exchange for tribute. It can force its clients to pay unless (and sometimes even if) they move out of its geographical jurisdiction. "Government is an organization that has the ability to finance its activities by compulsory contributions from all individuals in a given geographic area." Coercion distinguishes taxation from, for example, club dues (Holcombe 1994, quotation from p. 90). Almost equivalently, government is often defined as the organization claiming a monopoly on the legal use of force in a given geographic area (but with qualifications regarding different levels of government in a federal system). Unlike other wielders of coercion, such as the mafia, "government is the agency of coercion that has flags in front of its offices" (Browne 1995, p. 12).

233

Granted, the state can be a beneficial institution. Still, not even a democratic state is a mechanism voluntarily operated by its citizens to attend to their common concerns. Even under political democracy the essence of the state is compulsion.[1] Any call for a particular government activity is a call for supporting it, if ultimately necessary, by force. A person living within the geographical jurisdiction of a state has no choice about being subject to it and its laws. If obedience to government is not compulsory, then what is? What does the word "compulsory" mean? What happens to the distinction between what is voluntary and what is compulsory?

True enough, I am glad that the state exists; I prefer it to anarchy; but it is there whether I want it or not. My welcoming something does not keep it from being compulsory. I am glad to have seat belts in my car and would probably have bought them willingly if I had had a free choice, but the fact remains that I did not have a free choice and that the belts were installed under compulsion of law.

The cause of keeping force tightly restrained is ill served by the delusion that government embodies free exchange and that compliance with its orders is voluntary. The cause of human liberty gains scant support from attempts to talk coercion away, as by postulating that the consent of the governed, especially if only their tacit or putative or virtual or conceptual consent, makes submission voluntary after all. Tough-minded thinking and language better serve that cause. Society and the state are not and cannot be the results of a social contract. Their justification, and especially the justification of democratic government, rests on other grounds.

TYPES OF JUSTIFICATION: SOCIAL CONTRACT

Why are a government's subjects morally obliged, if they are, to respect its authority and obey its laws? Within what limits may a government rightly claim obedience? May exceptional circumstances override its subjects' obligation?

Perhaps the main rationale of government and political obligation is to deter and punish predation, help avoid private disputes or settle them peacefully, and so strengthen social cooperation. Why abridge native freedom by positive law, and why create magistrates, David Hume asked. Government could not exist if it were useless. "[T]he sole foundation of the duty of allegiance is the advantage, which it procures to society, by preserving peace and order among mankind" (1751/1777/1930, p. 39).

Brand Blanshard (1961, Chapter 14) reviews six doctrines of political obligation. He dismisses the anarchist denial of political rights and duties as "pathetically irresponsible". A second theory – might makes right – sets ethics aside. A third appeals to divine authority. A fourth, the theory of social contract, begs the question. Why are people obliged to abide by a social contract unless they already have the obligation to honor contracts? And if they do already have certain obligations, isn't social-contract theory superfluous?

Before moving on to the fifth and sixth doctrines on Blanshard's list, we should dwell on this fourth one. John Simmons (1979) reviews doctrines purporting to ground political obligation in consent, often supposed to be "tacit" or "conceptual" consent. (These doctrines apply to political philosophy the contractarian ethics reviewed in Chapter 10.) Or one might try to ground political obligation, if not quite in consent, then in fair play among participants in a scheme of cooperation, or in gratitude for benefits received from government. Simmons concludes that none of these theories works in general, although, by exception, naturalized citizens may indeed have consented to their political obligation.

While rejecting political authority and obligation, stringently construed, Simmons does not claim to justify disobedience or revolution. He recognizes that some theorists have sought to ground political obligation not in past words or deeds of individual citizens but in the good qualities of government (1979, pp. 197–8). He recognizes "strong reasons for supporting at least certain types of governments and for obeying the law" (p. 193). A government's actions may be morally justifiable, and rights violated by them may be less important than "other considerations, such as the need for order" (p. 199). Nevertheless, Simmons does say that the search for a utilitarian or some other basis of political obligation has failed (pp. 45–54).

Interpreted in what seems to me a sympathetic way, social-contract theory holds that most of us generally abide by the law and refrain from unconstitutional subversion of existing government in consideration or expectation of others' doing the same. But this nebulous contract, if a contract at all, is of the same sort as the one by which we generally observe ordinary ethical precepts and often extend the familiar little courtesies to one another. We ordinarily show some consideration for other people because we expect similar consideration ourselves, because mutual consideration yields gains from trade, and because behaving with consistency and decency serves our own self-esteem. To recognize convention and reciprocity and tacit consent of this sort is not to rely on fictions in the way contractarian political doctrine does.

It would really be reaching to interpret such implicit trading as a social contract by which each of us has consented to the existing constitution and so is deemed to have consented to government decisions made in accord with it. It is an exaggeration to call the government's laws and actions the result of collective decisionmaking in any literal sense. Government decisions are made by government officials, and the composite of those decisions undergoes some unintended drift over time. We ordinary citizens are not the government, even though many of us do vote in occasional elections.

Contractarian language about conceptual consent to the coercive powers of government is reminiscent of saying that a jailed criminal is not really being coerced because he has conceptually agreed to be punished if he commits crimes. Such language is dangerous. George Orwell (1946/1961, 1949) understood the affinity between dishonest politics or even totalitarian regimes and the abuse of language. It is safer to call a spade a spade.

Silence or passive acquiescence is no sign of consent especially if dissent would be difficult or would bring on serious consequences or heavy costs, as moving abroad might do (Simmons 1979, p. 98). Hume (essay of 1748 reprinted in Hume 1985, edited by Miller, p. 475) drew a parallel with the idea that a shanghaied sailor consents to the captain's authority over him by not jumping overboard. Jeremy Bentham mocked the notion of "virtual consent" used by a fellow controversialist:

> "Happily for you", said Muley Ishmael once to the people of Morocco, "Happily for you, you are bound by no laws but what have your virtual consent: for they are all made by your virtual representative, and I am he" (*Truth versus Ashhurst*, in Bentham's *Works*, Bowring edition, 1843, V, p. 235, quoted in Simmons 1979, p. 92n).

Thomas Hobbes is widely mentioned as the prototypical theorist of social contract. Yet we need not read Hobbes as tracing political obligation to an actual contract. For him as later for John Locke, the social contract is a metaphor (Gray 1989LEPP, p. 36). His fictions of the state of nature and the social contract (1651/1952) seem to be mere devices for dramatizing the great *utility* of acquiescing in government and accepting political obligation. Hobbes is indeed often classified not only as a contract theorist but also as a proto-utilitarian.

Before ever discussing the supposed social contract, Hobbes (1651/1952) describes the horrors of anarchy and of war of all against all. He states "laws of nature", ethical precepts conducive to peace (recall the section on Hobbes in my appendix to Chapter 6). Not until Chapter 17 of *Leviathan* does he discuss "a Commonwealth" as a means of reinforcing behavior and dispositions consonant with these precepts.

Government's rationale, which is the source of political obligation, is to provide this reinforcement. Hobbes goes on to imagine people behaving *as if* they had agreed among themselves to institute a sovereign and submit to his judgments. He does not say that governments derive their authority from an actual social contract, and he devotes little space to that device.

In the hypothetical absence of government coercion, people lived in "endless and oppressive insecurity". For Hobbes,

The fundamental dictate of the law of nature ... is that men should seek peace. ... [M]en ... perceive that civil society is the sole means of self-preservation and a contented life. ... [S]afety, Hobbes added, means not only bare preservation but happiness and living delightfully, so far as these are possible. ... The commonwealth is the work of men; its utility is its sole justification (Zagoria 1968, pp. 483–5).

Contractarian fictions (reviewed in Chapter 10) are unnecessary and futile as grounds for political obligation. I might obey the laws of an absolute monarchy and even consider such obedience in the general interest and for that reason morally obligatory, all while disapproving of that government's nondemocratic character and some of its actions. Theories centering on tacit consent really deal with reasons why people *ought* to give their consent and so why they may perhaps, in a strained sense, be deemed to have given it. Why not, then, emphasize those reasons? Beyond that, talk of consent is a diversionary flourish.

OTHER JUSTIFICATIONS: NATURAL RIGHTS, RATIONAL WILL, AND UTILITY

Fifth on Blanshard's list of possible grounds of political obligation comes the one stressed in the American Declaration of Independence: governments exist to secure certain self-evident rights. Although sympathetic to this idea of natural rights, Blanshard doubts that self-evidence is their true ground.

The Declaration also contains language that may seem to endorse a consent theory of political obligation: to secure certain unalienable rights, "Governments are instituted among Men, deriving their just Powers from the Consent of the Governed". The Declaration does not, however, trace these "just powers" to consent, actual or conceptual, by the individual citizen. (Neither does the Declaration suppose that persons' rights derive from mutual consent; it sets the question of rights apart from that of consent; Sedgwick 1980, p. 8.) In criticizing the rule of George III, the Declaration identifies the illegitimacy of tyrannical government scornful of its subjects' interests. By implication, the more extensive and wholehearted acquiescence the government earns by securing people's rights, the more nearly legitimate it is. The Declaration goes on to recognize the "prudence" of suffering endurable evils instead of overthrowing long-established institutions, but it also recognizes the right of the people to alter or replace their existing government in a way that seems likely to serve their "Safety and Happiness". These are broadly utilitarian ideas.

Sixth on Blanshard's list comes his own doctrine of "rational will". People have rights against one another deriving from a shared common moral end (which is social cooperation, although Blanshard does not use that term). The mission of the state is to further its realization. The state could not function if its citizens could individually pick and choose which laws they would obey. This is the ground for obedience in normal cases and for disobedience only in exceptional cases.

One's duties toward a reasonably decent government derive, then, from the obligation to support rather than subvert social cooperation, which intertwines with ordinary ethical precepts. Scorning that obligation by arrogating special privilege to oneself, picking and choosing what laws to obey, and making exceptions in one's own favor subverts a generally useful institution, which government is, even though perhaps only a "necessary evil". Respecting political obligation contributes to our own and our fellows' welfare – especially in view of the Hobbesian alternative, the war of all against all.

John J. Ford (1915/1970, p. 348) makes essentially this point, though in unnecessarily theological terms: the expressed will of the people is not what legitimizes civil authority of some sort or other. "Nature, or rather the author of nature, God, bids men live in civil society", which presupposes a ruling authority to preserve order. Civil authority is therefore natural. "The right to rule is not necessarily, however, bound up with any special form of government; nor, except in the case of the theocratic form, is the ruler immediately chosen by God."

We ordinary citizens find ourselves living under a government and laws that have evolved over decades and centuries without our having had any effective opportunity to give or withhold our individual consents. Even so, we generally acquiesce in the existing government and obey its laws because, first, we ordinarily have no real alternative. Revolt would be fruitless for an individual acting alone, and moving abroad too costly. Besides, where would we go? Second, and perhaps more important, we ordinarily prefer the existing system to general turmoil. Particularly (though not only) under a democratic system, sizable groups of us have some hope of influencing public opinion and the policies and even the character of government. Many laws conform to ethical precepts that we respect anyway. We individuals benefit from others' obeying the law and feel that making exceptions in our own favor at others' expense would be morally wrong. Those among us who behave otherwise are subject to penalties. In self-defense we apply force against criminals who flout such of the moral code as has been reinforced by law.

VALUES AND PUBLIC POLICY

Economists sometimes invoke the concepts of Pareto optimality and Pareto-optimal change – or, more broadly, the concepts of theoretical welfare economics – as supposed keys to a positive science of political economy. (A Pareto-optimal change benefits at least one person while harming no one; a

Pareto optimum is a situation from which no such change is possible.) The following are a few, though not all, inadequacies of this supposed policy criterion (see Yeager 1978).[2] The Pareto optimum is not unique; in principle, there are many Pareto-optimal states. Although any nonoptimal position is dominated by other positions reachable by Pareto-optimal moves, there is no presumption that *any* optimum is preferable to *any* nonoptimum. Applying the implied requirement of unanimous consent to a change, or at least unanimous acquiescence in it, is bedeviled by problems of knowledge, misrepresentation, negotiations, and enforcement. The requirement has a status-quo bias.

Sometimes the Pareto criterion is watered down to a "constitutional" approach recommending searches for policy *packages* yielding gain for all or some persons and loss for none. Unanimous consent is not expected for each separate feature of a policy change but only for the entire package. Further weakening the requirement to one not of actual unanimity but only of *near-unanimity* leaves questions dangling about whose opposition or what sort of opposition should not count, and why. A more appetizing escape from a literal to an honorary unanimity criterion looks for consensus in favor of the whole social-decision-making process and of the totality of policy measures (though not each one separately) evolving over time. That approach threatens, however, to empty the supposed Pareto criterion of meaning.

Understandably the "constitutional" political economist cherishes the ideals of consensus and of recommending broad lines of policy almost value-free. An Occam's Razor is handy for promoting economy in the appeal to value judgments. Confusion between disagreement over values and disagreement over positive propositions should be avoided, as should haste to chalk up disagreement over policies to an impasse over values. But attempts to banish value judgments, or programmatic pronouncements about doing so, tend in their own way to undermine scientific standards. All policy recommendations rest not only on positive propositions but also on conceptions, at least tacit, of desirable and undesirable states of affairs. Frankly, to recognize this necessary role of values is not to disparage scientific rigor but simply to avoid self-deception. The Pareto criterion itself involves value judgments, however hidden, including the judgment that all persons' tastes and preferences are to count equally according to their intensity (or, more exactly, according to the tradeoffs that people will make to gratify them), regardless of their content. Even tastes for meddlesomeness, nosiness, and Schadenfreude are to count.

As Clarence Philbrook says, "Only one type of serious defense of a policy is open to an economist or anyone else: he must maintain that the policy is good" (1953, p. 859). That claim logically has two bases: (1) a positive analysis predicting the results of the recommended policy, and (2) a judgment that those results cohere, at least on balance, with the advisor's conception of a good society, which he should be ready to avow openly. Positive analysis –

as in economics, physics, medical science, or whatever – explores how facts and events fit together and helps predict the effects of particular actions. But it alone cannot decree what *should* be done. What should be done depends also on how strongly people desire or deplore those effects, side effects as well as main ones and remote as well as immediate ones.

Positive analysis alone cannot even recommend a measure that would produce an overwhelmingly desired result; the judgment about desirability is also necessary. Suppose a marvelous invention enabled the government to abolish hurricanes at negligible cost. Should it do so? Some people would lose income or would need to switch jobs. No one can prove scientifically that the harm done to those few should count less heavily than the benefit to the majority. Nor can science prove that hurricanes should be abolished only if the gainers fully or more than fully compensate the losers or, on the other hand, that hurricanes should be abolished without compensation. Even if *no one* would feel any loss from abolition, someone could still maintain, immune from purely scientific refutation, that abolishing hurricanes would wickedly interfere with God's will.

In short, any policy recommendation or decision rests in part on judgments about what results are desirable, including benefits for some people at others' expense and, in general, about what makes a good society.

It by no means follows that everything bearing on policy is a matter of taste. Nor is anyone's opinion as good as anyone else's. If the respectability of disagreeing on values and therefore on policy extends to positive propositions in the same way, it undermines scientific standards. When policy disagreements trace to disagreements over fact and logic that further investigation and discussion might narrow, chalking disagreement up to differences of equally respectable personal opinions is anti-intellectual. Even when disagreement does hinge on value judgments, investigation and discussion may reveal hierarchies among value judgments, showing that some fit neatly together while others clash. Investigation and discussion may help systematize value judgments, weeding out both repetitions and contradictions. This is not the same as identifying one single correct set of mutually consistent values. An irreducible element of nonscientific preference remains. Still, it is reasonable to hope that discussion will often reveal a broad consensus on fundamental values.

Particular policies do not necessarily serve the common good or public interest merely because they are widely desired. Furthermore, policies may affect what people desire through affecting their tastes, values, attitudes, and personal characters. Effects like these may well enter into assessment of policies.

But does not saying so express an activist and almost totalitarian view of government? Is it not arrogant to speculate about objective truth in value judgments? An answer has three parts. First, if policies do unavoidably affect attitudes and tastes, it is perverse to pretend otherwise and recommend an impossible neutrality. Although individuals' tastes are largely a social product and may indeed be affected by policy, complacency about overriding them does not follow in the least. Regardless of just how a person's tastes were shaped, they are his own, and having them overridden is unpleasant for him at the time. There is no contradiction between wanting to let people gratify their own tastes and taking heed of influences on those tastes. A second part of the answer is that attention to these influences does not necessarily recommend hyperactive government. It might recommend restricting government's scope. Third, the working hypothesis of quasi-objective truth even in the realm of values does not arrogantly claim special insight for a dictatorial elite. It recommends the ordinary scientific procedures of investigation and discussion.

The policy advisor or social philosopher who respects the hypothesis of objective good and bad, right and wrong, does not thereby claim that his insights are infallibly superior to everyone else's. He is just forthrightly stating what they are. His views on topics in which he is a specialist are indeed probably more worth hearing than those of most other people, just as other people probably have better-based views than he does about the many fields in which he does not specialize. His particular job is to seek and communicate positive knowledge that, combined with frankly avowed and carefully examined value judgments, yields policy recommendations. Discussion would lose its main point unless participants were willing to lay out their judgments for inspection, instead of trying to adjust their own to those of everyone else. Frank if tentative advocacy of what one thinks good is part of the job.

Perhaps the political philosopher's job is 99 per cent positive analysis. The relevant analysis in positive political economy comes in assessing probable effects – ultimately, effects on happiness – not just in counting or conjecturing about votes. Perhaps the political philosopher's job consists only to a vanishingly small extent of offering his own carefully articulated value judgments in hopes that they will appeal to other people generally. His value judgments would not endorse specific tastes in detail; rather, they would endorse attainable conditions thought conducive to individuals' successful pursuit of happiness. Even so, his job would be a distinctive one, and it is absurd to urge him to abdicate it in favor of a supposedly purely positive political economy.

Especially as applied in political philosophy, discussion of values in hope that some may prove quasi-objectively valid is sometimes suspected of affinity with intolerance and authoritarianism. Yet this suspicion is unwarranted (or so argues the section on "Truth judgment and fallibilism" in Chapter 10).

RELATIONS BETWEEN LAW AND MORALITY

Besides informing the values that necessarily undergird policy, ethics intertwines with policymaking in another way. It is impossible to draft statutes and constitutional provisions so that they fully enforce themselves. Adherence to them presupposes a certain moral commitment to their spirit or intention. Discussions over a proposed balanced-budget amendment to the US Constitution illustrate the difficulties that arise when moral standards weaken. How does one draft an amendment to prevent evasions? A kind of ethical commitment to a balanced budget had long imposed a healthy discipline on the Federal government, as we came to realize only after that commitment had faded away late in the twentieth century. It is difficult to restore a lapsed ethical spirit.

Not only in implementing policies and financing them and not only in dealing with criminals but also in civil cases among private parties, law ultimately involves the exercise of coercion. To bring a lawsuit is to seek to enlist the governmental force, or the threat of it, that ultimately backs up court judgments. In what one would consider justified lawsuits, the force invoked is defensive, rectificatory, or retaliatory. In a predatory lawsuit the plaintiff *initiates* the use or threat of governmental force to redistribute wealth toward himself. (A story on TV headline news, 24 November 1995, dramatized this point by portraying Eufaula, Alabama, whether correctly or not, as a hotbed of such litigation.)

To a large extent the law serves to reinforce morality in relatively clear-cut cases (we scarcely want coercion to serve fuzzy rules). The law goes beyond, however, merely trying to reinforce ethical principles. In some cases it reinforces customs or even makes somewhat arbitrary stipulations, as in traffic rules and rules for property transfers. In such cases its purpose is to improve people's ability to predict each other's behavior, to reduce misunderstandings, to lessen action at cross-purposes, and otherwise to improve coordination.

Mary Ann Glendon (1991, esp. Chapter 4) makes much of the failure of law in the United States to impose a legal duty to come to the aid of a person in mortal danger. What significance she attaches to this failure is not entirely clear, but she apparently sees it as a symptom of something regrettable. Yet one might well regard the nonimposition of a legal duty to give help as an example of humility and restraint on the part of law and government. The absence of a legal requirement does not mean repudiating the *moral* duty to give help. To suppose it does – more broadly, to suppose that the law determines or at least registers what morality requires – is a tacitly statist notion. Government should not try, with coercion as its ultimate sanction, to enforce everything good and suppress everything bad. Taking on so broad a responsibility would worsen its dangerous aspects.

Although law does not determine morality, it should, in my view, try to reinforce it in clear-cut cases. Cases in which rescue might seem obligatory are far from clear-cut. How much and what sort of danger would legally entitle the victim to rescue? How would the authorities determine what knowledge a neglectful potential rescuer had of the victim's plight? How much and what sort of risk may a potential rescuer be required to run, and how are third parties to judge his knowledge and state of mind about this risk? What excuses are available to a nonrescuer? (Several come to mind that would be difficult to refute.) If several potential rescuers had been on the scene, on which one or ones did the legal duty fall?

If failure to rescue were a criminal offense, this vagueness and these difficulties of proving guilt or innocence would provide opportunities for selective prosecution. Even if that failure were only an actionable tort, unrescued victims or their heirs, along with clever lawyers, would be tempted to file suits on the off-chance of a big award or settlement.

Some matters, then, must be left outside the purview of the law, to be governed by the flexible precepts of morality. Morality does call for actions – like rescues in certain cases – that had best not be made *legally* obligatory. Legality and morality, illegality and immorality, simply could not be made to coincide completely. Attempts to enlist government power toward that end would risk leading to a totalitarian society. "Law seeks to establish and maintain only that minimum of actualized morality that is necessary for the healthy functioning of the social order. It does not look to what is morally desirable, or attempt to remove every moral taint from the atmosphere of society. It enforces only what is minimally acceptable, and in this sense socially necessary" (John Courtney Murray, quoted in Perry 1988, p. 101). Richard Epstein cautions against reflexively invoking the law – "collective might" – to enforce all conduct thought desirable. Too much reliance on coercion crowds out informal sanctions and narrows the scope for prized personal virtues. A social system is shaped not only by the law but also by social norms of approval and disapproval (Epstein 1995, esp. p. 326).

As Tom Beauchamp and James Childress similarly argue (1983, p. 12), what is moral or immoral cannot or should not be made to coincide with what is legal or illegal. To judge an act morally wrong does not necessarily entail wanting the government to prohibit it. (Their example is abortion. I would suggest surliness when being surly is immoral.) Nor does holding an act morally acceptable in some circumstances necessarily imply that the law should permit it. It is logically coherent, for example, to hold euthanasia morally justified in extreme circumstances yet also hold that it should remain illegal because legislators could not design a permissive law that would nevertheless prevent abuses.

A popular writer on etiquette has expressed such insights:

[T]he danger of attempting to expand the dominion of the law to take over the function of etiquette – to deal with such violations as students calling each other nasty names, or protesters doing provocative things with flags – is that it may compromise our constitutional rights. For all its strictness, a generally understood community standard of etiquette is more flexible than the law and, because it depends on voluntary compliance, less threatening (Judith Martin ("Miss Manners") 1996 essay; compare her excellent book of same date).

Hadley Arkes, whose book of 1986 served as an example of ethical intuitionism in Chapter 10, illustrates an extreme position on the relation between law and ethics. Arkes claims to agree with Aristotle that the justification for a polity goes beyond the need to provide security and a peaceful framework for commerce. The case arises from morality itself (Arkes 1986, p. 8). The mission of the polity is to render justice and to engage in moral teaching through the law (p. 14). Arkes risks breeding confusion, by the way, in dwelling on "the polity". The term presumably indicates organized society rather than government specifically, yet it does tend to focus attention on society's political, coercion-wielding, organs.

Arkes means more than that politics, like other human activities, should operate within ethical restraints. Politics should seek to promote morality. Law arises directly from the logic of morals. We have law only because some things are right and others are wrong. As for legislating morality, we may legislate *only* morality. Once we establish that "X is wrong", the logical implication is to remove X from the domain of personal taste or private choice. We may forbid X with the force of law (p. 162). Moral principles can define things that are wrong and ought to be forbidden (p. 328). (Arkes apparently wants government to be active in suppressing evil and promoting good as he conceives of it. He comes across as an activist conservative of a kind that is anathema to many libertarians.)

A utilitarian can wholeheartedly agree with Arkes (though on grounds different from his) that some things are right and ought to be encouraged or required, while other things are wrong and ought to be discouraged or forbidden. It does not follow, though, that the political bodies of society, the agencies legally authorized to employ coercion, are the best agencies to discern and enforce morality. One reason is that even though the basic truths of morality may objectively exist and be capable in principle of commanding recognition by almost everyone, how these principles apply in specific circumstances is by no means cut and dried. People can legitimately disagree on lower-level or relatively specific rules and their applications; they are open to discussion.

The supposition is arrogant, especially when reinforced by coercion, that one possesses detailed moral truth and that people who disagree are not merely mistaken but wicked. The political process operates with the various inaccuracies diagnosed by the public-choice school of economics. Other organs of society besides government can support morality. Unnecessarily to raise points of disagreement to the level of moral issues tends to embitter disputes and impair the cooperative search for mutual accommodations.

Arkes seems not to recognize any valid basis for law other than morality. But what about law to improve coordination, like the details of traffic law and commercial law? And Arkes does not recognize reasons for not wanting to erect government into the chief champion of morality and entrench all moral precepts as actual law. These reasons include concern for definiteness and enforceability and so for the rule of law, dangers of abuse of legalized coercion, and other reasons developed in public-choice theory and in economists' writings on the nature of man (see, for example, Brunner and Meckling 1977). He does not adequately distinguish government or state from polity or society and sometimes seems to think of society–polity–state–government all welded together.

Arkes seems not to recognize the fact, pregnant with implications, that governmental authorities, like other people, are fallible. What would the consequences be of people's feeling entitled to enlist governmental coercion in enforcing whatever they conceive of as moral truth? (Here, as elsewhere, Arkes shuns consequential arguments.) Even more so than already, government would be the object of struggle among all sorts of special interests, including hobbyist and moralistic interests. To recognize fallibility and, partly for that reason, to want to keep government constrained is not at all the same thing as being a moral relativist (on fallibilism, recall Chapter 10). I can believe in the existence of objective moral truth without also believing that I am already in such complete and infallible possession of it as to be entitled to enlist governmental coercion to enforce my understanding of it.

SOME CONTENTIOUS TERMS: DEMOCRACY

Use of terms vaguely or in multiple senses often impairs discussions of political philosophy, especially informal or popular ones. Some examples are "democracy", "liberty" or "freedom", "public interest", and "common good".

Democracy, compared with other political systems, does somewhat increase the scant influence that the individual citizen may have over his rulers. But the ordinary citizen's control over government is less precise and effective than his control over economic activity, as it affects him, through the way he earns and especially the way he spends his money ("voting in the marketplace"). Although some analogy does hold between political and economic processes, it is scarcely close.

Reviewing the case for democracy requires understanding the word. Of course, words do not come with their true meanings laid down in objective reality. A word derives its meaning from how it is used. The equivocation of blanketing multiple concepts under a single label confuses meaning and obstructs clear thought and communication. Not only a particular political method but also concepts related to liberty, equality, and fraternity are often lumped together under the label "democracy", impeding analysis of how well those distinct concepts actually cohere with one another.[3] Joseph Schumpeter's understanding of democracy (1950, p. 242) helps avoid this confusion.

> Democracy is a political *method*, that is to say, a certain type of institutional arrangement for arriving at political – legislative and administrative – decisions and hence incapable of being an end in itself, irrespective of what decisions it will produce under given historical conditions.

Schumpeter rejected what he called the "classical theory" of democracy, according to which the people "hold a definite and rational opinion about every individual question" and give it effect by choosing representatives to implement their will (p. 269). On Schumpeter's view, the people's role is to produce a government, a ruling body. He offers a definition: "[T]he democratic method is that institutional arrangement for arriving at political decisions in which individuals acquire the power to decide by means of a competitive struggle for the people's vote" – through "free competition for a free vote" (pp. 269, 271). "The principle of democracy ... merely means that the reins of government should be handed to those who command more support than do any of the competing individuals or teams" (p. 273). "Now one aspect of this may be expressed by saying that democracy is the rule of the politician" (p. 285).

Democracy is a particular *method*, then, of choosing and influencing those who wield government power. The rulers gain and hold office through success in periodic competitions for votes. Competition for the freely given votes of a broad electorate implies that public opinion and discussion are relevant and that the citizens thereby influence their rulers even between elections. Public opinion and electoral prospects exert influence on what decisions public officials will consider in their own personal interests.[4]

The key element in the case for democracy, so conceived, is that democracy lessens the necessity or desirability of violent rebellion. It makes an alternative relevant – discussion. If a law really is oppressively bad, citizens and their political representatives may come to understand why and may change it peacefully. This case for democracy is a far cry from asserting that all decisions made under democratic government are made in accordance with each citizen's will, or his real will, or are to be "deemed" so made. We need not appeal to any contractarian fiction about unanimous constitutional agreement to waive unanimous agreement on specific issues.

LIBERTY AND THE FORM OF GOVERNMENT

Like "democracy", the word "freedom" (or "liberty") provides examples of blanketing two or more distinct concepts under a single label. Often we hear that freedom is worth little to people who are too hungry, sick, miserable, ignorant, or otherwise disadvantaged to do the things that they are nominally free to do. A long tradition of such word abuse includes the proclamation of the "four freedoms" by President Roosevelt in 1941. People enslaved by addictions or other character flaws are likewise not "truly free". "True freedom" means more than mere absence of restraint; it presupposes some degree of well-being and opportunity.

With such rhetoric in mind, Sir Isaiah Berlin diagnoses a slide between "Two concepts of liberty". The first is a negative concept, the absence of restraint. This might seem valueless by itself; true freedom, positive freedom, presupposes some power, efficacy, self-realization, status. A truly free man has a voice in collective decisions. One might even drift into thinking (as J.-J. Rousseau apparently did) that a person partakes of the highest freedom as a member of the whole body of citizens expressing and implementing its general will (if perhaps only through its leaders). Positive freedom can become nearly the opposite of negative freedom (Berlin 1958/1969; compare Hayek 1944/1956, pp. 25–6).[5]

Again, we should beware of equivocations. Writers should make it clear, explicitly or by context, when they depart from a word's most usual meaning. In discussion of interpersonal relations and government actions, the central meaning of "freedom" does seem to be the negative one of absence of restraint or compulsion imposed on a person by other persons (cf. Hayek 1960, Chapter 1). Even a poor, sick, miserable person may be free of such restraint or compulsion. A mountain-climber trapped in a crevasse is physically unfree, yet not thereby stripped of his civil liberty. A subject of a tyrannical and totalitarian ruler may be rich – not yet plundered – while possessing scant political power and personal liberty.

Personal freedom, while a great value, is not the only value. Quite conceivably, in wretched circumstances, people might willingly trade away their freedom, *if* the tradeoff were genuinely available, for more food, clothing, shelter, and safety. But it clouds thinking to *define* freedom as embracing these other good things. It clouds thinking to suppose that a sacrifice of some freedom for a good reason spells no loss of freedom after all. (Sometimes, if not very clearly, Lord Acton's remark that freedom is the highest *political* value warns against these confusions.)[6] Sir Isaiah Berlin recognizes that in some circumstances it may be reasonable, perhaps even morally required, to sacrifice some freedom to reduce injustice or glaring inequality or widespread misery. "But a sacrifice is not an increase in what is being sacrificed, namely freedom, however great the moral need or the compensation for it. Everything is what it is: liberty is liberty, not equality or fairness or justice or culture, or human happiness or a quiet conscience" (1958/1969, p. 125). (Earlier, Bishop Joseph Butler had already cautioned that "every thing is what it is, and not another thing.")

John Gray warns against linking freedom and democracy almost by definition, a confusion he associates with contemporary "liberalism" as he understands it (what one might call left liberalism, as opposed to classical liberalism). He sees no good reason to regard the political or democratic liberties (perhaps better called rights to political participation) as being as basic as the civil and personal liberties. The classic negative liberties have flourished under a variety of political regimes, not just representative democracy. The connection between the two categories of liberties is that the political ones serve as means of protecting the civil and personal ones. While the basic liberties have sometimes flourished in the absence of democratic institutions, they have never existed without extensive rights of private property (Gray 1989LEPP, pp. 156-7).

Gray champions what he calls "civil society" and Michael Oakeshott called "civil association". This is the domain of voluntary associations and market exchanges through which individuals pursuing their own diverse purposes may live together in peace. Private property, the market, contractual liberty, and the rule of law count among its essential characteristics. Although most institutions of civil society are independent of the state, they do require the protection of law. Civil association contrasts with government as an enterprise association, as an instrument for pursuing specific collective goals (Gray 1993, pp. 246, 275, and *passim*).

Civil society may flourish under many types of government (p. 159). Gray mentions the authoritarian regimes of South Korea, Taiwan, and Singapore (p. 247) and even has some kind words for empires and monarchies in general (pp. 213, 268-9, 278). "In all its varieties ... liberal political philosophy has failed to establish its fundamental thesis: that liberal democracy is the only form of government that can be sanctioned by reason and morality" (p. 246). One who shares Gray's unsentimental understanding of democracy and alternative political regimes would hardly suppose that submitting large parts of life to the majority vote of electorates or legislatures is central to classical liberalism or the American dream.

Gray sympathizes with the conception of government that he attributes to Thomas Hobbes – a strong but strictly limited state that secures peace and leaves most other activities to private agents enjoying liberty of thought and action (p. 270). He identifies a *new Hobbesian dilemma*: To defend their own assets, citizens are driven nowadays to organize to capture government power. The state itself is becoming the chief weapon in *a political war of all against all* (pp. 211–12).

Gray's and Oakeshott's civil society or civil association is practically the same as a framework of social cooperation. Gray does not make this identification, however, and might not accept the implied utilitarian gloss on his own position.

Neither does he accept a purely rights-based or justice-based view of political morality. Rights are never foundational; instead, they "gain their content from the requirements of human well-being" (1993, p. 303). An overblown rhetoric of rights, as Gray implies, consorts with legalism and runs counter to a spirit of mutual accommodation (cf. Glendon 1991).

David Hume, although evidently a forerunner or founder of the classical-liberal tradition, did not adhere to what Gray berates as foundationalist liberalism. Hume does not try to describe an ideal social order founded on first principles. (In our own day and earlier, examples of foundationalism appeal to a postulated original contract, self-evident rights, or what agreement would emerge from discussion under ideal conditions, such as imagined by John Rawls 1971 or Bruce Ackerman 1980.) Although Hume was willing to examine existing institutions critically and propose reforms, he warned against rash overthrow of inherited traditions and customs, which do, after all, enjoy a presumption of some value. Like Adam Smith, he welcomed the emerging commercial society as part of the practice of liberty, but he also thought that substantial moral traditions and respect for traditional virtues were required. In our day, he would not have ranked mass political democracy high on the list of features of a good society. He does not argue that the liberal state is the only legitimate state. In short, Hume's position is classical liberalism heavily tinged with conservatism. (This interpretation, consistent with my reading of Hume, derives from a Symposium in *Hume Studies*, November 1995, particularly the contributions of Donald W. Livingston and John B. Stewart; compare Varco 1994.)

PUBLIC INTEREST, COMMON GOOD, AND PUBLIC POLICY

An examination of several related terms may begin with examples of their use. As Alexander Hamilton recognized, people commonly intend the public good but sometimes err about how best to promote it. What should legislators do then? What weight should they give to ignorant or ill-advised preferences?

Hamilton thought they should "withstand the [people's] temporary delusion in order to give them time and opportunity for more cool and sedate reflection" (Sedgwick 1980, pp. 2, 7, quoting Hamilton in "Publius" 1787–8 from *The Federalist*, No. 71). Similarly, James Madison found public opinion or preference an uncertain basis for decent government. He suggested that the opinions of the citizenry, like the interests or passions of a minority or a majority or a coalition of factions, do not necessarily articulate the long-term or permanent or aggregate interests of the nation; they may even override justice and minority rights (*The Federalist*, No. 10, interpreted by Sedgwick 1980, pp. 8–10, 13).

Do views like Hamilton's and Madison's imply that when the correct or effective policy and the one commanding popular consent diverge, the former should be enacted? No. That would come close to saying that if officials or legislators who sincerely deem a particular policy best can manage to get it enacted even contrary to the wishes of most people, they are right in doing so; lack of popular consent should not block the policy. I would endorse neither that view nor roughly the opposite: that current majority opinion should immediately prevail. The case for checks and balances and for "refining" the will of the people is a strong one.

The will of the people is not the test of the correctness, effectiveness, or desirability of a policy and so is not the criterion of what an expert or policy advisor should recommend. A system that permits ramming policies down the throats of unwilling majorities (or substantial minorities) ill serves social cooperation. Yet despite unpopularity, a particular policy may be good and worth recommending. The recommender does not necessarily want to impose his judgment by force. He hopes that the people will eventually come to see the merits of the recommended policy and will accept it willingly.

In short, consent is not the criterion of goodness, although it may be a clue. Imposing policies contrary to popular will is bad, but this badness is not the same as badness of the policies themselves.

It is scarcely possible to have a political system that always serves truth and beauty and the true public interest rather than, in case of clash, mere popular desire. Procedures are almost bound to operate perversely sometimes, and officials to decide unjustly. Operationally, the public interest cannot be made the decisive feature of a structure and procedure. Still, this is no reason for political philosophers to abandon that criterion in their theorizing and discussions. The lack of any infallible way to enforce some criterion does not in itself invalidate the criterion; no criterion is infallibly enforceable.

Aping much policy discussion, I have been using terms like "common good" or "public interest". Such expressions may sometimes betray a collectivist conception of society as a higher entity transcending its individual members and having a "good" or "interest" of its own. But they need not have such a meaning. The "common good" is the good that individuals share in common, and "public interest" is practically a synonym – the state of affairs, such as social cooperation or a healthy society, that is in the interest of practically everyone. A nearly equivalent formulation refers to the state of affairs that affords the individual chosen at random the best prospects of achieving his goals. (Koppl 1992 provides an example of such a formulation, giving credit to F.A. Hayek.)

Cost/benefit analysis can be useful on relatively specific issues, such as whether to build a particular dam or to issue a particular environmental regulation. Such analysis cannot be scientific or even as rigorous as, say, accounting. Furthermore, it may – though it need not – seem to dignify the idea of sacrificing the interests of some people to the supposedly greater interests of other people. Still, pressure to ponder various costs and benefits and put warranted dollar figures on them brings a certain discipline into policy discussions and lessens the role of sheer eloquence, poetry, and emotion. Anyway, neither cost/benefit analysis nor any other form of welfare economics is a substitute for ethics, which remains indispensable to policy judgments.

CRIME, PUNISHMENT, AND RETRIBUTION

Closely related to the rationale of government as a protective institution is punishment of criminals. A magazine reader (Richard Samuelson 1995), commenting on the O.J. Simpson acquittal of 1995, rehearsed one of the traditional rationales of punishment by law. Since ancient Greece we have known that government must prosecute murder so that private citizens will not. Justice requires punishing murderers, but private performance of that function may trigger a cycle of revenge. The state, by contrast, treats murder as a crime against society rather than merely against an individual.[7] Relatives of murder victims can see justice done without drawing retaliation against themselves.

Similarly, and at greater length, Jeffrey Sedgwick (1980) finds the rationale of punishment inadequate if it leaves out retribution and includes only rehabilitation and deterrence (p. 1). Understandably finding little support for the rehabilitation theory, Sedgwick focuses his critical attention on deterrence. Trying to deter crime by increasingly severe punishment runs into the problem that punishments seen as unfairly harsh impose psychic costs on judges and juries (p. 42 and Chapter 4 generally). Furthermore, trying to deter crime mainly by making it costly for the criminal is an excessively economistic approach. "[L]aw enforcement cannot succeed where obedience to law is understood in purely self-interested terms" (Sedgwick 1980, p. 34, and Chapter 4 on the whole; I would say *narrowly* self-interested).

These remarks need elaboration. Treating criminal penalties as a mere price list is subversive of a good society if it invites calculation – of benefits, costs, and probabilities – instead of *un*calculating rejection of certain activities as simply wrong. Calculation of whether to commit a crime is itself a moral defect. True, there are morally defective persons who make such calculations, and others must defend themselves by recognizing what kind of persons they are and how they respond to incentives; but we should not suppose that a calculating response to incentives is itself always admirable. An economist should appreciate the importance of rules, stable institutions, and moral characters; not everything should be the subject of case-by-case calculation.

Dissenting from much of modern criminology, Sedgwick explains the scope for retribution in a criminal-justice system. Most noncriminals see crime as not merely disadvantageous but morally wrong, which suggests that crime might increase if this feeling were weakened. Retribution demands punishment to fit the crime. Retribution provides the satisfaction of seeing a criminal get his just deserts. "[T]he desire for retribution (that is, righteous indignation) is a characteristic of any healthy legal system. Without a sense of retribution, there would be no respect for law, no ability to impose punishment, and no civil society" (p. 43). Without it, resolve actually to impose punishment softens and disrespect for the legal system widens. Retribution grows out of a sense of right, deterrence out of a sense of self-interest. Yet no legal system can survive as long as it is understood simply in terms of self-interest (Sedgwick 1980, esp. pp. 35, 43–5).

People come to respect the law, Sedgwick continues, as an articulation of the good or proper. Besides being a deterrent, punishment helps promote the internalization of norms. Once a person believes crime is decisively wrong, he is less likely to commit it. Even when he might occasionally escape detection and gain by breaking the law, the law-abiding person forgoes this opportunity. Crime makes him either feel outrage at the unjust advantage seized by the criminal or else possibly see himself as too timid in pursuing his own advantage. Even people who would continue to obey the law would be demoralized by seeing violators go unpunished. Lack of punishment diminishes deterrence for the calculators and makes the law-abiding doubt their own sense of right (pp. 44–5).

Without retribution, society will be lax in imposing costly punishment. As criminals frequently escape due punishment, demoralization will set in, and righteous indignation will give way to envy of the successful criminal. Self-interest will crowd out the sense of right and wrong (pp. 46–7). "[M]oral commitment to a law is a much more effective deterrent than the belief that law-abiding behavior is in one's interest because of the certainty of punishment. Thus, the practice of punishing criminals reflects a merging of the deterrent and retribution approaches" (p. 47).

Law must sometimes help shape public preferences rather than simply reflect them. The moral values of a community do not trace merely to consent. If the civil-rights laws are promulgated precisely to change public preferences on race relations, basing their enforcement on public preferences would be irrational and self-defeating (Sedgwick, pp. 48–9).

The welfare-economics approach to law enforcement overlooks the possible conflict between wisdom and consent. By ignoring the formative effect of law on public character, the economist reduces the problem of law enforcement to considering what the public will pay for. "But good laws are good regardless of public willingness to see them enforced" (p. 49). "Clearly men may consent to bad laws or fail to consent to good laws, and so consent cannot be the final word in policy making" (p. 50). Rather than recognizing the need to conjoin consent and wise policy, welfare economics wholly embraces consent (p. 50).

Although Sedgwick does not explicitly say so, his argument for a retributive element in the criminal-justice system is a utilitarian one. Retribution reinforces attitudes that serve social cooperation and a good society.

Pondering the ethical basis of punishment prompts questioning whether the American criminal-justice system has operated in an ideal or even acceptable manner, particularly in recent decades. Robert Bidinotto (1996) faults the system for too much regard for expediency and not enough for proportionality. Felons are opportunistically processed through the system by plea bargains, probation, and parole. Punishment bears no due proportion to the heinousness of the offense or the suffering of the victims. So-called rights of criminals keep being expanded. Sociology, medicine, psychology, and chatter about "the so-called root causes of crime" are drafted into the service of "an excuse-making industry".

Questionably, I think, Bidinotto (p. 7) diagnoses the current approach as "a utilitarian scheme" that "does not allow for individual considerations of justice and proportionality". Its "utilitarian premise excludes moral considerations in punishment". It looks forward – to prevention, to deterrence, to possible rehabilitation of the criminal (as perhaps of the South Carolina woman who drowned her young children) – rather than backward to the crime and its victims. Proportionality, justice, and "the moral principle of accountability" are relatively neglected. The system botches the application of external constraints on behavior and overlooks or undermines the cultivation of internal constraints, which include morality or values and the capacity for feeling appropriate guilt and shame.

This message resonates with me, except that Bidinotto provides yet another example of giving utilitarianism an unfairly bad press. He sets utilitarianism in contrast to morality and diagnoses the ills of the current system as utilitarianism at work. He confuses an extremely crude, almost straw-man, interpretation of utilitarianism with the doctrine itself. Far from standing opposed to morality, it is a theory of the *grounding* of morality. Indirect utilitarianism pays due attention to the cultivation of character, including Bidinotto's "internal constraints on behavior". It does not rule out looking backward to the crime and its victims; indeed, it recognizes how doing so contributes to a good society. It even recognizes (with Sedgwick) how a retributive element in punishment can be healthy.

Much like Bidinotto, the *Economist* magazine ("Go directly to jail", 1996) contrasts what it calls "utilitarian" and "retributivist" theories of punishment. The latter or "just deserts" school requires "punishment ... for principle's sake" – "what criminals deserve, victims merit and society has to inflict if it is not to condone wrongdoing." "Utilitarians and retributivists have been at each other for centuries and are not likely to stop now."

This also is a narrow conception of utilitarianism, as if it weighed pain inflicted on criminals only against the good of observable reductions in crime. On the contrary, utilitarianism *is* concerned with principle, with not appearing to condone wrongdoing, with internalizing values, and with attitudes favorable to a good society.

To illustrate how utilitarian ethics may bear on a specific issue (rather than in hopes of settling it), I turn now to capital punishment. Chapter 10 already reviewed George Smith's (1996) rights-based rejection of it. Smith quite incidentally added a few unavowedly utilitarian arguments concerning how the death penalty perversely affects the incentives of someone who has already committed a capital crime (p. 54).

Agreeing with John Locke as he reads him, Smith maintains "that reparation (restitution) and restraint (self-defense) are the only justified uses of violence in a free society". One conceivably could argue for executing a villain whose past crimes showed him to be a "standing threat" to society in general. Doing so would be an act of self-defense, however, not of punishment (pp. 68–9).

Further considerations pull for and against the death penalty. Contingent empirical facts are relevant – for example, how real and strong the deterrent effect is, or how great the risk of miscarriages of justice. Retaliation or revenge enters the discussion. "Revenge", along with "vindicate", derives from Latin *revindicare*, in turn derived from the Indo-European root *deik-*, to show, pronounce solemnly. "Retribution" derives from *retribuere*, to pay back. Taken together in this context, these words refer to establishing and maintaining a claim to justice and to setting things right. The victims of crime, or their representatives (who may be primarily "society", the people in general who suffer from lawlessness), are entitled to put things to right so far as they can, even though in a murder case this extent is pitifully slight. It just is not right that a guilty criminal escape due punishment. A further reason is that the criminal had a chance of escaping detection and prospering from his deed. To the extent that a murderer escapes punishment commensurate with the harm imposed on his victims, he prospers relative to them.

It would detract from a good society if its authorities reacted too mildly to crime, perhaps out of misplaced sentimentality. In a good society, the legal authorities solemnly emphasize (remember *deik-*) the seriousness of crime, not resting content with words or inadequate gestures.

What bears emphasis here goes beyond a possible deterrent effect, narrowly considered, of capital punishment on capital crimes; it is an attitude that takes serious matters seriously, that prescribes punishment commensurate with crimes, and that deplores allowing criminals to seem to make out well, even if only relative to their victims. (It is probably only a minor point, but that attitude may help keep apparently successful or glamorous criminals from becoming role models for impressionable youth.) An unhealthy attitude, in contrast, waxes sentimental about condemned criminals while relatively neglecting the victims and their families.

If the murderer draws a life sentence (or shorter) and maintenance at public expense, he prospers relative to his victims; in that respect matters are not being set right to the extent possible. The expense of maintaining murderers for their whole lives is a relatively minor consideration (and the death-penalty system also has heavy costs, particularly when appeals and stays on death row drag on for years). More broadly, in escaping the fate he imposed on his victims, the criminal is further exploiting the public and possibly subjecting his victim's heirs to further anguish.

The last remark does not boil down to mere approval of the victims' heirs' possible enjoyment of the murderer's suffering and death. What it endorses is taking due claims seriously. The feelings of victims or of their bereaved of continuing to suffer from injustice through the relatively favorable treatment of criminals who have aggressed against them – these agonizing feelings get to some extent assuaged. As suggested above, moreover, much is to be said for institutionalizing revenge rather than leaving it to private activities, which invite counter-retaliation.

Despite Christian notions about turning the other cheek, desiring revenge is not to be wholly despised. That emotion helps maintain behavior that serves the public interest but that narrowly self-interested calculation might reject. Robert Frank (as noted in Chapter 8 above) has insightfully written about the personal and social value of emotions, even of the emotion of revenge.

Chapter 6 mentions reluctance to sacrifice an innocent known life, as distinguished from a "mere" statistical life. People feel general revulsion at anyone's exercising life-or-death power over specific individuals. They regret the lack of compassion shown in withholding even costly rescue from persons in mortal danger. Does some such revulsion properly apply to capital punishment? Some considerations suggest, although not decisively, that it does not. Capital punishment for atrocious crimes may be justified as defending social cooperation. When laws to that effect are enacted, the criminals to be executed are unknown; their lives are mere statistical lives. Legislators may even reasonably believe that a deterrent effect will save lives in total, including the lives of potential victims.

When the occasion does arise to convict and execute a murderer, this action merely implements decisions already made, and made without reference to known individuals. Murderers facing execution have not been selected by the legislators or any other specific authorities. (They have not been selected as long as no official has arbitrary power to impose or waive capital punishment. Even a state governor with pardon or commutation authority does not have such *arbitrary* power; for he is supposed to enforce the laws and to grant pardon or commutation only for exceptional reasons.) The criminals selected themselves for execution, or put themselves at risk, when they decided to commit their capital crimes.

None of this makes the case for capital punishment conclusive. Further facts remain relevant. How many innocent persons are executed, and how might those errors be reduced or eliminated? Is the system unfairly discriminatory; and if so, how might this defect be remedied? How effectively does the death penalty deter murder? How costly is the system compared with alternatives? How important is capital punishment for "closure" for the relatives and friends of murder victims? What are all the consequences of respecting the revenge motive that enters into the desire for closure? Questions like these further illustrate how utilitarianism meshes with social science. Rarely or never does disagreement center on values alone, leaving further facts irrelevant.

PROPERTY RIGHTS AND RECTIFICATION

Questions arise about property rights and rectifying past violations. The institution of private property, as opposed to socialism or communism, is necessary for prosperity and human happiness in a technologically advanced world. Economic theory and ample experience, old and new, support this proposition beyond any need for discussion here. Property rights lose their meaning if serious violations are tolerated. Private property presupposes that violations be reversed and punished; identifiable injustices must be set right.

But should public policy (or private initiative) try to undo injustices committed long ago? "It depends." The case is clear when the victim and the perpetrator can be identified. Stolen property should be returned to its owner, and the thief should probably be further punished by law to protect social cooperation.

Yet most existing property rights probably have aggression, force, fraud, and other evils in their backgrounds, if only in the remote past. How, then, can they be valid? Should not the victims of predation, or their heirs or successors, receive restitution? How can the mere passage of time turn the results of crime into venerable institutions? Well, time itself does not do so, but it makes the burden of proof more difficult for anyone challenging existing or *de facto* property rights. To avoid ongoing strife, custom and the law make a presumption, though a defeasible one, in favor of existing holdings of property. What would the alternative be? What consequences would flow from a presumption in favor of challenges? (Ludwig von Mises recognized propositions and questions like these; see Eshelman 1993, pp. 34–8.)

One occasionally finds a principle of restitution pressed to unrealistic lengths. An unpublished proposal that once came to my attention invokes John Locke's "proviso" that persons are entitled to appropriate previously unowned land, including natural resources, only to the extent that "enough and as good" remains for others. It supposedly follows that each person now has a rightful claim to an equal share of the world's land and resources. Implementing this conclusion would involve massive worldwide redistributions of wealth that many millions of persons would find deeply unjust.

While envisaging less drastic programs, some ethicists (including Murray Rothbard 1982, pp. 63–75, and to some extent Robert Nozick 1974, pp. 152–3) do urge that injustices more specific and brutal than supposed ancient violations of the Lockean proviso be rectified in favor of the victims' descendants or heirs. But would the consequences of such actions be acceptable or just? Remote injustices are not obviously relevant to what should be done now. As James Buchanan likes to say, we necessarily start from where we are. The case for rectification is weak indeed when the conjectured violation occurred so long ago that the heirs or successors of perpetrators and victims cannot be identified. Many people from whom rectificatory transfers would be taken would have acquired and invested their current wealth in ways considered perfectly respectable. It would be unjust to disappoint legitimate expectations by confiscating land from someone who had bought it in good faith with hard-earned money from someone who had in turn bought or inherited it in good faith in accordance with rules of title in effect at the time. Such action would introduce capriciousness, breed skepticism of titles, and impair contracting and coordination. It would encourage seeking wealth by receiving transfers, to be obtained for example by legal cleverness and litigation, rather than by actually producing wealth. It would do practically the opposite of what *timely* identification and rectification of injustices can do. Reshuffling property titles now could in no way compensate the claimants' ancestors, who were victimized long ago. Do the sins of earlier predators nevertheless attach to, and require expiation by, innocent and even unrelated members even of much later generations? The idea of inherited or collective guilt coheres badly with a society of individual responsibility and individual rights.

One might counter that no one, however good his own faith, can acquire good title to something whose holder's title to it was bad; no one can transfer better title to something than his own. And – so this counterargument might continue – this principle holds true no matter how far back in time the event invalidating the title occurred. But to argue this way is to argue in a circle, to argue that rectification is morally imperative despite the arguments against it. (For what the point is worth, furthermore, current law *does* recognize cases in which one can acquire good title from someone whose own title was dubious.)

A perhaps profounder objection has been raised by Loren Lomasky (1987), and earlier by Derek Parfit. Not even in principle, let alone in practice, can we identify the descendants of predators and victims. The very identities of all persons alive today depend on events of the recent and remote past, including injustices; for these events conditioned what men and women met each other, and when, and had children with what particular combinations of genes. These causal events are in turn partly the consequences of past property holdings, class relations, and migrations. If the past injustices had in fact never occurred, none of us persons living today, including the supposed heirs of past victims, would ever have been born as the individuals we biologically are.

If unscrambling long-past injustices is downright impossible, it cannot be morally obligatory; "ought implies can" (or better, "ought *presupposes* can").

Tolerating relatively recent injustices would be quite another matter. Trying to identify and reverse them is central to maintaining property rights and to resisting violations in the first place. Furthermore, *continuing* injustices cannot be excused merely by their having ancient roots. This remark might conceivably apply, for example, to continuing subjugation of a class of landless farm laborers or sharecroppers by a hereditary small class of owners of vast estates. Even though we cannot identify the individual heirs of individual victims of specific past transgressions, we can supposedly identify a class of victims, the "landless masses". True enough, these masses are not the victims of industrious persons who have innocently invested some of their savings in land. They are arguably the victims, rather, of an unsatisfactory institutional setup, one that might be improved, moreover, by tax reform. After all, taxes of some sort or other must be collected, and the case is strong for levying taxes that have relatively slight adverse side effects. If some of the effects are positively beneficial, so much the better. Under such circumstances, failure to introduce reform might plausibly count as continually repeating the injustice.

Again, utilitarianism looks to the facts of reality both in identifying ethical and legal principles and in applying principles to specific situations. A plausible case for land reform cannot rest on the rectification of injustice alone. Instead, it must involve examining the likely operating properties of the reformed institutions and comparing these new institutions with the existing ones. Also taking account of how well the proposed reforms would cohere with broad ethical principles, the case is not a narrowly act-utilitarian one.

COMMON LAW VERSUS LEGISLATION

Ancient Romans and the English shared the concept of law as something to be discovered more than enacted (Leoni 1961; cf. Rothbard's 1972 review). Anglo-Saxon common law was a structure of generally agreed principles arising from either age-old custom or the basic requirements for people's getting along with one another. Lawmaking involved millions of people over dozens of generations. In discovering and announcing the law, judges were more like spectators than actors; they resembled grammarians *recording* language or statisticians *recording* economic activity. Because people agree more nearly on what they do not want done to them than on what the law should positively require, law to protect people from harm is likely to be more identifiable and more nearly certain and stable than laws requiring positive behavior. Like scientific knowledge, language, customs, and fashions, law can develop through voluntary collaboration and not just through the deliberate decisions of specific authorities.

In recent times, Leoni complains, we have moved away from a state of affairs where, as on the market, individual choices adjust themselves to one another. We have shifted to passing laws in an atmosphere of campaigns, elections, and special-interest pressures. Statute law is more subject to sudden change than common law and so affords a less stable basis for long-term planning. (US tax law is perhaps a prime example.) The law lacks certainty whenever legislatures can change it as the spirit moves them. Legislation is far from an alternative to arbitrariness; it often ranks alongside orders of tyrants or arrogant majorities in overriding spontaneous processes. Whenever majority rule unnecessarily replaces individual choice, democracy conflicts with individual freedom. *Ideally*, lawmaking is more a theoretical process than an act of will; it is not the result of decisions issued by power groups at the expense of dissenting minorities (Leoni 1961; Rothbard 1972).

LEGAL POSITIVISM AND NATURAL LAW

Relations between law and ethics may be illuminated by contrasting two rather artificially polarized doctrines, legal positivism and natural law. (For some writers, however, one or the other of those labels is not too far-fetched.) Legal positivism consistently denies "that the reason for the validity of laws is to be found in nature". Their validity "derives instead from the authority of those who make, apply and/or enforce them" (van Dun 1994, pp. 269–70). The doctrine sees no sense in looking for law outside positive law itself – law in the strict sense, government law, law made within their authority by rulers, legislatures, and judges. Positive law encompasses constitutions and statutes, common or case law embodied in court decisions, and administrative regulations implementing these other strands of positive law. The existence and content of positive law can be empirically verified in a way that cannot apply to natural law. The validity of any purported law is tested only within, not outside, the legal system.

Legal positivism distinguishes sharply between questions of legal validity or invalidity and of right or wrong. We may hope that the right and the legal and the wrong and the illegal are generally consistent with one another and that lawmakers act accordingly, but confusing the moral and legal realms invites a hopeless muddle. (The adverb "generally" makes a qualification. On utilitarian grounds, as argued above, we do not want positive law to require everything that is right and prohibit everything wrong; we do not expect the power of government to enforce morality in detail.)

Legal positivism restricts its questions about actual law to what the law is and says. It asks only what rules of positive law prevail in virtue of their having been enacted or promulgated with formal validity, of being free from mutual contradiction, and of being actually enforced (rather than having lapsed into desuetude). (This is my understanding, anyway, of Kelsen, 1945/1949.) Positivism does not deny that the content of formally valid law, as well as government actions conforming to it, may be appraised on ethical grounds; but such appraisal is outside the scope of strict legal scholarship.

The contrasting doctrine of natural law comes in various and changing versions, so a description cannot be precise. It holds natural laws "more fundamental than mere enactments. Outside the context of natural law, legislation is nothing but an expression of sheer political power, of might, not of right" (van Dun 1994, p. 270). But might does not make right, not even the might of overwhelming majorities. In its most stringent version, the doctrine holds that wicked law – wicked *purported* law – is not valid and is not truly law. Some "higher law" overrides whatever the purported positive law may say. Government laws violating this higher law are not properly binding. The natural law is discoverable by reason and by observation of human life and society.

People disagree on the content and even the existence of natural law. Clearly it does not exist in the same verifiable sense that positive law does. (In R.M. Hare's view, appeal to it is nothing but an appeal to intuition; 1989EoPM, p. 74.) Still, disagreement over its content does not show that the concept or the investigation of natural law is nonsense. People disagree on propositions of physics or ethics, too, without making nonsense of those fields. Still, the uncertain character of natural law is one reason for not trying to enforce it in the same way as statutory and common law. One purpose of law is to improve predictability in human relations, and that purpose would be subverted by governmental enforcement of unenacted law about whose substance and even existence people disagree. For a similar reason, we would regret people's feeling free routinely to disregard government laws they considered contrary to natural law. For the sake of predictability and social stability, each person has some obligation to obey the positive law as it stands, bad though it may be, apart from truly exceptional cases. Before supposed precepts of natural law are treated as positive law, they might better be clearly identified and written into constitutions and statutes.

Positivists tend to relegate natural law to "a realm of pure oughtness", finding it "a woolly concoction of idealist speculation" divorced from facts and of no interest to science (van Dun, p. 271). Against this view, natural-law theory aims to spell out the principles that should inform the creative work of lawyers, judges, and legislators. Effective law must accord with nature; and for naturalists but not for positivists, effectiveness means more than the political power of man over man (van Dun, p. 271). As David Hume had insisted, an obvious and necessary human contrivance is as properly called natural as anything arising without thought and reflection. The rules of justice may be artificial, but they are not arbitrary. Including the rules of property, they are necessary for the maintenance of society, the survival of the human species, and the well-being of individuals. In that sense certain laws are natural. Hume invokes sympathy as a natural sentiment that helps explain why we feel we should respect the laws of justice (van Dun 1994, pp. 277–8, quoting and paraphrasing Hume's *A Treatise of Human Nature*, Book III, Part 2, Section 1, pp. 430–36 (Hume 1739–40/1961), esp. the last paragraph of the section).[8]

Loosely interpreted, natural-law doctrine recognizes the legitimacy of appraising positive laws not only for due enactment, mutual consistency, and actual enforcement but also for conformity to moral principles and other openly avowable value judgments. So interpreted, the doctrine nicely parallels F.A. Hayek's (1960) conception of the rule of law as a metalegal principle.[9] Natural law is not a particular strand or level of positive law but is something outside it. What the law *should be* is not the same as what it already *is*.

John Stuart Mill found it "universally admitted that there may be unjust laws and that law, consequently, is not the ultimate criterion of justice ...". In most languages, the word for "just" has an origin connected with what law requires. "[T]he primitive element ... in the notion of justice was conformity to law." Since it came to be recognized that some deliberately enacted laws might be bad laws, "the sentiment of injustice came to be attached not to all violations of law, but only to violations of such laws as *ought* to exist, including such as ought to exist but do not, and to laws themselves, if supposed to be contrary to what ought to be law" (Mill 1861/1863, *Utilitarianism*, Chapter V, pp. 284–5, 287–8 in Cowling edition).

Positive laws resemble commands, but they might also be interpreted as predictions of how the police and the courts will respond to specified behavior. Positive law and value judgments are different things. The is/ought gap yawns between describing what positive law requires and saying that positive law ought always to be obeyed. While positive law and value judgments are distinct, all enacting or acquiescing in positive law must involve value judgments somewhere. Why not openly recognize those judgments and discuss them to see which can command reasoned consensus?

FURTHER EXAMPLES OF NATURAL-LAW AND POSITIVIST THINKING

Some further samples of the two strands of doctrine follow. I cannot conveniently present first all of the one and then all of the other, for some of the samples include comments on the rival doctrine.

In asserting "certain unalienable Rights", the US Declaration of Independence is a natural-law document. Government's task is "to secure these Rights"; and whenever any government becomes destructive of this purpose, "it is the Right of the People to alter or abolish it, and to institute new Government" shaped as they consider "most likely to effect their Safety and Happiness". This assertion cannot be taken as literal fact, but it is a powerful statement (incidentally with a utilitarian tone) of values appropriate to a healthy political order.

A close association between morals and law is the distinguishing feature of natural-law theory, wrote A.P. d'Entrèves (1952, pp. 80, 83–4). Natural law derives from an ancient conviction that law's purpose is not only to make men obedient but to help them be virtuous. "Th[e] point where values and norms coincide, which is the ultimate origin of law ..., is ... what men for over two thousand years have indicated by the name of natural law" (concluding sentence of d'Entrèves 1952, p. 122). Whether the asserted point of intersection between law and morals actually exists is "the ultimate test of the validity of all natural law thinking" (p. 116). D'Entrèves calls legal and political philosophy "nothing else than natural law writ large" (1952, p. 14). He quotes Cicero on an "unchangeable law ... valid for all nations and for all times" (p. 21). Hugo Grotius maintained that natural law would remain valid even if God did not exist (d'Entrèves 1952, p. 70). The very condition of existence of natural law "is that the identification of law and command be overcome or abandoned" (p. 64). The doctrine "was an endeavour to formulate ... certain fundamental values which were believed to be absolutely valid" (p. 117). It asserts "the possibility of testing the validity of all laws by referring them ... to an ideal law which can be known and appraised with an even greater measure of certainty than all existing legislation. Natural law is the outcome of man's quest for an absolute standard of justice" (p. 95).

Challenging natural law, legal positivism sees law essentially as command entitled to obedience (d'Entrèves 1952, p. 65). It finds the study of the ideal law no longer relevant to the lawyer. "The juridical science of the nineteenth and twentieth century expressly declares itself incapable of drawing the problem of justice into the scope of its enquiries" (p. 96, quoting the positivist Hans Kelsen). "Modern jurists may be willing to leave the discussion of the ultimate reason why law should be regarded as binding to the legal philosopher, without taking a definite stand about the existence of natural law" (p. 97).

The task of legal positivism is to determine which laws are definite, binding, or positive enough to be called laws (p. 102). For positivists, recognizing a law's validity depends on tracing it to a common source from which all legal precepts ultimately proceed. Modern jurisprudence becomes "formal" as it strives to be a positive science, steering clear of any criterion of validity extraneous to the legal system (p. 103). For Kelsen and his followers, says d'Entrèves, a systematic construction of the legal order presupposes a "basic norm", a necessary hypothetical assumption. It "is the postulated ultimate rule according to which the norms of this order are established and annulled, receive and lose their validity". The basic norm of national law in the modern state is that the commands of the sovereign are to be obeyed; the basic norm of international law is that *pacta sunt servanda* (d'Entrèves 1952, p. 106, quoting from Kelsen).

Instead of trying to justify the basic norm, legal positivism treats it as a necessary presupposition. Trying to assess the basic norm merely returns to the old problem that used to be discussed under the heading of ideal or natural law. It is a natural-law proposition that the ultimate test of the validity of law lies *beyond* the law itself (pp. 107–8, in part quoting Kelsen).

For all practical purposes, says d'Entrèves, to deny the existence of any law but positive law amounts to saying that might equals right; modern legal positivism is a typical outcome of nineteenth century state worship (pp. 111, 119). (I disagree. To conceive of law in narrowly positivist terms is not necessarily to equate law so defined with what is morally right.)

David Lyons also contrasts legal positivism – or legal formalism, as he calls it, which is nearly if not exactly the same thing – with natural law. Formalism says that the law itself provides sufficient basis for deciding any case that arises. The law traces to an authoritative source. William Blackstone, on the other hand, denied any validity to human law contrary to the law of nature dictated by God; an atheist would refer to "moral law" instead. Blackstone may be reinterpreted as denying not the possible existence of morally objectionable law but any automatic moral obligation to obey it. Natural law bears on the question of when ordinary human law "binds in conscience". Aquinas developed this view: one has an obligation to obey just laws, but not all unjust laws (Lyons 1993, pp. 42–3).

Legal positivists are reputed to accept and natural-law adherents to reject the separation thesis, which distinguishes between the questions of the law's existence and of its merit or demerit; law is morally fallible (Lyons 1993, Chapter 4, quoting John Austin on p. 64). Lon Fuller considered himself a natural lawyer because he believed that there are moral conditions on what can count as law (Lyons 1993, p. 71).

H.L.A. Hart identified five strands of legal positivism: (1) the imperative theory: law is a coercive command; (2) the separation of law and morals; (3) the distinction between analytic jurisprudence and other studies of law; (4) formalism, or mechanical jurisprudence: correct legal decisions can be deduced logically from predetermined legal rules; (5) moral skepticism: moral judgments cannot be established the way statements of fact can be (paraphrased by Lyons 1993, pp. 72–3). Legal positivism holds that law consists of standards or rules identifiable by their pedigree rather than by content or moral acceptability (Ronald Dworkin as interpreted by Lyons 1993, p. 87).

Hart (1982) reviews Jeremy Bentham's positivistic attitude. Although denying any natural laws, Bentham did believe in rational principles for the criticism of law and the guidance of legislators. The principles of utility identify what is a good reason for a law. But a reason, even a good one, is not itself a law (p. 24). Bentham steadily refused to recognize that the morality of law is relevant to its validity. The existence of law is one thing, its merit or demerit another (p. 28).

According to Bentham, Cesare Beccaria never pretended that the reforms he advocated were already, in some transcendental sense, "really" law. Beccaria and Bentham stressed the distinction between what the law is and what it ought to be (Hart 1982, p. 41). Bentham insisted "that the foundations of a legal system are properly described in the morally neutral terms of a general habit of obedience ...". This position "opened the long positivist tradition in English jurisprudence" (p. 53).

Going beyond a mere reporting of the views of Bentham and John Austin and speaking for himself, Hart again makes similar points (1983, esp. Introduction and Essay 2). It seems shocking to recognize a truly iniquitous law as a law nevertheless. It is tempting to say that "what is utterly immoral cannot be law or lawful" (p. 77). But saying so encourages the romantic optimism that all cherished values ultimately fit into a single system. It glosses over moral quandaries. When life forces us to choose the lesser of two evils, we should recognize what we are doing (p. 77). Maintaining the distinction between actual and desirable law will help us steer between two dangers: that notions of what law ought to be may erode actual law and its authority and "that the existing law may supplant morality as a final test of conduct and so escape criticism" (p. 54). Bentham and Austin condemned natural-law thinkers for blurring this distinction (p. 50).

An anxious spectator of the French Revolution, Bentham was aware that the time might come when the law's commands were so evil as to raise the question of resistance. It was essential, then, that the issues be neither over-simplified nor blurred. Confusion between law and morals spreads in two different directions. On the one hand, an anarchist might argue that what ought not to be law is not law and may therefore be disregarded. On the other hand, the reactionary might argue that what is the law is what ought to be law and so is beyond criticism (Hart 1983, p. 53). Even such positivists as Austin and Bentham recognized that if a law were sufficiently evil and prospects of changing it through regular procedures sufficiently poor, disobedience might be morally required. (The US Fugitive Slave Act of 1850 comes to mind as a possible example.) Still, careful calculation and comparison of consequences would be necessary before disobedience was rationally justified (Hart 1983, p. 73; 1982, p. 81). No clear and simple rules tell us when the usual presumption in favor of obedience is overridden (although Rawls 1971, Chapter VI, did try to draw up some guidelines). We live in a complicated world, even a morally complicated world.

If we say that laws too evil to be obeyed are not even laws at all, we blunt a powerful form of moral criticism. Many people would not believe that assertion. We must not set plain speech aside and "present the moral criticism of institutions as propositions of a disputable philosophy" (Hart 1983, pp. 77–8, quotation from p. 78).

I'll interpret these ideas. Blurring the distinction between law and morality may promote belief that what should be law *is* law, while a purported but morally bad law is not actually law. What is distinctive about law authorized and enforced by the state becomes obscured. People confusing law with morality may regard law as the final test of conduct and let it escape criticism. The blurring reflects the rather statist attitude that the state's laws must necessarily enunciate morality or at least be compatible with it.

Hans Kelsen's book of 1945 requires further attention. Kelsen distinguishes a basic norm of a legal system from the specific positive laws that acquire their validity by deriving from it. The basic norm cannot get its validity in the same way. It is simply *presupposed* or *postulated* to be valid because otherwise no judgments could be made about the legal validity or invalidity of the derivative laws (Kelsen 1945, pp. 116–17). The theory of the basic norm might be considered a natural-law doctrine; still, a vast difference remains between the basic law which merely makes possible the cognition of positive law as a meaningful order and a doctrine which proposes to establish a just order beyond and independent of all positive law (pp. 437–8, in appendix). The validity of a legal norm cannot be questioned on the ground of incompatibility with some moral or political value. A legal norm (other than the basic one) is valid only by virtue of having been created according to a definite rule (p. 113). Legal norms are considered valid only if they belong to an order which is by and large efficacious. A legal order that goes unheeded or that prescribes only what happens anyway is not what we conceive of as a legal order (pp. 120–21; cf. pp. 436–7 in appendix). The positiveness of positive law lies in its being created and annulled by human beings. It is independent of morality and similar norm systems (p. 114). The essential characteristic distinguishing positivism from natural law is its self-imposed restriction: it does not go outside the legal system, and it contents itself with a merely hypothetical, formal foundation in the basic norm (p. 396 in appendix). The obligations imposed by positive law are only relative, relative to the assumed norm, and so can only be hypothetical (pp. 394–5 in appendix). According to natural law, the norm of justice is immanent in the nature of men and things; but this doctrine is an illusion (pp. 48–9). In the theory of positive law, a certain kind of behavior is a delict because it entails a sanction, and not the other way around. A distinction between *mala in se* and *mala prohibita* cannot be maintained; there are no *mala in se*, no acts that are inherently wrong even apart from being prohibited by law (pp. 51–3; this last remark is perhaps positivism at its worst).

Kelsen says that a state can do no wrong in terms of its own national law, as distinct from international law (p. 200), but he does not thereby mean that might makes right. He merely means that since the state is the national legal order personified for convenience in speech, it – the legal order – cannot be in violation of itself. Although he is not explicit on this point, Kelsen appears not to deny that ethical principles should apply to rulers, legislators, policemen, and others concerned with creating, modifying, or applying the legal order. His words seem wicked only out of context. In my impressionistic interpretation, anyway, Kelsen's denial of natural law is a denial that the propositions of natural and positive law belong to the same category. So-called natural law is metalaw, transcending law in the ordinary or strict sense and not part of it. This is not a particularly shocking proposition.

Ludwig von Mises, classical liberal and certainly no statist, respected Kelsen's work. He saw merit in natural-law thinking, also, despite what he considered fallacies in most lines of it. Long before the classical economists discovered regularity in the phenomena of human action, Mises says, the champions of natural law were dimly aware of this regularity. Several theorems emerged. First, successful human action presupposes taking account of a nature-given order of things. Second, no social institution is exempt from examination and appraisal. Third, no standard exists for appraising the actions of individuals and groups other than the effects produced. "Carried to its ultimate logical consequences, the idea of natural law led eventually to rationalism and utilitarianism" (Mises 1957/1985, p. 45).

This idea, Mises continues, countered the positivist doctrine that the ultimate source of statute law is the legislator's power to compel obedience. It taught that statutory laws can be bad. It contrasted positive laws promulgated by those in power with a "higher" law grounded in the innermost nature of man. It held that even every formally valid law is open to critical examination. Older members of the school had only vague notions about the standard to be applied; they referred to nature. But it is useless to look to nature as the ultimate arbiter of right and wrong. "Nature does not clearly reveal its plans and intentions to men." The doctrine merely substitutes dissent about interpretations of natural law for dissenting judgments of value. The ultimate standard of good and bad must be found in a law's effects. Utilitarianism completed the intellectual evolution inaugurated by the Greek sophists (Mises 1957/1985, pp. 47-9).

INSTRUCTIVE DISAGREEMENTS

A conception of law attributed to Judge Richard Posner, as well as Hadley Arkes's criticism of it, are both wrong, in my view (Arkes 1990, reviewing Posner 1990). Yet both are instructive, even if one of them is rather an invention. Entitling his review "The perils of legal positivism", Arkes seems not to appreciate how subtle and complex Posner's position is.

Actually, Posner does not articulate any definite and familiar position – or not, anyway, legal positivism in the style of Kelsen. He couples a flexible pragmatism with consequentialism and with a belief that economics is important to the work of the courts. He seems to welcome reinterpretation of the US Constitution to accommodate changed circumstances. He rejects a formalism that insists on the law's autonomy and objectivity. Decisions must often go beyond mere interpretation of statute or constitution; the judges must look at reality and employ "practical reason". (This remark seems to parallel M.J. Detmold's insistence, reviewed below, on the individual case in all its distinctive detail.) Posner finds natural law in fine shape in the sense that ethical (and policy) considerations do properly bear on judicial discretion. The dichotomy between legal positivism and natural law collapses. "Truth" is problematic for a pragmatist, whose real interest is in belief justified by social need. Moral beliefs held with great conviction gain no analytic strength by being called natural law. The underlying problem of moral objectivity is that there are neither facts to which moral principles correspond nor any strong tendency for moral principles to converge.

On Arkes's interpretation, Posner has persuaded himself "that there is no science of law, no serious moral philosophy that could furnish an understanding of the things that are in principle just and unjust". Persuaded "that the claims of natural law are irredeemably false", Posner is driven to legal positivism (Arkes 1990, pp. 132, 134). Even so, Posner does see the difficulty, says Arkes, of explaining people's moral obligation to obey the law, even against their own interests, if law is merely the command of the authorities.

> Something else is needed, something of irreducible moral significance, to explain the rightness of the law, or the wrongness of disobeying it until the law can be changed. That something else, he knows, is "a natural law that underwrites positive law". In rejecting natural law, he knows that the result is "a diminished sense of moral obligation to obey laws, [and] so it will have to be" (Arkes 1990, p. 135).

Arkes's own version of natural law recommends that "judges must ever be in the business of 'moral philosophy'" (1990, p. 133). (Chapters 1 and 10 above also discuss Arkes's views.)

M.J. Detmold would agree. In his *The Unity of Law and Morality* (1984), subtitled *A refutation of legal positivism*, Detmold stresses the primacy of the individual case, with all its relevant particulars. The values of continuity and predictability yield a presumption that judges should decide cases in conformity with the constitution, statutes, and precedents – a strong but not conclusive presumption. Judges are in the service of the law, which blends with morality, instead of sometimes serving morality in opposition to the law. Individual cases may arise, Detmold says, in which the ostensibly controlling law does not properly apply and so is not law after all. If a judge were not entitled to exercise his own professional craft in such a case – if, on the contrary, he had to grind out an unambiguously foreordained result as if he were a computer programmed with the constitution and all statutes and precedents – then there would be no point to having judges at all. His very office implies that a judge must pay attention to more than what is spelled out in the law books.

Detmold considers a hypothetical statute requiring execution of all blue-eyed babies. On the legal-positivist view as he interprets it, the statute is indeed law provided only that it conforms to the constitution and pertinent technicalities. A positivist judge might refuse to apply it: he might resign, or he might bypass or override it in deference to morality as he saw it; but he would not deny that what he thereby defies nevertheless is law. Detmold, on the other hand, would deny that the statute is law at all; it is just too iniquitous.

In refusing to apply the statute for this reason, a judge of Detmold's stripe would still be serving the law rather than serving morality as opposed to law. It is part of a judge's duty, in extreme cases like this one, to recognize and declare that the supposed statute is not in fact law.

But is the dispute between Detmold and the positivist any more than terminological? It seems plausible to agree with the positivist that the statute (if constitutional and so forth) is indeed law but that it is just too iniquitous to be obeyed and that it deserves to be overridden and to be denounced with all the resources at the judge's disposal. Detmold would say that its blatant clash with morality makes it not law at all. But what is the operational difference? Detmold tries to define away the very concept of a highly iniquitous but technically valid law; yet that concept can serve clear thought and discussion.

Robert Bork (1990) expresses views closer to those of Kelsen and Posner than to those of Arkes and Detmold. The theme of his book comes across to me as follows. Judges have the job of giving effect to legal documents as they are actually written, whether contracts, statutes, or constitutions. Their job is not to conjecture at the intentions of the authors. After all, most such documents express compromises among parties having divergent specific intentions or desires. If a document's words are open to different interpretations, judges should try to read them as their users understood them. When apparently key words are missing or are obstinately opaque, judges still should not take that fact as carte blanche to reach a decision according to their own or currently fashionable moral sentiments. Judges should not, despite Hadley Arkes, "ever be in the business of 'moral philosophy'". That responsibility lies elsewhere.

Obvious blunders or slips of the pen will occasionally occur in statutes or other documents, as well as interstitial cases covered neither by positive law nor by compelling analogies (Posner 1990 gives examples). In such cases, *faute de mieux*, judges should decide in accordance with, rather than contrary to, common sense and morality. But they should restrain any eagerness to imagine that such cases have in fact turned up. In most cases by far when a judge or an ordinary citizen is confronted by a palpably bad positive law, he should nevertheless conform to it while perhaps working to change it through established procedures. (Here I am using the word "should" in its ordinary moral sense, and I am interpreting rather than just strictly reporting Bork's view.) Judges should restrain themselves out of respect for their office and the law, whose purpose is to help shelter people from arbitrary victimization and to improve predictability and coordination and cooperation in human affairs. This is not to say that applying whatever law is formally, legally valid is the overriding virtue of a judge. Exceptional cases are indeed conceivable in which a judge's obligation as a moral human being may override his narrower professional duty to apply the law as it formally exists.

TOWARD RECONCILIATION

The Posner–Bork conception of law, as I perhaps too charitably interpret it, does not reject morality or deny its importance. It does, however, distinguish it from law. Law does, after all, invoke governmental coercion; and we want to tie down its application by relatively clear rules rather than allow judges to invoke and shape it according to their own notions of morality. Laws can indeed be appraised on moral grounds, but the authority to make these appraisals and accordingly to frame or change the law belongs primarily to legislators and constitution-makers rather than routinely to judges. (It is no contradiction to say that ordinary morality calls on judges to respect the law's function and their own professional responsibilities and so refrain from case-by-case application of their own moral notions even to the disregard of clear positive law. A general moral precept requires that much humility and restraint on the part of judges.) This conception of judges' duty coheres with a belief in the separation of governmental powers in service of the freedom of the individual. To deny judges the office of free-ranging moralizers in no way disparages morality.

When legal positivism and natural law are each interpreted in a less than polar way, they are complementary positions. Moral judgments, including judgments about what laws are morally required or acceptable or unacceptable, are distinct from laws in the strict sense, laws duly enacted in conformity with the legal system (including law inferred by analogy or "found" by judges acting within their authority). Useful research in the spirit of Hans Kelsen can be carried out on whether the body of positive law is coherent and how particular purported laws must be interpreted to render the system coherent. Some ostensible laws may turn out not to be laws after all because they contradict one another or have not been properly enacted; most obviously, they may be found unconstitutional. Most of the time or ordinarily, perhaps, jurists should concern themselves with these formal aspects of law and not promiscuously drag in their own ethical ideas.

If legal positivism recognizes no scope for evaluating a particular law beyond determining whether it was either duly enacted or found as an interpretation or extension of already existing law, then I reject that doctrine. But positivism need not be so interpreted. A law that is legally valid in the sense described may still be assessed as morally compelling or acceptable or reprehensible.

Some people – philosophers, constitution-makers, legislators, voters, or whoever – may legitimately conduct such assessments. Some duly enacted laws may be judged morally perverse and unacceptable on any plausible conception of morality. Shall we say, then, that such purported laws are not really laws at all, not even in the narrowly legal sense? I think not. It would hardly promote clear thinking to make the set of formally valid but morally unacceptable legal enactments empty by mere definition.

Even an overall legal system may legitimately be assessed from the ethical standpoint. Discussion of how ethical considerations apply even to legislators and judges can be fruitful. But it would be a sterile language game to deny the possibility that rulers or legislators may promulgate legally valid though morally reprehensible laws.

The polar and perhaps caricature version of natural-law doctrine borders, furthermore, on authoritarianism and opposition to free discussion. It may carry the implication that ultimate truth is known by an elect group and that rejecting it is wicked.

Still, not only authoritarian certainty but also nihilistic relativism is wrong. It remains sensible, at least as a heuristic principle, to suppose that some almost objectively valid value judgments exist to be found, ones fated to command practically universal assent if discussion could go on forever. (I am drawing an analogy with Charles Peirce's conception of truth in an 1878 article, reprinted 1955, pp. 38–9.) We need not imagine a natural law distinguishable from and somehow more lawlike than ordinary morality underwriting valid government law. Ordinary morality underwrites positive law in the tamer sense of establishing, in the interest of social cooperation, a powerful though rebuttable presumption in favor of obeying it. Natural law, so interpreted, does not rule out a utilitarian grounding of morality.

As already implied, the line between natural-law doctrine and legal positivism is not sharp. Some strands of positive law – common law or law declared by judges as they interpret or fill gaps in statutory law – reflect judges' perceptions of what custom or fairness or morality requires; in that sense they involve natural law. What shall we say, furthermore, about legal enactments that apparently incorporate parts of supposed natural law or of morality into positive law without actually spelling out just what is being incorporated? The Ninth Amendment to the US Constitution bars denial or disparagement not only of enumerated rights but also of unspecified further rights retained by the people. The Amendment thus seems in effect, though not explicitly, to invite judges to hold purported laws unconstitutional if they infringe those additional unspecified rights. (On this issue, contrast the views of Barnett 1989 and Bork 1990, pp. 183–5).

UTILITY-BASED LIBERTARIAN PRINCIPLES: AN EXAMPLE

Richard Epstein, a legal scholar of undoubtedly classical-liberal or libertarian orientation, has suggested six *Simple Rules for a Complex World* (1995; cf.

John Hospers's 1998 review). Briefly, they require: (1) autonomy or self-ownership; (2) ownership by first possession; (3) voluntary exchange, or contract; (4) protection against aggression; (5) limited privilege in cases of necessity ("take and pay"); and (6) the taking of property under eminent domain only with compensation.

The rules have a utilitarian basis (as acknowledged, for example, on p. 30). What might the alternatives to rule 1 be? If each person does not own his own body, who does? Other particular persons? If so, what decides which other person owns each one? Or is each person to be owned collectively, by everybody? How workable would each of these alternatives be? Would its consequences be coherent with a society of effective and happy men and women? Almost surely not.

Regarding rule 2, what alternative principles might govern the ownership of newly created or discovered or otherwise previously unvalued and unowned property? Ownership by *second* possession? If property were owned collectively, by everybody, difficulties would arise concerning obtaining permission for any particular use and concerning incentives.

Rule 3 vastly facilitates reaping the gains from specialization and trade and making provision for the future.

Rule 4 pertains to the probably fundamental rationale of government and to avoiding the horrors of the Hobbesian war of all against all. The rule must be extended to cover cases not strictly of aggression but of torts and infliction of dangers.

A case illustrating rule 5 is that of the man who breaks into a pharmacy closed at night as the only way to get medicine to save his dying wife. Considerations of reasonableness and human happiness recommend tolerating such an emergency infringement of property rights, subject to payment of compensation; but the concept of necessity must not be stretched too far.

Broadly utilitarian considerations also argue for rule 6, concerning restricted government exercise of eminent domain (as well as exercise of the police power in restricting use of property in ways that would inflict great harm or danger on others than the owner).

Complications arise regarding application of the "simple" rules to children and animals, the ownership of unsettled or only nomadically occupied land and of buried aboriginal artifacts, the division of property between divorcing persons who had not made contractual provision for the contingency, the regulation of labor contracts, secession by a part of a political entity, and so forth. As many examples argue, however – such as laws to bar discharge of employees without "just cause" – seeking a legal system that yields perfect results in all cases will result in destructive complexity and will multiply opportunities for gaming the system. If simple rules offer good solutions in 95 per cent of all possible situations, trying to clean up the remaining five per cent of cases will unravel the system for the 95 per cent. "No single, carefully constructed hypothetical case offers sufficient practical reason to overturn any rule that has stood the test of time" (Epstein 1995, p. 53, thus incidentally taking a jab at the method of philosophizing by lifeboat cases).

CONCLUSION

Ethics enters into competing views about the nature and origin of political obligation; legitimate and illegitimate uses of governmental coercion; crime and punishment, even retributive punishment; the concept of public interest or general welfare; the roles of welfare economics and values in policy espousal; property rights and the rectification of past violations; and the governing principles of a legal order. This chapter has warned against confusion between political democracy and other valued conditions, including personal and civil liberty. It has explored relations between common law and statutory law and has compared natural-law and positivist conceptions of the relation between law and ethics. On all these topics, I submit, a utilitarian approach is eminently sensible.

In economic-policy discussions, libertarians in particular tend to emphasize rights and freedoms over case-by-case calculation of supposed benefits and costs. Pointillistic arguments are likely to be of low intellectual quality because of the influence of special interests, the exploitable "rational ignorance" of the ordinary voter, and other reasons explained by public-choice economics. Even though reliance on case-by-case arguments and calculations is often stigmatized as a utilitarian approach, recognition of their likely low quality is actually an indirect-utilitarian reason for wariness about them and for emphasizing broad principles instead.

APPENDIX TO CHAPTER 11   LIBERTARIANISM AND CLASSICAL LIBERALISM

Liberalism Distinguished from the Pareto Criterion

Positive analysis of how the world works, coupled with the utilitarian fundamental value judgment, seems to me to support classical liberalism or the variant nowadays called libertarianism. In contrast with the Pareto criterion[10] that receives much lip service among economic theorists, classical liberalism is a set of positive propositions and value judgments adding up to a particular conception of the good society. It puts the happiness, freedom, and self-determination of the individual person, interacting with his fellows, at center stage. Although valuing the well-being of individuals as they themselves perceive it, liberalism does not necessarily scorn all efforts to distinguish between tastes worthy and tastes unworthy of counting in the shaping of social institutions and policies. It seeks institutions that minimize the scope for clashes among the freedoms of different persons. It calls for limiting man's power over man, for dispersing power, and, in turn, for avoiding unnecessary linkage of economic and political power. These criteria are best served by secure property rights, a free-market economy, and a government of limited powers and democratic elements devoted to protecting the security and rights of individuals.

Setting forth the argument for classical-liberal institutions and policies is secondary, however, to my present purpose of showing the utilitarian nature of a sound ethical doctrine and, in particular, of defending that doctrine against a supposed libertarian rival. Ludwig von Mises, both a staunch classical liberal and a staunch utilitarian, said he would embrace socialism if positive analysis should show it to be the system most conducive to human happiness (1919/1983, p. 221).

Libertarian Criticism of Utilitarianism

Some critics say that utilitarianism lacks a principled basis and so provides only meager, pragmatic defenses against bad policies. Yet such complaints might well be called "pragmatic" themselves. Ellen Paul (1979) explores the demise of laissez-faire in nineteenth century British political economy. Whereas early British economists like Adam Smith rested their preference for laissez-faire on a philosophy of natural law and natural rights, utilitarians like Jeremy Bentham, James and John Stuart Mill, and Henry Sidgwick later set that philosophy aside. They reduced the policy of nonintervention to a contingent, defeasible presumption at best. They no longer saw interventions as violations of the individual's rights to liberty and property. Once the empirical judgment that interventions would be counterproductive came into question, no natural-rights philosophy remained as a bulwark against government expansion. Paul observes this change in intellectual climate and traces it less to developments in economics than to an unhealthy change in moral perspective. (She focuses on the *act* version of utilitarianism, most explicitly on p. 111, n. 6. She neglects its rules or indirect version, possibly because it had not yet been presented explicitly enough in the period discussed to command her attention.)

Karen Vaughn (1976) regrets that Ludwig von Mises accepted the collectivists' and authoritarians' terms of debate by stressing how efficiently the free market serves well-being. Such a defense of freedom is doubly dangerous. "First, it is open to empirical refutation." Second, a utilitarian calculus might tip in favor of a nonliberal system if it counted even the bureaucrats' pleasure in controlling and regulating people. A less risky course simply postulates freedom as supremely "desirable for its own sake" and as "a moral value that, as a bonus, also happen[s] to lead to the well-being of society" (pp. 108-9). To paraphrase: empirically oriented arguments for economic freedom are risky because they might conceivably be refuted and the case for freedom embarrassed. It is safer simply to postulate freedom as a supreme value. Someone mounting no arguments need fear no refutations.

In a similar vein, Murray Rothbard (1973) objects that the utilitarian will rarely apply a principle to real world situations absolutely and consistently. For the utilitarian, a principle is a vague, overridable guideline or aspiration. He "cannot be 'trusted' to maintain libertarian principles in every specific application" (p. 24).

Such criticisms proceed backwards. Paul, Vaughn, and Rothbard are so devoted to laissez-faire that they test ethical doctrines by whether they appear to undermine or support it. But surely the doctrines bearing on a policy position, along with supposed facts, are themselves open to examination. How can doctrines like utilitarianism and natural law be appraised by their supposed policy implications rather than by their own content? It is easy to invent a doctrine that, if valid, would support one's favorite policy. Surely, though, that potential support is not enough to validate the doctrine. Yet the pragmatic critics do seem to suppose that some alternative to utilitarianism could protect its adherents from policy errors.

No doctrine can provide built-in protection against its being misunderstood, misused, ignored, underappreciated, or rejected. It is idle to test a doctrine by whether it does what no doctrine can do. Although it might be convenient for adherents of a particular policy stance if a supportive philosophical doctrine were both true and generally accepted, that mere potential convenience is no evidence of its truth. Libertarians cannot defeat proposals for unfortunate economic interventions by reporting their intuitions about natural law or endangered rights (or by issuing methodological pronouncements, either). Nothing can substitute for the constant discipline of fact, logic, and frankly avowed value judgments.

The pragmatic critics distinguish sharply, if sometimes only implicitly, between ethically principled and utilitarian approaches to policy (Eshelman 1993 comes close to making the distinction explicit). They interpret the latter as the unprincipled case-by-case direct calculation of gains and losses of utility.

Yet utilitarianism neither challenges nor ignores ethical principle. Its very core is the *grounding* of ethics. Rules or indirect utilitarianism accepts the powerful case for abiding by established ethical principles on the level of practice (the intuitive level, as R.M. Hare calls it; recall Chapter 2). In all but exceptional cases, policymakers and people in general should follow these principles faithfully. The doctrine rejects displacing them by case-by-case *ad hoc* cost/benefit assessments. It is on Hare's reflective level that utilitarianism attends to the appraisal and grounding of these operational- or intuitive-level precepts.

A Supposed Libertarian Ethics

Not to favor government enforcement of morality in a certain area, say personal drug consumption or consensual sex, may imply but does not necessarily imply skepticism about morality in general or about its relevance to the area in question.[11] The contrary view, unduly confident in government's benevolence and competence, is a tacitly or even openly statist attitude.

The version of libertarian ethics that sets itself against utilitarianism is not so much a separate approach as one belonging to the first or the first two of Paul Edwards's categories, intuitionism and objective naturalism (recall Chapter 10). It is closely related to doctrines of rights, and it is expounded with particular attention to public policy. (Despite its title, Murray Rothbard's 1982 *The Ethics of Liberty* is not so much a work in ethical theory as an application to political philosophy of his version of Lockean natural rights.)

A few libertarians have tended to slide from judging that certain activities should not be made illegal into approving of them and perhaps even deeming them heroic. That slide involves an unintended, unrecognized, and paradoxical statism – the unarticulated idea that the state is responsible for suppressing all evil and promoting all good and that something the state should not suppress is by that very token not evil and perhaps even good after all.

Walter Block (1976) apparently exemplifies this thinking. His book includes chapters making heroes out of pimps, counterfeiters, litterbugs, blackmailers, and other types generally thought "undefendable".[12] Pimps and prostitutes, heroically braving obstacles and obloquy, are supplying demanded services and so are providing gains from trade and upholding the free market. Blackmailers, too, are supplying a demanded service, that of silence. They have a right to do research as long as they do not infringe on anyone's right to his own person and property; they have a right to publicize their findings; and they have a right to accept compensation for forbearing to exercise their right of free speech. Even litterbugs, if they confine their slovenliness to public property, are valuably helping demonstrate that public property is inexpedient and that even parks, roads, and sidewalks might better be privately owned. (Littering on private property against the owner's rules is different because it violates his property rights.)

Rothbard (1982), like Block, tries to deduce all sorts of specific judgments from a few axioms about rights. These include the right of self-ownership, the right to property acquired through the Lockean process of mixing one's labor with hitherto unowned resources, and the right to property acquired through voluntary transactions. The concept of property right, including property in one's own body, appears fundamental. Rights are violated only by actual or threatened physical aggression or by fraud, which resembles force and threats in essential respects.

Rothbard deduces that people have a right to commit libel and slander (a right rather different from my conception articulated in Chapter 10). Anyone has a property right to print and disseminate anything he wants – even deliberate falsehoods about another person. Neither the victim nor anyone has a right to the integrity of his reputation, for that would imply a preposterous right to control thoughts in the minds of other people. From the right to commit libel and slander Rothbard derives a right to commit blackmail; for a blackmailer has a right to engage in an agreed and therefore presumably mutually beneficial transaction whereby he forbears from an act that he would have a right to commit. As for invasion of privacy, well, no one has any right to privacy except the right to have one's person and other property free from physical invasion or trespass. If the blackmailer obtains his sensitive information by stealing letters or tapes or by bugging his victim's home or office, the theft or trespass is the actual offense, not the blackmail as such. If, however, the blackmailer obtains his information from old newspapers or other legally available records or by buying it from old associates of the victim (provided they have not contracted to maintain confidentiality), no rights are violated. On the contrary, to outlaw blackmail or the spreading of false libels against someone's person or product would itself be an aggressive violation of rights, for outlawing something means using force or the threat of force to suppress it.

Boycotts, including secondary boycotts, are a legitimate exercise of free speech and of property rights. Contracts should be legally enforceable only when nonperformance constitutes a straightforward or implicit theft of property (or, one might add, in the spirit of Rothbard's position, when nonperformance constitutes a physical invasion of person or property, if that is conceivable).

Rothbard arrives at his remarkable conclusions by trying to squeeze all issues into his property rights framework and by sharply distinguishing between physical and nonphysical (such as verbal) aggression. Such a sharp distinction between the material and the nonmaterial seems odd, incidentally, coming from an economist of the Austrian school, which puts so much emphasis on the subjective aspect of commodities and of human affairs generally.

Suppose Jones threateningly demands that I sell him my profitable business for one dollar. In a first case, he threatens violence – to trample my tomato plants, maybe, or kick me in the shins. Alternatively, he threatens to circulate, through his extensive network of contacts, stories – false ones, as it happens – about my alleged dishonesty, unreliability, and general immorality. Now, in which case do I suffer the more palpable coercion or the more extreme invasion of my rights?

To vary the example slightly, Jones makes the second threat, and I yield. In fact, however, Jones could not have carried out his threat effectively because he has no extensive network of contacts and because his acquaintances know him as a pathological liar and complete scoundrel. Now, does his successful threat become unacceptable merely because it involved fraud (the lie) and because he could not have damaged me in the threatened way and so was not actually providing me with the ostensible service of forbearance, whereas his threat would have been acceptable if he had been telling the truth and could indeed have ruined me with his stories?

Rothbard's answer (expressed in personal correspondence) is that committing or threatening physical violence (to my tomatoes or my shins) is an illegal violation of my rights, while accomplishing the same predation nonviolently, by threatening malicious stories, should not be so regarded. Nor should bolstering the second threat with a lie be illegal. (I might have protected myself by having the threatener sign a warranty contract to pay me a specified sum of money if he turned out not to have the claimed network of contacts.)

Rothbard agrees, of course, in condemning both the threat of violence and the threat of malicious stories and in condemning the latter whether or not it involves a lie about the effectiveness of the stories. In all those examples, the threatener's behavior is morally odious. Rothbard insists on a sharp distinction between legality or illegality on the one hand and morality or immorality on the other. (More must be said about that distinction later. Anyway, it appears inconsistent both with natural-law thinking and with the subtle statism attributed, above, especially to Walter Block. If a distinctively libertarian ethics appears inconsistent, well, that is my judgment also.)

Another questionable position of libertarian ethics of the Rothbardian stripe is to regard crime as a kind of private transaction between culprit and victim (recall the discussion earlier in Chapter 11). If the victim chooses to forgive him, the culprit is properly no more subject to legal prosecution than a debtor whose debt his creditor has forgiven.

But consider a mugging. Who happens to be the victim on a particular occasion is a matter of chance, and the victim is hardly entitled to forgive the mugger or make a private settlement with him. Potential victims and members of society in general have suffered invasion of their peace and security. Where does the accidental actual victim get authority to speak for them? To brush this question aside and suppose that crime is a private transaction between specific culprit and specific victim is to press the philosophy of individualism beyond where it fits. It is hardly benevolent, furthermore, to throw the additional agony of a decision about forgiveness onto someone already harmed, especially since pressing the case may expose him to retaliation. (Some crime other than mugging might make a better example in this latter respect, perhaps one committed by members of an organization.)

Rothbard has more to say about extortionary threats and crime. In the absence of laws against libel and slander, people would be less ready than now to believe damaging stories without solid evidence, and threats to circulate them would be less effective. Victims who habitually forgave their attackers would become known to criminals and become their favorite targets. Social Darwinism would operate until forgiving victims either perished or learned the appropriate lessons.

These latter arguments, whether persuasive or not, are utilitarian arguments. Resort to them almost concedes that the program of deriving all policy stances from a very few axioms about rights does not work after all.

Rothbard's sharp distinction between matters of morality and matters of law enables him to agree with the rest of us that certain actions are utterly reprehensible, yet also maintain that people should have a legal right to commit them. When he first asserted a right to blackmail, he "was met with a storm of abuse by critics who apparently believed that [he] was advocating the morality of blackmail. Again – a failure to make the crucial distinction between the legitimacy of a right and the morality or esthetics of exercising that right!" (Rothbard 1982, p. 127n.).

But the distinction is not always sharp. Agreed, the law forbids some actions not to reinforce morality but to improve interpersonal coordination, as in specifying which side of the road to drive on. However, the law forbids many actions, including murder, theft, and fraud, precisely because they are immoral. Weighty practical considerations do argue against having the law require everything good and forbid everything bad. They do argue for leaving much influence over behavior to the looser sanctions of morality. But these practical considerations do not suppose that law and morality are totally separate realms.

It is perverse, then, to trumpet arguments that the law should not forbid certain actions, even admittedly morally reprehensible ones, on the grounds that people have rights to commit them nevertheless. That emphasis is especially perverse when linked with scorn for utilitarian considerations and with a show of deducing numerous practical conclusions from axioms about rights.

The concept of rights does not imply that it is always right for a person to do what he has a right to do (cf. Chapter 10). To treat rights as only a legal concept and not at all a moral concept – which I surely do not recommend – should itself warn against that confusion. Yet the confusion keeps creeping back, for it is hard to maintain a sharp distinction between the legally right and the morally right. The confusion reaches perhaps its peak when Walter Block makes "heroes" of those who, like blackmailers and litterbugs, commit actions that, although immoral, should not be illegal in his opinion.

In trying to give ethics an entirely nonutilitarian natural-rights basis, the libertarian approach does not work. It yields some bizarre applications. Its exaggerated individualism dodges the full implications of man's being a social animal. A durable free society presupposes more than putting a very high value on freedom (as Shirley Letwin, John Davenport, and Ernest van den Haag properly recognized in their panel discussion at the 1984 Mont Pelerin meeting[13]). People must also share values more specific than freedom if a society is to cohere. Freedom allows diversity, but diversity extending even to the most basic ethical precepts can have regrettable consequences.

Libertarians deplore (properly in my view) making actual crimes out of victimless activities. Criminalizing them diverts resources away from suppressing crimes that do have victims and increases the intrusiveness and power of the state. But it is a mistake to slip almost into welcoming whatever activities the force of law should not suppress, like the drug culture. Encouraging the counterculture tends to erode shared values.

Probably the state should not try to suppress gambling, but it should not enhance its respectability by itself conducting lotteries. Nor should the state enforce contracts involving, say, sadism. (I have utilitarian reasons for these judgments. Anarchist libertarians would not have a state enforcing any contracts.)

Many libertarians and contractarians seem to think that any noncoercive private actions are acceptable, as well as any collective actions that command unanimous agreement, or agreement counted as essentially or honorarily unanimous. That is a shallow doctrine. A political philosopher cannot responsibly recommend or condemn a particular action or policy merely according to whether it is noncoercive or whether it commands essentially unanimous support. It is his job to strive for a coherent conception of the good society. He should strive for a picture, not for a mere ticket reading that the good society is whatever commands substantially unanimous agreement. This is not to say, of course, that he may impose his views in violation of democratic procedures.

Mises and Natural Rights

One potential embarrassment for Rothbardian natural-rights libertarianism is that Ludwig von Mises, eminent Austrian economist and Rothbard's mentor, scorned doctrines of natural law and natural rights except as interpreted in conformity with his own emphatic utilitarianism. Larry J. Eshelman tries to soften this embarrassment by reinterpreting Mises along the lines of Rothbard. Mises took a principled stance on social issues, much as if he had been an adherent of natural rights. Although he rejected natural law and natural rights because he equated them with intuitionism, "he did not reject the categorical moral framework that underlies much of that tradition". His moral utilitarianism "owes more to the principled, categorical moral framework of [Herbert] Spencer and [Auberon] Herbert, than to the maximizing, comparative moral framework of Bentham and Mill" (Eshelman 1993, p. 38).

This implied contrast between utilitarianism and morality is familiar but mistaken. Utilitarianism is a particular doctrine about the *grounding* of morality. Mises takes a principled, moral, stance, yes – and on utilitarian grounds.

Eshelman introduces the label "harmonist" for doctrines that focus on social cooperation and on arrangements, principles, and attitudes serving it. He also invents a distinction between "comparative" and "categorical" harmonists. Some comparative harmonists argue for maximizing happiness or minimizing pain, others for maximizing liberty. F.A. Hayek argues for maximizing the expectations or "chances of anyone selected at random". Jeremy Bentham supposed that happiness can be quantified and summed. Other comparativists resort to devices like the veil of ignorance or the impartial spectator. But all comparative harmonists are maximizers: they assume a moral framework in which the moral theorist chooses the best from among the alternatives.

Unlike these supposed maximizers, Eshelman's categorical harmonist – his better kind of harmonist – sees only the two moral alternatives of "social harmony or social chaos, the way of reason or the way of beasts". For him the primary moral relation is reciprocity: social harmony is possible only among people committed to it. The categorical harmonist classifies people into those willing to live in harmony with others and those unwilling or unable to do so. His moral world is more black and white than that of the comparativist, who creates the illusion of being more humane and tolerant. The categorical harmonist views punishment primarily as restitutional and retributive, while the comparativist views it primarily as a way to deter crime and reform criminals. The categorical harmonist measures justice against the law and the need to preserve social harmony, while the comparative harmonist measures it against the goal of maximum utility (Eshelman 1993, pp. 12–14).

Eshelman's distinction is contrived and unsuccessful. On most of the points supposedly distinguishing the two types of harmonist, I would count as categorical myself; yet, with Mises, I reject natural-law/natural-rights doctrines except as understood consonant with utilitarianism. On the question of punishment, Rothbard, with his conception of crime as a private transaction between offender and victim, seems not to fit into either of the harmonist camps. Furthermore, Eshelman's rejection of comparative harmonism seems to imply rejecting the comparative-institutions approach to policy. Yet no categorical or absolutist alternative is available. Absolute laissez-faire would mean anarchy, and Mises was no anarchist (he considered government force justified to defend society against its enemies). Government interventions come in various kinds and degrees of desirability or expediency. As long as any government at all exists, it must make decisions. What alternative is there to appraising – comparing – alternative courses of action, with due regard, of course, to applicable moral principles?

The comparative harmonist, says Eshelman (p. 16), is always a tinkerer who sees preserving society as only a first step toward the more ambitious goal of increasing social welfare. The comparativist insists on weighing the evidence in each case of possible action; he dismisses any claim to a priori knowledge of the right action as an appeal to intuition or "an infallible pipeline to the truth" (p. 24). Cleared of all euphemisms, the comparative approach boils down to saying that the decision rests with whoever can gain control of government (p. 27). Again, Eshelman draws too sharp a distinction. I, no absolutist, certainly do not suppose that every proposal for government intervention must be judged on the separate merits of the particular case. Utilitarianism takes principle seriously.

Mises was no comparativist, Eshelman insists, but rather an astute critic of any maximizing moral framework. (That remark tacitly recognizes, by the way, that a utilitarian need not be a maximizer in the sense examined in Chapter 6.) Mises's categorical approach shows up in his claim that "freedom is indivisible" and in his rejection of any middle way between socialism and capitalism (Eshelman 1993, p. 22). The basis for his principled stance is the same as that developed by John Locke (and others before him) and generalized by Herbert Spencer and Auberon Herbert (p. 29). How then, Eshelman asks, could Mises have been both a principled defender of laissez faire and a defender of the doctrine of social expediency? Passages defending expediency can be interpreted as defending the functionalist doctrine that morality is concerned with preserving society and attacking any appeal to mysteriously intuited principles (p. 20).

Unfortunately, Eshelman says, Mises insisted that all values are arbitrary. When Mises attacks holding absolute values, however, he almost always has in mind the belief that such values are handed down from Providence and are independent of society. His target is the righteous nihilist or "theocrat". He speaks sarcastically of "those individuals to whom, by the mysterious decrees of some mysterious agency, the task of determining the collective will and directing the actions of the collective has been entrusted". Fortunately, Mises's argument for a principled, categorical approach to social harmony in no way depends upon his rejection of absolute values and would be strengthened without it (Eshelman 1993, pp. 31–3, with the quotation from Mises 1962/1977, p. 107).

But Mises is right about values, and without adhering to them only weakly. He is right, anyway, if he means that fundamental value judgments, being fundamental, cannot be established by positive argument alone. Eshelman himself reads Mises as believing "that it is impossible to give any ultimate reason why one should be committed to peaceful cooperation. Instead, he treats this commitment as a hypothetical imperative" (Eshelman 1993, p. 33). I would make one slight clarification: peaceful cooperation need not be taken as the utterly ultimate value, since it is instrumental to a more truly ultimate (and in that sense arbitrary) value, happiness.

Eshelman's scholarly documentation and style foster the illusion that he is rescuing Rothbard's position from the embarrassment posed by Mises, the hard-boiled utilitarianian critic of natural-rights doctrines. Eshelman's main device in this effort, however, his distinction between comparative and categorical harmonists, just does not work. Furthermore, he scarcely even tries to lay out a case for a natural-rights approach distinct from utilitarianism; perhaps he expects the reader to know such a case already.

Conclusion

Libertarian ethics, as already noted, is heavily slanted toward policy. As a political philosophy or program, libertarianism favors narrowly limited government – or none at all, in the view of Rothbard and a few other libertarians. Ethan O. Waters (1988; Waters is a pseudonym of R.W. Bradford) distinguishes between two types of argument for libertarian politics. "Libertarian moralism", as he calls it, bases its political position on the nonaggression axiom, the proposition that "no man has the right to initiate the use of physical force against another". (This proposition appears to be not an axiom, strictly speaking, but a corollary of the Lockean property-rights axioms.) "Libertarian consequentialism" bases its position on the contrasting performances of socialism and a society of free markets with limited government. This second position appeals to the consequentialism – to the utilitarianism, as Waters might have said more specifically – of such classical liberals as Ludwig von Mises, Friedrich A. Hayek, and Henry Hazlitt.

As Waters suggests, the "two libertarianisms" may possibly be reconciled. Their shared political position rests on ethics, as I think any political philosophy must ultimately do. They differ in the particular brand of ethics, one basing itself on the supposed axioms of nonaggression and rights, the other on utilitarian ethics. Their ultimate reconciliation hinges on recognizing that an ethics of nonaggression and rights, to the extent that those supposed axioms are valid and can carry the weight placed on them, itself has a utilitarian basis.

To become a card-carrying member of the US Libertarian Party, one must sign the following pledge: "I certify that I do not believe in or advocate the *initiation* of force as a means of achieving political or social goals". When asked to join the party, I have said that I could not conscientiously sign that pledge. I do not advocate actual anarchism. Some government is necessary, though only a government of limited purposes and powers, as envisaged by the American Founders. As I understand the world and human nature, government requires some tax revenues to operate. Collecting taxes ultimately requires the threat and potential exercise – and even the initiation – of force against recalcitrant persons. No one but an actual anarchist, then, could consistently disavow literally all initiation of force.

Let us describe and think about reality in straightforward language. Government, requiring tax revenues, necessarily though regrettably involves force, even initiatory force. We are better intellectually prepared to resist governmental overreaching if we identify force as what it is rather than try to talk it away in equivocal language.

NOTES

1. Jonathan Rauch (1993, p. 57 and *passim*) recognizes this point in describing democracy, one of the three pillars of a liberal society, as "an open-ended, decentralized process for legitimizing the use of force". (Rauch's other two pillars are capitalism, or the market system, and science, or the free market in ideas.)

2. This and the next several paragraphs treat rather technical material, and in a condensed way. The impatient reader may skip them with no great loss provided he understands the passages introduced by a quotation from Clarence Philbrook.

   I do not mean to disparage all uses of the Pareto conception of efficiency. It has pedagogical value in price theory. It can help one grasp the barebones logic of a competitive market economy or of a centrally administered economy successful in imitating certain of its features. Students may gain facility in price theory by studying it both backwards and forwards, not only starting with the concept of long-run competitive equilibrium and deriving its welfare properties but also starting with those properties and seeing how perfect competition would tend to achieve them.

All of this is quite different from erecting a Pareto-optimal state as a benchmark, in comparison with which states of affairs in the real world are to be approved or condemned. It is different from insisting that policy changes be Pareto-optimal. Elegant abstractions have an unquestioned role in theory, but they are far from the most important part of economics; and their direct and overriding application to policy in the real world is quite a jump.

If we must have a standard against which to appraise reality, we might better adopt the looser view of a competitive market economy as a device for gathering and transmitting information about not-yet-exhausted opportunities for gains from trade (including "trade" with nature through production, through rearrangements of the pattern of production and resource allocation, and through new production methods and new goods), for conveying incentives to exploit such opportunities, and for coordinating specialized and decentralized activities. Narrowly economic criteria cannot be conclusive, however; for sociological, psychological, and political considerations are also relevant to appraising how well various institutions and policies cohere with a good society.

3. George Orwell notices that *democracy, socialism, freedom, patriotic, realistic,* and *justice* have multiple and irreconcilable meanings. For "*democracy*, not only is there no agreed definition, but the attempt to make one is resisted from all sides. It is almost universally felt that when we call a country democratic we are praising it: consequently the defenders of every kind of régime claim that it is a democracy, and fear that they might have to stop using the word if it were tied down to any one meaning. Words of this kind are often used in a consciously dishonest way" (Orwell 1946/1961, p. 359).

4. John Stuart Mill (1861/1991) thought that representative government presupposes a certain stage of civilization; not all countries are ready for it. He favored adult suffrage, including women's suffrage, with no property requirement but with some sort of educational requirement. Better-informed citizens might have multiple votes, either explicitly or by belonging to multiple constituencies, for example, as graduates of specific universities. Recipients of public welfare payments would be excluded from the vote. On balance, Mill preferred public or open voting to secret voting (pp. 353ff.) He favored proportional representation. With minor exceptions, he saw no value in indirect voting, for example, in electing electors who in turn elect members of parliament. He stressed the educational value of political participation, including holding office on the local if not national level. Like Edmund Burke, he thought that a legislator should exercise his own judgment rather than be a mere delegate following the instructions of his constituents (pp. 373ff.).

    Mill expressed himself in a way suggestive of Lord Acton's dictum that power corrupts. Men holding power come to attribute an entirely new degree of importance to their own interests. Finding themselves worshiped by others, they "think themselves entitled to be counted at a hundred times the value of other people". Being able to do as they like without regard to consequences, they drift away from due attention even to consequences affecting themselves. Universal experience testifies to "men's being corrupted by power" (p. 297).

5. Charles Taylor identifies extreme conceptions of negative and positive liberty and then suggests that some intermediate conception is the right one. For example, "Freedom can't be just the absence of external obstacles, for there may also be internal ones. ... For freedom now involves my being able to recognise adequately my more important purposes, and my being able to overcome or at least neutralise my motivational fetters, as well as my being free of external obstacles. ... I must be actually exercising self-understanding in order to be truly or fully free" (1979, p. 193).

    Well, it is nice to be "free" of psychological hang-ups; but it invites confusion to include psychological well-being in one's conception of freedom, especially political freedom. Taylor's apparent mistake is to be searching for a correct "theory" of freedom. The relevant question in our context, however, is: how shall we use words like "freedom" to avoid confusing our analysis by blanketing distinct concepts under a single label?

6. One must wonder, though, about how consistent Acton's understanding was if he is correctly quoted on the fund-raising envelope of the Acton Institute for the Study of Religion and Liberty: "Liberty is not the power of doing what we like, but the right of being able to do what we ought".

7. Some libertarians, however, occasionally recommend treating crime as a private transaction

between culprit and victim. Whatever restitution or compensation is satisfactory for the victim (or for the heirs of a murder victim) should be satisfactory to the agencies of society, if it is any of their business at all. I wonder. Quite possibly the victim does not want the option of requiring or waiving compensation; perhaps he reasonably fears retaliation. Many victims are not specifically chosen by their attackers; the victim of a mugging just happened to be in the wrong place at the wrong time. In such cases, the culprit is aggressing against people in general; he is contributing to a general atmosphere of insecurity. Furthermore, culprits should not be allowed to balance the chance of gain by either escaping detection or being forgiven against the mere risk of being caught and having to pay compensation.

On these issues, compare this chapter's appendix on "Libertarianism and classical liberalism".

8. Hume's consequentialist argument, as interpreted by van Dun, recognizes that humans, as social beings endowed with a capacity for sympathy, cannot help but appraise actions and institutions according as they contribute to supporting or to destroying social order. What tends to benefit society helps solve problems that we all face. "It is ... a mistake", van Dun nevertheless says, "to claim that Hume gave a utilitarian account of morality and law". No one calculates the maximization of any sort of utility. The argument for liberty or justice depends not on valuations of expected consequences "but on the conditions for the existence of the social order itself" (Van Dun, pp. 278, 282).

Obviously, then, van Dun has a narrow conception of what counts as utilitarian argument.

9. Van Dun (1994, p. 269) finds natural-law thinking present in Hayek's work in the sense that since a functioning society is a precondition for the achievement of whatever ends human beings may pursue, society and therefore law to maintain it ought to exist.

10. A Pareto-optimal state of affairs is one from which no Pareto-optimal move is available. Any such available move should be made (according to a rather tame value judgment, anyway); for, by definition, it would benefit at least one person while harming no one. Although these concepts enter into certain strands of abstract economic theory, they rarely if ever have any application in policy decisions. Recall the discussion earlier in Chapter 11.

11. The head of George Washington University's student libertarians provided an apparent example of such skepticism in a TV discussion on 25 January 1998 of alleged White House sex and perjury scandals. The student said in effect that someone's private behavior is no one else's business, or not a legitimate topic of political discussion.

12. Not even Block, however, attempted anything so preposterous as making a hero out of the itchy-fingered copyeditor.

13. The Mont Pelerin Society is an international society of classical-liberal economists and others, founded in 1947 on the Mont Pèlerin in Switzerland. The Society holds its "general meetings" every other year and "regional meetings" in the intervening years.

12.   Utilitarianism after all

Summarizing ideas from earlier chapters and putting them in close contact with one another may further illuminate them.

RELATIONS BETWEEN ECONOMICS AND ETHICS

Economists have been writing sensibly on moral philosophy at least as far back as David Hume and Adam Smith. This book has mentioned other notable economist-ethicists also, as well as several moral and political philosophers who have taken the trouble to learn the essentials of economics. This overlap of interests is no coincidence. The same conditions provide the subject matter of both branches of social science. The fact of scarcity, man's nature as a social animal, with genuine but only limited benevolence toward his fellows, and the benefits of trade and other forms of cooperation require people to get along with one another somehow. Ethics and economics both bear on easing tensions and coordinating decentralized activities as individuals pursue their own goals. Such insights have a venerable history. David Hume judged three conditions essential to long-run planning, saving and investment, and cooperation in large projects. These are the stability of possessions, the transfer of ownership by consent (rather than by force or fraud), and the performance of promises. Earlier, Thomas Hobbes stressed the importance of peace and security, presupposing, as he thought, a government strong enough to suppress the war of all against all. Where every man is enemy to every man and each must look to himself alone for security, Hobbes's much-quoted description of life under such conditions is apt. Peace and security, however, permit industriousness and "commodious living", which is Hobbes's term for economic development. Already in 1651 Hobbes thus set forth the bare essentials of development economics. Many Third World countries today illustrate, by tragic contrast, the importance of Hobbes's insight.

A double relation holds between ethics and the rest of social science. First, ethics enters into elucidating the conditions necessary for prosperity and progress; ethical standards condition how well economies perform. Finding appropriate trading partners, negotiating and enforcing contracts, complying with government regulations, coping with unexpected contingencies, avoiding litigation – all are easier if the parties can trust one another. The assumption of honesty, if warranted, reduces the need to spell out contract terms at length. Partially implicit bargains figure in relaxed employer–employee relations. Shared moral values help hold down transactions costs. Even money has moral significance. It is both tool and symbol of the kind of society where men and women benefit from and contribute to one another's excellences, voluntarily trading value for value.

The second part of the double relation has been the larger theme of this book: social science helps face some central questions of ethics. What sorts of knowledge do ethical precepts constitute? How are they grounded? How can traditional precepts and suggested modifications to them be judged wise or perverse?

VALUE JUDGMENTS

Its involving value judgments does not remove ethics from the purview of social science. Also called normative propositions, these stand in contrast with positive propositions of fact and logic. No conclusion about what is good or desirable, or the opposite, follows from facts and logic alone; one cannot derive an "ought" from an "is". That alcohol *is* dangerous to an unborn child does not itself imply that the pregnant woman *ought* to abstain from it. That conclusion presupposes not only the medical facts but also a value judgment about the child's health relative to the mother's pleasure in drinking. Solely from the conclusion of fact and economic theory that a certain policy would bring general misery and an alternative general happiness, one cannot judge the first policy bad and its alternative good; a judgment against misery and for happiness is also necessary.

As these examples suggest, one can assess relatively specific judgments, like ones about specific policies, by invoking facts and logic *and also* other and deeper value judgments. One can condemn lying, cheating, and stealing by fact-based argument that such behavior tends to subvert general happiness, *along with* a judgment in favor of happiness. For most people, probably, that judgment is a *fundamental* one. By definition of a fundamental judgment, one cannot argue for it; one has reached the end of arguing; one must appeal to direct observation or intuition. But as this example also suggests, disputes about fundamental value judgments are rare. Almost no one would doubt that misery is bad and happiness is good, but almost no one would think of *demonstrating* that judgment; such a demonstration would require appealing to a still more fundamental judgment, which is hard to imagine.

THE SOCIAL-SCIENCE APPROACH TO ETHICS

Economics and other social and natural sciences shed light on the origins of ethical precepts and on why they command whatever consensus they do. Long before the sociobiologists, Charles Darwin argued the role of biology. Of course, as Darwin recognized, explaining behavior is not the same as justifying it. Still, facts do enter into examining how values interrelate and what the likely consequences are of heeding or scorning particular values. Nothing impossible can be morally obligatory. For example, probably, policymakers can hardly be obliged to achieve high degrees of both personal freedom and equality of income and wealth.

Social science investigates what conditions promote and what ones undermine a well-functioning society, "civil society", as some have called it, or "social cooperation". The natural and social sciences, including psychology, find common ground with ethics in investigating what supports and what undercuts opportunities for individuals peacefully to benefit from specialization and trade and their other interactions. Actions, institutions, rules, principles, customs, ideals, dispositions, and character traits count as good or bad according as they support or undercut such a society.

Social cooperation, so conceived, is merely the *quasi*-ultimate ethical criterion because it is merely a means, though an indispensable means, to what is ultimately desired. The latter, in utilitarian ethics, is human happiness in a suitably stretched sense of the word. Social science, including psychology, helps investigate interactions between the characteristics and values prevailing in society and those of its individual members. It helps investigate what reason, if any, the individual has for respecting and generally abiding by ethical precepts. No guarantees are available that "virtue pays", but empirical argument is relevant to the probabilities.

RECIPROCITY

Philosophers and social scientists have investigated how cooperation might evolve "spontaneously". Computer tournaments and simulations have illuminated the game of prisoners' dilemma. In a single round, considered alone, the better move for each of the two players, regardless of what the other does, is to try to exploit the other. Yet when both act that way, the result for both is worse than if they had cooperated. Still, if either forgoes the narrowly self-interested strategy, he risks winding up the victim. What incentive, then, does each player have to subordinate his own narrow immediate advantage to a broader perspective? A solution appears in multiple repetitions of the game. Each player's moves transmit signals to the other. In Robert Axelrod's experiments, the most successful strategy is "tit for tat": one begins by playing cooperatively but retaliates on the next round if the other player acts exploitatively. If the other then returns to cooperation, the first does so too.

This strategy of cooperating without letting oneself be victimized contrasts with the Christian principle of turning the other cheek. That conduct might seem comfortable on a single occasion, or even generous and noble. On the contrary, though, cheek-turning invites further predation not only against oneself but also against other innocent persons. It is thus *anti*social. The truly social strategy for the long run is to reciprocate cooperation and punish predation.

Axelrod's experiments merely stylize some aspects of society. Additional twists of reality allow players to opt out of moves or to shun undesirable partners. Would-be exploiters get eliminated by others' refusal to play with them, and more cooperation results than in the original game. Though far from fully mirroring reality, such games are an instructive metaphor. Even if each individual pursues only his own interest, due regard for the long run and for the reactions of other persons can promote reciprocal benevolence.

Reciprocity need not mean insisting on strict equivalence of benefits received and furnished, all measured in money. It is the exchange – not necessarily strictly calculated – of appropriate attitudes and actions. Similarly, the word "market" need not be confined to narrowly economic transactions. In an extended sense, the "market" is a metaphor for all voluntary interpersonal relations, in contrast to relations imposed by force or fraud or rigid and oppressive custom.

Part of the rationale of ethical standards is that positive law just could not codify and enforce all desirable character traits and behavior in all imaginable and unimaginable circumstances. The logic of an ethical code requires flexibility in application and adherence to its spirit rather than to minute specifications. People's moral obligations toward one another depend on many circumstances, including the kind and degree of solidarity or loyalty expected among them. Much behavior must be left to the informal pressures of moral judgments and reputation effects. We would scarcely like – would we? – the consequences of having government agencies appraise the moral correctness of every action or every payment passing between persons. Institutions and policies simply cannot be devised to guarantee ethically appealing detailed outcomes in each individual case.

Very productive of gains from specialization and trade is worldwide multilateral exchange among millions and billions of persons unknown to one another. In this "great society" or "extended order" (as F.A. Hayek calls it), monetary evaluations – prices and costs, profits and losses – are indispensable. No special solidarity among the traders is needed – nothing beyond honorable dealing and refraining from lying, cheating, stealing, violence, and coercion.

Although the market, business, and money are indispensable to human survival and comfort, they should not dominate all human relations; in some contexts, regrets about "commercialism" are pertinent. Not all behavior conforming to the logic and ethics of a capitalist system is ethically correct for that reason alone. As Hayek said, an ethics of solidarity is proper within the small special groups embedded in the great society of worldwide business exchanges – groups like the family, good friends, and, perhaps, enthusiasts in a common cause. To a degree, one might add, the same holds among professional colleagues and among employees and employers associated for a long time. In the great society or extended order, the individual also belongs to several smaller orders. The intimacy available within special groups has psychological value. To pursue one's narrow and immediate personal interest, to insist on monetary calculations of costs and benefits, and to insist on narrowly conceived reciprocity even among members of such groups – all that would destroy great values. "If we were always to apply the rules of the extended order to our more intimate groupings, *we would crush them.* So we must learn to live in two sorts of world at once" (Hayek 1989, p. 18). (These generalizations about reciprocity may be wrong, but evidence supports them, and they are amenable to research.)

UTILITARIANISM UNDER ATTACK

An ethics centering on social cooperation is more soundly based than the ethics of, say, theologians. Yet it draws criticisms. "Why bother answering?" one might ask. Admittedly, the word "utilitarianism" is ugly. Still, it is historically warranted: a favorable attitude toward utility or happiness, broadly conceived, is the doctrine's fundamental value judgment. Abandoning the word would seem to yield to the critics. Besides, what other label would be equally descriptive yet more generally acceptable? Finally, facing criticisms is a way of more fully examining the doctrine itself.

Besides taking casual jabs as if simply to remind readers of the doctrine's already familiar evils, superficial critics imagine utilitarians going around looking for opportunities to torture redheads for the amusement of the multitude or to approve of rape when the rapist's pleasure outweighs his victim's distress. Or critics find utilitarianism guilty by association with Jeremy Bentham, whose supposed personality flaws they proceed to rehearse. Joseph Schumpeter, fortunately restricting his assessment mostly to the Benthamite version, called utilitarianism "the shallowest of all conceivable philosophies of life" (1954, p. 133; cf. p. 407).

Policy-oriented objections find utilitarianism offering no principled defense against bad policies. Some libertarian economists regret abandonment of a laissez-faire stance based on a philosophy of natural law and natural rights and reducing the policy of nonintervention to an *ad hoc*, contingent, defeasible presumption at best. Such critics thus appraise ethical systems according to whether they infallibly support preconceived policy recommendations. This seems backward. It seems more plausible to appraise policies according to how well they accord with a well-grounded ethical system. Furthermore, the lines of criticism mentioned sometimes distinguish between ethically principled and utilitarian approaches to policy, interpreting the latter as the unprincipled case-by-case direct calculation of gains and losses of utility. Actually, far from rejecting principles, utilitarianism seeks their sound basis.

Criticisms deeper than those just sampled fall into four further groups. One may label them as charging (1) aggregation, (2) miscellaneous immoralities, (3) rules fetishism, and (4) vacuity.

Aggregation

According to the first of these further charges, utilitarianism purports to measure, compare, and add up the utilities of different persons. It is collectivistic, valuing individuals only as devices for processing goods and experiences into contributions to aggregate utility. Individuals are like branch plants that might properly be shut down for the greater efficiency of the company or industry as a whole. Such criticism traffics in caricature. Utilitarians know as well as anyone else that the happiness of individuals is the only kind available; no distinct kind pertains to some sort of social aggregate instead. (Ludwig von Mises, an avowed utilitarian, was explicit on this point; 1957/1985, p. 58.) Utilitarians recognize that individuals are their own men and women with distinct and diverse personalities who are properly partial to their own interests and projects and those of their relatives and friends.

Utilitarians are charged with unconcern about the distribution of welfare (or of income or wealth). Many utilitarians presumably do have a taste for lesser inequality than they currently observe, but a taste tempered by concern for what measures and what institutions would be required to seek equality. More broadly, what are the likely consequences of making government responsible for kinds and degrees of equality and inequality? Questions might seem to arise about choice between maximum aggregate or per capita utility on the one hand and lesser aggregate or per capital utility distributed more nearly equally on the other hand. I conjecture, however, that such questions simply dissolve in the face of detailed institutional investigation. Facts and theory from various fields suggest that arrangements at either the egalitarian or the antiegalitarian extreme of the range of possibilities would yield less total or per capita utility (supposing for the sake of argument that such measurements could even be made), or less attractive prospects for either the person considered at random or the least advantaged stratum of society, than some intermediate arrangement. Similar considerations would still apply, if less decisively, to comparisons between alternative intermediate or nonextreme arrangements. Scope will remain for positive research bearing on how attractive the associated kind of society would be. It is unlikely that people will be at loggerheads over a fundamental value judgment of happiness versus equality. The question of making such judgments can appear to arise only from neglect of the prior question of in what *context* it could relate to a genuine issue.

Miscellaneous Immoralities

A second group of objections finds utilitarianism immoral in various further respects. Critics contrive "lifeboat cases" in a stretched sense of the term: in each of them, utilitarians would allegedly recommend sacrificing an innocent victim for the sake of greater aggregate utility. (Broadly similar cases feature deathbed promises.) The critic, so runs a veiled hint, would never act so shamefully as to make the decision allegedly recommended by the crass utilitarians. Chapter 7 reviews two of Bernard Williams's favorite cases, that of George, who needs a job in research for chemical and biological warfare but who conscientiously opposes such work, and that of Jim, who faces a choice between himself killing a single innocent prisoner to save nineteen others or seeing their captor kill all twenty. How should each respond to his dilemma? Williams makes much of "integrity", or moral purity, implying that George or Jim would impair his own by making the alleged utilitarian choice and implying that utilitarians are deficient in this virtue.

    R.M. Hare (1981, pp. 59–60, 139) has identified the "fraudulence" of such lifeboat cases. It is fraudulent for a critic to hint that he, in a cooked-up dilemma and in contrast with a utilitarian, would preserve his own moral purity – somehow. In tragic cases, *prima facie* principles can indeed clash (as benevolence or loyalty with truthfulness); and one or more must give way. Yet an ethical principle does not cease being just that merely because another principle may be more pressing and so override it in a special case. No alternative to utilitarian ethics can conjure away moral dilemmas.

    Just as utilitarianism does not render compellingly clear lifeboat verdicts, so, critics sometimes object, it fails to settle the controversy over abortion – or, one might add, over capital punishment. Intuitions do deliver clear verdicts. Awkwardly, opposite sides have opposite intuitions. Pondering such specific issues may require looking beyond the proxy moral criterion of social cooperation to more nearly direct effects on happiness and to particular facts of specific cases (but to say so is not to repudiate principle and call for case-by-case unprincipled judgments). Judgments like ones about abortion or capital punishment can be agonizing; but even in tough cases, what ethical system works better than utilitarianism? The factual questions bearing on such issues (noted in Chapters 10 and 11) further illustrate utilitarianism's affinity with social science. Rarely or never does disagreement center on values alone, with further facts irrelevant.

Critics charge that utilitarianism could condone slavery in certain circumstances. But in grinding out the same old verdict even for fantastic imagined circumstances in which slavery would serve happiness and abolishing it would cause misery, the critics show loss of contact with what their intuitions are supposed to cope with. Utilitarians, in contrast, know that they must check their intuitions against reality. They recognize that the circumstances required to make slavery acceptable would be so peculiar as to warrant a practically absolute condemnation.

Rules Fetishism

A third group of criticisms imputes to rules utilitarianism a fetish about sticking to rules regardless of consequences (even when, for example, making an exception to a traffic rule could avoid a crash). The contrasting position of extreme act utilitarianism, even though nowadays scarcely more than a straw man for superficial critics, can serve as a device to illuminate more sensible versions of utilitarianism by contrast. Anyway, the act version calls for the action in each individual case that seems, even apart from any general principles, to promise the best results on the whole. It thereby encourages each person to follow his own moral intuitions as if they were infallible and as if he had more factual and theoretical knowledge and more prodigious ability to calculate even remote and subtle consequences than anyone really could have. It overlooks the temptations and excuses that people find to make exceptions in their own favor. It also overlooks the coordinative value of familiar rules and conventions: confidence in their being generally heeded makes people better able to predict each other's behavior and so avoid acting at cross-purposes.

A realistic version of rules utilitarianism neither commits these errors nor insists on rigid adherence to rules regardless of consequences. Instead, it condemns violating an applicable rule on whim or on scanty information. It stresses that people cannot have full knowledge and cannot predict soundly in each separate case. It stresses the coordinative value of rules generally heeded (and of respect, though not rigid respect, for tradition). It knows that people must sometimes make exceptions (as to avoid a car crash, or when rules clash, as in lifeboat cases); but it expects that any exceptions, instead of being made *ad hoc*, should have a principled rationale. R.M. Hare distinguishes between two levels of ethical thinking. In day-to-day practice, the very rationale of rules requires a strong though not absolute presumption that they are binding.

Appraisal belongs on the reflective level, where rules are criticized or justified or even rejected in particular applications.

Rules are recommended not for their own sakes – not as fetishes – but for their usual good results. They are no mere rule-of-thumb substitutes for case-by-case calculations that would be preferable if time, information, and freedom from bias permitted. No; ordinarily to take them as conclusive helps focus expectations and otherwise serve interpersonal coordination.

Rules utilitarianism is better interpreted as, or broadened into, indirect utilitarianism (so called by John Gray, attributing it to John Stuart Mill). That version inquires not merely into what rules but also and especially into what character traits, habits, attitudes, and dispositions are likely to serve both a person's own happiness and the general happiness. These inclinations and dispositions include sympathy (as conceived by David Hume and Adam Smith) and a disinclination to grab special privilege and make unfair exceptions in one's own favor. Such dispositions condition the application of rules in special cases.

The rules of morality have wider scope than laws made by legislatures and judges; they are also looser and more flexible and adaptable. Utilitarians understand why these features are useful and why it would be impossible legally to codify and rigidly to enforce all precepts of decent behavior. It is scarcely fair, then, to accuse them of insisting on conformity to rules, come what may.

Vacuousness

A fourth line of criticism finds utilitarianism all-accommodating to the point of being vacuous: it wriggles away or transforms itself when challenged. But its defensive maneuvers, if such they are, accord with the world's complexity. On what contributes to and what detracts from social cooperation and happiness, utilitarianism invokes social science to compare how well alternative sets of institutions and practices are likely to function. Psychology joins in suggesting that fairness or unfairness and interpersonal distribution of well-being do affect a society's functioning and its members' happiness. Utilitarianism can acknowledge possible objective aspects to what promotes human flourishing, such as Aristotle's notions of human distinctiveness, natural ends, and fulfillment. At least some of those topics are researchable. Each of us, with his own particular character and background, may have his own particular views on detailed proper ends for the individual. Still, we may broadly agree on what characteristics a society must have to afford an individual good chances of pursuing his ends.

The criterion of a society affording good prospects for happiness is no mere tautology. Rival criteria are readily conceivable. One is a just society in the sense of John Rawls (1971), who rejects viewing justice as a mere means to happiness. Other alternative criteria center on duty or on religion. Still others posit conformity to traditional ethical precepts, even if only intuition rather than analysis of consequences has tested the precepts; or respect for individual rights that have simply been postulated rather than argued for; or conduciveness to the special flourishing of the few highest and noblest specimens of the human race. Or one might conceivably make the criterion the happiness not of people in general but of oneself or some other specific person. That such alternative criteria are conceivable shows that utilitarianism is not vacuous, while their scant appeal strengthens the utilitarian case.

NATURAL LAW AND RIGHTS

Rival doctrines, as just suggested, further illuminate utilitarianism. Murray Rothbard emphasized a conception of rights purportedly deriving from Locke's axioms of self-ownership and homesteading. A loosely compatible approach seeks to reason out what actions are "natural" and therefore ethically acceptable by reflecting on the nature of human beings, their shared aspirations and fundamental values, and their interactions in community (Piderit 1993). Yet one can scarcely mean that whatever is natural is right and good. An acceptable doctrine must not, of course, require impossible actions or behavior enforceable only at excessive cost; but respecting the facts of nature and human interaction does not distinguish the natural-law approach from utilitarianism. If the two really are different, the former boils down to a promiscuous if tacit appeal to specific intuitions.

Natural law does make sense if it means merely that all sorts of behavior and precepts, including laws made by legislatures and judges, are open to appraisal on moral grounds. Nothing becomes ethically acceptable merely by due enactment into positive law. That formulation does not rule out a utilitarian grounding of morality. But if the doctrine says that whatever is morally right (or wrong) has all (or none) of the force of positive law for that reason alone, it is fatuously trying to deny a live distinction.

The meaning of natural (or human or individual) rights that seems to fit the typical context is this: a right is a person's entitlement to others' treatment of him that is binding on those others with compelling moral force. Some rights are positive entitlements, like a child's right to support by his parents or each party's right to performance by the other party to a contract. The rights mentioned in the Declaration of Independence are negative rights, rights to forbearances, rights not to be coerced or victimized by other persons, notably including agents of the state. One reason why negative rights are especially stringent is that they are relatively easy to honor – by simply not interfering.

Anyway, rights, being moral entitlements, *presuppose* an ethical system and cannot provide its very grounding. (On what principles or intuitions provide the basis of rights, "the rhetoric of rights sheds no light whatever"; Hare 1989EoPM, p. 194 and Chapters 7-9. Richard Epstein finds a utilitarian grounding for natural law and natural rights, sensibly interpreted, and even for the Lockean axioms of self-ownership or personal autonomy and home-steading or first possession; Epstein 1989 and Epstein 1995, pp. 30, 55, 68, 311-13, and *passim*.)

Making natural rights the very foundation of ethics substitutes intuition for factual research and reasoning. Furthermore, some strands of "rights talk" (as Glendon 1991 calls it) debase political discussion. To demand a particular line of policy as a matter of right is to deploy pretty heavy artillery, portraying one's opponents not merely as mistaken or obtuse but as moral transgressors. Such rhetoric obstructs the democratic processes of public justification, communication, and deliberation; it subverts a creative search for mutually beneficial accommodations. "Behind the rights talk lurks a class prejudice in favor of minting fresh rights to fuel judicial activism" (George Will 1992, p. 176, agreeing with Glendon). (Hypotheses like these about the subversion of politics may turn out to be wrong, but they are researchable.)

CONTRACTARIANISM

Several versions of "contractarianism" challenge utilitarianism. John Rawls (1971) imagines persons negotiating a social contract behind a "veil of ignorance" about their future positions in society and even about their distinctive personal characteristics. I see no operational difference, however, between Rawls's appeal to this *conceptual* social contract and doing what I interpret him as actually doing – asking himself what he can in good conscience recommend on his own responsibility when in a duly detached frame of mind. Rawls's "original position" comes across to me merely as a device for evoking that frame of mind. But utilitarians value a duly philosophical frame of mind no less than he.

James Buchanan and the public-choice school are another fount of contractarian thinking (and of more nearly genuine contractarianism than Rawls's). Acceptable principles of social organization are those that people did agree on or could agree on or would agree on if they were adequately informed, had taken enough time for reflection and discussion, and were negotiating in a frame of mind sufficiently detached from their own individual idiosyncrasies and preferences.

It is unnecessary to choose among these different formulations, for the same question applies in any case: how can the theorist know what the contracting parties could or would or should agree on? *In view of what* would they reject some principles and accept others? In view – is this not so? – of how well society would function, affecting people's prospects of happiness, under one or another set of principles. What, then, are the operational – not merely rhetorical – differences between contractarianism and utilitarianism?

Rather than a substantively distinct position, contractarianism is an attitude, one located at the individualistic opposite pole from a desire to maximize the welfare of some collective entity transcending individuals. (This charitable interpretation, as I consider it, derives partly from Lomasky 1987, Narveson 1988, and Sugden 1989.) Contractarianism inquires how institutions and customs can promote or subvert voluntary and mutually beneficial cooperation among distinct individuals pursuing their diverse goals. Whereas the utilitarian supposedly speaks as if to a benevolent despot eager to learn and implement the findings of science, the contractarian tentatively and modestly explores with people how they might possibly agree on social changes to their shared benefit. In truth, though, both are typically speaking to their colleagues in philosophical discussions. Neither aspires to impose his own views on everyone else, or so one hopes. Precisely utilitarian considerations condemn having authorities empowered to do any such thing. In academic discussion, at its best, anyway, each participant lays out his evidence and arguments for inspection by his colleagues, hoping, yes, to persuade them, but also willing to learn and to revise his own views. Far from expressing arrogance and an eagerness to impose one's views coercively, forthrightness about what one recommends, and on what basis, serves clarity. Communication suffers if discussants suppress their own views and modestly defer to what others supposedly do or could agree on.

Contractarians and wise utilitarians agree on essential points, including these. First, subordinating the interests of individuals pursuing their own diverse projects to some supposed transcendent general interest would undercut the happiness of individuals, which is the only kind available. Second, institutions, policies, ethical precepts, behavioral dispositions, and the like are to be appraised according as they enhance or detract from prospects for voluntary and beneficial cooperation among individuals seeking to make good lives for themselves in their own ways. Finally, a value-free political economy is impossible. Contractarians and utilitarians share the fundamental or nearly fundamental value of wishing individuals well as they pursue their diverse but reconcilable goals.

Similarities with utilitarianism would be even more evident if the contractarians would occasionally drop their metaphorical language about conceptual unanimous agreement, social contract on the constitutional level, and propositions that are not actually true but avowedly only "conceptually" true, and if instead they would use hard-boiled, literal language.

UTILITARIANISM AFTER ALL

The social scientist's concern with cooperation, including impersonal cooperation among vast numbers of mutually unknown persons, helps elucidate a broadly utilitarian approach to ethics and its application to political philosophy. This approach invokes fact and logic to appraise institutions, policies, rules, character traits, and dispositions according to how well they serve peaceful cooperation among individuals pursuing their own diverse goals in life.

Ethical systems and policy recommendations necessarily involve value judgments. Most of these, instead of being fundamental, are amenable to being argued for (or against) by appeal to facts and logic and still deeper values. Only fundamental value judgments cannot be further argued for and must rest, instead, on intuition or direct perception. Utilitarianism is parsimonious with value judgments and specific intuitions. Its fundamental value judgment is to regret misery and value happiness, broadly interpreted. It stands in contrast with ethical systems that do traffic promiscuously in specific intuitions conveyed with rhetoric and bombast, notably systems that would locate the very basis of ethics in notions about natural law and natural rights, conceived of as floating without any utilitarian basis. Yet natural law and rights are important, and enough so to deserve a sensible interpretation and grounding. The appeal to numerous specific intuitions is the opposite of disciplined argument.

Another prominent rival of utilitarianism, namely contractarianism, turns out to be utilitarianism disguised by verbal fictions. All the criticisms of utilitarianism known to me fail to discredit it in favor of some genuinely rival doctrine. In particular, the objection that it is so plastic and all-accommodating as to be vacuous falls because genuinely distinct doctrines do exist, unappealing though they may be. In its detailed content and applications, utilitarianism is fact-oriented and welcomes the ongoing discoveries of social science.

Let whoever rejects a utilitarian grounding of ethics clearly articulate what distinct alternative he accepts, making sure that it is not, after all, utilitarianism in disguise.

References

Ackerman, Bruce A. (1980), *Social Justice in the Liberal State*, New Haven: Yale University Press.

Adler, Mortimer J. (1970), *The Time of Our Lives*, New York: Holt, Rinehart, and Winston.

Alexander, Richard D. (1987), *The Biology of Moral Systems*, Hawthorne, NY: Aldine De Gruyter.

Alexander, Sidney S. (1967), "Human values and economists' values", in Sidney Hook (ed.), *Human Values and Economic Policy*, New York: New York University Press, pp. 101–16.

Alsop, Stewart (1970), "Let's raise more hell", *Newsweek*, 9 March, p. 100.

Anschutz, Richard Paul (1981), "Mill, John Stuart", *Encyclopaedia Britannica*, 15th ed., Vol. 12, pp. 197–200.

Arkes, Hadley (1986), *First Things: An Inquiry into the First Principles of Morals and Justice*, Princeton: Princeton University Press.

Arkes, Hadley (1990), "The perils of legal positivism" (review of Richard A. Posner, *The Problems of Jurisprudence*, Harvard University Press, 1990), *The Public Interest*, **101**, Fall, pp. 132–9.

Arrow, Kenneth J. (1963), *Social Choice and Individual Values*, 2nd edn, New York: Wiley.

Atkinson, R.F. (1961), "Hume on 'is' and 'ought': A reply to Mr. MacIntyre", *Philosophical Review*, 70. Reprinted in V.C. Chappell (ed.), *Hume: A Collection of Critical Essays*, Garden City: Anchor Books/Doubleday, 1966, pp. 265–77.

Axelrod, Robert (1984), *The Evolution of Cooperation*, New York: Basic Books.

Axelrod, Robert (1997), *The Complexity of Cooperation*, Princeton: Princeton University Press.

Ayer, A.J. (1936), *Language, Truth, and Logic*. Reprinted New York: Dover, 1952.

Badhwar, Neera Kapur (1993), "Altruism versus self-interest: Sometimes a false dichotomy", *Social Philosophy & Policy*, **10**(1), Winter, pp. 90–117.

Baier, Kurt (1965), *The Moral Point of View*, Abridged edition, with a new preface, New York: Random House, fourth printing, 1967.

Baier, Kurt (1967), "Welfare and preference", in Sidney Hook (ed.), *Human Values and Economic Policy*, New York: New York University Press, pp. 120–35. Reprinted in Brian Barry and Russell Hardin (eds), *Rational Man and Irrational Society?* Beverly Hills: Sage Publications, 1982, pp. 284–95.

Banfield, Edward C., assisted by Laura C. Banfield (1958), *The Moral Basis of a Backward Society*, New York: Free Press, paperback 1967.

Banfield, Edward C. (1970), *The Unheavenly City*, Boston: Little, Brown.

Barnett, Randy (1989), *The Rights Retained by the People: The History and Meaning of the Ninth Amendment*, Fairfax, VA: George Mason University Press.

Barry, B.M. (1977), "Justice between generations", in P.M.S. Hacker and J. Raz (eds), *Law, Morality, and Society*, Essays in honour of H.L.A. Hart, Oxford: Clarendon Press, pp. 268–84.

Bartley, William Warren, III (1985), *The Retreat to Commitment*, 2nd edn, La Salle: Open Court.

Bartley, William Warren, III (1990), *Unfathomed Knowledge, Unmeasured Wealth*, La Salle: Open Court.

Bauer, P.T. (1981), "Western guilt and Third World poverty", in his *Equality, the Third World, and Economic Delusion*. Reprinted in Franky Schaeffer (ed.), *Is Capitalism Christian?* Westchester, IL: Crossway Books, 1985, pp. 115–37.

Bauer, P.T. (1984), "Ecclesiastical economics: Envy legitimized", in his *Reality and Rhetoric: Studies in the Economics of Development*. Reprinted in Franky Schaeffer (ed.), *Is Capitalism Christian?* Westchester, IL: Crossway Books, 1985, pp. 327–43.

Beauchamp, Tom L. and James F. Childress (1983), *Principles of Biomedical Ethics*, New York: Oxford University Press.

Bedau, Hugo (1995–96), "A tragic choice: Jim and the natives in the jungle", *The Key Reporter*, **61**(2), Winter, pp. 1, 3–6.

Bedau, Hugo (1996), Response to readers' letters, *The Key Reporter*, **61**(3), Spring, p. 15.

Benne, Robert (1987), "Two cheers for the bishops", in Charles P. Lutz (ed.), *God, Goods, and the Common Good*, Minneapolis: Augsburg, pp. 44–59.

Bentham, Jeremy (1780, 1789, 1823), *An Introduction to the Principles of Morals and Legislation*. Reprinted New York: Hafner, 1948.

Bentham, Jeremy (1973), *Bentham's Political Thought*, Ed. by Bhiku Parekh. New York: Barnes & Noble.

Bergstrom, Theodore C. (1995), "On the evolution of altruistic ethical rules for siblings", *American Economic Review*, **85**, March, pp. 58–81.

Bergstrom, Theodore C. and Oded Stark (1993), "How altruism can prevail in an evolutionary environment", *American Economic Review*, **83**, May, pp. 149–55.

Berlin, Isaiah (1958), "Two concepts of liberty". Reprinted in his *Four Essays on Liberty*, Oxford: Oxford University Press, 1969, pp. 118–72.

Bidinotto, Robert J. (1996), "Civil liberties and criminal justice", *Cato Policy Report*, **18**, January/February, pp. 6–8.

Binmore, Ken (1994), *Playing Fair*, Vol. I of his *Game Theory and the Social Contract*, Cambridge: MIT Press.

Binswanger, Harry (ed.) (1986), *The Ayn Rand Lexicon*, New York: New American Library.

Binswanger, Harry (1990), *The Biological Basis of Teleological Concepts*, Los Angeles: Ayn Rand Institute Press.

Blanshard, Brand (1961), *Reason and Goodness*, London: Allen & Unwin; New York: Macmillan.

Blanshard, Brand (1966), "Morality and politics", in Richard T. De George (ed.), *Ethics and Society*, Garden City: Anchor Books/Doubleday, pp. 1–23.

Blanshard, Brand (1980), "Replies to my critics", sections following the commentaries of individual critics, in Paul Arthur Schilpp (ed.), *The Philosophy of Brand Blanshard*, La Salle: Open Court.

Block, Walter (1976), *Defending the Undefendable: The Pimp, Prostitute, Scab, Slumlord, Libeler, Moneylender, and Other Scapegoats in the Rogue's Gallery of American Society*, New York: Fleet Press.

Blum, L.A. (1980), *Friendship, Altruism, and Morality*, London and Boston: Routledge & Kegan Paul, paperback, 1982.

Bok, Sissela (1979), *Lying*, New York: Vintage Books.

Boonin-Vail, David (1994), *Thomas Hobbes and the Science of Moral Virtue*, New York: Cambridge University Press.

Bork, Robert H. (1990), *The Tempting of America: The Political Seduction of the Law*, New York: Free Press.

Boyle, Joseph M., Jr, Germain Grisez, and Olaf Tollefsen (1976), *Free Choice: A Self-referential Argument*, Notre Dame: University of Notre Dame Press.

Brandt, Richard B. (1979), *A Theory of the Good and the Right*, Oxford: Clarendon Press.

Brandt, Richard B. (1992), *Morality, Utilitarianism, and Rights*, New York: Cambridge University Press.

Brink, David O. (1989), *Moral Realism and the Foundations of Ethics*, New York: Cambridge University Press, reprinted 1991, 1994.

Brittan, Samuel (1983), "Two cheers for utilitarianism", *Oxford Economic Papers*, **35**, November, pp. 331–50.

Brown, David M. (1992), "Rand on Rand (almost)" (review of Leonard Peikoff, *Objectivism: The Philosophy of Ayn Rand*, New York: Dutton, 1991), *Reason*, **23**, February, pp. 62–4.

Browne, Harry (1995), *Why Government Doesn't Work*, New York: St. Martin's Press.

Brownlee, Shannon (1998), "Of males and tails", *U.S. News & World Report*, 6 July, pp. 60–61.

Brunner, Karl and William H. Meckling (1977), "The perception of man and the conception of government", *Journal of Money, Credit and Banking*, **9**(1), Part 1, February, pp. 70–85.

Buchanan, James M. (1965), "Ethical rules, expected values, and large numbers", *Ethics*, **76**, October, pp. 1–13.

Buchanan James M. (1975), *The Limits of Liberty*, Chicago: University of Chicago Press.

Buchanan James M. (1977), *Freedom in Constitutional Contract*, College Station: Texas A&M University Press.

Buchanan James M. (1979), *What Should Economists Do?*, Indianapolis: Liberty Press.

Buchanan James M. (1984), "Sources of opposition to constitutional reform", in Richard B. McKenzie (ed.), *Constitutional Economics*, Lexington, MA: Lexington Books, pp. 21–34.

Campbell, C.A. (1951), "Is 'freewill' a pseudo-problem?", *Mind*, **60**, October. Reprinted in part in Bernard Berofsky (ed.), *Free Will and Determinism*, New York: Harper & Row, 1966, pp. 112–35.

Castelli, Jim (1983), *The Bishops and the Bomb*, Garden City: Image Books.

Catlin, George (1939), *The Story of the Political Philosophers*, New York: Tudor Publishing Co., n.d. (c. 1939 by McGraw-Hill).

Copleston, Frederick (1985), *A History of Philosophy*, Vols IV, V, and VI in one book, New York: Doubleday, Image Book.

Copp, David (1985), "Introduction", in David Copp and David Zimmerman (eds), *Morality, Reason and Truth*, Totowa: Rowman & Allanheld, pp. 1–24.

Cowen, Tyler (1993), "The scope and limits of preference sovereignty", *Economics and Philosophy*, **9**, October, pp. 253–69.

Cowley, Geoffrey (1996), "The roots of good and evil", *Newsweek*, **127**(9), 26 February, pp. 52–4.

Cramp, A.B. (1991), "Pleasures, prices and principles", in J. Gay Tulip Meeks (ed.), *Thoughtful Economic Man*, Cambridge and New York: Cambridge University Press, pp. 50–73.

d'Amour, Gene (1976), "Research programs, rationality, and ethics", in R.S. Cohen et al. (eds), *Essays in Memory of Imre Lakatos*, Dordrecht and Boston: Reidel, pp. 87–98.

Danto, Arthur C. (1984), "Constructing an epistemology of human rights: A pseudo problem?", *Social Philosophy & Policy*, **1**(2), Spring, pp. 25–30.

Darwin, Charles (1859 and 1871)), *The Origin of Species* and *The Descent of Man*, combined in one volume, New York: Modern Library, 1936.

Davie, William (1987), "Hume's apology", *Hume Studies*, **13**(1), April, pp. 30–45.

Davis, Harry R. (1967/68), "Toward justifying democracy", *The Key Reporter*, **33**, Winter, pp. 2–4, 8.

Dawkins, Richard (1978), *The Selfish Gene*, New York: Oxford University Press, paperback.

d'Entrèves, A.P. (1952), *Natural Law: An Introduction to Legal Philosophy*, London: Hutchinson's University Library.

Detmold, M.J. (1984), *The Unity of Law and Morality: A Refutation of Legal Positivism*, London: Routledge & Kegan Paul.

de Waal, Frans (1989), *Chimpanzee Politics*, Baltimore: Johns Hopkins University Press.

Dworkin, Gerald (1970), "Acting freely", *Nous*, 4, pp. 367–83. Reprinted in Steven M. Cahn, Patricia Kitcher, and George Sher (eds), *Reason at Work: Introductory Readings in Philosophy*, New York: Harcourt Brace Jovanovich, 1984, pp. 509–22.

Dworkin, Ronald (1977), *Taking Rights Seriously*, Cambridge: Harvard University Press.

Dworkin, Ronald (1981), "Rights as trumps". Reprinted in Jeremy Waldron (ed.), *Theories of Rights*, Oxford and New York: Oxford University Press, 1984, pp. 153–67.

Eberly, Don (1995), "Even Newt can't save us", *Wall Street Journal*, 3 February, p. A12.

Edgeworth, Francis Y. (1881), *Mathematical Psychics*, London: Kegan Paul. Photoreprint, New York: Kelley, 1967.

Edwards, Paul (1965), *The Logic of Moral Discourse*, New York: Free Press.

Elbert, Fred (1989), Talk at the meeting of the Alabama Philosophical Society in Auburn, AL, 18 November.

Epstein, Richard A. (1989), "The utilitarian foundations of natural law" and "Postscript: Subjective utilitarianism", *Harvard Journal of Law & Public Policy*, **12**, pp. 713–51, 769–73.

Epstein, Richard A. (1995), *Simple Rules for a Complex World*, Cambridge: Harvard University Press.

Eshelman, Larry J. (1993), "Ludwig von Mises on principle", *Review of Austrian Economics*, **6**(2), pp. 3–41.

Etzioni, Amitai (1988), *The Moral Dimension*, New York: Free Press.

Eucken, Walter (1950), *The Foundations of Economics*, Trans. by T.W. Hutchison, London: Hodge.

Eucken, Walter (1954), *Kapitaltheoretische Untersuchungen*, 2nd edn, Tübingen: Mohr (Siebeck).

Ezorsky, Gertrude (1968), Review of David Lyons, *Forms and Limits of Utilitarianism* (Oxford: Clarendon Press, 1965), *Journal of Philosophy*, **65**, pp. 533–44.

Festinger, Leon (1962), *A Theory of Cognitive Dissonance*, Stanford: Stanford University Press.

Finnis, John (1983), *Fundamentals of Ethics*, Oxford: Clarendon Press.

Flam, Faye (1994), "Artificial-life researchers try to create social reality", *Science*, **265**, 12 August, pp. 868–9.

Fletcher, Joseph (1966), *Situation Ethics*, 1st British edn, London: SCM Press, 4th impression, 1974.

Flew, Antony (1963), "On the interpretation of Hume", *Philosophy*, **38**. Reprinted in V.C. Chappell (ed.), *Hume: A Collection of Critical Essays*, Garden City: Anchor Books/Doubleday, 1966, pp. 278–86.

Flew, Antony (1966), "'Not Proven' – at most", newly written for V.C. Chappell (ed.), *Hume: A Collection of Critical Essays*, Garden City: Anchor Books/Doubleday, pp. 291–4.

Flew, Antony (1971), *An Introduction to Western Philosophy*, Indianapolis and New York: Bobbs-Merrill.

Flew, Antony (1986), *David Hume: Philosopher of Moral Science*, Oxford and New York: Basil Blackwell.

Foot, Philippa (1958), "Moral beliefs", *Proceedings of the Aristotelian Society*, **59**. Reprinted in W.D. Hudson (ed.), *The Is/Ought Question*, New York: St. Martin's Press, 1969, reprinted 1973, pp. 196–213.

Foot, Philippa (1988), "Utilitarianism and the virtues", in Samuel Scheffler (ed.), *Consequentialism and Its Critics*, Oxford and New York: Oxford University Press, pp. 224–42.

Ford, John J. (1915), "A defense of capital punishment", *Catholic Mind*, 18 March. Reprinted in Robert N. Beck and John B. Orr (eds), *Ethical Choice*, New York: Free Press, 1970, pp. 345–55.

Frank, Robert H. (1988), *Passions within Reason*, New York: Norton.

Frankel, S. Herbert (1978), *Two Philosophies of Money*, New York: St. Martin's Press.

Frey, R.G. (ed.) (1984), *Utility and Rights*, Minneapolis: University of Minnesota Press.

Friedman, Milton (1953), *Essays in Positive Economics*, Chicago: University of Chicago Press.

Fukuyama, Francis (1995), *Trust: The Social Virtues and the Creation of Prosperity*, New York: Free Press.

Galbraith, John Kenneth (1958), *The Affluent Society*, Boston: Houghton Mifflin.

Gannon, Thomas M., S.J. (ed.) (1987), *The Catholic Challenge to the American Economy*, New York: Macmillan.

Gauthier, David (1985), "Bargaining and Justice", *Social Philosophy & Policy*, **2**, Spring, pp. 29–47.

Gauthier, David (1986), *Morals by Agreement*, Oxford: Clarendon Press.

Georgescu-Roegen, Nicholas (1971), *The Entropy Law and the Economic Process*, Cambridge: Harvard University Press, 2nd printing 1974.

Gewirth, Alan (1978), *Reason and Morality*, Chicago: University of Chicago Press.

Gewirth, Alan (1982), *Human Rights*, Chicago: University of Chicago Press.

Gewirth, Alan (1984ATAAR), "Are there any absolute rights?", in Jeremy Waldron (ed.), *Theories of Rights*, Oxford and New York: Oxford University Press, pp. 91–109.

Gewirth Alan (1984EHR), "The epistemology of human rights" and "A reply to Danto", *Social Philosophy & Policy*, **1**(2), Spring, pp. 1–24, 31–4.

Gewirth, Alan (1987), "Private philanthropy and positive rights", *Social Philosophy & Policy*, **4** (2), Spring, pp. 55–78.

Gigerenzer, Gerd, Zeno Swijtink, Theodore Porter, Lorraine Daston, John Beatty, and Lorenz Krüger (1989), *The Empire of Chance*, Cambridge and New York: Cambridge University Press, reprinted 1993.

Glendon, Mary Ann (1991), *Rights Talk*, New York: Free Press.

"Go directly to jail" (1996) (a review of six books on punishment), *The Economist*, **338**, 16 March, special section, pp. 3–4.

"Going ape" (1996), *The Economist*, **338**(7953), 17–23 February, p. 78.

Golding, Martin P. (1984), "The primacy of welfare rights", *Social Philosophy & Policy*, **1**(2), Spring, pp. 119–36.

Goodman, John C. (1997), "Do inalienable rights outlaw punishment?", *Liberty*, **10**(5), May, pp. 47–9.

Gordon, Scott (1976), "The new contractarians", *Journal of Political Economy*, **84**, June, pp. 573–90.

Gray, John (1979), "John Stuart Mill: Traditional and revisionist interpretations", *Literature of Liberty*, **2**, April–June, pp. 7–37.

Gray, John (1983), *Mill on Liberty: A Defence*, London and Boston: Routledge & Kegan Paul.

Gray, John (1984), "Indirect utility and fundamental rights", *Social Philosophy & Policy*, **1**(2), Spring, pp. 73–91.

Gray, John (1986), *Liberalism*, 2nd edn, Minneapolis: University of Minnesota Press, 1995.

Gray, John (1989BoL), "Buchanan on liberty", Manuscript for conference in honor of James M. Buchanan, Roanoke, VA, 28 September to 1 October.

Gray, John (1989LEPP), *Liberalisms: Essays in Political Philosophy*, London & New York: Routledge.

Gray, John (1989LS), "The last socialist?", *National Review*, **41**, 30 June, pp. 27–9, 31.

Gray, John (1993), *Post-liberalism: Studies in Political Thought*, New York and London: Routledge.

Griffin, James (1986), *Well-being: Its Meaning, Measurement, and Moral*

Importance, Oxford: Clarendon Press.

Halévy, Elie (1955), *The Growth of Philosophic Radicalism*, Trans. by Mary Morris, Boston: Beacon Press, 3rd printing, 1966.

Hamilton, W.D. (1996), *Narrow Roads of Gene Land*, Collected Papers, Vol. I of his *Evolution of Social Behavior*, Oxford and New York: Freeman.

Hamlin, Alan A. (1986), *Ethics, Economics and the State*, Brighton: Wheatsheaf Books.

Hardin, Garrett (1968), "The tragedy of the commons", *Science*, **162**, 13 December, pp. 1243-8. Reprinted in his *New Ethics for Survival*, New York: Viking, 1972, pp. 250-64.

Hardin, Russell (1989), "Ethics and stochastic processes", *Social Philosophy & Policy*, **7**, Autumn, pp. 69-80.

Hardin, Russell (1995), *One for All: The Logic of Group Conflict*, Princeton: Princeton University Press.

Hare, R.M. (1964), "The promising game", *Revue Internationale de Philosophie*, **18**. Reprinted in Kenneth Pahel and Marvin Schiller (eds), *Readings in Contemporary Ethical Theory*, Englewood Cliffs: Prentice-Hall, 1970, pp. 168-79.

Hare, R.M. (1981), *Moral Thinking*, Oxford: Clarendon Press; New York: Oxford University Press.

Hare, R.M. (1984), "Rights, utility, and universalization: Reply to J.L. Mackie", in R.G. Frey (ed.), *Utility and Rights*, Minneapolis: University of Minnesota Press, pp. 106-20.

Hare, R.M (1989EiET), *Essays in Ethical Theory*, Oxford: Clarendon Press; New York: Oxford University Press.

Hare, R.M. (1989EoPM), *Essays on Political Morality*, Oxford: Clarendon Press.

Hare, R.M. (1997), *Sorting Out Ethics*, Oxford: Clarendon Press.

Harman, Gilbert (1977), *The Nature of Morality*, New York: Oxford University Press.

Harman, Gilbert and Judith Jarvis Thomson (1996), *Moral Relativism and Moral Objectivity*, Oxford: Blackwell.

Harrison, Lawrence E. (1985), *Underdevelopment Is a State of Mind*, Lanham, MD: Madison Books.

Harrison, Lawrence E. (1992), *Who Prospers? How Cultural Values Shape Economic and Political Success*, New York: Basic Books.

Harrod, R.F. (1936), "Utilitarianism revised", *Mind*, **45**, April, pp. 137-56. Excerpted in Sissela Bok, *Lying*, New York: Vintage Books, 1979, pp. 293-301.

Harsanyi, John C. (1955), "Cardinal welfare, individualistic ethics, and interpersonal comparisons of utility", *Journal of Political Economy*, **63**, August, pp. 309-21. Reprinted in Edmund S. Phelps (ed.), *Economic*

Justice, Baltimore: Penguin, 1973, Selection 10, pp. 266–85.

Harsanyi, John C. (1975), "Can the maximin principle serve as a basis for morality? A critique of John Rawls's theory", *American Political Science Review*, **69**, pp. 594–606.

Harsanyi, John C. (1976), *Essays on Ethics, Social Behavior, and Scientific Explanation*, Dordrecht and Boston: Reidel.

Harsanyi, John C. (1977MTRB), "Morality and the theory of rational behavior", *Social Research*, **44**, pp. 623–56. Reprinted in Amartya Sen and Bernard Williams (eds), *Utilitarianism and Beyond*, London, New York, and Paris: Cambridge University Press and Editions de la Maison des Sciences de l'Homme, 1982, pp. 39–62.

Harsanyi, John C. (1977RUDT), "Rule utilitarianism and decision theory", *Erkenntnis*, **11**, pp. 25–53.

Harsanyi, John C. (1985), "Rule utilitarianism, equality, and justice", *Social Philosophy & Policy*, **2**, Spring, pp. 115–27.

Harsanyi, John C. (1987), Review of David Gauthier, *Morals by Agreement* (Clarendon, 1986), *Economics and Philosophy*, **3**, October, pp. 339–51.

Hart, H.L.A. (1979), "Between utility and rights" (expansion of a lecture at the Columbia University Law School in November 1978), in Alan Ryan (ed.), *The Idea of Freedom: Essays in Honour of Isaiah Berlin*, Oxford and New York: Oxford University Press, pp. 77–98.

Hart, H.L.A. (1982), *Essays on Bentham*, Oxford: Clarendon Press.

Hart, H.L.A. (1983), *Essays in Jurisprudence and Philosophy*, Oxford: Clarendon Press. (Essay 9, "Between utility and rights", from *Columbia Law Review*, **79**, 1979, pp. 828–46, is a version of the article cited in Hart 1979 above.)

Hartmann, Nicolai (1932), "Truthfulness and uprightness" (a selection from his *Ethics*). Reprinted in Robert N. Beck and John B. Orr (eds), *Ethical Choice*, New York: Free Press, 1970, pp. 39–42.

Haslett, D.W. (1990), "What is utility?", *Economics and Philosophy*, **6**, April, pp. 65–94.

Haslett, D.W. (1994), *Capitalism with Morality*, Oxford: Clarendon Press; New York: Oxford University Press.

Hayek, F.A. (1944), *The Road to Serfdom*, Chicago: University of Chicago Press/Phoenix Books, 1956.

Hayek, F.A. (1945), "The use of knowledge in Society", *American Economic Review*, **35**, September, pp. 519–30.

Hayek, F.A. (1960), *The Constitution of Liberty*, Chicago: University of Chicago Press.

Hayek, F.A (1961), "The non sequitur of the 'Dependence Effect'", *Southern Economic Journal*, **27**, April. Reprinted in his *Studies in Philosophy, Politics and Economics*, Chicago: University of Chicago Press, 1967, pp. 313–17.

Hayek, F.A. (1967), *Studies in Philosophy, Politics and Economics*, Chicago: University of Chicago Press. (Especially pertinent are Chapter 4, "Notes on the evolution of systems of rules of conduct", Chapter 6, "The results of human action but not of human design", and Chapter 7, "The legal and political philosophy of David Hume".)

Hayek, F.A. (1976), *The Mirage of Social Justice*, Vol. 2 of *Law, Legislation and Liberty*, Chicago: University of Chicago Press.

Hayek, F.A. (1978), *New Studies in Philosophy, Politics, Economics and the History of Ideas*, Chicago: University of Chicago Press.

Hayek, F.A. (1984), "The origins and effects of our morals: A problem for science", in Chiaki Nishiyama and Kurt R. Leube (eds), *The Essence of Hayek*, Stanford: Hoover Institution Press, Chapter 17.

Hayek, F.A. (1989), *The Fatal Conceit*, Vol. 1 of the Collected Works of F.A. Hayek, Ed. by W.W. Bartley III, Chicago: University of Chicago Press.

Hayek, F.A. (1994), *Hayek on Hayek: An Autobiographical Dialogue*, Ed. by Stephen Kresge and Leif Wenar, Chicago: University of Chicago Press.

Hazlitt, Henry (1964), *The Foundations of Morality*, Princeton: Van Nostrand. 2nd edn, with a new preface, sponsored by Institute for Humane Studies, Los Angeles: Nash, 1972.

Helburn, Suzanne W. (1992), "On Keynes's Ethics", in Philip Arestis and Victoria Chick (eds), *Recent Developments in Post-Keynesian Economics*, Aldershot, UK and Brookfield, VT: Edward Elgar, pp. 27–46.

Heyne, Paul (1998), Review of Richard B. McKenzie, *The Paradox of Progress: Can Americans Regain Their Confidence in a Prosperous Future?* (Oxford University Press, 1997), *The Freeman*, **48**, April, pp. 252–4.

Himmelfarb, Gertrude (1974), *On Liberty and Liberalism: The Case of John Stuart Mill*, New York: Knopf.

Hobart, R.E. (1934) [pseudonym of Dickinson Miller], "Free will as involving determination and inconceivable without it", *Mind*, **43**, January, pp. 169ff. Reprinted in Bernard Berofsky (ed.), *Free Will and Determinism*, New York: Harper & Row, 1966, pp. 63–95. Partially reprinted in Steven M. Cahn, Patricia Kitcher, and George Sher (eds), *Reason at Work: Introductory Readings in Philosophy*, New York: Harcourt Brace Jovanovich, 1984, pp. 494–508.

Hobbes, Thomas (1651), *Leviathan*, Great Books of the Western World, Vol. 23, Chicago: Encyclopaedia Britannica, 1952.

Holcombe, Randall G. (1994), *The Economic Foundations of Government*, New York: New York University Press.

Horwitz, Steven (1996), "Liberty and the domain of self-interest", *The Freeman*, **46**, November, pp. 726–30.

Hospers, John (1961), "What means this freedom?", in Sidney Hook (ed.), *Determination and Freedom in the Age of Modern Science*, New York: Collier Books, pp. 126–42. Reprinted in Bernard Berofsky (ed.), *Free Will and Determinism*, New York: Harper & Row, 1966. pp. 26–45.

Hospers, John (1998), "Simplicity Rules" (review of Richard A. Epstein, *Simple Rules for a Complex World* (Harvard University Press, 1995), *Liberty*, **11**, May, pp. 58–61.

Hudson, W.D. (1964), "Hume on Is and Ought", *Philosophical Quarterly*, **14**. Reprinted in V.C. Chappell (ed.), *Hume: A Collection of Critical Essays*, Garden City: Anchor Books/Doubleday, 1966, pp. 295–307.

Hudson, W.D. (ed.) (1969), *The Is–Ought Question*, New York: St. Martin's Press.

Hudson, W.D. (1970), *Modern Moral Philosophy*, Garden City: Doubleday/Anchor Books.

Hume, David (1739/1740), *A Treatise of Human Nature*, Garden City: Doubleday/Dolphin Books, 1961. Key sections reprinted in Alasdair MacIntyre (ed.), *Hume's Ethical Writings*, New York: Collier Books, 1965, pp. 177–252.

Hume, David (1751/1777), *An Enquiry Concerning the Principles of Morals*, Chicago: Open Court, 1930. Key sections reprinted in Alasdair MacIntyre (ed.), *Hume's Ethical Writings*, New York: Collier Books, 1965, pp. 22–156.

Hume, David (1955), *Writings on Economics*, edited and with an introduction by Eugene Rotwein, Madison: University of Wisconsin Press, reprinted 1970.

Hume, David (1985), *Essays Moral, Political, and Literary*, Ed. by Eugene F. Miller, Indianapolis: Liberty Classics. (Includes "Of the first principles of government", 1741, pp. 32–6, and "Of the original contract", 1748, pp. 465–87.)

Hunter, Geoffrey (1963), "Reply to Professor Flew", *Philosophy*, **38**. Reprinted in V.C. Chappell (ed.), *Hume: A Collection of Critical Essays*, Garden City: Anchor Books/Doubleday, 1966, pp. 287–90.

Jewkes, John (1968), *The New Ordeal by Planning*, London: Macmillan. Selections reprinted as "Moral values in a socialist society", Chapter 8. In Robert L. Schuettinger (ed.), *The Conservative Tradition in European Thought*, New York: Putnam, 1970.

Johnson, Conrad D. (1988), "The authority of the moral agent", in Samuel Scheffler (ed.), *Consequentialism and Its Critics*, Oxford and New York: Oxford University Press, pp. 261–87.

Kant, Immanuel (ca. 1775–80), *Lectures on Ethics*, Trans. by Louis Infield, New York: Harper Torchbooks, 1963.

Kant, Immanuel (1785MFM), *Metaphysical Foundations of Morals*, Trans. by

Carl J. Friedrich in Carl J. Friedrich (ed.), *The Philosophy of Kant*, New York: Modern Library, 1949, pp. 140–208.

Kant, Immanuel (1785GMM), *Groundwork of the Metaphysic of Morals*, another translation of the preceding item, trans. and with analysis and notes by H.J. Paton, New York: Harper Torchbooks, 1964.

Kaplan, Morton A. (1959–60), "Some problems of the extreme utilitarian position", *Ethics*, **70**, pp. 228–32.

Katz, S.H., M.L. Hediger, and L.A. Valleroy (1974), "Traditional maize processing techniques in the New World", *Science*, **184**, 17 May, pp. 765–73.

Kavka, Gregory S. (1985), "The reconciliation project", in David Copp and David Zimmerman (eds), *Morality, Reason and Truth*, Totowa: Rowman & Allanheld, pp. 297–319.

Kekes, John (1987), "Benevolence: A minor virtue", *Social Philosophy & Policy*, **4**, Spring, pp. 21–36.

Kelley, David (1994), Review of J.Q. Wilson, *The Moral Sense* (New York: Macmillan, 1993), *Cato Journal*, **13**, Winter, pp. 455–8.

Kelley, David (1996), *Unrugged Individualism: The Selfish Basis of Benevolence*, Poughkeepsie: Institute for Objectivist Studies.

Kelsen, Hans (1945), *General Theory of Law and State*, Trans. by Anders Wedberg, Cambridge: Harvard University Press, 1949. (An appendix, pp. 389–446, is "Natural law doctrine and legal positivism", 1929, trans. by W.H. Kraus.)

Kemp, J. (1970), *Ethical Naturalism: Hobbes and Hume*, London: Macmillan.

Keynes, John Maynard (1936), *The General Theory of Employment, Interest, and Money*, New York: Harcourt, Brace.

Kincaid, Harold (1993), Review of David Levy, *The Economic Ideas of Ordinary People* (London: Routledge, 1992), *Economics and Philosophy*, **9**, October, pp. 328–33.

King, J. Charles (1988), "Contract, utility, and the evaluation of institutions", *Cato Journal*, **8**, Spring/Summer, pp. 29–52.

Koppl, Roger (1992), "What is the public interest?", in Robert W. McGee (ed.), *Business Ethics and Common Sense*, Westport, CT: Quorum Books, pp. 89–98.

Kupperman, Joel J. (1983), *The Foundations of Morality*, London: Allen & Unwin.

Kymlicka, Will (1990), *Contemporary Political Philosophy*, Oxford: Clarendon Press; New York: Oxford University Press.

Laycock, Douglas (1985), "The ultimate unity of rights and utilities", *Texas Law Review*, **64**, August, pp. 407–13.

Leoni, Bruno (1961), *Freedom and the Law*, Princeton: Van Nostrand.

Lewis, Marlo, Jr. (1985), "The Achilles heel of F.A. Hayek", *National Review*,

37(9), 17 May, pp. 32-6.

Lindbeck, Assar (1995), "Hazardous welfare-state dynamics", *American Economic Review*, **85**, May, pp. 9-15.

Little, I.M.D. (1950), *A Critique of Welfare Economics*, Oxford: Clarendon Press.

Livingston, Donald W. (1995), "On Hume's conservatism", *Hume Studies*, **21**, November, pp. 151-64.

Lomasky, Loren E. (1987), *Persons, Rights, and the Moral Community*, New York: Oxford University Press.

Lomasky, Loren (1989), "A pilgrim's progress" (review of Jan Narveson, *The Libertarian Idea*, Philadelphia: Temple University Press, 1988), *Reason*, **21**, December, pp. 45-7.

Lomasky, Loren E. (1993), "Sense and sensibilities: Knowing right from wrong" (review of James Q. Wilson, *The Moral Sense*, New York: Macmillan, 1993), *Reason*, **25**, December, pp. 41-4.

Lorenz, Edward N. (1993), *The Essence of Chaos*, Seattle: University of Washington Press.

Lucas, J.R. (1980), *On Justice*, Oxford: Clarendon Press.

Lyons, David (1965), *Forms and Limits of Utilitarianism*, Oxford: Clarendon Press.

Lyons, David (1984), "Utility and rights", in Jeremy Waldron (ed.), *Theories of Rights*, Oxford and New York: Oxford University Press, pp. 110-36.

Lyons, David (1993), *Moral Aspects of Legal Theory*, New York: Cambridge University Press.

Mabbott, J.D. (1956), "Interpretations of Mill's utilitarianism", *Philosophical Quarterly*, **6**. Reprinted in J.B. Schneewind (ed.), *Mill: A Collection of Critical Essays*, Garden City: Doubleday/Anchor, 1968, pp. 190-98.

Machan, Tibor R. (1975), *Human Rights and Human Liberties*, Chicago: Nelson Hall.

Machan, Tibor R. (1988), "Government regulation of business", in Tibor R. Machan (ed.), *Commerce and Morality*, Totowa, NJ: Rowman & Littlefield, pp. 161-79.

Machan, Tibor R. (1989), *Individuals and Their Rights*, La Salle: Open Court.

MacIntyre, Alasdair C. (1959), "Hume on 'Is' and 'Ought'", *Philosophical Review*, **68**. Reprinted in V.C. Chappell (ed.), *Hume: A Collection of Critical Essays*, Garden City: Anchor Books/Doubleday, 1966, pp. 240-64.

MacIntyre, Alasdair C. (1981), *After Virtue*, Notre Dame: University of Notre Dame Press, 1984.

Mack, Eric (1988), "Preference utilitarianism, prior existence and moral replaceability", *Reason Papers*, **13**, Spring, pp. 120-31.

Mackie, J.L. (1977), *Ethics: Inventing Right and Wrong*, Harmondsworth: Penguin Books.

Mackie, J.L. (1978), "Can there be a right-based moral theory?" Reprinted in Jeremy Waldron (ed.), *Theories of Rights*, Oxford and New York: Oxford University Press, 1984, pp. 168–81.

Mackie, J.L (1980), *Hume's Moral Theory*, London and Boston: Routledge & Kegan Paul.

Mackie, J.L. (1984), "Rights, utility, and universalization", in R.G. Frey (ed.), *Utility and Rights*, Minneapolis: University of Minnesota Press, pp. 86–105.

Marshall, Eliot (1996), "Probing primate morality", *Science*, **271**, 16 February, p. 904.

Martin, Judith ("Miss Manners") (1996), Essay in *The Responsive Community*, Spring, Washington, DC: the Center for Political Research. Excerpted in *Wall Street Journal*, 16 August, 1996, p. A10.

Martin, Judith ("Miss Manners") (1996), *Miss Manners Rescues Civilization from Sexual Harassment, Frivolous Lawsuits, Dissing and other Lapses in Civility*, New York: Crown.

Mayr, Ernst (1997), *This Is Biology*, Cambridge: Belknap Press of Harvard University Press.

McCloskey, Herbert J. (1969), *Meta-ethics and Normative Ethics*, The Hague: Martinus Nijhoff.

McCloskey, Herbert J. (1984), "Respect for human moral rights versus maximizing good", in R.G. Frey (ed.), *Utility and Rights*, Minneapolis: University of Minnesota Press, pp. 121–36.

McKenzie, Richard B. (1997), *The Paradox of Progress: Can Americans Regain Their Confidence in a Prosperous Future?*, New York: Oxford University Press.

Merrill, Ronald E. (1991), *The Ideas of Ayn Rand*, La Salle: Open Court.

Meyer, Frank S. (1960), "Freedom, tradition, conservatism", *Modern Age*, **4**, Fall. Reprinted as Chapter 1 in Frank S. Meyer (ed.), *What Is Conservatism?*, New York: Holt, Rinehart and Winston, 1964.

Meyer, Frank S. (1962), *In Defense of Freedom*, Chicago: Regnery.

Meyerson, Émile (1921), *Explanation in the Sciences*, Trans. from French by Mary-Alice and David A. Sipfle, Dordrecht and Boston: Kluwer, 1991.

Midgley, Mary (1994), *The Ethical Primate*, London and New York: Routledge.

Mill, John Stuart (1838), "Bentham", in Maurice Cowling (ed.), *Selected Writings of John Stuart Mill*, New York: New American Library/Mentor Books, 1968, pp. 15–56.

Mill, John Stuart (1859), *On Liberty*. Reprinted in many places, including Maurice Cowling (ed.), *Selected Writings of John Stuart Mill*, New York: New American Library, 1968, pp. 121–229.

Mill, John Stuart (1861/1863), *Utilitarianism*. Reprinted in many places, including Maurice Cowling (ed.), *Selected Writings of John Stuart Mill*,

New York: New American Library, 1968, pp. 243–304, and John Gray (ed.), *On Liberty and Other Essays*, Oxford and New York: Oxford University Press, 1991, pp. 129–201.

Mill, John Stuart (1861), *Considerations on Representative Government*. Reprinted in John Gray (ed.), *On Liberty and Other Essays*, Oxford and New York: Oxford University Press, 1991, pp. 203–467.

Mill, John Stuart (1874), "Nature", in his *Three Essays on Religion* (but completed in 1854). Reprinted in many places, including Jack Stillinger (ed.), *Autobiography and Other Writings*, Boston: Houghton Mifflin, 1969, pp. 313–48.

Miller, Harlan B. and William H. Williams (eds) (1982), *The Limits of Utilitarianism*, Minneapolis: University of Minnesota Press.

Mills, Frederick C. (1938), *Statistical Methods Applied to Economics and Business*, Revised edition, New York: Holt.

Mirrlees, J.A. (1982), "The economic uses of utilitarianism", in Amartya Sen and Bernard Williams (eds), *Utilitarianism and Beyond*, London, New York, and Paris: Cambridge University Press and Editions de la Maison des Sciences de l'Homme, pp. 63–84.

Mises, Ludwig von (1919), *Nation, State, and Economy*, Trans. by Leland B. Yeager, New York: New York University Press, 1983.

Mises, Ludwig von (1922), *Socialism*, Trans. by J. Kahane, Indianapolis: Liberty Classics, 1981.

Mises, Ludwig von (1927), *Liberalism in the Classical Tradition*, Trans. by Ralph Raico. 3rd edn, Irvington-on-Hudson: Foundation for Economic Education; San Francisco: Cobden Press, 1985.

Mises, Ludwig von (1949), *Human Action*, 2nd edn, New Haven: Yale University Press, 1963.

Mises, Ludwig von (1957), *Theory and History*, New Haven: Yale University Press. Reprinted Auburn, AL: Ludwig von Mises Institute, 1985.

Mises, Ludwig von (1962), *The Ultimate Foundation of Economic Science*, 2nd edn, Kansas City, KS: Sheed Andrews and McMeel, 1977.

Mitchell, W.C. (1937), "Bentham's felicific calculus", in his *The Backward Art of Spending Money and Other Essays*, New York: McGraw-Hill.

Moore, George Edward (1903), *Principia Ethica*, Cambridge: Cambridge University Press, paperback, 1960.

Murphy, Jeffrie G. (1977), "Rights and borderline cases", *Arizona Law Review*, **19**(1), pp. 228–41.

Murphy, Jeffrie (1982), *Evolution, Morality, and the Meaning of Life*, Totowa, NJ: Rowan and Littlefield.

Nagel, Ernest (1954), *Sovereign Reason*, Glencoe: Free Press.

Naipaul, V.S. (1964), *An Area of Darkness*, New York: Vintage Books/ Random House, 1981.

Narveson, Jan (1967), *Morality and Utility*, Baltimore: Johns Hopkins Press.

Narveson, Jan (1979), "Rights and utilitarianism", *Canadian Journal of Philosophy*, Supplementary Vol. V (W.E. Cooper et al. (eds), *New Essays on John Stuart Mill and Utilitarianism*), pp. 137–60.

Narveson, Jan (1984), "Contractarian Rights", in R.G. Frey (ed.), *Utility and Rights*, Minneapolis: University of Minnesota Press, pp. 161–74.

Narveson, Jan (1988), *The Libertarian Idea*, Philadelphia: Temple University Press.

National Conference of Catholic Bishops (1986), "Economic justice for all: Catholic social teaching and the U.S. economy", © United States Catholic Conference. Reprinted as an unpaginated appendix in Thomas M. Gannon, S.J. (ed.), *The Catholic Challenge to the American Economy*, New York: Macmillan, 1987.

National Conference of Catholic Bishops on War and Peace (1983), "The challenge of peace: God's promise and our response", © United States Catholic Conference. Reprinted in Jim Castelli, *The Bishops and the Bomb*, Garden City: Image Books, 1983, pp.185–283.

Ng, Yew-Kwang (1989), "What should we do about future generations?", *Economics and Philosophy*, **5**, October, pp. 235–53.

Nielsen, Kai (1985), "Must the immoralist act contrary to reason?", in David Copp and David Zimmerman (eds), *Morality, Reason and Truth*, Totowa: Rowman & Allanheld, pp. 212–27.

Nielsen, Kai (1990), *Ethics without God*, revised edition, Buffalo: Prometheus Books.

Norton, David Fate (1993), "Hume, human nature, and the foundations of morality", in D.F. Norton (ed.), *The Cambridge Companion to Hume*, New York: Cambridge University Press, pp. 148–81.

Nozick, Robert (1974), *Anarchy, State, and Utopia*, New York: Basic Books.

Nozick, Robert (1989), *The Examined Life: Philosophical Meditations*, New York: Simon and Schuster.

Nutter, G. Warren (1983), *Political Economy and Freedom*, Ed. by Jane Couch Nutter, Indianapolis: Liberty Press.

O'Hear, Anthony (1980), *Karl Popper*, London: Routledge and Kegan Paul.

Okun, Arthur M. (1975), *Equality and Efficiency*, Washington: Brookings Institution.

Okun, Arthur M. (1981), *Prices and Quantities*, Washington: Brookings Institution.

Oldenquist, Andrew (1990), "The origins of morality: An essay in philosophical anthropology", *Social Philosophy & Policy*, **8**, Autumn, pp. 121–40.

Olson, Mancur (1982), *The Rise and Decline of Nations*, New Haven: Yale University Press.

Olson, Robert G. (1965), *The Morality of Self-interest*, New York: Harcourt, Brace & World.

Orwell, George (1946), "Politics and the English Language". Reprinted in his *Collected Essays*, London: Secker & Warburg, 1961, pp. 353–67. Also in *A Collection of Essays*, Garden City: Doubleday Anchor Books, 1954, pp. 162–77.

Orwell, George (1949), *Nineteen Eighty-four, a Novel*, New York: Harcourt, Brace.

Overman, Dean L. (1997), *A Case Against Accident and Self-organization*, Lanham: Rowman & Littlefield.

Parfit, Derek (1982), "Future generations: Further problems", *Philosophy & Public Affairs*, **11**, Spring, pp. 113–72.

Parfit, Derek (1984), *Reasons and Persons*, Oxford: Clarendon Press.

Paul, Ellen Frankel (1979), *Moral Revolution and Economic Science*, Westport, CT: Greenwood Press.

Peikoff, Leonard (1991), *Objectivism: The Philosophy of Ayn Rand*, New York: Dutton.

Peirce, Charles S. (1955), "The scientific attitude and fallibilism", in Justus Buchler (ed.), *Philosophical Writings of Peirce*, New York: Dover, pp. 42 59.

Peirce, Charles S. (1958), *Values in a Universe of Chance*, Ed. by Philip P. Wiener, Garden City: Doubleday Anchor Books.

Perry, M.J. (1988), *Morality, Politics, and Law*, Oxford and New York: Oxford University Press, paperback 1990.

Philbrook, Clarence (1953), "'Realism' in Policy Espousal", *American Economic Review*, **43**, December, pp. 846–59.

Piaget, Jean and seven collaborators (1975), *The Moral Judgment of the Child*, Trans. by Marjorie Gabain, New York: Free Press.

Piderit, John Jay (1993), *The Ethical Foundations of Economics*, Washington: Georgetown University Press.

Pitson, A.E. (1989), "Projectionism, realism, and Hume's moral sense theory", *Hume Studies*, **15**(1), April, pp. 61–92.

Plato (4th century BC), *The Republic*, in *Great Books of the Western World*, Chicago: Encyclopaedia Britannica, 1952, 21st printing, 1977, Vol. 7, pp. 295–441.

Popper, Karl (1972), "Indeterminism is not enough" (lecture at the Mont Pelerin Society meeting in Munich, September), in his *The Open Universe*, Totowa, NJ: Rowan and Littlefield, 1982, pp. 20–26.

Popper, Karl (1982), *Unended Quest*, Revised edn, La Salle: Open Court.

Popper, Karl (1985), *Popper Selections*, Ed. by David Miller, Princeton: Princeton University Press.

Posner, Richard A. (1990), *The Problems of Jurisprudence*, Cambridge:

Harvard University Press.

"Publius" (1787–8) (Alexander Hamilton, John Jay, and James Madison), *The Federalist*, New York: Modern Library, n.d.

Quinton, Anthony (1973), *Utilitarian Ethics*, London: Macmillan. Reprinted La Salle: Open Court, 1988.

Rand, Ayn (1957), *Atlas Shrugged*, New York: Random House.

Rand, Ayn (1964), *The Virtue of Selfishness*, New York: New American Library.

Rand, Ayn (1979), *Introduction to Objectivist Epistemology*, New American Library. 2nd edn, Ed. by Harry Binswanger and Leonard Peikoff, New York: Meridian (Penguin Books), 1990.

Rapoport, Anatol (1987), "Prisoner's dilemma", *The New Palgrave*, **3**, pp. 973–6.

Rasmussen, Douglas B. and Douglas J. Den Uyl (1991), *Liberty and Nature: An Aristotelian Defense of Liberal Order*, La Salle: Open Court.

Rauch, Jonathan (1993), *Kindly Inquisitors*, Chicago: University of Chicago Press.

Rawls, John (1955), "Two concepts of rules", *Philosophical Review*. Reprinted in M.D. Bayles (ed.), *Contemporary Utilitarianism*, Garden City: Anchor Books, 1968, pp. 59–98.

Rawls, John (1971), *A Theory of Justice*, Cambridge: Belknap Press of Harvard University Press.

Raz, Joseph (1984), "Right-based moralities", in Jeremy Waldron (ed.), *Theories of Rights*, New York: Oxford University Press, pp. 182–200. Also in R.G. Frey (ed.), *Utilities and Rights*, Minneapolis: University of Minnesota Press, 1984, pp. 42–60.

Regan, Donald (1980), *Utilitarianism and Co-operation*, Oxford: Clarendon Press.

Reiman, Jeffrey (1990), *Justice and Modern Moral Philosophy*, New Haven: Yale University Press.

Reiners, Ludwig (1975), *Stilfibel*, 14th edn, Munich: Deutscher Taschenbuch Verlag.

Rescher, Nicholas (1966), *Distributive Justice: A Constructive Critique of the Utilitarian Theory of Distribution*, Indianapolis: Bobbs-Merrill.

Rescher, Nicholas (1975), *Unselfishness*, Pittsburgh: University of Pittsburgh Press.

Rhinelander, Philip (1977), Seminar presentation for newspaper editors quoted in "Notable & Quotable", *Wall Street Journal*, 16 December, p. 14.

Rhoads, Steven E. (1985), *The Economist's View of the World*, New York: Cambridge University Press.

Ridley, Matt (1996), *The Origins of Virtue*, London and New York: Viking.

Robinson, Joan (1963), *Economic Philosophy*, Chicago: Aldine.

Rollins, L.A. (1983), *The Myth of Natural Rights*, Port Townsend, WA: Loompanics Unlimited.

Röpke, Wilhelm (1958), *A Humane Economy: The Social Framework of the Free Market*, Trans. by Elizabeth Henderson, Chicago: Regnery, 1960; Indianapolis: Liberty Fund, 1971.

Rorty, Richard (1991), *Objectivity, Relativism, and Truth*, New York: Cambridge University Press.

Rosenberg, Alexander (1990), "The biological justification of ethics: A best-case scenario", *Social Philosophy & Policy*, **8**, Autumn, pp. 86–101.

Rothbard, Murray N. (1972), "Free law in a free society" (review of Bruno Leoni, *Freedom and the Law*, Princeton: Van Nostrand, 1961), *National Review*, 21 July, pp. 803, 805.

Rothbard, Murray N. (1973), *For a New Liberty*, New York: Macmillan.

Rothbard, Murray N. (1982), *The Ethics of Liberty*, Atlantic Highlands, NJ: Humanities Press.

Rothbard, Murray N. (1995), *An Austrian Perspective on the History of Economic Thought*, Vol. II, *Classical Economics*, Aldershot, UK and Brookfield, VT: Edward Elgar.

Rotwein, Eugene (ed.) (1955), Editor's Introduction to David Hume, *Writings on Economics*, Madison: University of Wisconsin Press, reprinted 1970.

Rotwein, Eugene (1968), "Hume, David", *International Encyclopedia of the Social Sciences*, **6**, pp. 546–50.

Rotwein, Eugene (1987), "Hume, David", *The New Palgrave*, **3**, pp. 692–5.

Ruse, Michael (1990), "Evolutionary ethics and the search for predecessors: Kant, Hume, and all the way back to Aristotle?", *Social Philosophy & Policy*, **8**, Autumn, pp. 59–85.

Rushton, J. Philippe (1995), *Race, Evolution, and Behavior*, New Brunswick: Transaction Publishers.

Ryan, Alan (ed.) (1979), *The Idea of Freedom: Essays in Honour of Isaiah Berlin*, Oxford and New York: Oxford University Press. (Includes H.L.A. Hart, "Between Utility and Rights", pp. 77–98, and Richard Wollheim, "John Stuart Mill and Isaiah Berlin", pp. 253–69.)

Ryan, Alan (ed.) (1987), J.S. Mill and J. Bentham, *Utilitarianism and Other Essays*, Harmondsworth: Penguin Books.

Samuelson, Paul A. (1993), "Altruism as a problem involving group versus individual selection in economics and biology", *American Economic Review*, **83**, May, pp. 143–8.

Samuelson, Richard (1995), Letter to *National Review*, *National Review*, **47**, 27 November, p. 2.

Sartorius, Rolf E. (1975), *Individual Conduct and Social Norms*, Encino and Belmont, CA: Dickenson.

Sartorius, Rolf E. (1984), "Persons and Property", in R.G. Frey (ed.), *Utility and Rights*, Minneapolis: University of Minnesota Press, pp. 196–214.

Scanlon, T.M. (1982), "Contractualism and utilitarianism", in Amartya Sen and Bernard Williams (eds), *Utilitarianism and Beyond*, London, New York, and Paris: Cambridge University Press and Editions de la Maison des Sciences de l'Homme, pp. 103–28.

Scanlon, T.M. (1984), "Rights, goals, and fairness", in Jeremy Waldron (ed.), *Theories of Rights*, Oxford and New York: Oxford University Press, pp. 137–52.

Scheffler, Samuel (1988), "Agent-centred restrictions, rationality, and the virtues", in S. Scheffler (ed.), *Consequentialism and Its Critics*, Oxford and New York: Oxford University Press, pp. 243–60.

Schelling, Thomas C. (1968), "The life you save may be your own", in Samuel B. Chase (ed.), *Problems in Public Expenditure Analysis*, Washington: Brookings Institution, pp. 127–62.

Schlick, Moritz (1930), *Problems of Ethics*, Trans. by David Rynin, 1939, New York: Dover, 1961.

Schmidtz, David (1990), "Justifying the state", *Ethics*, **101**, October, pp. 89–102. Revised in John T. Sanders and Jan Narveson (eds), *For and Against the State: New Philosophical Readings*, Lanham, MD: Rowman & Littlefield, 1996, pp. 81–97.

Schmidtz, David (1993), "Reasons for altruism", *Social Philosophy & Policy*, **10**(1), Winter, pp. 52–68.

Schopenhauer, Arthur (1841), *On the Basis of Morality*, Trans. by E.F.J. Payne, Indianapolis: Bobbs-Merrill, 1965.

Schuettinger, Robert L. (ed.) (1970), *The Conservative Tradition in European Thought*, New York: Putnam.

Schumpeter, Joseph A. (1950), *Capitalism, Socialism and Democracy*, 3rd edition, New York: Harper & Row, paperback 1962.

Schumpeter, Joseph A. (1954), *History of Economic Analysis*, New York: Oxford University Press.

Seanor, Douglas and N. Fotion (eds) (1990), *Hare and Critics: Essays on Moral Thinking*, with comments by R.M. Hare, Oxford: Clarendon Press, 1990.

Searle, John R. (1964), "How to derive 'ought' from 'is'", *Philosophical Review*, **73**. Reprinted in W.D. Hudson (ed.), *The Is–Ought Question*, New York: St. Martin's Press, 1969, pp. 120–43, and followed by discussions by Antony Flew, R.M. Hare, and others. Also reprinted in Kenneth Pahel and Marvin Schiller (eds), *Readings in Contemporary Ethical Theory*, Englewood Cliffs: Prentice-Hall, 1970, pp. 156–68.

Searle, John R. (1969), *Speech Acts*, Cambridge: Cambridge University Press.

Searle, John R. (1970), "Reply to 'The Promising Game'", in Kenneth Pahel and Marvin Schiller (eds), *Readings in Contemporary Ethical Theory,*

Englewood Cliffs: Prentice-Hall, pp. 180–82.

Sedgwick, Jeffrey Leigh (1980), *Deterring Criminals: Policy Making and the American Political Tradition*, Washington: American Enterprise Institute.

Sen, Amartya K. (1970), *Collective Choice and Social Welfare*, San Francisco: Holden-Day.

Sen, Amartya K. (1973), *On Economic Inequality*, Oxford: Clarendon Press.

Sen, Amartya K. and Bernard Williams (eds) (1982), *Utilitarianism and Beyond*, London, New York, and Paris: Cambridge University Press and Editions de la Maison des Sciences de l'Homme.

Sidgwick, Henry (1907), *The Methods of Ethics*, 7th edn, Chicago: University of Chicago Press, reissued 1962.

Simmonds, N.E. (1987), "Natural Law", *The New Palgrave*, **3**, pp. 602–3.

Simmons, A. John (1979), *Moral Principles and Political Obligations*, Princeton: Princeton University Press.

Simon, Herbert A. (1990), "A mechanism for social selection and successful altruism", *Science*, **250**, 21 December, pp. 1665–8.

Simons, Henry C. (1948), *Economic Policy for a Free Society*, Chicago: University of Chicago Press.

Singer, Peter (1982), *The Expanding Circle: Ethics and Sociobiology*, New York: New American Library/Meridian Books.

Slote, Michael (1990), "Ethics without free will", *Social Theory and Practice*, **16**, Fall, pp. 369–83. Followed by Peter van Inwagen, "Response to Slote", pp. 385–95.

Smart, J.J.C. (1956), "Extreme and restricted utilitarianism", *Philosophical Quarterly*, **6**. Revised in Kenneth Pahel and Marvin Schiller (eds), *Readings in Contemporary Ethical Theory*, Englewood Cliffs: Prentice-Hall, 1970, pp. 249–60.

Smart, J.J.C. (1961), "An outline of a system of utilitarian ethics". Reprinted in J.J.C. Smart and Bernard Williams, *Utilitarianism: For and Against*, Cambridge: Cambridge University Press, 1973, pp. 1–74.

Smart, J.C.C. and Bernard Williams (1973), *Utilitarianism: For and Against*, New York: Cambridge University Press.

Smith, Adam (1759), *The Theory of Moral Sentiments*, Indianapolis: Liberty Classics, 1976.

Smith, Adam (1776), *The Wealth of Nations*, New York: Modern Library, 1937.

Smith, George (1996), "A killer's right to life", *Liberty*, **10**(2), November, pp. 46–54, 68–9.

Sommers, Christina Hoff (1993), "Teaching the virtues", *The Public Interest*, **111**, Spring, pp. 3–13.

Spencer, Herbert (1897), *The Principles of Ethics*, Two vols, Indianapolis: Liberty Classics, 1978.

Squire, John Collings (1931), *If, or History Rewritten*, New York: Viking Press.

Sterba, James P. (1980), *The Demands of Justice*, Notre Dame: University of Notre Dame Press.

Stevenson, Charles L. (1944), *Ethics and Language*, New Haven: Yale University Press, paperback 1960.

Stewart, John B. (1995), "The public interest vs. old rights", *Hume Studies*, **21**, November, pp. 165-88.

Sugden, Robert (1986), *The Economics of Rights, Co-operation and Welfare*, Oxford and New York: Basil Blackwell.

Sugden, Robert (1989), Review of James Griffin, *Well-being: Its Meaning, Measurement and Moral Importance* (1986), *Economics and Philosophy*, **5**, April, pp. 103-8.

Sumner, L.W. (1984), "Rights denaturalized", in R.G. Frey (ed.), *Utility and Rights*, Minneapolis: University of Minnesota Press, pp. 20-41.

Taylor, Charles (1979), "What's wrong with negative liberty", in Alan Ryan (ed.), *The Idea of Freedom*, Oxford and New York: Oxford University Press, pp. 175-93.

Taylor, Richard (1970), *Good and Evil: A New Direction*, New York: Macmillan.

Teller, Edward (1980), *The Pursuit of Simplicity*, Malibu: Pepperdine University Press.

Toulmin, Stephen (1960), *Reason in Ethics*, Cambridge: Cambridge University Press.

Tullock, Gordon (1985), "Adam Smith and the Prisoners' Dilemma", *Quarterly Journal of Economics*, **100**(5), Supplement, pp. 1073-81.

Urmson, J.O. (1953), "The interpretation of the moral philosophy of J.S. Mill", *Philosophical Quarterly* **3**. Reprinted in J.B. Schneewind (ed.), *Mill: A Collection of Critical Essays*, Garden City: Doubleday/Anchor, 1968, pp. 179-89.

Usher, Dan (1985), "The value of life for decision making in the public sector", *Social Philosophy and Policy*, **2**, Spring, pp. 168-91.

Vanberg, Viktor (1987), *Morality and Economics: De Moribus Est Disputandum*, Social Philosophy & Policy Center Original Papers No. 7, New Brunswick: Transaction Books.

Vanberg, Viktor (1994), "Social contract theory", in Peter J. Boettke (ed.), *The Elgar Companion to Austrian Economics*, Aldershot, UK and Brookfield, VT: Edward Elgar, pp. 337-42.

van Dun, Frank (1994), "Hayek and natural law: The Humean connection", in Jack Birner and Rudy van Zijp (eds), *Hayek, Co-ordination and Evolution*, London and New York: Routledge, pp. 269-86.

van Inwagen, Peter (1990), "Response to Slote", *Social Theory and Practice*,

16, Fall, pp. 385-95.

Varco, Richard L. III (1994), "Stability within common life: The standard of Hume's reflections", *LockeSmith Review*, **1**, pp. 64-80.

Vaughn, Karen (1976), "Critical discussion of the four papers", in Laurence S. Moss (ed.), *The Economics of Ludwig von Mises*, Kansas City: Sheed and Ward, pp. 101-10.

Veatch, Henry B. (1962), *Rational Man*, Bloomington: Indiana University Press, 5th printing 1971.

Veatch, Henry B. (1971), *For an Ontology of Morals*, Evanston: Northwestern University Press.

Veatch, Henry B. (1985), *Human Rights: Fact or Fancy*, Baton Rouge: Louisiana State University Press.

Vickrey, William S. (1961), "Risk, utility and social policy", *Social Research*, **28**, July, pp. 205-17. Reprinted in Edmund S. Phelps (ed.), *Economic Justice*, Baltimore: Penguin, 1973, pp. 286-97.

Vining, Rutledge (1984), *On Appraising the Performance of an Economic System*, New York: Cambridge University Press.

Virkkala, Timothy (1997), "The hollow ring of inalienability", *Liberty*, **10**(5), May, pp. 49-50.

Voss, Peter (1995), "Freewill and determinism", revised 1996. Accessed from the Objectivism home page on the Internet. <http://www.vix.com/pub/objectivism/writing/PeterVoss/FreeWillAnd Determinism.html>

Waldron, Jeremy (ed.) (1984), *Theories of Rights*, Oxford and New York: Oxford University Press. (Includes an Editor's Introduction, pp.1-20.)

Walker, Graham (1986), *The Ethics of F.A. Hayek*, Lanham, MD: University Press of America.

Walker, Ralph C.S. (1978), *Kant*, London: Routledge & Kegan Paul.

Waters, Ethan O. (1988) [pseudonym of R.W. Bradford], "The two libertarianisms", *Liberty*, May. Reprinted in *Liberty*, **6**, September 1992, pp. 62-7.

Welch, C. (1987), "Utilitarianism", *The New Palgrave*, **4**, pp. 770-76.

Westermarck, Edward (1960), *Ethical Relativity*, Paterson, NJ: Littlefield, Adams.

Wiener, Philip P. (1968), "Charles Sanders Peirce", *International Encyclopedia of the Social Sciences*, **11**, pp. 511-13.

Will, George F. (1992), *Restoration: Congress, Term Limits and the Recovery of Deliberative Democracy*, New York: Free Press.

Williams, Bernard (1972), *Morality: An Introducttion to Ethics*, New edition, Cambridge: Cambridge University Press, 1993.

Williams, Bernard (1973ACU), "A critique of utilitarianism", in J.J.C. Smart and Bernard Williams (eds), *Utilitarianism: For and Against*, Cambridge:

Cambridge University Press, pp. 75–150.

Williams, Bernard (1973CI), "Consequentialism and integrity". Reprinted in Samuel Scheffler (ed.), *Consequentialism and Its Critics*, Oxford and New York: Oxford University Press, 1988, pp. 20–50.

Williams, Bernard (1985), *Ethics and the Limits of Philosophy*, London: Fontana Press/Collins.

Wilson, James Q. (1993), *The Moral Sense*, New York: Macmillan/Free Press.

Wolff, Robert Paul (1969), Editor's comment on J.S. Mill's *Utilitarianism*, in R.P. Wolff (ed.), *Ten Great Works of Philosophy*, New York: New American Library, pp. 400–402.

Wollheim, Richard (1979), "John Stuart Mill and Isaiah Berlin: The ends of life and the preliminaries of morality", in Alan Ryan (ed.), *The Idea of Freedom: Essays in Honour of Isaiah Berlin*, Oxford and New York: Oxford University Press, pp. 253–69.

Wright, Robert (1994), *The Moral Animal: The New Science of Evolutionary Psychology*, New York: Pantheon Books.

Yeager, Leland B. (1978), "Pareto optimality in policy espousal", *Journal of Libertarian Studies*, 2, Fall, pp. 199–216.

Yeager, Leland B. (1984), "Utility, rights, and contract: Some reflections on Hayek's work", in Kurt R. Leube and Albert H. Zlabinger (eds.), *The Political Economy of Freedom: Essays in Honor of F.A. Hayek*, Munich: Philosophia Verlag, pp. 61–80.

Yeager, Leland B. (1985), "Rights, contract, and utility in policy espousal", *Cato Journal*, 5, Spring/Summer, pp. 259–94.

Yeager, Leland B. (1988EHD), "Ethics in the history and doctrine of the Virginia School", Fourth annual Virginia Political Economy lecture, Fairfax: Center for Study of Public Choice, George Mason University.

Yeager, Leland B. (1988USWF), "Utility and the social welfare function", in Walter Block and Llewellyn H. Rockwell, Jr. (eds), *Man, Economy, and Liberty: Essays in Honor of Murray N. Rothbard*, Auburn, AL: Ludwig von Mises Institute, pp. 175–91.

Yeager, Leland B. (1993M&C), "Mises and his critics on ethics, rights, and law", in Jeffrey M. Herbener (ed.), *The Meaning of Ludwig von Mises*, Auburn, AL: Ludwig von Mises Institute; Norwell, MA: Kluwer, pp. 321–44.

Yeager, Leland B. (1993R&C), "Racism and civility", *Liberty*, 6, February, pp. 45–6, 76.

Yeager, Leland B. (1994), "Tautologies in economics and the natural sciences", *Eastern Economic Journal*, 20, Spring, pp. 157–69.

Zagoria, Peter (1968), "Hobbes, Thomas", *International Encyclopedia of the Social Sciences*, 6, pp. 481–7.

Index